W9-BBL-212

CROSSWORD

PUZZLE

DICTIONARY

STAFF

EXECUITVE EDITOR
Edward G. Finnegan

ADMINISTRATION EDITOR
Thomas Vadakelalam

EDITORS
Marilyn Finnegan
Rhonda Heisler
Judy Van Wie
McVey Associates

Copyright © 1982, 1980
This edition by DPC, 1987
All rights reserved under the international and
Pan American Copyright Conventions.
Manufactured in the U.S.A.

Library of Congress Catalog Card Number: 77-82270
International Standard Book Number: 0-8326-2221-4

CONTENTS

1. SYNONYMS AND ANTONYMS

abandon, SYN.—abdicate, abjure, relinquish, renounce, resign, surrender, vacate, waive; desert, forsake, leave, quit. ANT.—defend, maintain, uphold; stay, support.

abate, SYN.—assuage, decrease, diminish, lessen, lower, moderate, reduce, suppress. ANT.—amplify, enlarge, increase, intensify, revive.

abbey, SYN.—cloister, convent, hermitage, monastery, nunnery, priory.

abbreviate, SYN.—abridge, condense, contract, curtail, diminish, lessen, limit, reduce, restrict, shorten. ANT.—elongate, extend, lengthen.

abbreviation, SYN.—abridgement, contraction, reduction, shortening. ANT.—amplification, enlargement, expansion, extension.

abdicate, SYN.—abjure, abolish, relinquish, renounce, resign, surrender, vacate, waive; desert, forsake, leave, quit. ANT.—defend, maintain, uphold; stay.

aberrant, SYN.—abnormal, capricious, devious, eccentric, irregular, unnatural, unusual, variable. ANT.—fixed, methodical, ordinary, regular, usual.

abet, SYN.—aid, assist, encourage, help, incite. ANT.—discourage, hinder, oppose, resist.

abettor, SYN.—accessory, accomplice, ally, assistant, associate, confederate. ANT.—adversary, enemy, opponent, rival.

ability, SYN.—aptitude, aptness, capability, capacity, dexterity, efficiency, faculty, power, qualification, skill, talent. ANT.—disability, incapacity, incompetency, unreadiness.

abjure, SYN.—abandon, abdicate, relinquish, renounce, resign, surrender, vacate, waive; desert, forsake, leave, quit. ANT.—defend, maintain, uphold; stay.

abode, SYN.—domicile, dwelling, habitat, hearth, home, quarters, residence, seat.

abolish, SYN.—destroy, end, eradicate, obliterate, overthrow; abrogate, annul, cancel, invalidate, revoke. ANT.—continue, establish, promote, restore, sustain.

abominable, SYN.—detestable, execrable, foul, hateful, loathsome, odious, revolting, vile. ANT.—agreeable, commendable, delightful, pleasant.

abominate, SYN.—abhor, despise, detest, dislike, hate, loathe. ANT.—

admire, approve, cherish, like, love.

abroad, SYN.—away, departed; absent, absent-minded, abstracted, distracted, inattentive, preoccupied. ANT.—attending, present; attentive, watchful.

abrupt, SYN.—hasty, precipitate, sudden, unannounced, unexpected; blunt, brusque, curt, rude; craggy, harsh, precipitous, rough, rugged, sharp, steep. ANT.—anticipated, expected; courteous, gradual, smooth.

absent, SYN.—abroad, away, departed; absent-minded, abstracted, distracted, inattentive, preoccupied. ANT.—attending, present; attentive, watchful.

absolute, SYN.—actual, complete, entire, perfect, pure, ultimate, unconditional, unqualified, unrestricted; arbitrary, authoritative, despotic, tyrannous. ANT.—accountable, conditional, contingent, dependent, qualified.

absorb, SYN.—assimilate, consume, engulf, imbibe, swallow up; engage, engross, occupy. ANT.—discharge, dispense, emit, expel, exude.

abstinence, SYN.—abstention, continence, fasting, forbearance, moderation, self-denial, sobriety, temperance. ANT.—excess, gluttony, greed, intoxication, self-indulgence.

abstract, SYN.—draw from, part, remove, separate; appropriate, purloin, steal; abridge, summarize. ANT.—add, replace, restore, return, unite.

abstracted, SYN.—drawn from, parted, removed, separated; appropriated, purloined, stolen; abridged, summarized. ANT.—added, replaced, restored, returned, united.

abstraction, SYN.—concept, conception, fancy, idea, image, impression, notion, opinion, sentiment, thought. ANT.—entity, matter, object, substance, thing.

absurd, SYN.—foolish, inconsistent, irrational, nonsensical, preposterous, ridiculous, self-contradictory, silly, unreasonable. ANT.—consistent, rational, reasonable, sensible, sound.

abundant, SYN.—ample, bountiful, copious, overflowing, plenteous, plentiful, profuse, rich, teeming. ANT.—deficient, insufficient, scant, scarce.

abuse, SYN.—aspersion, defamation, desecration, dishonor, disparagement, insult, invective, maltreatment, misuse, outrage, perversion, profanation, reproach, reviling, upbraiding. ANT.—approval, commendation, laudation, plaudit, respect.

abuse, SYN.—asperse, defame, disparage, ill-use, malign, revile, scandalize, traduce, vilify; misapply, misemploy, misuse. ANT.—cherish, honor, praise, protect, respect.

academic, SYN.—bookish, erudite, formal, learned, pedantic, scholarly, scholastic, theoretical. ANT. — common-sense, ignorant, practical, simple.

accelerate, SYN.—dispatch, expedite, facilitate, forward, hasten, hurry, push, quicken, rush, speed. ANT.—block, hinder, impede, retard, slow.

accident, SYN.—calamity, casualty, contingency, disaster, fortuity, misfortune, mishap. ANT.—calculation, design, intention, purpose.

accidental, SYN.—casual, chance, contingent, fortuitous, incidental, undesigned, unintended. ANT.—calculated, decreed, intended, planned, willed.

acclaim, SYN.—credit, distinction, eminence, fame, glory, honor, notoriety, renown, reputation. ANT.—disrepute, ignominy, infamy, obscurity.

accompany, SYN.—associate with, attend, chaperone, consort with, convoy, escort, go with. ANT.—abandon, avoid, desert, leave, quit.

accomplice, SYN.—abettor, accessory, ally, assistant, associate, confederate. ANT.—adversary, enemy, opponent, rival.

accomplish, SYN.—achieve, attain, complete, consummate, do, effect, execute, finish, fulfill, perfect, perform. ANT.—block, defeat, fail, frustrate, spoil.

accomplishment, SYN.—act, action, deed, doing, execution, feat, operation, performance, transaction; decree, edict, law, statute. ANT.—cessation, deliberation, inactivity, inhibition, intention.

accost, SYN.—address, approach, greet, hail, speak to. ANT.—avoid, pass by.

account, SYN.—chronicle, description, detail, history, narration, narrative, recital, relation; computation, reckoning, record. ANT.—caricature, confusion, distortion, misrepresentation.

account, SYN.—believe, consider, deem, esteem, estimate, hold, judge, rate, reckon, regard, think, view; elucidate, explain, expound.

accrue, SYN.—accumulate, amass, collect, gather, heap, hoard, increase, store. ANT.—diminish, disperse, dissipate, scatter, waste.

accumulate, SYN.—accrue, amass, collect, gather, heap, hoard, increase, store. ANT.—diminish, disperse, dissipate, scatter, waste.

accusation, SYN.—arraignment, charge, imputation, incrimination, indictment. ANT.—exculpation, exoneration, pardon.

accuse, SYN.—arraign, censure, charge, incriminate, indict. ANT.—absolve, acquit, exonerate, release, vindicate.

achieve, SYN.—accomplish, acquire, do, effect, execute, gain, obtain, realize, win. ANT.—fail, fall short, lose, miss.

achievement, SYN.—deed, exploit, feat; accomplishment, attainment, completion, performance, realization. ANT.—neglect, omission; defeat, failure.

acquaintance, SYN.—cognizance, companionship, familiarity, fellowship, friendship, intimacy, knowledge. ANT.—ignorance, inexperience, unfamiliarity.

acquire, SYN.—assimilate, attain, earn, get, obtain, procure, secure, win. ANT.—forego, forfeit, lose, miss, surrender.

act, SYN.—accomplishment, action, deed, doing, execution, feat, operation, performance, transaction; decree, edict, law, statute. ANT.—cessation, deliberation, inactivity, inhibition, intention.

action, SYN.—achievement, activity, deed, exercise, exploit, feat, motion, movement, performance, play, procedure. ANT.—idleness, inactivity, inertia, repose, rest.

active, SYN.—operative, working; busy, industrious; agile, alert, brisk, lively, nimble, quick, sprightly, supple. ANT.—dormant, inactive; indolent, lazy, passive.

activity, SYN.—action, agility, briskness, energy, enterprise, exercise, intensity, liveliness, motion, movement, quickness, rapidity, vigor. ANT.—dullness, idleness, inactivity, inertia, sloth.

actuality, SYN.—certainty, fact, reality, truth; act, circumstance, deed, event, incident, occurrence. ANT.—fiction, supposition, theory; delusion, falsehood.

adapt, SYN.—accommodate, adjust, conform, fit, suit. ANT.—disturb, misapply, misfit.

add, SYN.—adjoin, affix, append, attach, augment, increase, sum, total. ANT.—deduct, detach, reduce, remove, subtract.

address, SYN.—accost, approach, greet, hail, speak to. ANT.—avoid, pass by.

adequate, SYN.—ample, capable, commensurate, enough, fitting, satisfactory, sufficient, suitable. ANT.—deficient, lacking, scant.

adhere, SYN.—clasp, clutch, grasp, grip; have, hold, keep, maintain, occupy, possess, retain, support; check, confine, curb, detain, restrain; accommodate, carry, contain, receive, stow. ANT.—abandon, relinquish, surrender, vacate.

adjoin, SYN.—add, affix, append, attach, augment, increase, sum, total. ANT.—deduct, detach, reduce, remove, subtract.

admire, SYN.—appreciate, approve, esteem, respect, venerate, wonder. ANT.—abhor, despise, dislike.

admissible, SYN.—allowable, fair, justifiable, permissible, probable, tolerable, warranted. ANT.—inadmissible, irrelevant, unsuitable.

admit, SYN.—accept, acknowledge, agree, allow, assent, concede, confess, grant, permit, welcome. ANT.—deny, dismiss, reject, shun.

adorn, SYN.—beautify, bedeck, decorate, embellish, garnish, gild, ornament, trim. ANT.—deface, deform, disfigure, mar, spoil.

advance, SYN.—aggrandize, elevate, forward, further, promote; adduce, allege, assign, bring forward, offer, propose, propound; improve, proceed, progress, rise, thrive; augment, enlarge, increase. ANT.—hinder, oppose, retard, retreat, withhold.

advantage, SYN.—edge, mastery, superiority; benefit, good, profit, service, utility. ANT.—detriment, handicap, harm, impediment, obstruction.

adventurous, SYN.—bold, chivalrous, daring, enterprising, foolhardy, precipitate, rash. ANT.—cautious, hesitating, timid.

adverse, SYN.—antagonistic, contrary, hostile, opposed, opposite; counteractive, disastrous, unfavorable, unlucky. ANT.—benign, favorable, fortunate, lucky, propitious.

advice, SYN.—admonition, caution, counsel, exhortation, instruction, recommendation, suggestion, warning; information, intelligence, notification.

affect, SYN.—alter, change, influence, modify, transform; concern, interest, regard; impress, melt, move, soften, subdue, touch; adopt, assume, feign, pretend.

affection, SYN.—attachment, endearment, fondness, kindness, love, tenderness; disposition, emotion, feeling, inclination. ANT.—aversion, hatred, indifference, repugnance, repulsion.

affirm, SYN.—assert, aver, declare, maintain, protest, state, swear.

ANT.—contradict, demur, deny, dispute, oppose.

afraid, SYN.—apprehensive, fainthearted, fearful, frightened, scared, timid, timorous. ANT.—assured, bold, composed, courageous, sanguine.

age, SYN.—dotage, senescence, senility, seniority; antiquity, date, epoch, era, generation, period, time. ANT.—childhood, infancy, youth.

aggravate, SYN.—heighten, increase, intensify, magnify; annoy, chafe, embitter, exasperate, inflame, irritate, nettle, provoke, vex. ANT.—appease, mitigate, palliate, soften, soothe.

aggregate, SYN.—amount, collection, conglomeration, entirety, sum, total, whole. ANT.—element, ingredient, part, particular, unit.

agility, SYN.—action, activity, briskness, energy, enterprise, exercise, intensity, liveliness, motion, movement, quickness, rapidity, vigor. ANT.—dullness, idleness, inactivity, inertia, sloth.

agitate, SYN.—arouse, disconcert, disturb, excite, jar, perturb, rouse, ruffle, shake, trouble. ANT.—calm, ease, placate, quiet.

agony, SYN.—ache, anguish, distress, misery, pain, suffering, throe, torment, torture, woe.

ANT.—comfort, ease, mitigation, relief.

agree, SYN.—accede, acquiesce, assent, comply, consent; coincide, concur, conform, tally. ANT.—contradict, differ, disagree, dissent, protest.

agreeable, SYN.—acceptable, amiable, charming, gratifying, pleasant, pleasing, pleasurable, suitable, welcome. ANT.—disagreeable, obnoxious, offensive, unpleasant.

agreement, SYN.—accordance, coincidence, concord, concurrence, harmony, understanding, unison; bargain, compact, contract, covenant, pact, stipulation. ANT.—difference, disagreement, discord, dissension, variance.

agriculture, SYN.—agronomy, cultivation, farming, gardening, horticulture, husbandry, tillage.

alarm, SYN.—affright, apprehension, consternation, dismay, fright, signal, terror, warning. ANT.—calm, composure, quiet, security, tranquility.

alien, SYN.—adverse, contrasted, extraneous, foreign, irrelevant, remote, strange, unconnected. ANT.—akin, germane, kindred, relevant.

allege, SYN.—advance, affirm, assign, cite, claim, declare, maintain.

ANT.—contradict, deny, disprove, gainsay, refute.

allegory, SYN.—chronicle, fable, fiction, legend, myth, parable, saga. ANT.—fact, history.

alleviate, SYN.—abate, allay, assuage, diminish, extenuate, mitigate, relieve, soften, solace, soothe. ANT.—aggravate, agitate, augment, increase, irritate.

alliance, SYN.—association, coalition, combination, confederacy, entente, federation, league, partnership, union; compact, covenant, marriage, treaty. ANT.—divorce, schism, separation.

allot, SYN.—apportion, deal, dispense, distribute, divide, mete; allocate, appropriate, assign, give, grant, measure. ANT.—confiscate, keep, refuse, retain, withhold.

allow, SYN.—let, permit, sanction, suffer, tolerate; authorize, give, grant, yield; acknowledge, admit, concede. ANT.—forbid, object, protest, refuse, resist.

allude, SYN.—advert, hint, imply, insinuate, intimate, refer, suggest. ANT.—declare, demonstrate, specify, state.

ally, SYN.—abettor, accessory, accomplice, assistant, associate, confederate. ANT.—adversary, enemy, opponent, rival.

alone, SYN.—deserted, desolate, isolated, lonely, secluded, unaided; lone, only, single, sole, solitary. ANT.—accompanied, attended, surrounded.

also, SYN.—besides, furthermore, in addition, likewise, moreover, similarly, too.

altruism, SYN.—beneficence, benevolence, charity, generosity, humanity, kindness, liberality, magnanimity, philanthropy, tenderness. ANT.—cruelty, inhumanity, malevolence, selfishness, unkindness.

always, SYN.—constantly, continually, eternally, ever, evermore, forever, incessantly, perpetually, unceasingly. ANT.—fitfully, never, occasionally, rarely, sometimes.

amalgamate, SYN.—blend, coalesce, combine, commingle, conjoin, consolidate, fuse, mingle, mix, merge, unify, unite. ANT.—analyze, decompose, disintegrate.

amateur, SYN.—apprentice, beginner, dabbler, dilettante, learner, neophyte, novice. ANT.—adept, authority, expert, master, professional.

ambiguous, SYN.—dubious, enigmatical, equivocal, obscure, uncertain, vague. ANT.—clear, explicit, obvious, plain, unequivocal.

ambition, SYN.—aspiration, eagerness,

emulation, goal, incentive, pretension. ANT.—contentment, indifference, indolence, resignation, satisfaction.

amiable, SYN.—agreeable, engaging, friendly, good-natured, gracious, pleasing. ANT.—churlish, disagreeable, hateful, ill-natured, surly.

among, SYN.—amid, amidst, between, betwixt, mingled, mixed. ANT.—apart, separate.

amount, SYN.—aggregate, number, quantity, sum, total, whole.

ample, SYN.—broad, extensive, great, large, spacious, wide; abundant, bountiful, copious, full, generous, liberal, plentiful, profuse, rich. ANT.—constricted, limited, small; insufficient, lacking, meager.

amplification, SYN.—accrual, augmentation, enhancement, enlargement, expansion, extension, growth, heightening, increase, intensification, magnification, multiplication, raising, waxing. ANT.—atrophication, contraction, decrease, diminishing, reduction.

analogous, SYN.—akin, alike, allied, comparable, correlative, correspondent, corresponding, like, parallel, similar. ANT.—different, dissimilar, divergent, incongruous, opposed.

anger, SYN.—animosity, choler, exasperation, fury, indignation, ire, irritation, passion, petulance, rage, resentment, temper, wrath. ANT.—conciliation, forbearance, patience, peace, self-control.

angry, SYN.—enraged, exasperated, furious, incensed, indignant, irate, maddened, provoked, wrathful, wroth. ANT.—calm, happy, pleased, satisfied.

anguish, SYN.—agony, distress, grief, misery, suffering, torment, torture. ANT.—comfort, joy, relief, solace.

animosity, SYN.—bitterness, enmity, grudge, hatred, hostility, malevolence, rancor, spite. ANT.—friendliness, goodwill, love.

announce, SYN.—advertise, declare, give out, herald, make known, notify, proclaim, promulgate, publish, report. ANT.—bury, conceal, stifle, suppress, withhold.

announcement, SYN.—advertisement, bulletin, declaration, notification, promulgation. ANT.—hush, muteness, silence, speechlessness.

annoy, SYN.—bother, chafe, disturb, inconvenience, irk, irritate, molest, pester, tease, trouble, vex. ANT.—accommodate, console, gratify, soothe.

answer, SYN.—rejoinder, reply, response, retort;

defense, rebuttal. ANT.—inquiry, questioning, summoning; argument.

anticipation, SYN.—contemplation, expectation, foresight, forethought, hope, preconception, prescience, presentiment. ANT.—doubt, dread, fear, worry.

anticipated, SYN.—contemplated, expected, foresought, forethought, hoped, preconceived. ANT.—doubted, dreaded, feared, worried.

anxiety, SYN.—apprehension, care, concern, disquiet, fear, solicitude, trouble, worry. ANT.—assurance, confidence, contentment, equanimity, nonchalance.

aperture, SYN.—abyss, cavity, chasm, gap, gulf, hole, opening, pore, void. ANT.—bridge, connection, link.

apology, SYN.—alibi, confession, defense, excuse, explanation, justification. ANT.—accusation, complaint, denial, dissimulation.

apostate, SYN.—dissenter, heretic, nonconformist, schismatic, sectarian, sectary, unbeliever. ANT.—believer, conformist, saint.

appalling, SYN.—awful, dire, dreadful, fearful, frightful, ghastly, hideous, horrible, horrid, repulsive, terrible. ANT.—beautiful, enchanting, enjoyable, fascinating.

apparent, SYN.—clear, evident, manifest, obvious, palpable, plain, self-evident, transparent, unambiguous, unmistakable, visible; illusory, ostensible, seeming. ANT.—ambiguous, dubious, indistinct, real, uncertain.

appear, SYN.—look, seem; arise, arrive, emanate, emerge, issue. ANT.—be, exist; disappear, vanish, withdraw.

appearance, SYN.—advent, apparition, arrival; air, aspect, demeanor, look, manner, mien; fashion, guise, pretense, semblance. ANT.—departure, disappearance; reality.

appease, SYN.—allay, alleviate, assuage, calm, compose, lull, pacify, placate, quell, quiet, relieve, satisfy, soothe, still, tranquilize. ANT.—arouse, excite, incense, inflame.

appetite, SYN.—hunger, relish, stomach, thirst, zest; craving, desire, inclination, liking, longing, passion. ANT.—disgust, distaste, renunciation, repugnance, satiety.

apply, SYN.—administer, affix, allot, appropriate, assign, attach, avail, devote, direct, employ, use; bear, pertain, refer, relate; appeal, petition, request. ANT.—detach, give away; demand.

appreciate, SYN.—admire, cherish, enjoy, esteem, prize, regard, value; appraise, estimate, evaluate, rate; apprehend, comprehend, understand; go up, improve, rise. ANT.—belittle, degrade, depreciate; misapprehend, misunderstand.

approach, SYN.—accost, address, greet, hail, speak to. ANT.—avoid, pass by.

appropriate, SYN.—applicable, apt, becoming, fitting, particular, proper, suitable. ANT.—contrary, improper, inappropriate.

appropriate, SYN.—burglarize, embezzle, loot, pilfer, pillage, plagiarize, plunder, purloin, rob, snitch, steal, swipe. ANT.—buy, refund, repay, restore, return.

approval, SYN.—approbation, assent, commendation, consent, endorsement, praise, sanction, support. ANT.—censure, reprimand, reproach, stricture.

approve, SYN.—appreciate, commend, like, praise; authorize, confirm, endorse, ratify, sanction. ANT.—criticize, disparage; condemn, nullify.

aptness, SYN.—ability, aptitude, capability, capacity, dexterity, efficiency, faculty, power, qualification, skill, talent. ANT.—disability, incapacity, incompetency, unreadiness.

arbitrary, SYN.—

unconditional, unqualified, unrestricted; absolute, authoritative, despotic, tyrannous. ANT.—accountable, conditional, contingent, dependent, qualified.

ardent, SYN.—eager, enthusiastic, fervent, fervid, fiery, glowing, hot, impassioned, intense, keen, passionate, vehement, zealous. ANT.—apathetic, cool, indifferent, nonchalant.

ardor, SYN.—devotion, eagerness, enthusiasm, fervor, fire, passion, rapture, spirit, zeal. ANT.—apathy, disinterest, indifference, unconcern.

argue, SYN.—debate, discuss, dispute, plead, reason, wrangle; denote, imply, indicate, prove, show. ANT.—ignore, overlook, reject, spurn.

arise, SYN.—begin, commence, enter, inaugurate, initiate, institute, open, originate, start. ANT.—close, complete, end, finish, terminate.

arraign, SYN.—accuse, censure, charge, incriminate, indict. ANT.—absolve, acquit, exonerate, release, vindicate.

arraignment, SYN.—accusation, charge, imputation, incrimination, indictment. ANT.—exculpation, exoneration, pardon.

arrange, SYN.—adjust, assort, classify, dispose, organize, place, regulate; devise, organize, plan, prepare. ANT.—confuse, disorder, disturb, jumble, scatter.

arrest, SYN.—apprehend, check, detain, hinder, interrupt, obstruct, restrain, seize, stop, withhold. ANT.—activate, discharge, free, liberate, release.

arrive, SYN.—appear, attain, come, emerge, land, reach, visit. ANT.—depart, exit, leave.

art, SYN.—adroitness, aptitude, cunning, knack, skill, tact; artifice, duplicity, guile, shrewdness, subtlety. ANT.—clumsiness, unskillfulness; forthrightness, honesty, innocence.

artificial, SYN.—affected, assumed, bogus, counterfeit, ersatz, fake, feigned, fictitious, phony, sham, spurious, synthetic, unreal. ANT.—genuine, natural, real, true.

ascend, SYN.—climb, mount, rise, scale, soar, tower. ANT.—descend, fall, sink.

ask, SYN.—beg, claim, demand, entreat, invite, request, solicit; inquire, interrogate, query, question. ANT.—command, dictate, insist, order, reply.

aspersion, SYN.—abuse, defamation, desecration, dishonor, disparagement, insult, invective, maltreatment, misuse, outrage, perversion, profanation, reproach, reviling, upbraiding. ANT.—approval, commendation, laudation, plaudit, respect.

aspiration, SYN.—aim, ambition, craving, desire, goal, hope, longing, objective, passion.

assault, SYN.—assail, attack, bombard, charge, invade, pound, storm, strike. ANT.—defend, oppose, protect.

assert, SYN.—affirm, allege, aver, claim, declare, express, maintain, state; defend, support, uphold, vindicate. ANT.—contradict, deny, refute.

assess, SYN.—appraise, assign, calculate, compute, estimate, evaluate, fix, levy, reckon, tax.

assign, SYN.—allot, apportion, appropriate, ascribe, attribute, cast, designate, distribute, specify. ANT.—discharge, release, relieve, unburden.

assist, SYN.—abet, aid, back, further, help, promote, serve, support, sustain. ANT.—hamper, hinder, impede, prevent.

assistance, SYN.—aid, alms, backing, furtherance, help, patronage, relief, succor, support. ANT.—antagonism, counteraction, defiance, hostility, resistance.

assistant, SYN.—abettor, accessory, accomplice, ally, associate, confederate. ANT.—adversary, enemy, opponent, rival.

associate, SYN.—affiliate,

ally, combine, conjoin, connect, join, link, mingle, mix. ANT.—disrupt, divide, estrange, separate.

assume, SYN.—appropriate, arrogate, take, usurp; adopt, affect, pretend, simulate, wear; postulate, presume, suppose. ANT.—concede, grant, surrender; doff; demonstrate, prove.

assurance, SYN.—assuredness, certainty, confidence, conviction, courage, firmness, security, self-reliance, surety; pledge, promise, word; assertion, declaration, statement. ANT.—bashfulness, humility, modesty, shyness, suspicion.

attach, SYN.—adjoin, affix, annex, append, connect, join, stick, unite; assign, associate, attribute. ANT.—detach, disengage, separate, unfasten, untie.

attachment, SYN.—adherence, affection, affinity, devotion, friendship, liking, regard. ANT.—alienation, aversion, estrangement, opposition, separation.

attack, SYN.—aggression, assault, criticism, denunciation, invasion, offense, onslaught; convulsion, fit, paroxysm. ANT.—defense, opposition, resistance, surrender, vindication.

attack, SYN.—assail, assault, besiege, charge, encounter, invade; abuse, censure, impugn. ANT.—aid, defend, protect, repel, resist.

attain, SYN.—accomplish, achieve, acquire, arrive, effect, gain, get, obtain, procure, reach, secure, win. ANT.—abandon, desert, discard, relinquish.

attainment, SYN.—achievement, deed, exploit, feat; accomplishment, completion, performance, realization. ANT.—neglect, omission; defeat, failure.

attempt, SYN.—effort, endeavor, essay, experiment, trial, undertaking. ANT.—inaction, laziness, neglect.

attend, SYN.—accompany, escort, follow, guard, lackey, protect, serve, tend, watch; be present, frequent. ANT.—abandon, avoid, desert.

attention, SYN.—alertness, care, circumspection, consideration, heed, mindfulness, notice, observance, watchfulness; application, contemplation, reflection, study. ANT.—disregard, indifference, negligence, omission, oversight.

attentive, SYN.—alert, alive, awake, aware, careful, considerate, heedful, mindful, observant, thoughtful, wary, watchful; assiduous, diligent, studious. ANT.—apathetic, indifferent, oblivious, unaware.

attitude, SYN.—disposition,

standpoint, viewpoint; aspect, pose, position, posture, stand.

attract, SYN.—allure, captivate, charm, enchant, entice, fascinate, lure. ANT.—alienate, deter, repel, repulse.

attractive, SYN.—alluring, charming, enchanting, engaging, inviting, magnetic, pleasant, pleasing, seductive, winning. ANT.—forbidding, obnoxious, repellent, repulsive.

audacity, SYN.—boldness, effrontery, fearlessness, hardihood, temerity. ANT. — circumspection, fearfulness, humility, meekness.

authentic, SYN.—genuine, pure, real, true, verifiable; accurate, authoritative, correct, reliable, trustworthy. ANT.—counterfeit, erroneous, false, spurious.

author, SYN.—composer, creator, father, inventor, maker, originator, writer.

authoritative, SYN.—certain, dependable, safe, secure, sure, tried, trustworthy, trusty. ANT.—dubious, fallible, questionable, uncertain, unreliable.

authority, SYN.—control, domination, dominion, force, justification, power, supremacy; authorization, license, permission, sanction; ground, importance, influence, prestige, weight. ANT.—impotence, incapacity, weakness; denial, prohibition.

auxiliary, SYN.—ancillary, assisting, conducive, furthering, helping, instrumental, subsidiary. ANT.—cumbersome, obstructive, opposing, retarding.

available, SYN.—accessible, handy, obtainable, prepared, ready, usable. ANT.—inaccessible, unavailable.

average, SYN.—fair, intermediate, mean, median, mediocre, medium, middling, moderate, ordinary. ANT.—exceptional, extraordinary, outstanding.

aversion, SYN.—abhorrence, antipathy, disgust, disinclination, dislike. distaste, dread, hatred, loathing, repugnance, repulsion, reluctance. ANT.—affection, attachment, devotion, enthusiasm.

avoid, SYN.—avert, dodge, escape, eschew, elude, forbear, forestall, free, shun, ward. ANT.—confront, encounter, meet, oppose.

aware, SYN.—apprised, cognizant, conscious, informed, mindful, observant, perceptive, sensible. ANT.—ignorant, insensible, oblivious, unaware.

away, SYN.—abroad, absent, departed; absentminded, abstracted, distracted, inattentive, preoccupied. ANT.—

attending, present, attentive, watchful.

awful, SYN.—appalling, dire, dreadful, frightful, horrible, terrible; awe-inspiring, imposing, majestic, solemn. ANT.—commonplace, humble, lowly, vulgar.

awkward, SYN.—clumsy, gauche, inept, rough, unpolished, untoward. ANT.—adroit, graceful, neat, polished, skillful.

axiom, SYN.—adage, aphorism, apothegm, byword, fundamental, maxim, principle, proverb, saw, saying, theorem, truism.

B

backward, SYN.—regressive, retrograde, revisionary; dull, sluggish, stupid; disinclined, hesitating, indisposed, loath, reluctant, unwilling, wavering. ANT.—advanced, civilized, progressive.

bad, SYN.—baleful, base, deleterious, evil, immoral, iniquitous, noxious, pernicious, sinful, unsound, unwholesome, villainous, wicked. ANT.—excellent, good, honorable, moral, reputable.

balance, SYN.—composure, equilibrium, poise, stability, steadiness, proportion, symmetry; excess, remainder, remains, residue, rest. ANT.—fall, imbalance, instability, unsteadiness.

baleful, SYN.—bad, base,

deleterious, evil, immoral, iniquitous, noxious, pernicious, sinful, unsound, unwholesome, villainous, wicked. ANT.—excellent, good, honorable, moral, reputable.

banal, SYN.—commonplace, hackneyed, inane, insipid, trite, vapid. ANT.—fresh, novel, original, stimulating, striking.

banish, SYN.—deport, dismiss, dispel, eject, exclude, exile, expatriate, expel, ostracize, oust. ANT.—accept, admit, harbor, receive, shelter.

banquet, SYN.—celebration, dinner, entertainment, feast, festival, regalement.

barbarous, SYN.—barbarian, barbaric, brutal, crude, cruel, inhuman, merciless, remorseless, rude, ruthless, savage, uncivilized, uncultured, unrelenting. ANT.—civilized, humane, kind, polite, refined.

base, SYN.—abject, contemptible, despicable, dishonorable, groveling, ignoble, ignominious, low, lowly, mean, menial, servile, sordid, vile, vulgar. ANT.—esteemed, exalted, honored, lofty, noble, righteous.

bashful, SYN.—abashed, coy, diffident, embarrassed, humble, modest, recoiling, shamefaced, sheepish, shy, timid, timorous. ANT.—adventurous, daring, fearless, gregarious, outgoing.

basis, SYN.—base, bottom, foundation, ground, groundwork, support, underpinning, assumption, postulate, premise, presumption, presupposition, principle. ANT.—derivative, implication, superstructure, trimming.

battle, SYN.—combat, conflict, contest, fight, fray, skirmish, strife, struggle. ANT.—agreement, concord, peace, truce.

bear, SYN.—support, sustain, uphold; allow, brook, endure, permit, stand, suffer, tolerate, undergo; carry, convey, take, transport; produce, spawn, yield. ANT.—avoid, dodge, evade, refuse, shun.

beat, SYN.—belabor, buffet, dash, hit, knock, pound, pummel, punch, smite, strike, thrash, thump; conquer, defeat, overpower, overthrow, rout, subdue, vanquish; palpitate, pulsate, pulse, throb. ANT.—defend, shield, stroke; fail, surrender.

beautiful, SYN.—beauteous, charming, comely, elegant, fair, fine, handsome, lovely, pretty. ANT.—foul, hideous, homely, repulsive, unsightly.

beauty, SYN.—attractiveness, charm, comeliness, elegance, fairness, grace, hand-

someness, loveliness, pulchritude. ANT.—deformity, disfigurement, eyesore, homeliness, ugliness.

because, SYN.—as, for, inasmuch as, since.

bed, SYN.—berth, bunk, cot, couch, cradle; accumulation, deposit, layer, stratum, vein.

beg, SYN.—adjure, ask, beseech, crave, entreat, implore, importune, petition, pray, request, solicit, supplicate. ANT.—bestow, cede, favor, give, grant.

beget, SYN.—breed, create, engender, father, generate, originate, procreate, produce, propagate, sire. ANT.—abort, destroy, extinguish, kill, murder.

beggar, SYN.—mendicant, pauper, ragamuffin, scrub, starveling, tatterdemalion, vagabond, wretch.

begin, SYN.—arise, commence, enter, inaugurate, initiate, institute, open, originate, start. ANT.—close, complete, end, finish, terminate.

beginning, SYN.—commencement, inception, opening, origin, outset, source, start. ANT.—close, completion, consummation, end, termination.

behave, SYN.—act, bear, carry, comport, conduct, demean, deport, interact, manage, operate.

behavior, SYN.—action, bearing, carriage, conduct, deed, demeanor, deportment, disposition, manner.

belief, SYN.—certitude, confidence, conviction, credence, faith, feeling, opinion, persuasion, reliance, trust. ANT.—denial, doubt, heresy, incredulity.

believe, SYN.—accept, apprehend, conceive, credit, fancy, hold, imagine, support, suppose. ANT.—distrust, doubt, question, reject.

belittle, SYN.—decry, depreciate, disparage, minimize, underrate. ANT.—admire, appreciate, esteem.

belongings, SYN.—commodities, effects, estate, goods, merchandise, possessions, property, stock, wares, wealth; attribute, characteristic, peculiarity, quality.

beloved, SYN.—dear, esteemed, precious, valued; costly, expensive, valuable. ANT.—despised, unwanted; cheap.

below, SYN.—beneath, lower, under, underneath. ANT.—above, aloft, over, overhead.

bend, SYN.—bow, crook, curve, deflect, incline, lean, stoop, turn, twist; influence, mold; submit, yield. ANT.—break, resist, stiffen, straighten.

beneath, SYN.—below, under, underneath. ANT.—above, over.

beneficial, SYN.—advantageous, good, helpful, profitable, salutary, serviceable, useful, wholesome. ANT.—deleterious, destructive, detrimental, harmful, injurious.

benefit, SYN.—account, advantage, avail, behalf, favor, gain, good, interest, profit, service. ANT.—calamity, distress, handicap, trouble.

benevolence, SYN.—altruism, beneficence, charity, generosity, humanity, kindness, liberality, magnanimity, philanthropy, tenderness. ANT.—cruelty, inhumanity, malevolence, selfishness, unkindness.

benevolent, SYN.—altruistic, benign, charitable, friendly, generous, humane, kind, liberal, merciful, obliging, philanthropic, tender, unselfish. ANT.—greedy, harsh, malevolent, wicked.

benign, SYN.—altruistic, benevolent, charitable, friendly, generous, humane, kind, liberal, merciful, obliging, philanthropic, tender, unselfish. ANT.—greedy, harsh, malevolent, wicked.

bias, SYN.—bent, disposition, inclination, leaning, partiality, penchant, predilection, predisposition, prejudice, proclivity, proneness, propensity, slant, tendency, turn.

ANT.—equity, fairness, impartiality, justice.

big, SYN.—august, bulky, colossal, enormous, grand, great, huge, hulking, immense, large, majestic, massive, monstrous. ANT.—little, petite, small, tiny.

bigoted, SYN.—dogmatic, fanatical, illiberal, intolerant, narrow-minded, prejudiced. ANT.—liberal, progressive, radical, tolerant.

bind, SYN.—attach, connect, engage, fasten, fetter, join, link, oblige, restrain, restrict, tie. ANT.—free, loose, unfasten, untie.

bite, SYN.—champ, chew, crunch, gnash, gnaw, nibble, nip, pierce, rend, tear.

bitter, SYN.—acrid, biting, distasteful, pungent, sour, tart; galling, grievous, painful, poignant; cruel, fierce, relentless, ruthless; acrimonious, caustic, harsh, sardonic, severe. ANT.—delicious, mellow, pleasant, sweet.

blame, SYN.—accuse, censure, condemn, implicate, rebuke, reproach, upbraid. ANT.—absolve, acquit, exonerate.

blemish, SYN.—blot, speck, stain; defect, disgrace, fault, flaw, imperfection. ANT.—adornment, embellishment, perfection, purity.

blend, SYN.—amalgamate, coalesce, combine, commingle, conjoin, consolidate, fuse, mingle, mix, merge, unify, unite. ANT.—analyze, decompose, disintegrate, separate.

bless, SYN.—adore, celebrate, delight, exalt, extol, gladden, glorify. ANT.—blaspheme, curse, denounce, slander.

blind, SYN.—ignorant, oblivious, sightless, undiscerning, unmindful, unseeing; headlong, heedless, rash. ANT.—aware, calculated, discerning, perceiving, sensible.

bliss, SYN.—blessedness, blissfulness, ecstasy, felicity, happiness, joy, rapture. ANT.—grief, misery, sorrow, woe, wretchedness.

block, SYN.—bar, barricade, clog, close, stop; impede; hinder, obstruct. ANT.—clear, open; aid, further, promote.

blunt, SYN.—dull, edgeless, obtuse, pointless, stolid, thick-witted, unsharpened; abrupt, bluff, brusque, impolite, outspoken, plain, rough, rude, unceremonious. ANT.—polished, polite, suave, subtle, tactful.

boast, SYN.—brag, crow, flaunt, glory, vaunt. ANT.—apologize, deprecate, humble, minimize.

body, SYN.—carcass, corpse, remains; form, frame, torso; bulk, corpus, mass; aggregate, association, company, society. ANT.—intellect, mind, soul, spirit.

bold, SYN.—adventurous, audacious, brave, courageous, daring, dauntless, fearless, intrepid; brazen, forward, impudent, insolent, pushy, rude; abrupt, conspicuous, prominent, striking. ANT.—cowardly, flinching, timid; bashful, retiring.

bondage, SYN.—captivity, confinement, imprisonment, serfdom, servitude, slavery, thralldom, vassalage. ANT.— freedom, liberation.

book, SYN.—booklet, brochure, compendium, handbook, manual, monograph, pamphlet, textbook, tract, treatise, volume, work.

bookish, SYN.—academic, erudite, formal, learned, pedantic, scholarly, scholastic, theoretical. ANT. — common-sense, ignorant, practical, simple.

border, SYN.—boundary, brim, brink, edge, fringe, frontier, limit, margin, outskirts, rim, termination, verge. ANT.— center, core, interior, mainland.

boredom, SYN.—doldrums, dullness, ennui, tedium, weariness. ANT.—activity, excitement, motive, stimulus.

bother, SYN.—annoy, disturb, harass, haunt, inconvenience, molest, perplex, pester, plague, tease, trouble, upset, worry. ANT.—gratify, please, relieve, soothe.

bottom, SYN.—base, basis, foot, foundation, fundament, groundwork. ANT.—apex, peak, summit, top.

bound, SYN.—hop, jerk, jump, leap, skip; spring, start, vault. ANT.—crawl, walk.

bountiful, SYN.—abundant, ample, copious, overflowing, plenteous, plentiful, profuse, rich, teeming. ANT.—deficient, insufficient, scant, scarce.

brag, SYN.—bluster, boast, crow, flaunt, flourish, vaunt. ANT.—debase, degrade, demean, denigrate.

brave, SYN.—adventurous, audacious, bold, chivalrous, courageous, daring, dauntless, fearless, gallant, heroic, intrepid, magnanimous, valiant, valorous. ANT.— cowardly, cringing, fearful, timid, weak.

break, SYN.—burst, crack, crush, demolish, destroy, fracture, infringe, pound, rack, rend, rupture, shatter, smash, squeeze; disobey, transgress, violate. ANT.—join, mend, renovate, repair, restore.

breed, SYN.—bear, beget, conceive, engender, generate, procreate, propagate; foster, nurture, raise, rear, train. ANT.— abort, kill, murder.

brief, SYN.—compendious, concise, curt, laconic, pithy, short, succinct, terse; fleeting, momentary, passing, transient. ANT.—extended, lengthy, long, prolonged, protracted.

bright, SYN.—brilliant, clear, gleaming, lucid, luminous, lustrous, radiant, shining, translucent, transparent; clever, intelligent, witty. ANT.—dark, dull, gloomy, murky, sullen.

brisk, SYN.—cool, fresh, refreshing. ANT.—decayed, faded, hackneyed, musty, stagnant.

briskness, SYN.—action, activity, agility, energy, enterprise, exercise, intensity, liveliness, motion, movement, quickness, rapidity, vigor. ANT.—dullness, idleness, inactivity, inertia, sloth.

brittle, SYN.—breakable, crisp, crumbling, delicate, fragile, frail, splintery, ANT.—enduring, thick, tough, unbreakable.

broad, SYN.—expanded, extensive, large, sweeping, vast, wide; liberal, tolerant. ANT.—confined, narrow, restricted.

broken, SYN.—crushed, destroyed, flattened, fractured, interrupted, reduced, rent, ruptured, separated, shattered, smashed, wrecked. ANT.—integral, repaired, united, whole.

brook, SYN.—bear, endure, permit, stand, suffer, tolerate, undergo. ANT.—avoid, dodge, evade, refuse, shun.

brotherhood, SYN.—brotherliness, fellowship, kindness, solidarity; association, clan, fraternity, society. ANT.—acrimony, discord, opposition, strife.

brusque, SYN.—hasty, precipitate, sudden, unannounced, unexpected; abrupt, blunt, curt, rude; craggy, harsh, precipitous, rough, rugged, sharp, steep. ANT.—anticipated, expected; courteous, gradual, smooth.

brutal, SYN.—barbarous, bestial, brute, brutish, carnal, coarse, cruel, ferocious, gross, inhuman, merciless, remorseless, rough, rude, ruthless, savage, sensual. ANT.—civilized, courteous, gentle, humane, kind.

build, SYN.—construct, erect, establish, found, raise, rear. ANT.—demolish, destroy, overthrow, raze, undermine.

bulky, SYN.—big, enormous, great, huge, hulking, immense, large, massive, monstrous. ANT.—little, petite, small, tiny.

bunk, SYN.—bed, berth, cot, couch.

buoyant, SYN.—effervescent, light, resilient; animated, blithe, cheerful, elated, hopeful, jocund, lively, spirited, sprightly, vivacious. ANT.—dejected, depressed, despondent, hopeless, sullen.

burden, SYN.—afflict, encumber, load, oppress, overload, tax, trouble, weigh. ANT.—alleviate, console, ease, lighten, mitigate.

burn, SYN.—blaze, char, consume, incinerate, scald, scorch, sear, singe. ANT.—extinguish, put out, quench.

bury, SYN.—conceal, cover, entomb, hide, immure, inhume, inter. ANT.—display, exhume, expose, open, reveal.

business, SYN.—art, commerce, employment, engagement, enterprise, job, occupation, profession, trade, trading, vocation, work. ANT.—avocation, hobby, pastime.

busy, SYN.—active, assiduous, careful, diligent, hard-working, industrious, patient, perseverant. ANT.—apathetic, careless, indifferent, lethargic, unconcerned.

butcher, SYN.—assassinate, execute, kill, massacre, murder, put to death, slaughter, slay. ANT.—animate, protect, resuscitate, save, vivify.

buy, SYN.—acquire, get, obtain, procure, purchase. ANT.—dispose of, sell, vend.

by, SYN.—beside, near, next to; by means of, through, with; according to; from.

C

cabal, SYN.—collusion, combination, conspiracy, intrigue, machination, plot, treachery, treason.

calamity, SYN.—adversity, casualty, catastrophe, disaster, mishap, ruin. ANT.—advantage, fortune, welfare.

calculate, SYN.—compute, consider, count, estimate, figure, reckon. ANT.—conjecture, guess, miscalculate.

calculation, SYN.—computation, consideration, count, estimation, figure, reckoning. ANT.—conjecture, guess, miscalculation.

caliber, SYN.—attribute, characteristic, distinction, feature, peculiarity, property, quality, trait; grade, value. ANT.—being, essence, nature, substance.

callous, SYN.—hard, impenitent, indurate, insensible, insensitive, obdurate, tough, unfeeling. ANT.—compassionate, sensitive, soft, tender.

calm, SYN.—alloy, alleviate, appease, assuage, compose, lull, pacify, placate, quell, quiet, relieve, satisfy, soothe, still, tranquilize. ANT.—arouse, incite, incense, inflame.

calm, SYN.—composed, dispassionate, imperturbable, pacific, peaceful, placid, quiet, serene, still, tranquil, undisturbed, unruffled. ANT.—excited, frantic, stormy, turbulent, wild.

calumny, SYN.—aspersion, backbiting, defamation, libel, scandal, slander, vilification. ANT.—applause, commendation, defense, flattery, praise.

cancel, SYN.—cross out, delete, eliminate, erase, expunge, obliterate; abolish, abrogate, annul, invalidate, nullify, quash, repeal, rescind, revoke. ANT.—confirm, enact, enforce, perpetuate.

candid, SYN.—frank, free, honest, ingenuous, open, plain, sincere, straightforward, truthful; fair, impartial, just, unbiased. ANT.—contrived, scheming, sly, wily.

candor, SYN.—fairness, frankness, honesty, integrity, justice, openness, rectitude, responsibility, sincerity, trustworthiness, uprightness. ANT.—cheating, deceit, dishonesty, fraud, trickery.

cant, SYN.—deceit, dissimulation, hypocrisy, pretense, sanctimony. ANT.—candor, frankness, honesty, openness, truth.

capability, SYN.—ability, aptitude, aptness, capacity, dexterity, efficiency, faculty, power, qualification, skill, talent. ANT.—disability, incapacity, incompetency, unreadiness.

capable, SYN.—able, clever, competent, efficient, fitted, qualified, skillful. ANT.—inadequate, incapable, incompetent, unfitted.

capacity, SYN.—ability, capability, faculty, power, skill, talent; magnitude, size, volume. ANT.—impotence, inability, incapacity, stupidity.

capitulate, SYN.—abandon, acquiesce, capitulate, cede, relinquish, renounce, resign, sacrifice, submit, surrender, yield. ANT.—conquer, overcome, resist, rout.

caprice, SYN.—face, humor, inclination, notion, quick, vagary, whim, whimsy.

capricious, SYN.—changeable, fickle, fitful, inconstant, restless, unstable, variable. ANT.—constant, reliable, stable, steady, trustworthy.

captivity, SYN.—bondage, confinement, imprisonment, serfdom, servitude, slavery, thralldom, vassalage. ANT.—freedom, liberation.

capture, SYN.—apprehend, arrest, catch, clutch, grasp, grip, lay hold of, seize, snare, trap. ANT.—liberate, lose, release, throw.

carcass, SYN.—corpse, remains; form, frame, torso; bulk, corpus, mass; aggregate, association, company, society.

ANT.—intellect, mind, soul, spirit.

care, SYN.—anxiety, concern, solicitude, worry; attention, caution, regard, vigilance, wariness; charge, custody, guardianship, ward. ANT.—disregard, indifference, neglect, negligence.

careful, SYN.—attentive, heedful, prudent, scrupulous, thoughtful; cautious, circumspect, discreet, guarded, vigilant, wary. ANT.—forgetful, improvident, indifferent, lax.

careless, SYN.—heedless, imprudent, inattentive, inconsiderate, indiscreet, reckless, thoughtless, unconcerned; desultory, inaccurate, lax, neglectful, negligent, remiss. ANT.—accurate, careful, meticulous, nice.

carelessness, SYN.— default, disregard, failure, heedlessness, neglect, negligence, oversight, slight. ANT.— attention, care, diligence, thoughtfulness, watchfulness.

caress, SYN.—coddle, cuddle, embrace, fondle, hug, kiss, pet. ANT.— annoy, buffet, spurn, tease, vex.

carnal, SYN.—animal, base, bodily, corporeal, fleshly, gross, lustful, sensual, voluptuous, worldly. ANT.—exalted, intellectual, refined, spiritual, temperate.

carping, SYN.—accurate, discerning, discriminating, exact, fastidious, particular; captious, caviling, censorious, faultfinding, hypercritical; acute, crucial, decisive, hazardous, important, momentous. ANT.— cursory, shallow, superficial, uncritical; appreciative, approving, commendatory, encouraging, insignificant; unimportant.

carriage, SYN.—action, bearing, behavior, conduct, deed, demeanor, deportment, disposition, manner.

carry, SYN.—bring, convey, transmit, transport; bear, support, sustain. ANT.—abandon, drop.

caste, SYN.—category, class, denomination, genre, kind; grade, order, rank, set; elegance, excellence.

casual, SYN.—accidental, chance, fortuitous, unexpected; incidental, informal, nonchalant, offhand, relaxed, unconcerned, unpremeditated. ANT.—expected, intended; formal, planned, pretentious.

casualty, SYN.—accident, calamity, contingency, disaster, fortuity, misfortune, mishap. ANT.— calculation, design, intention, purpose.

catastrophe, SYN.— adversity, calamity, casualty, disaster, mishap, ruin. ANT.—advantage, fortune, welfare.

catch, SYN.—apprehend, arrest, capture, clutch, grasp, grip. lay hold of, seize, snare, trap. ANT.—liberate, lose, release, throw.

catching, SYN.—communicable, contagious, infectious, pestilential, virulent. ANT.—healthful, hygienic, noncommunicable.

category, SYN.—caste, class, denomination, genre, kind; grade, order, rank, set; elegance, excellence.

cause, SYN.—agent, determinant, incentive, inducement, motive, origin, principle, reason, source. ANT.—consequence, effect, end, result.

cause, SYN.—create, effect, evoke, incite, induce, make, occasion, originate, prompt.

caustic, SYN.—acrid, bitter, biting, distasteful, pungent, sour, tart; galling, grievous, painful, poignant; cruel, fierce, relentless, ruthless; acrimonious, harsh, sardonic, severe. ANT.—delicious, mellow, pleasant, sweet.

caution, SYN.—care, heed, prudence, vigilance, wariness, watchfulness; admonition, counsel, injunction, warning. ANT.—abandon, carelessness, recklessness.

cautious, SYN.—attentive, heedful, prudent, scrupulous, thoughtful; careful, circumspect, discreet, guarded, vigilant, wary. ANT.—forgetful, improvident, indifferent.

cease, SYN.—abandon, desist, discontinue, stop; give up, relinquish, resign, surrender; abandon, depart, leave, withdraw. ANT.—continue, endure, occupy, persist, stay.

celebrate, SYN.—commemorate, honor, keep, observe, solemnize; commend, extol, glorify, honor, laud, praise. ANT.—disregard, overlook; decry, disgrace, dishonor, profane.

celebrated, SYN.—distinguished, eminent, famous, glorious, illustrious, noted, renowned, well known. ANT.—hidden, ignominious, infamous, obscure, unknown.

celestial, SYN.—divine, godlike, heavenly, holy, superhuman, supernatural, transcendant. ANT.—blasphemous, diabolical, mundane, profane, wicked.

censure, SYN.—blame, condemn, denounce, reprehend, reproach, reprobate, reprove, upbraid; convict, sentence. ANT.—approve, commend, condone, forgive, praise; absolve, acquit, exonerate, pardon.

center, SYN.—core, heart, middle, midpoint, midst, nucleus. ANT.—border, boundary, outskirts, periphery, rim.

ceremonious, SYN.—affected, correct, decorous, exact, formal, methodical, precise, proper, regular, solemn, stiff; external, outward, perfunctory. ANT.—easy, material, unconstrained, unconventional; heartfelt.

ceremony, SYN.—formality, observance, parade, pomp, protocol, rite, ritual, solemnity. ANT.—casualness, informality.

certain, SYN.—assured, definite, fixed, indubitable, inevitable, positive, secure, sure, undeniable, unquestionable. ANT.—doubtful, probable, questionable, uncertain.

certainty, SYN.—assuredness, confidence, conviction, courage, firmness, security, self-reliance, surety; pledge, promise, word; assertion, declaration, statement. ANT.—bashfulness, humility, modest, shyness, suspicion.

certitude, SYN.—belief, confidence, conviction, credence, faith, feeling, opinion, persuasion, reliance, trust. ANT.—denial, doubt, heresy, incredulity.

challenge, SYN.—object to, question; brave, dare, defy; call, invite, summon; demand, require.

chance, SYN.—accident, bechance, befall, betide, calamity, casualty, contingency, disaster, fortu-

ity, happen, misfortune, mishap, occur, take place, transpire. ANT.—calculation, design, intention, purpose.

change, SYN.—alteration, alternation, modification, mutation, substitution, variation, variety, vicissitude. ANT.—monotony, stability, uniformity.

change, SYN.—exchange, substitute; alter, convert, modify, shift, transfigure, transform, vary, veer. ANT.—retain; continue, establish, preserve, settle, stabilize.

changeable, SYN.—fickle, fitful, inconstant, shifting, unstable, vacillating, variable, wavering. ANT.—constant, stable, steady, unchanging, uniform.

chaos, SYN.—anarchy, confusion, disorder, disorganization, jumble, muddle. ANT.—order, organization, system.

chaperone, SYN.—accompany, associate with, attend, consort with, convoy, escort, go with. ANT.—abandon, avoid, desert, leave, quit.

character, SYN.—class, description, disposition, individuality, kind, nature, reputation, repute, sort, standing, mark, sign, symbol.

characteristic, SYN.—attribute, feature, mark, peculiarity, property, quality, trait.

charge, SYN.—accusation,

arraignment, imputation, incrimination, indictment. ANT.—exculpation, exoneration, pardon.

charge, SYN.—accuse, arraign, censure, incriminate, indict. ANT.—absolve, acquit, exonerate, release, vindicate.

charitable, SYN.—altruistic, benevolent, benign, friendly, generous, humane, kind, liberal, merciful, obliging, philanthropic, tender, unselfish. ANT.—greedy, harsh, malevolent, wicked.

charity, SYN.—altruism, beneficence, benevolence, generosity, humanity, kindness, liberality, magnanimity, philanthropy, tenderness. ANT.—cruelty, inhumanity, malevolence, selfishness, unkindness.

charming, SYN.—alluring, attractive, bewitching, captivating, enchanting, engaging, fascinating, winning. ANT.—repugnant, repulsive, revolting.

chart, SYN.—cabal, conspiracy, design, intrigue, machination, plan, plot, scheme, stratagem; diagram, graph, sketch.

chase, SYN.—follow, hunt, persist, pursue, track, trail. ANT.—abandon, elude, escape, evade, flee.

chaste, SYN.—clean, clear, genuine, immaculate, spotless, unadulterated; guiltless, innocent, modest, sincere, undefiled, virgin; absolute, bare, sheer. ANT.—foul, polluted, sullied, tainted; corrupt, defiled.

chastise, SYN.—castigate, correct, discipline, pummel, punish, strike. ANT.—acquit, exonerate, free, pardon, release.

chat, SYN.—colloquy, conference, conversation, dialogue, interview, parley, talk.

chat, SYN.—blab, converse, gossip, jabber, mutter, prattle, speak, talk, tattle; argue, comment, claim, discourse, harangue, lecture, plead, preach, rant, spout; confer, consult, deliberate, discuss.

chatter, SYN.—conference, conversation, dialogue, discourse, discussion, gossip, lecture, report, rumor, speech, talk. ANT.—correspondence, meditation, silence, writing.

cheap, SYN.—inexpensive, low-priced, poor; beggarly, common, inferior, mean, shabby. ANT.—costly, dear, expensive; dignified, honorable, noble.

cheat, SYN.—bilk, circumvent, deceive, defraud, dupe, fool, gull, hoax, hoodwink, outwit, swindle, trick, victimize.

check, SYN.—analyze, assess, audit, contemplate, dissect, examine, inquire, interrogate, notice, question, quiz, review, scan, scrutinize, survey, view, watch. ANT.—disregard, neglect, omit, overlook.

cheer, SYN.—comfort, console, encourage, gladden, solace, soothe, sympathize. ANT.—antagonize, aggravate, depress, dishearten.

cheerful, SYN.—gay, glad, happy, jolly, joyful, lighthearted, merry, sprightly. ANT.—depressed, glum, mournful, sad, sullen.

cherish, SYN.—appreciate, hold dear, prize, treasure, value; foster, nurture, sustain. ANT.—dislike, disregard, neglect; abandon, reject.

chief, SYN.—captain, chieftain, commander, head, leader, master, principal, ruler. ANT.—attendant, follower, servant, subordinate.

chilly, SYN.—arctic, cold, cool, freezing, frigid, frozen, icy, wintry; passionless, phlegmatic, stoical, unfeeling. ANT.—burning, fiery, heated, hot, torrid; ardent, passionate.

choice, SYN.—alternative, election, option, preference, selection.

choice, SYN.—dainty, delicate, elegant, exquisite, fine, nice, pure, refined, splendid, subtle; beautiful, handsome, pretty; minute, powdered, pulverized, sharp, slender, small, thin. ANT.—blunt, coarse, large, rough, thick.

choose, SYN.—cull, elect, opt, pick, select. ANT.—refuse, reject.

chronicle, SYN.—account, description, detail, history, narration, narrative, recital, relation; computation, reckoning, record. ANT.—caricature, confusion, distortion, misrepresentation.

cinema, SYN.—appearance, drawing, effigy, engraving, etching, film, illustration, image, likeness, painting, panorama, photograph, picture, portrait, portrayal, print, representation, resemblance, scene, sketch, view.

circuitous, SYN.—crooked, devious, distorted, erratic, indirect, roundabout, swerving, tortuous, wandering, winding; crooked, cunning, tricky. ANT.—direct, straight; honest, straightforward.

circular, SYN.—bulbous, chubby, complete, curved, cylindrical, entire, globular, plump, rotund, round, spherical.

circumspection, SYN.—anxiety, care, concern, solicitude, worry; attention, caution, regard, vigilance, wariness; charge, custody, guardianship, ward. ANT.—disregard, indifference, neglect, negligence.

circumstance, SYN.—condition, event, fact, happening, incident, occurrence, position, situation.

cite, SYN.—advance, affirm, allege, assign, claim, declare, maintain. ANT.—contradict, deny, disprove, gainsay, refute.

civil, SYN.—accomplished, considerate, courteous, cultivated, genteel, polite, refined, urbane, well-bred, well-mannered. ANT.—boorish, impertinent, rude, uncivil, uncouth.

civilization, SYN.—breeding, cultivation, culture, education, enlightenment, refinement. ANT.—boorishness, ignorance, illiteracy, vulgarity.

claim, SYN.—affirm, allege, assert, aver, declare, express, maintain, state; defend, support, uphold, vindicate. ANT.—contradict, deny, refute.

clamor, SYN.—babel, cry, din, noise, outcry, racket, row, sound, tumult, uproar. ANT.—hush, quiet, silence, stillness.

clan, SYN.—brotherliness, fellowship, kindness, solidarity; association, brotherhood, fraternity, society. ANT.—acrimony, discord, opposition, strife.

clandestine, SYN.—concealed, covert, hidden, latent, private, secret, surreptitious, unknown. ANT.—conspicuous, disclosed, exposed, known, obvious.

clarify, SYN.—decipher, educate, explain, expound, illustrate, interpret, resolve, unfold, unravel. ANT.—baffle, confuse, darken, obscure.

clasp, SYN.—adhere, clutch, grasp, grip, hold, have, keep, maintain, occupy, possess, retain, support; check confine, curb, detain, restrain; accommodate, carry, contain, receive, stow. ANT.—abandon, relinquish, surrender, vacate.

class, SYN.—caste, category, denomination, genre, kind; grade, order, rank, set; elegance, excellence.

clean, SYN.—cleanse, mop, purify, scrub, sweep, wash. ANT.—dirty, pollute, soil, stain, sully.

cleanse, SYN.—clean, mop, purify, scrub, sweep, wash. ANT.—dirty, pollute, soil, stain, sully.

clear, SYN.—cloudless, fair, sunny; limpid, transparent; apparent, distinct, evident, intelligible, lucid, manifest, obvious, plain, unmistakable, visible; open, unobstructed. ANT.—cloudy, foul, overcast, ambiguous, obscure, unclear, vague.

clemency, SYN.—charity, compassion, forgiveness, grace, leniency, mercy, mildness, pity. ANT.—cruelty, punishment, retribution, vengeance.

clever, SYN.—adroit, apt, dexterous, quick, quick-witted, skillful, talented, witty; bright, ingenious, sharp, smart. ANT.—awkward, bungling, clumsy, slow, unskilled; dull, foolish, stupid.

cleverness, SYN.—comprehension, intellect, intelligence, mind, perspicacity, reason, sagacity, sense, understanding; banter, fun, humor, irony, pleasantry, raillery, sarcasm, satire, wit, witticism. ANT.— commonplace, platitude, sobriety, solemnity, stupidity.

climax, SYN.—acme, apex, consummation, culmination, height, peak, summit, zenith. ANT.—anticlimax, base, depth, floor.

climb, SYN.—ascend, mount, rise, scale, soar, tower. ANT.—descend, fall, sink.

cloak, SYN.—clothe, conceal, cover, curtain, disguise, envelop, guard, hide, mask, protect, screen, shield, shroud, veil. ANT.—bare, divulge, expose, reveal, unveil.

cloister, SYN.—abbey, convent, hermitage, monastery, nunnery, priory.

close, SYN.—abutting, adjacent, adjoining, immediate, impending, near, nearby, neighboring; confidential, dear, devoted, intimate. ANT.—afar, distant, faraway, removed.

close, SYN.—occlude, seal, shut; clog, obstruct, stop; cease, complete, conclude, end, finish, terminate. ANT.—open, unbar, unlock; begin, commence, inaugurate, start.

clothes, SYN.—apparel, array, attire, clothing, drapery, dress, garb, garments, raiment, vestments, vesture. ANT.—nakedness, nudity.

clothing, SYN.—apparel, array, attire, clothes, drapery, dress, garb, garments, raiment, vestments, vesture. ANT.—nakedness, nudity.

cloudy, SYN.—dark, dim, indistinct, murky, mysterious obscure, overcast, shadowy. ANT.—bright, clear, distinct, limpid, sunny.

clumsy, SYN.—awkward, gauche, inept, rough, unpolished, untoward. ANT.—adroit, graceful, neat, polished, skillful.

coalition, SYN.—alliance, association, combination, confederacy, entente, federation, league, partnership, union; compact, covenant, marriage, treaty. ANT.—divorce, schism, separation.

coarse, SYN.—crude, impure, rough, rugged, unrefined; gross, gruff, immodest, indelicate, rude, unpolished, vulgar. ANT.—fine, polished, refined, smooth; cultivated, cultured, delicate.

coerce, SYN.—compel, constrain, drive, enforce, force, impel, oblige. ANT.—allure, convince, induce, persuade, prevent.

coercion, SYN.—dint, emphasis, energy, intensity, might, potency, power, strength, vigor; compulsion, constraint, force, violence, ANT.—feebleness, frailty, impotence, weakness; persuasion.

cognizance, SYN.—acquaintance, apprehension, erudition, information, knowledge, learning, lore, scholarship, science, understanding, wisdom. ANT.—ignorance, illiteracy, misunderstanding, stupidity.

cognizant, SYN.—apprised, aware, conscious, informed, mindful, observant, perceptive, sensible. ANT.—ignorant, insensible, oblivious, unaware.

coincide, SYN.—accede, acquiesce, agree, assent, comply, consent; concur, conform, tally. ANT.—contradict, differ, disagree, dissent, protest.

coincident, SYN.—equal, equivalent, identical, indistinguishable, like, same. ANT.—contrary, disparate, dissimilar, distinct, opposed.

cold, SYN.—arctic, chilly, cool, freezing, frigid, frozen, icy, wintry; pas-

sionless, phlegmatic, stoical, unfeeling. ANT.—burning, fiery, heated, hot, torrid; ardent, passionate.

collapse, SYN.—decline, decrease, descend, diminish, drop, fall, sink, subside; stumble, topple, tumble; droop, extend downward, hang. ANT.—arise, ascend, climb, mount, soar; steady.

colleague, SYN.—associate, attendant, companion, comrade, consort, crony, friend, mate, partner. ANT.—adversary, enemy, stranger.

collect, ANT.—accumulate, amass, assemble, concentrate, congregate, consolidate, gather, heap, hoard, mass, pile. ANT.—assort, disperse, distribute, divide, dole.

collected, SYN.—calm, composed, cool, imperturbable, peaceful; placid, quiet, sedate, tranquil, unmoved. ANT.—agitated, aroused, excited, perturbed, violent.

collection, SYN.—aggregate, amount, conglomeration, entirety, sum, total, whole. ANT.—element, ingredient, part, particular, unit.

collision, SYN.—battle, combat, conflict, duel, encounter, fight, struggle; contention, controversy, discord, inconsistency, interference, opposition, variance. ANT.—amity, concord, consonance, harmony.

collusion, SYN.—cabal, combination, conspiracy, intrigue, machination, plot, treachery, treason.

color, SYN.—complexion, dye, hue, paint, pigment, shade, stain, tincture, tinge, tint. ANT.— achromatism, paleness, transparency.

colossal, SYN.—elephantine, enormous, gargantuan, gigantic, huge, immense, large, prodigious, vast. ANT.—diminutive, little, minute, small, tiny.

combat, SYN.—battle, collision, conflict, duel, encounter, fight, struggle; contention, controversy, discord, inconsistency, interference, opposition, variance. ANT.—amity, concord, consonance, harmony.

combat, SYN.—battle, brawl, conflict, contend, dispute, encounter, fight, quarrel, scuffle, skirmish, squabble, struggle, wrangle.

combination, SYN.—alliance, association, coalition; confederacy, entente, federation, league, partnership, union; compact, covenant, marriage, treaty. ANT.—divorce, schism, separation.

combine, SYN.—accompany, adjoin, associate, attach, conjoin, connect, couple, go with, join, link, unite. ANT.—detach, disconnect, dis-

join, separate.

comely, SYN.—beauteous, beautiful, charming, elegant, fair, fine, handsome, lovely, pretty. ANT.—foul, hideous, homely, repulsive, unsightly.

comfort, SYN.—consolation, contentment, ease, enjoyment, relief, solace, succor. ANT.—affliction, discomfort, misery, suffering, torment, torture.

comfort, SYN.—cheer, console, encourage, gladden, solace, soothe, sympathize. ANT.—antagonize, aggravate, depress, dishearten.

comfortable, SYN.—acceptable, agreeable, convenient, cozy, gratifying, pleasing, pleasurable, relaxed, restful, welcome. ANT.—distressing, miserable, troubling, uncomfortable, wretched.

comical, SYN.—amusing, droll, farcical, funny, humorous, laughable, ludicrous, ridiculous, witty; curious, odd, queer. ANT.—melancholy, sad, serious, sober, solemn.

command, SYN.—arrangement, class, method, plan, rank, regularity, sequence, series, succession, system; bidding, decree, dictate, injunction, instruction, mandate, order, requirement. ANT.—confusion, disarray, disorder, irregularity; consent, license, permission.

command, SYN.—aim, level, point, train; conduct, govern, guide, manage, regulate, rule; bid, direct, instruct, order. ANT.—deceive, distract, misdirect, misguide.

commensurate, SYN.—celebrate, honor, keep, observe, solemnize; commend, extol, glorify, honor, laud, praise. ANT.—disregard, overlook; decry, disgrace, dishonor, profane.

commence, SYN.—arise, begin, enter, inaugurate, initiate, institute, open, originate, start. ANT.—close, complete, end, finish, terminate.

commencement, SYN.—beginning, inception, opening, origin, outset, source, start. ANT.—close, completion, consummation, end, termination.

commend, SYN.—appreciate, approve, like, praise; authorize, confirm, endorse, ratify, sanction. ANT.—criticize, disparage; condemn, nullify.

commendable, SYN.—acceptable, agreeable, amiable, charming, gratifying, pleasant, pleasing, pleasurable, suitable, welcome. ANT.—disagreeable, obnoxious, offensive, unpleasant.

commendation, SYN.—acclaim, adulation, applause, approval, compliment, eulogy, flattery, laudation, praise.

ANT.—abuse, censure, condemnation, disapproval.

comment, SYN.—annotation, assertion, declaration, observation, remark, statement, utterance.

commerce, SYN.—art, business, employment, engagement, enterprise, job, occupation, profession, trade, trading, vocation, work. ANT.—avocation, hobby, pastime.

commit, SYN.—do, perform, perpetrate; commend, consign, entrust, relegate, trust; bind, obligate, pledge. ANT.—fail, miscarry, neglect, mistrust, release, renounce; free, loose.

commodious, SYN.—accessible, adapted, advantageous, appropriate, favorable, fitting, handy, suitable, timely. ANT.—awkward, inconvenient, inopportune, troublesome.

common, SYN.—familiar, frequent, general, ordinary, popular, prevalent, universal, usual; low, mean, vulgar. ANT.—exceptional, extraordinary, odd, scarce; noble, refined.

common-sense, SYN.—appreciable, apprehensible, perceptible; alive, awake, aware, cognizant, comprehending, conscious, perceiving, sentient; discreet, intelligent, judicious, practical, prudent, reasonable, sagacious, sage, sensible, sober, sound, wise. ANT.—absurd, impalpable, imperceptible, stupid, unaware.

commotion, SYN.—agitation, chaos, confusion, disarrangement, disarray, disorder, ferment, jumble, stir, tumult, turmoil. ANT.—certainty, order, peace, tranquility.

communicable, SYN.—catching, contagious, infectious, pestilential, virulent. ANT.—healthful, hygienic, noncommunicable.

communicate, SYN.—confer, convey, disclose, divulge, impart, inform, notify, relate, reveal, tell, transmit. ANT.—conceal, hide, withhold.

communion, SYN.—association, fellowship, intercourse, participation, sacrament, union. ANT.—alienation, nonparticipation.

compact, SYN.—close, constricted, contracted, firm, narrow, snug, stretched, taught, tense, tight; closefisted, niggardly, parsimonious, penny-pinching, stingy. ANT.—lax, loose, open, relaxed, slack.

compact, SYN.—accordance, coincidence, concord, concurrence, harmony, understanding, unison; agreement, bargain, contract, covenant, pact, stipulation. ANT.—difference, disagreement, discord, dissension, variance.

companion, SYN.—associate, attendant, colleague, comrade, consort, crony, friend, mate, partner. ANT.—adversary, enemy, stranger.

companionship, SYN.—acquaintance, cognizance, familiarity, fellowship, friendship, intimacy, knowledge. ANT.—ignorance, inexperience, unfamiliarity.

company, SYN.—assemblage, band, crew, group, horde, party, throng, troop; association, fellowship, society, corporation, firm. ANT.—dispersion, individual, seclusion, solitude.

comparable, SYN.—akin, alike, allied, analogous, correlative, correspondent, corresponding, like, parallel, similar. ANT.—different, dissimilar, divergent, incongruous, opposed.

compare, SYN.—contrast, differentiate, discriminate, distinguish, oppose.

compassion, SYN.—commiseration, condolence, mercy, pity, sympathy. ANT.—brutality, cruelty, hardness, inhumanity, ruthlessness.

compassionate, SYN.—affable, benevolent, benign, forbearing, gentle, good, humane, indulgent, kind, kindly, merciful, sympathetic, tender, thoughtful. ANT.—cruel, inhuman, merciless, severe, unkind.

compatible, SYN.—accordant, agreeing, consistent, conforming, congruous, consonant, constant, correspondent. ANT.— contradictory, discrepant, incongruous, inconsistent, paradoxical.

compel, SYN.—coerce, constrain, drive, enforce, impel, oblige. ANT.—allure, convince, induce, persuade, prevent.

compensation, SYN.—allowance, earnings, fee, pay, payment, recompense, salary, stipend, wages. ANT.—gift, gratuity, present.

competent, SYN.—able, capable, clever, efficient, fitted, qualified, skillful. ANT.—inadequate, incapable, incompetent, unfitted.

complain, SYN.—grouch, grumble, lament, murmur, protest, regret, remonstrate, repine, whine. ANT.—applaud, approve, praise, rejoice.

complete, SYN.—concluded, consummate, ended, entire, finished, full, perfect, thorough, total, unbroken, undivided. ANT.—imperfect, lacking, unfinished.

complete, SYN.—accomplish, achieve, close, conclude, consummate, do, end, execute, finish, fulfill, get done, perfect, perform, terminate.

completion, SYN.—accomplishment, achievement, attainment, realization, ANT.—neglect, omission; defeat, failure.

complex, SYN.—complicated, compound, intricate, involved, perplexing. ANT.—plain, simple, uncompounded.

complexion, SYN.—color, dye, hue, paint, pigment, shade, stain, tincture, tinge, tint. ANT.—achromatism, paleness, transparency.

compliant, SYN.—humble, lowly, meek, modest, plain, simple, submissive, unassuming, unostentatious, unpretentious. ANT.—arrogant, boastful, haughty, proud, vain.

complicated, SYN.—complex, compound, intricate, involved, perplexing. ANT.—plain, simple, uncompounded.

compliment, SYN.—adulation, commendation, eulogy, flattery, praise, tribute. ANT.—affront, criticism, insult, taunt.

comply, SYN.—accede, acquiesce, agree, assent, consent; coincide, concur, conform, tally. ANT.—contradict, differ, disagree, dissent, protest.

component, SYN.—allotment, apportionment, division, fragment, moiety, piece, portion, scrap, section, segment, share; element, ingredient, member, organ; concern, faction, interest, party, side; character, lines, role. ANT.—entirety, whole.

comport, SYN.—act, bear, behave, carry, conduct, demean, deport, interact, manage, operate.

compose, SYN.—construct, create, fashion, forge, make, mold, produce, shape; constitute, form, make up; arrange, combine, organize; devise, frame, invent. ANT.—destroy, disfigure, dismantle, misshape, wreck.

composed, SYN.—calm, collected, cool, imperturbable, peaceful, placid, quiet, sedate, tranquil, unmoved. ANT.—agitated, aroused, excited, perturbed, violent.

composer, SYN.—author, creator, father, inventor, maker, originator, writer.

composure, SYN.—balance, calmness, carriage, equanimity, equilibrium, poise, self-possession. ANT.—agitation, anger, excitement, rage, turbulence.

compound, SYN.—alloy, amalgamate, blend, combine, commingle, concoct, confound, fuse, jumble, mingle, mix; associate consort, fraternize, join. ANT.—dissociate, divide, segregate, separate, sort.

comprehend, SYN.—appreciate, apprehend, conceive, discern, grasp, know, learn, perceive, realize, see, understand. ANT.—ignore, misapprehend, mistake, misunderstand.

comprehension, SYN.—apprehension, cognizance, conception, discernment, insight, perception, understanding. ANT.—ignorance, insensibility, misapprehension, misconception.

comprise, SYN.—accommodate, contain, embody, embrace, hold, include; repress, restrain. ANT.—discharge, emit, exclude, encourage, yield.

compulsion, SYN.—dint, emphasis, energy, intensity, might, potency, power, strength, vigor; coercion, constraint, force, violence. ANT.—feebleness, frailty, impotence, weakness; persuasion.

computation, SYN.—account, reckoning, record. ANT.—misrepresentation.

compute, SYN.—calculate, consider, count, estimate, figure, reckon. ANT.—conjecture, guess, miscalculate.

comrade, SYN.—associate, attendant, colleague, companion, consort, crony, friend, mate, partner. ANT.—adversary, enemy, stranger.

conceal, SYN.—cloak, cover, disguise, hide, mask, screen, secrete, suppress, veil, withhold. ANT.—disclose, divulge, expose, reveal, show, uncover.

concede, SYN.—let, permit, sanction, suffer, tolerate; authorize, give, grant, yield; acknowledge, admit, allow. ANT.—forbid, object, protest, refuse, resist.

conceit, SYN.—complacency, egotism, pride, self-esteem, vanity; caprice, conception, fancy, idea, imagination, notion, whim. ANT.—diffidence, humility, meekness, modesty.

conceited, SYN.—abortive, bootless, empty, fruitless, futile, idle, ineffectual, pointless, unavailing, useless, valueless, vapid, worthless; proud, vain, vainglorious. ANT.—effective, potent, profitable; meek, modest.

conceive, SYN.—concoct, contrive, design, devise, fabricate, frame, invent. ANT.—copy, imitate, reproduce.

concentrated, SYN.—close, compact, compressed, crowded, dense, thick; dull, obtuse, slow, stupid. ANT.—dispersed, dissipated, sparse; clever, quick.

concept, SYN.—abstraction, conception, fancy, idea, image, impression, notion, opinion, sentiment, thought. ANT.—entity, matter, object, substance, thing.

conception, SYN.—cogitation, consideration, contemplation, deliberation, fancy, idea, imagination, impression, judgment, meditation, memory, notion, opinion, recollection, reflection, regard, retrospection, sentiment, thought, view.

concern, SYN.—affair, business, matter, transaction; anxiety, care, solicitude, worry. ANT.—apathy, indifference, negligence, unconcern.

concise, SYN.—brief, compact, condensed, incisive, neat, pithy, succinct, summary, terse. ANT.—lengthy, prolix, verbose, wordy.

conclude, SYN.—accomplish, achieve, close, complete, consummate, do, end, execute, finish, fulfill, get done, perfect, perform, terminate.

concluding, SYN.—extreme, final, hindmost, last, latest, terminal, ultimate, utmost. ANT.—beginning, first, foremost, initial, opening.

conclusion, SYN.—close, completion, end, finale, issue, settlement, termination; decision, deduction, inference, judgment. ANT.—beginning, commencement, inception, prelude, start.

conclusive, SYN.—concluding, decisive, ending, eventual, final, last, latest, terminal, ultimate. ANT.—first, inaugural, incipient, original, rudimentary.

concord, SYN.—accordance, agreement, coincidence, concord, concurrence, harmony, understanding, unison; bargain, compact, contract, covenant, pact, stipulation. ANT.—difference, disagreement, discord, dissension, variance.

concur, SYN.—accede, acquiesce, agree, assent, comply, consent; coincide, conform, tally. ANT.—contradict, differ, disagree, dissent, protest.

condemn, SYN.—blame, censure, denounce, reprehend, reproach, reprobate, reprove, upbraid; convict, sentence. ANT.—approve, commend, condone, forgive, praise; absolve, acquit, exonerate, pardon.

condition, SYN.—case, circumstance, plight, predicament, situation, state; provision, requirement, stipulation, term.

condition, SYN.—concoct, contrive, equip, fit, furnish, get ready, make ready, predispose, prepare, provide, qualify, ready.

conditional, SYN.—contingent, dependent, depending, relying, subject, subordinate. ANT.—absolute, autonomous, casual, independent, original.

condolence, SYN.—affinity, agreement, commiseration, compassion, concord, congeniality, empathy, harmony, pity, sympathy, tenderness, warmth. ANT.—antipathy, harshness, indifference, malevolence, unconcern.

conduct, SYN.—action, bearing, behavior, carriage, deed, demeanor, deportment, disposition, manner.

conduct, SYN.—direct, escort, guide, lead, steer; control, manage, regulate, supervise.

confederate, SYN.—abettor, accessory, accomplice, ally, assistant, associate. ANT.—adversary, enemy, opponent; rival.

confederation, SYN.—alliance, association, coalition, combination, confederacy, entente, federation, league, partnership, union; compact, covenant, marriage, treaty. ANT.—divorce, schism, separation.

confer, SYN.—blab, chat, converse, gossip, jabber, mutter, prattle, speak, tattle; argue, comment, declaim, discourse, harangue, lecture, plead, preach, rant, spout; consult, deliberate, discuss, reason, talk.

confess, SYN.—acknowledge, admit, allow, avow, concede, divulge, grant, own, reveal. ANT.—conceal, deny, disclaim, disown, renounce.

confession, SYN.—alibi,

apology, defense, excuse, explanation, justification. ANT.—accusation, complaint, denial, dissimulation.

confidence, SYN.—assurance, assuredness, certainty, conviction, courage, firmness, security, self-reliance, surety; pledge, promise, word; assertion, declaration, statement. ANT.—bashfulness, humility, modesty, shyness, suspicion.

confine, SYN.—bound, circumscribe, enclose, encompass, envelop, fence, limit, surround. ANT.—develop, distend, enlarge, expand, expose, open.

confirm, SYN.—corroborate, substantiate, verify; acknowledge, assure, establish, settle; approve, fix, ratify, sanction; strengthen.

confirmation, SYN.—corroboration, demonstration, evidence, experiment, proof, test, testimony, trial, verification. ANT.—failure, fallacy, invalidity.

conflict, SYN.—battle, collision, combat, duel, encounter, fight, struggle; contention, controversy, discord, inconsistency, interference, opposition, variance. ANT.—amity, concord, consonance, harmony.

confiscate, SYN.—appropriate, capture, catch, ensnare, gain, purloin, remove, steal, take; clasp, clutch, grasp, grip, seize; accept, get, obtain, receive; bear, endure, stand, tolerate; bring, carry, convey, escort; attract, captivate, charm, delight, interest; claim, demand, necessitate, require; adopt, assume, choose, espouse, select.

conflagration, SYN.—blaze, burning, combustion, fire, flame, glow, heat, warmth; ardor, fervor, intensity, passion, vigor. ANT.—cold; apathy, quiescence.

conform, SYN.—accommodate, adapt, adjust, fit, suit. ANT.—disturb, misapply, misfit.

confront, SYN.—bar, combat, confront, contradict, counteract, defy, hinder, osbtruct, resist, thwart, withstand. ANT.—agree, cooperate, submit, succumb, support.

confuse, SYN.—bewilder, confound, confuse, dumbfound, mystify, nonplus, perlex, puzzle. ANT.—clarify, explain, illumine, instruct, solve.

confused, SYN.—bewildered, deranged, disconcerted, disordered, disorganized, indistinct, mixed, muddled, perplexed. ANT.—clear, lucid, obvious, organized, plain.

confusion, SYN.—agitation, chaos, commotion, disarrangement, disarray, disorder, ferment, jumble, stir, tumult, turmoil.

congruous, SYN.—accordant, agreeing, compatible, conforming, consonant, consistent, constant, correspondent. ANT.— contradictory, discrepant, incongruous, inconsistent, paradoxical.

conjecture, SYN.—hypothesis, law, supposition, theory. ANT.—certainty, fact, proof.

conjecture, SYN.—chance, dare, endanger, hazard, imperil, jeopardize, peril, risk, venture. ANT.—determine, guard, insure, know.

connect, SYN.—adjoin, affix, annex, append, attach, join, stick, unite; assign, associate, attribute. ANT.—detach, disengage, separate, unfasten, untie.

connection. SYN.—affinity, alliance, association, bond, conjunction, link, relationship, tie, union. ANT.—disunion, isolation, separation.

conquer, SYN.—beat, crush, defeat, humble, master, overcome, quell, rout, subdue, subjugate, surmount, vanquish. ANT.—capitulate, cede, lose, retreat, surrender.

conquest, SYN.—achievement, jubilation, ovation, triumph, victory. ANT.—defeat, failure.

conscious, SYN.—apprised, aware, cognizant, informed, mindful, observant, perceptive, sensible. ANT.—ignorant, insensible, oblivious, unaware.

consecrate, SYN.—adore, dignify, enshrine, enthrone, exalt, extol, glorify, hallow, honor, revere, venerate. ANT.—abuse, debase, degrade, dishonor, mock.

consecrated, SYN.—blessed, devout, divine, hallowed, holy, pious, religious, sacred, saintly, spiritual. ANT.—evil, profane, sacrilegious, secular, worldly.

consent, SYN.—authority, authorization, leave, liberty, license, permission, permit. ANT.—denial, opposition, prohibition, refusal.

consent, SYN.—accede, acquiesce, agree, assent, comply, coincide, concur, conform, tally. ANT.—contradict, differ, disagree, dissent, protest.

consequently, SYN.—accordingly, hence, so, then, thence, therefore.

conserve, SYN.—maintain, preserve, save; confine, hold, reserve, retain; keep, guard, protect; support, sustain. ANT.—discard, reject; dismiss, relinquish; neglect.

consider, SYN.—contemplate, deliberate, examine, heed, meditate, ponder, reflect, study, weigh; esteem, regard, respect. ANT.—ignore, neglect, overlook.

considerate, SYN.—attentive, careful, cautious, concerned, considerate, heedful, provident, prudent; contemplative, dreamy, introspective, meditative, pensive, reflective. ANT.—heedless, inconsiderate, precipitous, rash, thoughtless.

consideration, SYN.—attention, care, circumspection, consideration, heed, mindfulness, notice, observance, watchfulness; application, contemplation, reflection, study. ANT.—disregard, indifference, negligence, omission, oversight.

consistent, SYN.—accordant, agreeing, compatible, conforming, congruous, consonant, constant, correspondent. ANT.— contradictory, discrepant, incongruous, inconsistent, paradoxical.

consolation, SYN.—comfort, contentment, ease, enjoyment, relief, solace, succor. ANT.—affliction, discomfort, misery, suffering, torment, torture.

console, SYN.—allay, assuage, comfort, solace, soothe. ANT.—annoy, distress, worry.

consolidate, SYN.—amalgamate, blend, coalesce, combine, commingle, conjoin, fuse, mingle, mix, merge, unify, unite. ANT.—analyze, decompose, disintegrate, separate.

consort, SYN.—associate, attendant, colleague, companion, comrade, crony, friend, mate, partner. ANT.—adversary, enemy, stranger.

conspicuous, SYN.—clear, distinguished, manifest, noticeable, obvious, prominent, salient, striking, visible. ANT.—common, hidden, inconspicuous, obscure.

conspiracy, SYN.—cabal, collusion, combination, intrigue, machination, plot, treachery, treason.

constancy, SYN.—allegiance, devotion, faithfulness, fealty, fidelity, loyalty; accuracy, exactness, precision. ANT.—disloyalty, faithlessness, perfidy, treachery.

constant, SYN.—abiding, ceaseless, continual, enduring, faithful, fixed, immutable, invariant, permanent, perpetual, persistent, unalterable, unchanging, unwavering. ANT.—fickle, mutable, vacillating, wavering.

constantly, SYN.—always, continually, eternally, ever, evermore, forever, incessantly, perpetually, unceasingly. ANT.—fitfully, never, occasionally, rarely, sometimes.

consternation, SYN.—alarm, apprehension, cowardice, dismay, dread, fear, fright, horror, panic, scare, terror, timidity, trepidation. ANT.—assurance, boldness, bravery, courage, fearlessness.

constrain, SYN.—destiny, fate, necessity, requirement, requisite; exigency, indigence, need, poverty, want. ANT.—choice, freedom, luxury, option, uncertainty.

construct, SYN.—build, erect, fabricate, form, frame, make, raise. ANT.—demolish, destroy, raze.

construe, SYN.—decipher, decode, elucidate, explain, explicate, interpret, render, solve, translate, unravel. ANT.—confuse, distort, falsify, misconstrue, misinterpret.

consult, SYN.—chatter, conference, conversation, dialogue, discourse, discussion, gossip, lecture, report, rumor, speech, talk. ANT.—correspondence, meditation, silence, writing.

consume, SYN.—absorb, assimilate, engulf, imbibe, swallow up; engage, engross, occupy. ANT.—discharge, dispense, emit, expel, exude.

consummate, SYN.—accomplish, achieve, close, complete, conclude, do, end, execute, finish, fulfill, get done, perfect, perform, terminate.

consummation, SYN.—acme, apex, climax, cul-mination, height, peak, summit, zenith. ANT.—anticlimax, base, depth, floor.

contagious, SYN.—catching, communicable, infectious, pestilential, virulent. ANT.—healthful, hygienic, noncommunicable.

contain, SYN.—accommodate, comprise, embody, embrace, hold, include; repress, restrain. ANT.—discharge, emit, exclude; encourage, yield.

contaminate, SYN.—befoul, corrupt, defile, infect, poison, pollute, sully, taint. ANT.—disinfect, purify.

contaminated, SYN.—corrupt, corrupted, crooked, debased, depraved, dishonest, impure, profligate; putrid, spoiled, tainted, unsound, venal, vitiated.

contamination, SYN.—contagion, germ, pest, virus; ailment, disease, infection, poison, pollution, taint.

contemplate, SYN.—conceive, imagine, picture, recall, recollect, remember; cogitate, deliberate, meditate, muse, ponder, reason, reflect, speculate, think; apprehend, believe, consider, deem, esteem, judge, opine, reckon, regard, suppose; devise, intend, mean, plan, purpose. ANT.—conjecture, forget, guess.

contemplative, SYN.— attentive, careful, cautious, concerned, considerate, heedful, provident, prudent; dreamy, introspective, meditative, pensive. reflective, thoughtful. ANT.— heedless, inconsiderate, precipitous, rash, thoughtless.

contemporary, SYN.— current, modern, new, novel, present, recent. ANT.—ancient, antiquated, bygone, old, past.

contempt, SYN.—contumély, derision, detestation, disdain, hatred, scorn. ANT.—awe, esteem, regard, respect, reverence.

contemptible, SYN.— average, medium, middle; base, despicable, low, mean, sordid, vile, vulgar, malicious, nasty, offensive, selfish. ANT.—admirable, dignified, exalted, generous, noble.

contented, SYN.—blessed, cheerful, delighted, fortunate, gay, glad, happy, joyful, joyous, lucky, merry, opportune, propitious. ANT.—blue, depressed, gloomy, morose.

contention, SYN.—battle, collision, combat, conflict, duel, encounter, fight, struggle; controversy, discord, inconsistency, interference, opposition, variance. ANT.—amity, concord, consonance, harmony.

contentment, SYN.— beatitude, blessedness, bliss, delight, felicity, gladness, happiness, pleasure, satisfaction, well-being. ANT.— despair, grief, misery, sadness, sorrow.

contest, SYN.—altercate, argue, bicker, contend, debate, discuss, dispute, quarrel, squabble, wrangle. ANT.—agree, allow, assent, concede.

continence, SYN.— abstention, abstinence, fasting, forbearance, moderation, self-denial, sobriety, temperance. ANT.—excess, gluttony, greed, intoxication, self-indulgence.

contingent, SYN.—conditional, dependent, depending, relying, subject, subordinate. ANT.— absolute, autonomous, casual, independent, original.

contingency, SYN.—conditionality, dependency, reliance on, subject to, subordination. ANT.— absoluteness, autonomousness, casuality, independence, originality.

continual, SYN.—ceaseless, constant, continuous, endless, everlasting, incessant, perennial, perpetual, unceasing, uninterrupted, unremitting. ANT.—interrupted, occasional, periodic, rare.

continue, SYN.—advance, extend, proceed; endure, last, remain; persevere, persist, prolong, pursue.

ANT.—arrest, check, interrupt; cease, defer, halt, stop, suspend.

contract, SYN.—abbreviate, abridge, condense, curtail, diminish, lessen, limit, reduce, restrict, shorten. ANT.—elongate, extend, lengthen.

contract, SYN.—agreement, bargain, compact, covenant, pact, promise, stipulation, treaty.

contraction, SYN.—abbreviation, abridgment, reduction, shortening. ANT.—amplification, enlargement, expansion, extension.

contradict, SYN.—confute, controvert, counter, dispute, gainsay, oppose. ANT.—agree, confirm, support, verify.

contradictory, SYN.—contrary, discrepant, illogical, incompatible, incongruous, inconsistent, irreconcilable, paradoxical, unsteady, vacillating, wavering. ANT.—compatible, congruous, consistent, correspondent.

contrary, SYN.—adverse, antagonistic, hostile, opposed, opposite; counteractive, disastrous, unfavorable, unlucky. ANT.—benign, favorable, fortunate, lucky, propitious.

contrast, SYN.—compare, differentiate, discriminate, distinguish, oppose.

contrite, SYN.—penitent, regretful, remorseful, repentant, sorrowful, sorry. ANT.—obdurate, remorseless.

contrition, SYN.—compunction, grief, penitence, qualm, regret, remorse, repentance, self-reproach, sorrow. ANT.—complacency, impenitence, obduracy, self-satisfaction.

contrive, SYN.—delineate, design, devise, intend, outline, plan, plot, prepare, project, scheme, sketch.

control, SYN.—command, direct, dominate, govern, manage, regulate, rule, superintend; bridle, check, curb, repress, restrain. ANT.—abandon, follow, forsake, ignore, submit.

controversy, SYN.—argument, contention, debate, disagreement, dispute, quarrel, squabble. ANT.—agreement, concord, decision, harmony.

convenient, SYN.—accessible, adapted, advantageous, appropriate, commodious, favorable, fitting, handy, suitable, timely. ANT.—awkward, inconvenient, inopportune, troublesome.

conversant, SYN.—acquainted, aware, cognizant, familiar, intimate, knowing, versed; affable, amicable, close, courteous, friendly, informal, sociable, unreserved. ANT.—affected, cold, distant, reserved, unfamiliar.

conversation, SYN.—chat, colloquy, conference, dialogue, interview, parley, talk.

converse, SYN.—blab, chat, gossip, jabber, mutter, prattle, speak, talk, tattle; argue, comment, declaim, discourse, harangue, lecture, plead, preach, rant, spout; confer, consult, deliberate, discuss, reason.

convert, SYN.—exchange, substitute; alter, change, modify, shift, transfigure, transform, vary, veer. ANT.—retain; continue, establish, preserve, settle, stabilize.

convey, SYN.—bring, carry, transmit, transport; bear, support, sustain. ANT.—abandon, drop.

convict, SYN.—criminal, culprit, delinquent, felon, malefactor, offender, transgressor.

convict, SYN.—blame, censure, denounce, reprehend, reproach, reprobate, reprove, upbraid, condemn, sentence. ANT.—approve, commend, condone, forgive, praise; absolve, acquit, exonerate, pardon.

conviction, SYN.—belief, certitude, confidence, credence, faith, feeling, opinion, persuasion, reliance, trust. ANT.—denial, doubt, heresy, incredulity.

convince, SYN.—allure, coax, entice, exhort, incite, induce, influence, persuade, prevail upon, urge, win over. ANT.—coerce, compel, deter, dissuade, restrain.

convoy, SYN.—accompany, associate with, attend, chaperone, consort with, escort, go with. ANT.—abandon, avoid, desert, leave, quit.

copious, SYN.—abundant, ample, bountiful, overflowing, plenteous, plentiful, profuse, rich, teeming. ANT.—deficient, insufficient, scant, scarce.

copy, SYN.—duplicate, exemplar, facsimile, imitation, replica, reproduction, transcript. ANT.—original, prototype.

cordial, SYN.—ardent, earnest, gracious, hearty, sincere, sociable, warm. ANT.—aloof, cool, reserved, taciturn.

core, SYN.—center, heart, middle, midpoint, midst, nucleus. ANT.—border, boundary, outskirts, periphery, rim.

corporal, SYN.—bodily, carnal, corporeal, physical, somatic; material, natural. ANT.—mental, spiritual.

corporation, SYN.—assemblage, band, crew, group, horde, party, throng, troop; association, fellowship, society; company, firm. ANT.—dispersion, individual, seclusion, solitude.

corpse, SYN.—body, carcass, remains; form, frame, torso; bulk, corpus, mass; aggregate, association, company, society. ANT.—intellect, mind, soul, spirit.

corpulent, SYN.—chubby, fat, obese, paunchy, plump, portly, pudgy, rotund, stocky, stout, thickset. ANT.—gaunt, lean, slender, slim, thin.

correct, SYN.—accurate, exact, faultless, impeccable, precise, proper, right, strict. ANT.— erroneous, false, faulty, untrue, wrong.

correct, SYN.—amend, mend, rectify, reform, right; admonish, discipline, punish. ANT.— aggravate, ignore, spoil; condone, indulge.

correction, SYN.—control, order, regulation, restraint, self-control; exercise, instruction, practice, training; discipline, punishment. ANT.— chaos, confusion, turbulence.

correlative, SYN.—akin, alike, allied, analogous, comparable, correspondent, corresponding, like, parallel, similar. ANT.—different, dissimilar, divergent, incongruous, opposed.

correspondent, SYN.—akin, alike, allied, analogous, comparable, corresponding, like, parallel, similar. ANT.—different, dissimilar, divergent, incongruous, opposed.

corrupt, SYN.—contaminated, corrupted, crooked, debased, depraved, dishonest, im-

pure, profligate, putrid, spoiled, tainted, unsound, venal, vitiated.

corrupted, SYN.—contaminated, crooked, debased, depraved, dishonest, impure, profligate, putrid, spoiled, tainted, unsound, venal, vitiated.

cost, SYN.—charge, expense, price, value, worth.

council, SYN.—admonition, advice, caution, counsel, exhortation, instruction, recommendation, suggestion, warning; information, intelligence, notification.

counsel, SYN.—advise, allude, hint, imply, insinuate, intimate, offer, propose, recommend, refer, suggest. ANT.—declare, demand, dictate, insist.

count, SYN.—calculate, compute, consider, estimate, figure, reckon. ANT.—conjecture, guess, miscalculate.

countenance, SYN.—face, mug, visage; assurance, audacity, cover, exterior, front, surface. ANT.— timidity; back, interior, rear.

counterfeit, SYN.—affected, artificial, assumed, bogus, ersatz, fake, feigned, fictitious, phony, sham, spurious, synthetic, unreal. ANT.— genuine, natural, real, true.

couple, SYN.—accompany, adjoin, associate, attach, combine, conjoin, connect, go with, join, link, unite. ANT.—detach, disconnect, disjoin, separate.

courage, SYN.—boldness, bravery, chivalry, fearlessness, fortitude, intrepidity, mettle, prowess, resolution. ANT.—cowardice, fear, pusillanimity, timidity.

courageous, SYN.—adventurous, audacious, bold, brave, chivalrous, daring, dauntless, fearless, gallant, heroic, intrepid, magnanimous, valiant, valorous. ANT.—cowardly, cringing, fearful, timid, weak.

course, SYN.—avenue, channel, passage, path, road, route, street, thoroughfare, track, trail, walk, way.

courteous, SYN.—accomplished, civil, considerate, cultivated, genteel, polite, refined, urbane, wellbred, well-mannered. ANT.—boorish, impertinent, rude, uncivil, uncouth.

covenant, SYN.—accordance, agreement, coincidence, concord, concurrence, harmony, understanding, unison; bargain, compact, contract, pact, stipulation. ANT.—difference, disagreement, discord, dissension, variance.

cover, SYN.—cloak, clothe, conceal, curtain, disguise, envelop, guard, hide, mask, protect, screen, shield, shroud, veil. ANT.—bare, divulge, expose, reveal, unveil.

covert, SYN.—concealed, dormant, hidden, inactive, potential, quiescent, secret, undeveloped, unseen. ANT.—conspicuous, evident, explicit, manifest, visible.

covetousness, SYN.—envy, jealousy, spitefulness. ANT.—generosity, geniality, indifference.

cowardice, SYN.—alarm, apprehension, consternation, dismay, dread, fear, fright, horror, panic, scare, terror, timidity, trepidation. ANT.—assurance, boldness, bravery, courage, fearlessness.

coy, SYN.—abashed, bashful, diffident, embarrassed, humble, modest, recoiling, shamefaced, sheepish, shy, timid, timorous. ANT.—adventurous, daring, fearless, gregarious, outgoing.

crafty, SYN.—artful, astute, clandestine, covert, cunning, foxy, furtive, guileful, insidious, shrewd, stealthy, subtle, surreptitious, sly, tricky, underhand, wily. ANT.—candid, frank, ingenuous, open, sincere.

craggy, SYN.—irregular, jagged, rough, rugged, scratchy, uneven; unpolished; harsh, severe. ANT.—even, level, sleek, slippery, smooth; fine, finished, polished, refined; gentle, mild.

crass, SYN.—coarse, green, harsh, ill-prepared, raw, rough, unfinished, unpolished, unrefined; crude, uncouth, unrefined. ANT.—finished, well-prepared; cultivated, refined.

craving, SYN.—appetite, hunger, relish, stomach, thirst, zest; desire, inclination, liking, longing, passion. ANT.—disgust, distaste, renunciation, repugnance, satiety.

crazy, SYN.—delirious, demented, deranged, foolish, idiotic, imbecilic, insane, mad, maniacal. ANT.—rational, reasonable, sane, sensible, sound.

create, SYN.—cause, engender, fashion, form, formulate, generate, invent, make, originate, produce; appoint, constitute, ordain. ANT.—annihilate, demolish, destroy; disband, terminate.

creative, SYN.—clever, fanciful, imaginative, inventive, mystical, poetical, visionary. ANT.—dull, literal, prosaic, unromantic.

credence, SYN.—belief, certitude, confidence, conviction, faith, feeling, opinion, persuasion, reliance, trust. ANT.—denial, doubt, heresy, incredulity.

credit, SYN.—accept, apprehend, believe, conceive, fancy, hold, imagine, support, suppose. ANT.—distrust, doubt, question, reject.

creed, SYN.—belief, doctrine, dogma, precept, teaching, tenet. ANT.—conduct, deed, performance, practice.

crest, SYN.—acme, head, pinnacle, summit, top. ANT.—base, bottom, foot.

crime, SYN.—affront, atrocity, indignity, insult, outrage; aggression, injustice, misdeed, offense, sin, transgression, trespass, vice, wrong. ANT.—gentleness, innocence, morality, right.

criminal, SYN.—convict, culprit, delinquent, felon, malefactor, offender, transgressor.

crippled, SYN.—defective, deformed, disabled, feeble, halt, hobbling, lame, limping, maimed, unconvincing, unsatisfactory, weak. ANT.—agile, athletic, robust, sound, vigorous.

crisis, SYN.—acme, conjuncture, contingency, emergency, exigency, juncture, pass, pinch, strait. ANT.—calm, equilibrium, normality, stability.

crisp, SYN.—breakable, brittle, crumbling, delicate, fragile, frail, splintery. ANT.—enduring, thick, tough, unbreakable.

criterion, SYN.—gauge, law, measure, principle, proof, rule, standard, test, touchstone. ANT.—

chance, fancy, guess, supposition.

critical, SYN.—accurate, discerning, discriminating, exact, fastidious, particular; captious, carping, caviling, censorious, faultfinding, hypercritical; acute, crucial, decisive, hazardous, important, momentous. ANT.—cursory, shallow, superficial, uncritical; appreciative, approving, commendatory, encouraging, insignificant, unimportant.

criticize, SYN.—analyze, appraise, evaluate, examine, inspect, scrutinize; blame, censure, reprehend. ANT.—approve, neglect, overlook.

critique, SYN.—commentary, criticism, examination, inspection, reconsideration, retrospect, retrospection, review, revision, survey, synopsis.

crony, SYN.—associate, attendant, colleague, companion, comrade, consort, friend, mate, partner. ANT.—adversary, enemy, stranger.

crooked, SYN.—abased, adulterated, corrupt, defiled, degraded, depraved, impaired, lowered, perverted, vitiated. ANT.—enhanced, improved, raised, restored, vitalized.

crop, SYN.—fruit, harvest, proceeds, produce, product, reaping, result, store, yield.

crowd, SYN.—bevy, crush, horde, host, masses, mob, multitude, populace, press, rabble, swarm, throng.

crown, SYN.—apex, chief, crest, head, pinnacle, summit, top, zenith. ANT.—base, bottom, foot, foundation.

crude, SYN.—coarse, green, harsh, ill-prepared, raw, rough, unifinished, unpolished, unrefined; crass, uncouth, unrefined. ANT.—finished, well-prepared; cultivated, refined.

crucial, SYN.—acute, critical, decisive, hazardous, important, momentous. ANT.—cursory, shallow, superficial, uncritical; insignificant, unimportant.

cruel, SYN.—barbarous, brutal, ferocious, inhuman, malignant, merciless, ruthless, savage. ANT.—benevolent, compassionate, forbearing, gentle, humane, kind, merciful.

crumb, SYN.—bit, grain, iota, jot, mite, particle, scrap, shred, smidgen, speck. ANT.—aggregate, bulk, mass, quantity.

crunch, SYN.—bite, champ, chew, gnash, gnaw, nibble, nip, pierce, rend, tear.

cuddle, SYN.—caress, coddle, embrace, fondle, hug, kiss, pet. ANT.—annoy, buffet, spurn, tease, vex.

cull, SYN.—choose, elect,

opt, pick, select. ANT.—
refuse, reject.

culmination, SYN.—acme,
apex, climax, consum-
mation, height, peak,
summit, zenith. ANT.—
anticlimax, base, depth,
floor.

culprit, SYN.—convict,
criminal, delinquent, felon, malefactor, offender,
transgressor.

cultivation, SYN.—agriculture, agronomy, farming,
gardening, horticulture,
husbandry, tillage.

culture, SYN.—breeding,
civilization, cultivation,
education, enlighten-
ment, refinement.
ANT.—boorishness, ig-
norance, illiteracy, vul-
garity.

cultured, SYN.—blasé, cultivated, sophisticated,
worldly, worldly-wise.
ANT.—crude, ingenuous,
naive, simple, uncouth.

cunning, SYN.—crooked,
devious, tricky. ANT.—
direct, straight; honest,
straightforward.

cunning, SYN.—aptitude,
cleverness, faculty, in-
geniousness, ingenuity,
inventiveness, resource-
fulness, skill. ANT.—
clumsiness, dullness, in-
eptitude, stupidity.

curb, SYN.—bridle, check,
constrain, hinder, hold
back, inhibit, limit, re-
press, restrain, stop, suppress. ANT.—aid, en-
courage, incite, loosen.

cure, SYN.—antidote, help,
medicant, restorative;
redress, relief, remedy,

reparation.

curiosity, SYN.—marvel,
miracle, phenomenon,
prodigy, rarity, specta-
cle; admiration, amaze-
ment, astonishment,
awe, bewilderment, sur-
prise, wonder, wonder-
ment. ANT.—familiarity,
triviality; apathy, expectation, indifference.

curious, SYN.—inquiring,
inquisitive, interrogative,
meddling, nosy, peeping,
peering, prying, search-
ing, snoopy; odd, pecu-
liar, queer, strange, unusual. ANT.—incurious,
indifferent, uncon-
cerned, uninterested;
common, ordinary.

current, SYN.—contem-
porary, modern, new,
novel, present, recent.
ANT.—ancient, anti-
quated, bygone, old,
past.

cursory, SYN.—exterior,
flimsy, frivolous, imper-
fect, shallow, slight, superficial. ANT.—
abstruse, complete,
deep, profound, thor-
ough.

curt, SYN.—abrupt, hasty,
precipitate, sudden;
blunt, brusque, rude;
harsh, rough, sharp.
ANT.—courteous, gradu-
al, smooth.

curtail, SYN.—abbreviate,
abridge, condense, con-
tract, diminish, lessen,
limit, reduce, restrict,
shorten. ANT.—elongate,
extend, lengthen.

curve, SYN.—bend, bow,
crook, deflect, incline,

lean, stoop, turn, twist.
ANT.—break, resist,
stiffen, straighten.

custody, SYN.—care,
charge, guardianship,
ward. ANT.—disregard,
indifference, neglect,
negligence.

custom, SYN.—fashion,
habit, practice, routine,
usage, use, wont.

customary, SYN.—accustomed, common, everyday, familiar, general,
habitual, normal, ordinary, usual. ANT.—abnormal, exceptional,
extraordinary, irregular,
rare.

cylindrical, SYN.—bulbous,
chubby, circular, complete, curved, entire,
globular, plump, rotund,
round, spherical.

D

dainty, SYN.—delicate, elegant, exquisite, fastidious, frail, slender, slight,
pleasant, pleasing.
ANT.—brutal, coarse,
rude, tough, vulgar

damage, SYN.—deface,
harm, hurt, impair, injure, mar, spoil. ANT.—
ameliorate, benefit, enhance, mend, repair.

damaging, SYN.—deleterious, detrimental, harmful, hurtful, injurious,
mischievous. ANT.—
advantageous, beneficial, helpful, profitable,
salutary.

danger, SYN.—hazard,
jeopardy, peril, risk.
ANT.—defense, immunity, protection, safety.

dangerous, SYN.—critical,
hazardous, insecure,
menacing, perilous, precarious, risky, threatening, unsafe. ANT.—firm,
protected, safe, secure.

dare, SYN.—object to,
question, brave, challenge, defy, call, invoke,
summon.

daring, SYN.—adventurous, bold, chivalrous,
enterprising, foolhardy, precipitate, rash.
ANT.—cautious, hesitating, timid.

dark, SYN.—black, dim,
gloomy, murky, obscure,
shadowy, unilluminated;
dusky, opaque, sable,
swarthy; dismal, gloomy,
mournful, somber, sorrowful; evil, sinister, sullen, wicked; hidden,
mystic, occult, secret.
ANT.—light; bright,
clear; pleasant, lucid.

dash, SYN.—beat, buffet,
hit, knock, pound, pummel, punch, smite, strike,
thrash, thump. ANT.—
defend, shield, stroke.

dead, SYN.—deceased, defunct, departed, dull,
gone, inanimate, insensible, lifeless, spiritless,
unconscious. ANT.—
alive, animate, living,
stirring.

deafening, SYN.—clamorous, loud, noisy, resounding, sonorous,
stentorian, vociferous.
ANT.—dulcet, inaudible,
quiet, soft, subdued.

dear, SYN.—beloved, esteemed, precious, val

ued; costly, expensive, valuable. ANT.—despised, unwanted; cheap.

debase, SYN.—abase, adulterate, alloy, corrupt, defile, degrade, deprave, depress, humiliate, impair, lower, pervert, vitiate. ANT.—enhance, improve, raise, restore, vitalize.

debate, SYN.—argue, discuss, dispute, plead, reason, wrangle. ANT.—ignore, overlook, reject, spurn.

decay, SYN.—decline, decompose, crease, disintegrate, dwindle, ebb, putrefy, rot, spoil, wane, waste. ANT.—flourish, grow, increase, luxuriate, rise.

deceased, SYN.—dead, defunct, departed, dull, gone, inanimate, insensible, lifeless, spiritless, unconscious. ANT.—alive, animate, living, stirring.

deceit, SYN.—beguilement, cheat, chicanery, cunning, deceitfulness, deception, duplicity, fraud, guile, sham, trick, wiliness. ANT.—candor, honesty, openness, sincerity, truthfulness.

deceitful, SYN.—deceptive, delusive, delusory, fallacious, false, illusive, misleading, spacious. ANT.—authentic, genuine, honest, real, truthful.

decent, SYN.—adequate, becoming, befitting, comely, decorous, fit,

proper, respectable, seemly, suitable, tolerable. ANT.—coarse, gross, indecent, reprehensible, vulgar.

deception, SYN.—beguilement, cheat, chicanery, cunning, deceit, deceitfulness, duplicity, fraud, guile, sham, trick, wiliness. ANT.—candor, honesty, openness, sincerity, truthfulness.

deceptive, SYN.—deceitful, delusive, delusory, fallacious, false, illusive, misleading, specious. ANT.—authentic, genuine, honest, real, truthful.

decide, SYN.—adjudicate, close, conclude, determine, end, resolve, settle, terminate. ANT.—doubt, hesitate, suspend, vacillate, waver.

decipher, SYN.—construe, decode, elucidate, explain, explicate, interpret, render, solve, translate, unravel. ANT.—confuse, distort, falsify, misconstrue, misinterpret.

declare, SYN.—affirm, announce, assert, aver, broadcast, express, make known, proclaim, profess, promulgate, protest, state, tell. ANT.—conceal, repress, suppress, withhold.

declaration, SYN.—allegation, announcement, mention, report, assertion, proposition, statement, thesis.

decline, SYN.—incline, slant, slope; descend,

sink, wane; decay, decrease, degenerate, depreciate, deteriorate, diminish, dwindle, weaken; refuse, reject. ANT.—ameliorate, appreciate, ascend, increase; accept.

decorate, SYN.—adorn, beautify, deck, embellish, enrich, garnish, ornament, trim. ANT.—debase, defame, expose, strip, uncover.

decoration, SYN.—adornment, embellishment, garnish, ornament, ornamentation.

decrease, SYN.—abate, curtail, decline, deduct, diminish, dwindle, lessen, reduce, remove, shorten, subtract, wane. ANT.—amplify, enlarge, expand, grow, increase.

decree, SYN.—act, edict, law, statute. ANT.—inactivity.

decree, SYN.—decide, determine; adjudicate, arbitrate, condemn, judge.

decrepit, SYN.—delicate, enervated, exhausted, faint, feeble, forceless, impaired, infirm, languid, powerless, puny, weak. ANT.—forceful, lusty, stout, strong, vigorous.

decry, SYN.—belittle, depreciate, derogate, discredit, lower, minimize, undervalue. ANT.—aggrandize, commend, exalt, magnify, praise.

dedicated, SYN.—affectionate, ardent, attached, devoted, disposed, earnest, faithful, fond, given

up to, inclined, loyal, prone, true, wedded. ANT.—detached, disinclined, indisposed, untrammeled.

deduct, SYN.—abate, curtail, decrease, diminish, dwindle, lessen, reduce, remove, shorten, subtract. ANT.—amplify, enlarge, expand, grow, increase.

deed, SYN.—accomplishment, act, action, doing, execution, feat, operation, performance, transaction. ANT.—cessation, deliberation, inactivity, inhibition, intention.

deem, SYN.—account, believe, consider, esteem, estimate, hold, judge, rate, reckon, regard, think, view; elucidate, explain, expound.

deface, SYN.—damage, harm, hurt, impair, injure, mar, spoil. ANT.—ameliorate, benefit, enhance, mend, repair.

defamation, SYN.—abuse, aspersion, desecration, dishonor, disparagement, insult, invective, maltreatment, misuse, outrage, perversion, profanation, reproach, reviling, upbraiding. ANT.—approval, commendation, laudation, plaudit, respect.

default, SYN.—dereliction, failure, omission, deficiency, lack, loss, want. ANT.—achievement, success, victory, sufficiency.

defeat, SYN.—beat, conquer, crush, humble, master, overcome, quell, rout, subdue, subjugate, surmount, vanquish. ANT.—capitulate, cede, lose, retreat, surrender.

defect, SYN.—blemish, error, failure, fault, flaw, imperfection, mistake, omission, shortcoming, vice. ANT.—completeness, correctness, perfection.

defend, SYN.—fortify, guard, protect, safeguard, screen, shield; assert, espouse, justify, maintain, uphold, vindicate. ANT.—assault, attack, deny, oppose, submit.

deference, SYN.—admiration, adoration, dignity, esteem, fame, glory, homage, honor, praise, renown, respect, reverence, worship. ANT.—contempt, derision, disgrace, dishonor, reproach.

defense, SYN.—bulwark, fence, refuge, safeguard, shelter, shield; guard, protection, security.

deficient, SYN.—defective, inadequate, incomplete, insufficient, lacking, scanty, short. ANT.—adequate, ample, enough, satisfactory, sufficient.

definite, SYN.—certain, correct, determined, exact, explicit, fixed, precise, prescribed, specific. ANT.—ambiguous, confused, dubious, equivocal, indefinite.

defunct, SYN.—dead, deceased, departed, dull, gone, inanimate, insensible, lifeless, spiritless, unconscious. ANT.—alive, animate, living, stirring.

defy, SYN.—attack, confront, hinder, impede, obstruct, oppose, resist, thwart, withstand. ANT.—accede, allow, cooperate, relent, yield.

degenerate, SYN.—decay, decrease, decline, depreciate, deteriorate, diminish, dwindle, weaken. ANT.—ameliorate, appreciate, ascend, increase.

degrade, SYN.—abase, abash, break, crush, debase, humble, humiliate, mortify, shame, subdue. ANT.—elevate, exalt, honor, praise.

delay, SYN.—defer, postpone, procrastinate; arrest, detain, hinder, impede, retard, stay; dawdle, linger, loiter, tarry. ANT.—expedite, hasten, precipitate, quicken.

delectable, SYN.—delightful, delicious, luscious, palatable, savory, sweet, tasty. ANT.—acrid, distasteful, nauseous, unpalatable, unsavory.

deleterious, SYN.—bad, baleful, base, evil, immoral, iniquitous, noxious, pernicious, sinful, unsound, unwholesome, villainous, wicked. ANT.—excellent, good, honorable, moral, reputable.

deliberate, SYN.—contemplated, designed, intended, intentional, premeditated, studied, voluntary, wilful. ANT.—accidental, fortuitous.

deliberate, SYN.—consider, contemplate, examine, heed, meditate, ponder, reflect, study, weigh. ANT.—ignore, neglect, overlook.

delicate, SYN.—dainty, elegant, exquisite, fastidious, feeble, frail, sensitive, slender, slight, weak; pleasant, pleasing, savory. ANT.—brutal, coarse, rude, tough, vulgar.

delicious, SYN.—delectable, delightful, luscious, palatable, savory, sweet, tasty. ANT.—acrid, distasteful, nauseous, unpalatable, unsavory.

delight, SYN.—bliss, ecstasy, enjoyment, gladness, happiness, joy, pleasure, rapture, transport. ANT.—annoyance, dejection, melancholy, misery, sorrow.

delighted, SYN.—blessed, cheerful, contented, fortunate, gay, glad, happy, joyful, lucky, merry, opportune, propitious. ANT.—blue, depressed, gloomy, morose.

delightful, SYN.—acceptable, amiable, agreeable, charming, gratifying, pleasant, pleasing, pleasurable, suitable, welcome. ANT.—disagreeable, obnoxious, offensive, unpleasant.

deliver, SYN.—commit, give, impart, transfer, yield; announce, communicate, impart, proclaim, publish; emancipate, free, liberate, release, rescue, save. ANT.—confine, withhold; capture, imprison, restrict.

delusion, SYN.—dream, fantasy, hallucination, illusion, mirage, phantom, vision. ANT.—actuality, reality, substance.

demand, SYN.—ask, ask for, challenge, claim, exact, require; inquire, necessitate. ANT.—give, offer, present, tender.

demean, SYN.—act, bear, behave, carry, comport, conduct, deport, interact, manage, operate.

demolish, SYN.—annihilate, destroy, devastate, eradicate, exterminate, extinguish, obliterate, ravage, raze, ruin, wreck. ANT.—construct, establish, make, preserve, save.

demonstrate, SYN.—display, exhibit, show; establish, evince, manifest, prove. ANT.—conceal, hide.

demur, SYN.—delay, doubt, falter, hesitate, pause, scruple, stammer, stutter, vacillate, waver. ANT.—continue, decide, persevere, proceed, resolve.

denounce, SYN.—blame, censure, condemn, reprehend, reproach, reprobate, reprove, upbraid. ANT.—approve, commend, condone, forgive, praise.

dense, SYN.—close, compact, compressed, concentrated, crowded, thick; dull, obtuse, slow, stupid. ANT.—dispersed, dissipated, sparse; clever, quick.

deny, SYN.—contradict, contravene, gainsay, refute; abjure, disavow, disown, forbid; refuse, repudiate, withhold. ANT.—affirm, assert, concede, confirm.

depart, SYN.—abandon, desert, forsake, give up, go, leave, quit, relinquish, renounce, withdraw. ANT.—abide, remain, stay, tarry.

departure, SYN.—farewell, good-by, leave-taking, valediction. ANT.—greeting, salutation, welcome.

dependable, SYN.—certain, reliable, safe, secure, sure, tried, trustworthy, trusty. ANT.—dubious, fallible, questionable, uncertain, unreliable.

dependent, SYN.—conditional, contingent, depending, relying, subject, subordinate. ANT.—absolute, autonomous, casual, independent, original.

depict, SYN.—characterize, describe, explain, narrate, portray, recount, relate.

deplore, SYN.—bemoan, bewail, grieve, lament, mourn, repine, wail, weep.

deport, SYN.—banish, dismiss, dispel, eject, exclude, exile, expatriate, expel, ostracize, oust. ANT.—accept, admit, harbor, receive, shelter.

deportment, SYN.—action, bearing, behavior, carriage, conduct, deed, demeanor, disposition, manner.

depreciate, SYN.—descend, sink, wane; decay, decline, decrease, degenerate, deteriorate, diminish, dwindle, weaken. ANT.—ameliorate, appreciate, ascend, increase.

depression, SYN.—despair, desperation, despondency, discouragement, gloom, hopelessness, pessimism. ANT.—confidence, elation, hope, optimism.

dereliction, SYN.—failure, fiasco, miscarriage; default, omission; decay, decline; deficiency, lack, loss, want. ANT.—achievement, success, victory; sufficiency.

derision, SYN.—banter, gibe, irony, jeering, mockery, raillery, ridicule, sarcasm, satire, sneering.

derivation, SYN.—beginning, birth, commencement, cradle, foundation, inception, origin, source, spring, start. ANT.—end, harvest, issue, outcome, product.

descend, SYN.—incline, slant, slope; decline, sink, wane. ANT.—ameliorate, appreciate, ascend, increase.

description, SYN.—account, chronicle, detail, history, narration, narrative, recital, relation; computation, reckoning, record. ANT.—caricature, confusion, distortion, misrepresentation.

desecration, SYN.—abuse, aspersion, defamation, dishonor, disparagement, insult, maltreatment, misuse, outrage, perversion, profanation, reviling. ANT.—approval, commendation, laudation, respect.

desert, SYN.—abandon, abdicate, abjure, relinquish, renounce, resign, surrender, vacate, waive; forsake, leave, quit. ANT.—defend, maintain, uphold; stay, support.

design, SYN.—delineation, draft, drawing, outline, plan, sketch; artfulness, contrivance, cunning, objective, purpose. ANT.—result, candor, sincerity; accident, chance.

design, SYN.—contrive, create, devise, invent, plan, scheme; intend, mean, purpose; draw, sketch.

designate, SYN.—denote, disclose, imply, indicate, intimate, manifest, reveal, show, signify, specify. ANT.—conceal, distract, divert, falsify, mislead.

desire, SYN.—appetite, aspiration, craving, hungering, longing, lust, urge, wish, yearning. ANT.—abomination, aversion, distaste, hate, loathing.

desist, SYN.—abstain, arrest, bar, cease, check, close, cork, discontinue, end, halt, hinder, impede, interrupt, obstruct, plug, seal, stop, terminate. ANT.—begin, proceed, promote, speed, start.

desolate, SYN.—abandoned, bare, bleak, deserted, forlorn, forsaken, lonely, solitary, uninhabited, waste, wild. ANT.—attended, cultivated, fertile.

despair, SYN.—depression, desperation, despondency, discouragement, gloom, hopelessness, pessimism. ANT.—confidence, elation, hope, optimism.

desperate, SYN.—audacious, daring, despairing, despondent, determined, hopeless, reckless, wild. ANT.—assured, composed, confident, hopeful, optimistic.

desperation, SYN.—depression, despair, despondency, discouragement, gloom, hopelessness, pessimism. ANT.—confidence, elation, hope, optimism.

despicable, SYN.—base, contemptible, low, mean, sordid, vile, vulgar; malicious, nasty, offensive, selfish. ANT.—admirable, dignified, exalted, generous, noble.

despise, SYN.—abhor, abominate, detest, dislike, hate, loathe. ANT.—admire, approve, cherish, like, love.

despondent, SYN.—dejected, depressed, disconsolate, dismal, dispirited, doleful, gloomy, glum, melancholy, moody, sad, somber, sorrowful. ANT.—cheerful, happy, joyous, merry.

despotic, SYN.—absolute, complete, entire, ultimate, unconditional, unqualified, unrestricted; arbitrary, authoritative, tyrannous. ANT.—accountable, conditional, contingent, dependent, qualified.

destiny, SYN.—consequence, doom, fate, fortune, lot, portion; issue, necessity, outcome, result.

destitute, SYN.—impecunious, indigent, needy, penniless, poor, poverty-stricken. ANT.—affluent, opulent, rich, wealthy.

destroy, SYN.—annihilate, demolish, devastate, eradicate, exterminate, extinguish, obliterate, ravage, raze, ruin, wreck. ANT.—construct, establish, make, preserve, save.

destroyed, SYN.—broken, crushed, flattened, fractured, interrupted, reduced, rent, ruptured, separated, shattered, smashed, wrecked. ANT.—integral, repaired, united, whole.

destructive, SYN.—baneful, deadly, deleterious, detrimental, devastating, fatal, injurious, noxious, pernicious, ruinous. ANT.—beneficial, constructive, creative, profitable, salutary.

detach, SYN.—curtail, decrease, deduct, diminish, lessen, reduce, remove, shorten, subtract. ANT.—amplify, enlarge, expand, grow, increase.

detain, SYN.—arrest, delay, hinder, impede, retard, stay. ANT.—expedite, hasten, precipitate, quicken.

detail, SYN.—circumstance, item, minutia, part, particular; detachment, party, squad. ANT.—generality.

detect, SYN.—ascertain, devise, discover, expose, find, find out, invent, learn, originate, reveal. ANT.—cover, hide, lose, mask, screen.

determinant, SYN.—agent, cause, incentive, inducement, motive, origin, principle, reason, source. ANT.—consequence, effect, end, result.

determination, SYN.—courage, decision, firmness, fortitude, persistence, resolution, resolve, steadfastness. ANT.—inconstancy, indecision, vacillation.

determine, SYN.—conclude, decide, end, fix, resolve, settle; ascertain, verify; incline, induce, influence; condition, define, limit; compel, necessitate.

detest, SYN.—abhor, abominate, despise, dislike, hate, loathe. ANT.—admire, approve, cherish, like, love.

detestable, SYN.—abominable, execrable, foul, hateful, loathsome, odious, revolting, vile. ANT.—agreeable, commendable, delightful, pleasant.

detriment, SYN.—damage, evil, harm, hurt, ill, infliction, injury, mischief, misfortune, mishap, wrong. ANT.—benefit, boon, favor, kindness.

detrimental, SYN.—damaging, deleterious, harmful, hurtful, injurious, mischievous. ANT.—advantageous, beneficial, helpful, profitable, salutary.

develop, SYN.—amplify, create, elaborate, enlarge, evolve, expand, mature, unfold. ANT.—compress, contract, restrict, stunt, wither.

development, SYN.—elaboration, expansion, unfolding, unraveling; evolution, growth, maturing, progress. ANT.—abbreviation, compres-

sion, curtailment.

deviate, SYN.—bend, crook, deflect, digress, diverge, divert, sidetrack, stray, wander. ANT.—continue, follow, persist, preserve, remain.

device, SYN.—agent, apparatus, channel, instrument, means, medium, tool, utensil, vehicle. ANT.—hindrance, impediment, obstruction, preventive.

devious, SYN.—circuitous, crooked, distorted, erratic, indirect, roundabout, swerving, tortuous, wandering, winding; crooked, cunning, tricky. ANT.—direct, straight, honest, straightforward.

devoted, SYN.—addicted, affectionate, ardent, attached, dedicated, disposed, earnest, faithful, fond, given up to, inclined, loyal, prone, true, wedded. ANT.—detached, disinclined, indisposed, untrammeled.

devotion, SYN.—affection, ardor, attachment, consecration, dedication, devoutness, fidelity, love, loyalty, piety, religiousness, zeal. ANT.—alienation, apathy, aversion, indifference, unfaithfulness.

devout, SYN.—holy, pietistic, pious, religious, reverent, sacred, sanctimonious, spiritual, theological. ANT.—atheistic, impious, profane, secular, skeptical.

dexterity, SYN.—ability, aptitude, aptness, capability, efficiency, faculty, power, qualification, skill, talent. ANT.—disability, incapacity, incompetency, unreadiness.

dialect, SYN.—cant, diction, idiom, jargon, language, lingo, phraseology, slang, speech, tongue, vernacular. ANT.—babble, drivel, gibberish, nonsense.

dialogue, SYN.—chat, colloquy, conference, conversation, interview, parley, talk.

dictator; SYN.—autocrat, despot, oppressor, persecutor, tyrant.

die, SYN.—cease, decay, decease, decline, depart, expire, fade, languish, perish, sink, wane, wither. ANT.—begin, flourish, grow, live, survive.

difference, SYN.—disparity, dissimilarity, distinction, separation, variety; disagreement, discord, dissension. ANT.—identity, resemblance, similarity; agreement, harmony.

different, SYN.—contrary, dissimilar, distinct, diverse, incongruous, opposite, unlike, variant; divers, miscellaneous, sundry, various. ANT.—alike, congruous, identical, same, similar.

differentiate, SYN.—detect, discern, discriminate, distinguish, perceive, recognize, separate. ANT.—confound, confuse, mingle, omit, overlook.

difficult, SYN.—arduous, complicated, demanding, hard, intricate, involved, laborious, obscure, perplexing, toilsome, trying. ANT.—easy, effortless, facile, simple.

digress, SYN.—bend, crook, deflect, deviate, diverge, divert, sidetrack, stray, wander. ANT.—continue, follow, persist, preserve, remain.

dilate, SYN.—amplify, augment, distend, enlarge, expand, increase, magnify, widen. ANT.—abridge, contract, diminish, restrict, shrink.

dilemma, SYN.—condition, difficulty, fix, plight, predicament, scrape, situation, strait. ANT.—calmness, comfort, ease, satisfaction.

diligent, SYN.—active, assiduous, busy, careful, hard-working, industrious, patient, perseverant. ANT.—apathetic, careless, indifferent, lethargic, unconcerned.

dim, SYN.—faded, faint, indistinct, pale. ANT.—conspicuous, glaring.

diminish, SYN.—abate, assuage, decrease, lessen, lower, moderate, reduce, suppress. ANT.—amplify, enlarge, increase, intensify, revive.

din, SYN.—babble, clamor, noise, outcry, racket, row, sound, tumult, uproar. ANT.—hush, quiet, silence, stillness.

diplomacy, SYN.—address, adroitness, dexterity, finesse, knack, poise, savoir fair, skill, tact. ANT.— awkwardness, blunder, incompetence, rudeness, vulgarity.

diplomatic, SYN.—adroit, discreet, discriminating, judicious, politic, tactful. ANT.—boorish, churlish, coarse, gruff, rude.

dire, SYN.—appalling, awful, dreadful, fearful, frightful, ghastly, hideous, horrible, horrid, repulsive, terrible. ANT.— beautiful, enchanting, enjoyable, fascinating, lovely.

direct, SYN.—aim, level, point, train; conduct, govern, guide, manage, regulate, rule; bid, command, instruct, order. ANT.—deceive, distract, misdirect, misguide.

direction, SYN.—course, inclination, tendency, trend, way; administration, management, superintendence; guidance, instruction, order.

dirty, SYN.—filthy, foul, grimy, muddy, soiled, squalid; indecent, nasty, obscene; base, contemptible, despicable, low, mean, pitiful, shabby. ANT.—clean, neat, presentable; pure, wholesome.

disability, SYN.—handicap, impotence, inability, incapacity, incompetence, weakness. ANT.—ability, capability, power,

disabled, SYN.—crippled, defective, deformed, feeble, halt, hobbling, lame, limping, maimed, unconvincing, unsatisfactory, weak. ANT.— agile, athletic, robust, sound, vigorous.

disagreement, SYN.— challenge, difference, dissent, dissentience, noncompliance, nonconformity, objection, protest, recusancy, rejection, remonstrance, variance. ANT.—acceptance, agreement, assent, compliance.

disaster, SYN.—adversity, calamity, casualty, catastrophe, mishap, ruin. ANT.—advantage, fortune, welfare.

disavow, SYN.—disclaim, disown, reject, renounce, retract, revoke. ANT.—acknowledge, assert, recognize.

discern, SYN.—descry, detect, differentiate, discriminate, distinguish, observe, perceive, recognize, see, separate. ANT.—confound, confuse, mingle, omit, overlook.

discerning, SYN.—accurate, critical, discriminating, exact, fastidious, particular. ANT.—cursory, shallow, superficial, uncritical.

discernment, SYN.— acumen, insight, intuition, penetration, perspicuity. ANT.—obtuseness.

discharge, SYN.—banish,

discard, dismiss, eject, exile, oust, remove, send off. ANT.—accept, detain, recall, retain.

disciple, SYN.—adherent, devotee, follower, supporter, votary; learner, pupil, scholar, student.

discipline, SYN.—control, order, regulation, restraint, self-control; exercise, instruction, practice, training; correction, punishment. ANT.— chaos, confusion, turbulence.

disclaim, SYN.—deny, disavow, disown, reject, renounce, retract, revoke. ANT.—acknowledge, assent, recognize.

disclose, SYN.—betray, discover, divulge, expose, impart, reveal, show, uncover. ANT.—cloak, conceal, cover, hide, obscure.

disconsolate, SYN.—cheerless, dejected, depressed, despondent, dismal, doleful, downcast, gloomy, lugubrious, melancholy, mournful, sad, somber, sorrowful. ANT.—cheerful, glad, happy, joyous, merry.

discontinue, SYN.—adjourn, defer, delay, interrupt, postpone, stay, suspend. ANT.—continue, maintain, persist, proceed, prolong.

discourage, SYN.—block, check, hamper, hinder, impede, obstruct, prevent, resist, restrain, retard, stop, thwart. ANT.—assist, expedite, facilitate, further, promote.

discourteous, SYN.—blunt, boorish, gruff, impolite, impudent, insolent, rough, rude, saucy, surly, uncivil, vulgar. ANT.—civil, genteel, polished, courtly, dignified, noble, stately.

discover, SYN.—ascertain, detect, devise, expose, find, find out, invent, learn, originate, reveal. ANT.—cover, hide, lose, mask, screen.

discreet, SYN.—adroit, diplomatic, discriminating, judicious, politic, tactful. ANT.—boorish, churlish, coarse, gruff, rude.

discrepant, SYN.—contradictory, contrary, illogical, incompatible, incongrouous, inconsistent, irreconcilable, paradoxical, unsteady, vacillating, wavering. ANT.—compatible, congruous, consistent, correspondent.

discriminate, SYN.—descry, detect, differentiate, discern, distinguish, perceive, recognize, separate. ANT.—confound, confuse, mingle, omit, overlook.

discriminating, SYN.—accurate, critical, discerning, exact, fastidious, particular. ANT.—cursory, shallow, superficial, uncritical, insignificant, unimportant.

discrimination, SYN.—discernment, intelligence, judgment, perspicacity, sagacity, understanding, wisdom. ANT.—arbitrariness, senselessness, stupidity, thoughtlessness.

discuss, SYN.—blab, chat, converse, gossip, jabber, mutter, prattle, speak, tattle; argue, comment, declaim, discourse, harangue, lecture, plead, preach, rant, spout; confer, consult, deliberate, reason, talk.

discussion, SYN.—chatter, conference, conversation, dialogue, discourse, gossip, lecture, report, rumor, speech, talk. ANT.— correspondence, meditation, silence, writing.

disdain, SYN.—contempt, contumely, derision, detestation, hatred, scorn. ANT.—awe, esteem, regard, respect, reverence.

disease, SYN.—ailment, complaint, disorder, illness, infirmity, malady, sickness. ANT.—health, healthiness, soundness, vigor.

disgrace, SYN.—abashment, chagrin, humiliation, mortification, dishonor, disrepute, ignominy, odium, opprobrium, scandal, shame. ANT.—dignity, glory, honor, praise, renown.

disgraceful, SYN.—discreditable, dishonorable, disreputable, ignominious, scandalous, shameful. ANT.—esteemed, honorable, renowned, respectable.

disguise, SYN.—affectation, cloak, excuse, garb, mask, pretense, pretension, pretext, semblance, show, simulation, subterfuge. ANT.—actuality, fact, reality, sincerity, truth.

disguise, SYN.—cloak, conceal, cover, hidden, mask, screen, secrete, suppress, veil, withhold. ANT.—disclose, divulge, expose, reveal, show, uncover.

dishonest, SYN.—contaminated, corrupt, corrupted, crooked, debased, depraved, impure, profligate, putrid, spoiled, tainted, unsound, venal, vitiated.

dishonor, SYN.—abashment, chagrin, humiliation, mortification; disgrace, disrepute, ignominy, odium, opprobrium, scandal, shame. ANT.—dignity, glory, honor, praise, renown.

disintegrate, SYN.—decay, decline, decompose, decrease, dwindle, ebb, putrefy, rot spoil, wane, waste. ANT.—flourish, grow, increase, luxuriate, rise.

dislike, SYN.—abhorrence, antipathy, aversion, disgust, disinclination, distaste, dread, hatred, loathing, repugnance, repulsion, reluctance. ANT.—affection, attachment, devotion, enthusiasm.

dislike, SYN.—abhor, abominate, despise, detest, dislike, hate, loathe. ANT.—admire, approve, cherish, like, love.

disloyal, SYN.—apostate, faithless, false, perfidious, recreant, traitorous, treacherous, treasonable. ANT.—constant, devoted, loyal, true.

dismal, SYN.—bleak, cheerless, dark, doleful, dreary, dull, funereal, gloomy, lonesome, melancholy, sad, somber. ANT.—cheerful, gay, joyous, lively.

dismiss, SYN.—banish, discard, discharge, eject, exile, oust, remove, send off. ANT.—accept, detain, recall, retain.

disobedient, SYN.—defiant, forward, insubordinate, rebellious, refractory, undutiful, unruly. ANT.—compliant, dutiful, obedient, submissive.

disobey, SYN.—break, infringe, invade, transgress, violate, defile.

disorder, SYN.—anarchy, chaos, confusion, disorganization, jumble, muddle. ANT.—order, organization, system.

disorganization, SYN.—anarchy, chaos, confusion, disorder, jumble, muddle. ANT.—order, organization, system.

disorganized, SYN.—bewildered, confused, deranged, disconcerted, disordered, indistinct, mixed, muddled, perplexed. ANT.—clear, lucid, obvious, organized, plain.

disparage, SYN.—belittle, decry, depreciate, derogate, discredit, lower, minimize, undervalue. ANT.—aggrandize, commend, exalt, magnify, praise.

disparagement, SYN.—belittling, decrying, depreciation, derogation, discredit, lowering, minimizing, undervaluing. ANT. — aggrandizement, commendation, exalting, magnification, praise.

dispatch, SYN.—cast, discharge, emit, impel, propel, send, throw, transmit. ANT.—bring, get, hold, receive, retain.

dispel, SYN.—diffuse, disperse, disseminate, dissipate, scatter, separate. ANT.—accumulate, amass, assemble, collect, gather.

dispense, SYN.—allot, apportion, deal, distribute, divide, mete; allocate, appropriate, assign, give, grant, measure. ANT.—confiscate, keep, refuse, retain, withhold.

disperse, SYN.—diffuse, dispel, disseminate, dissipate, scatter, separate. ANT.—accumulate, amass, assemble, collect, gather.

displace, SYN.—dislodge, move, remove, shift, transfer, transport. ANT.—leave, remain, stay, retain.

display, SYN.—exhibit, expose, flaunt, parade, reveal, show, spread out.

ANT.—conceal, cover, disguise, hide.

disposition, SYN.—action, bearing, behavior, carriage, conduct, deed, demeanor, deportment, manner.

dispute, SYN.—argument, contention, controversy, debate, disagreement, quarrel, squabble. ANT.—agreement, concord, decision, harmony.

dispute, SYN.—altercate, argue, bicker, contend, contest, debate, discuss, quarrel, squabble, wrangle. ANT.—agree, allow, assent, concede.

disregard, SYN.—ignore, neglect, omit, overlook, skip, slight. ANT.—include, notice, regard.

dissent, SYN.—challenge, difference, disagreement, dissentience, noncompliance, nonconformity, objection, protest, recusancy, rejection, remonstrance, variance. ANT.—acceptance, agreement, assent, compliance.

dissimilar, SYN.—contrary, different, distinct, divergent, diverse, incongruous, opposite, unlike, variant; divers, miscellaneous, sundry, various. ANT.—alike, congruous, identical, same, similar.

dissimulation, SYN.—cant, deceit, hypocrisy, pretense, sanctimony. ANT.—candor, frankness, honesty, openness, truth.

dissipate, SYN.—consume, lavish, misuse, scatter, spend, squander, waste, wear out; diminish, dwindle. ANT.—accumulate, conserve, economize, preserve, save.

distant, SYN.—far, faraway, remote, removed; aloof, cold, reserved, stiff, unfriendly. ANT.—close, near, nigh, cordial, friendly.

distinct, SYN.—apparent, clear, evident, intelligible, lucid, manifest, obvious, plain, unmistakable, visible. ANT.—ambiguous, obscure, unclear, vague.

distinction, SYN.—attribute, characteristic, feature, peculiarity, property, quality, trait. ANT.—being, essence, nature, substance.

distinctive, SYN.—eccentric, exceptional, extraordinary, odd, rare, singular, strange, striking, unusual; characteristic, individual, particular, peculiar, special. ANT.—common, general, normal, ordinary.

distinguish, SYN.—descry, detect, differentiate, discern, discriminate, perceive, recognize, separate. ANT.—confound, confuse, mingle, omit, overlook.

distinguished, SYN.—conspicuous, elevated, eminent, famous, glorious, illustrious, noted, prominent, renowned. ANT.—common, obscure, ordinary, unimportant, unknown.

distracted, SYN.—absent, absent-minded, abstracted, inattentive, preoccupied. ANT.—attending, present; attentive, watchful.

distress, SYN.—agony, anguish, grief, misery, suffering, torment, torture. ANT.—comfort, joy, relief, solace.

distribute, SYN.—allot, apportion, deal, dispense, divide, dole, mete, scatter, spread; classify, group, sort.

district, SYN.—country, division, domain, dominion, land, place, province, quarter, region, section, territory.

distrust, SYN.—ambiguity, doubt, hesitation, incredulity, scruple, skepticism, suspense, suspicion, unbelief, uncertainty. ANT.—belief, certainty, conviction, determination, faith.

disturb, SYN.—agitate, annoy, confuse, derange, discompose, interrupt, perplex, perturb, rouse, trouble, unsettle, vex, worry. ANT.—order, pacify, quiet, settle, soothe.

divide, SYN.—part, separate, sever, sunder; allot, deal out, dispense, distribute, share. ANT.—combine, convene, gather, join, unite.

divine, SYN.—celestial, godlike, heavenly, holy, superhuman, supernatural, transcendent.

ANT.—blasphemous, diabolical, mundane, profane, wicked.

diverse, SYN.—contrary, different, dissimilar, distinct, divergent, incongruous, opposite, unlike, variant; divers, miscellaneous, sundry, various. ANT.—alike, congruous, identical, same, similar.

diversity, SYN.—assortment, change, difference, dissimilarity, heterogeneity, medley, miscellany, mixture, multifariousness, variety, variousness. ANT.—homogeneity, likeness, monotony, sameness, uniformity.

divert, SYN.—avert, deflect, deviate, swerve, turn; alter, change, transmute. ANT.—arrest, fix, stand, stop; continue, proceed; endure, perpetuate.

divulge, SYN.—betray, disclose, discover, expose, impart, reveal, show, uncover. ANT.—cloak, conceal, cover, hide, obscure.

do, SYN.—accomplish, complete, conclude, consummate, effect, execute, finish, fulfill, perform, settle, terminate; carry on, conduct, discharge, transact; observe, perform, practice; make, produce, work; answer, serve, suffice.

docile, SYN.—compliant, obedient, pliant, submissive, tame, teachable, tractable, yielding.

ANT.—mulish, obstinate, stubborn, ungovernable, unruly.

doctrine, SYN.—belief, creed, dogma, precept, teaching, tenet. ANT.—conduct, deed, performance, practice.

doctrinaire, SYN.—arrogant, authoritarian, dictatorial, dogmatic, domineering, magisterial, opinionated, overbearing, positive; authoritative, doctrinal, formal. ANT.—fluctuating, indecisive, open-minded, questioning, skeptical.

document, SYN.—account, archive, chronicle, memorandum, minute, note, record, report, register; mark, memorial, trace, vestige.

dogma, SYN.—belief, creed, doctrine, precept, teaching, tenet. ANT.—conduct, deed, performance, practice.

dogmatic, SYN.—arrogant, authoritarian, dictatorial, doctrinaire, domineering, magisterial, opinionated, overbearing, positive; authoritative, doctrinal, formal. ANT.—fluctuating, indecisive, open-minded, questioning, skeptical.

doing, SYN.—accomplishment, act, action, deed, execution, feat, operation, performance, transaction. ANT.—cessation, deliberation, inactivity, inhibition, intention.

dole, SYN.—allot, apportion, deal, dispense, distribute, divide, mete, scatter, spread.

doleful, SYN.—bleak, cheerless, dark, dismal, dreary, dull, funereal, gloomy, lonesome, melancholy, sad, somber. ANT.—cheerful, gay, joyous, lively.

domain, SYN.—country, district, division, dominion, land, place, province, quarter, region, section, territory.

dominate, SYN.—command, control, direct, govern, manage, regulate, rule, superintend. ANT.—abandon, follow, forsake, ignore, submit.

domination, SYN.—ascendancy, mastery, predominance, sovereignty, supremacy, sway, transcendence. ANT.—inferiority.

donation, SYN.—benefaction, bequest, boon, charity, endowment, favor, gift, grant, gratuity, largess, present. ANT.—deprivation, earnings, loss, purchase.

doom, SYN.—consequence, fate, fortune, lot, portion; destiny, issue, necessity, outcome, result.

dormant, SYN.—idle, inactive, indolent, inert, lazy, slothful, unemployed, unoccupied. ANT.—active, employed, industrious, occupied, working.

doubt, SYN.—ambiguity, distrust, hesitation, incredulity, scruple, skepticism, suspense, suspicion, unbelief, uncertainty. ANT.—belief, certainty, conviction, determination, faith.

doubt, SYN.—hesitate, question, waver; distrust, mistrust, suspect. ANT.—believe, confide, decide, rely on, trust.

dour, SYN.—crabbed, fretful, gloomy, glum, moody, morose, sulky, surly. ANT.—amiable, gay, joyous, merry, pleasant.

draw, SYN.—drag, haul, pull, tow, tug; extract, remove, take out, unsheathe; allure, attract, entice, induce, lure, persuade; delineate, depict, sketch, trace; compose, draft, formulate, write; deduce, derive, get, infer, obtain; extend, lengthen, prolong, protract, stretch. ANT.—alienate, contract, drive, propel, shorten.

draw from, SYN.—extract, remove, withdraw. ANT.—leave, remain, stay; retain.

drawing, SYN.—engraving, etching, illustration, image, likeness, panorama, picture, portrait, portrayal, print, representation, resemblance, scene, sketch, view.

dread, SYN.—alarm, apprehension, awe, fear, foreboding, horror, reverence, terror. ANT.—assurance, boldness, confidence, courage.

dreadful, SYN.—appalling, awful, dire, fearful, frightful, ghastly, hideous, horrible, horrid, repulsive, terrible. ANT.—beautiful, enchanting, enjoyable, fascinating, lovely.

dreary, SYN.—bleak, cheerless, dark, dismal, doleful, dull, funereal, gloomy, lonesome, melancholy, sad, somber. ANT.—cheerful, gay, joyous, lively.

dress, SYN.—apparel, array, attire, clothing, drapery, garb, garments, raiment, vestments, vesture. ANT.—nakedness, nudity.

drill, SYN.—activity, application, employment, exercise, exertion, lesson, operation, performance, practice, task, training, use. ANT.—idleness, indolence, relaxation, repose, rest.

drive, SYN.—coerce, compel, constrain, enforce, force, impel, oblige. ANT.—allure, convince, induce, persuade, prevent.

droll, SYN.—amusing, comical, farcical, funny, humorous, laughable, ludicrous, ridiculous, witty. ANT.—melancholy, sad, serious, sober, solemn.

drop, SYN.—collapse, decline, decrease, descend, diminish, fall, sink, subside; stumble, topple, tumble, droop, extend downward, hang. ANT.—arise, ascend, climb, mount, soar, steady.

drudgery, SYN.—effort, endeavor, exertion, labor, striving, task, toil, travail, work. ANT.—idleness, indolence, leisure, recreation.

drunk, SYN.—drunken, high, inebriated, intoxicated, tight, tipsy. ANT.—clear-headed, sober, temperate.

dry, SYN.—arid, dehydrated, desiccated, drained, parched, thirsty; barren, dull, insipid, plain, tedious, tiresome, uninteresting, vapid. ANT.—damp, moist; fresh, interesting, lively.

dull, SYN.—dense, slow, stupid; blunt, obtuse; boring, commonplace, dismal, dreary, monotonous, sad, tedious. ANT.—animated, lively, sharp; clear, interesting.

dumb, SYN.—brainless, crass, dense, dull, foolish, obtuse, senseless, stupid, witless. ANT.—alert, bright, clever, discerning, intelligent.

dunk, SYN.—dip, douse, immerse, plunge, sink, submerge. ANT.—elevate, recover, uplift.

duplicate, SYN.—copy, exemplar, facsimile, imitation, replica, reproduction, transcript. ANT.—original, prototype.

durability, SYN.—force, fortitude, intensity, lustiness, might, potency, power, stamina, stout-ness, strength, sturdiness, toughness, vigor. ANT.—feebleness, frailty, infirmity, weakness.

durable, SYN.—abiding, changeless, constant, enduring, fixed, indestructible, lasting, permanent, unchangeable. ANT.—ephemeral, temporary, transient, transitory, unstable.

duration, SYN.—boundary, limit, period, term, time.

dusky, SYN.—dark, dim, gloomy, murky, obscure, shadowy, unilluminated; opaque, sable, swarthy; dismal, gloomy, mournful, somber. ANT.—light; bright, clear, pleasant; lucid.

duty, SYN.—accountability, bond, compulsion, contract, engagement, obligation, responsibility. ANT.—choice, exemption, freedom.

dwelling, SYN.—abode, domicile, habitat, hearth, home, quarters, residence, seat.

E

eager, SYN.—anxious, ardent, avid, enthusiastic, fervent, hot, impassioned, impatient, keen, yearning. ANT.—apathetic, indifferent, unconcerned, uninterested.

early, SYN.—beforehand, betimes, shortly, soon. ANT.—belated, late, overdue, tardy.

earn, SYN.—achieve, acquire, attain, deserve, gain, get, merit, obtain, win. ANT.—consume, forfeit, lose, spend, waste.

earned, SYN.—adequate, condign, deserved, merited, proper, suitable. ANT.—improper, undeserved, unmerited.

earnest, SYN.—candid, frank, genuine, heartfelt, honest, open, sincere, straightforward, true, truthful, unfeigned, upright. ANT.—affected, dishonest, hypocritical, insincere, untruthful.

earth, SYN.—continent, country, field, ground, island, land, plain, region, soil, tract.

ease, SYN.—allay, alleviate, assuage, calm, comfort, facilitate, lighten, mitigate, pacify, relieve, soothe. ANT.—confound, distress, disturb, trouble, worry.

easy, SYN.—facile, light, pleasant, relaxed, simple, uncomplicated. ANT.—arduous, demanding, difficult, hard.

eccentric, SYN.—bizarre, curious, odd, peculiar, quaint, queer, singular, strange, unique, unusual. ANT.—common, familiar, normal, regular, typical.

economical, SYN.—frugal, niggardly, provident, saving, sparing, thrifty. ANT.—extravagant, improvident, lavish, prodigal, wasteful.

ecstasy, SYN.—delight, exaltation, gladness, rapture, transport; frenzy, madness, trance. ANT.—depression, melancholy.

edge, SYN.—border, boundary, brim, brink, extremity, hem, margin, periphery, rim, verge; intensity, keenness, sharpness, sting. ANT.—center, interior; bluntness, dullness.

edict, SYN.—act, decree, law, statute. ANT.—deliberation, inactivity, intention.

educate, SYN.—inculcate, inform, instill, instruct, school, teach, train, tutor. ANT.—misguide, misinform.

education, SYN.—cultivation, development, instruction, knowledge, learning, schooling, study, training, tutoring.

effect, SYN.—achieve, accomplish, attain, complete, consummate, do, execute, finish, fulfill, perfect, perform. ANT.—block, defeat, fail, frustrate, spoil.

effective, SYN.—adept, capable, competent, effectual, efficacious, efficient, proficient, skillful. ANT.—incompetent, ineffectual, inefficient, unskilled.

efficacy, SYN.—ability, capability, competency, effectiveness, efficiency, potency, skillfulness. ANT.—inability, ineptitude, wastefulness.

efficiency, SYN.—clarify,

decipher, explain, expound, illustrate, interpret, resolve, unfold, unravel. ANT.—baffle, confuse, darken, obscure.

efficient, SYN.—adept, capable, competent, effective, effectual, efficacious, proficient, skillful. ANT.—incompetent, ineffectual, inefficient, unskilled.

effort, SYN.—attempt, endeavor, essay, exertion, trial; labor, pains, strain, strife, struggle, toil, trouble.

effrontery, SYN.—assurance, audacity, boldness, impertinence, impudence, insolence, presumption, rudeness, sauciness. ANT.—diffidence, politeness, subserviency, truckling.

egotism, SYN.—conceit, pride, self-esteem, vanity. ANT.—diffidence, humility, meekness, modesty.

elastic, SYN.—compliant, ductile, flexible, lithe, pliable, pliant, resilient, supple, tractable. ANT.—brittle, hard, rigid, stiff, unbending.

elect, SYN.—choose, cull, opt, pick, select. ANT.—refuse, reject.

elegance, SYN.—attractiveness, beauty, charm, comeliness, fairness, grace, handsomeness, loveliness, pulchritude. ANT.—deformity, disfigurement, eyesore, homeliness, ugliness.

elegant, SYN.—beauteous, beautiful, charming, comely, fair, fine, handsome, lovely, pretty. ANT.—foul, hideous, homely, repulsive, unsightly.

elementary, SYN.—basic, fundamental, primary, rudimentary, simple. ANT.—abstract, abstruse, complex, elaborate, intricate.

elevate, SYN.—erect, exalt, heave, heighten, hoist, lift, uplift; breed, cultivate, grow, produce, raise. ANT.—abase, depreciate, depress, destroy.

elevated, SYN.—lofty, tall, towering; eminent, exalted, high, proud. ANT.—small, stunted, tiny; base, low, mean.

eliminate, SYN.—dislodge, eject, eradicate, erase, exclude, expel; extirpate, oust, remove. ANT.—accept, admit, include, involve.

elongate, SYN.—distend, distort, expand, extend, lengthen, protract, spread, strain, stretch. ANT.—contract, loosen, shrink, slacken, tighten.

elucidate, SYN.—clarify, decipher, explain, expound, illustrate, interpret, resolve, unfold, unravel. ANT.—baffle, confuse, darken, obscure.

elude, SYN.—avert, avoid, dodge, escape, eschew, forbear, forestall, free, shun, ward. ANT.—

confront, encounter, meet, oppose.

emanate, SYN.—belch, breathe, discharge, eject, emit, expel, hurl, shed, shoot, spurt, vent.

emancipate, SYN.—deliver, discharge, free, let go, liberate, release, set free. ANT.—confine, imprison, oppress, restrict, subjugate.

embarrass, SYN.—abash, discomfit, distress, entangle, fluster, hamper, hinder, mortify, perplex, rattle, trouble. ANT.—cheer, encourage, help, relieve.

embellish, SYN.—adorn, beautify, deck, decorate, enrich, garnish, ornament, trim. ANT.—debase, defame, expose, strip, uncover.

embody, SYN.—accommodate, comprise, contain, embrace, hold, include. ANT.—discharge, emit, exclude.

embrace, SYN.—clasp, hug; accept, adopt, espouse, receive, welcome; comprehend, comprise, contain, embody, include, incorporate, subsume. ANT.—reject, renounce, repudiate, scorn, spurn.

emerge, SYN.—appear, arise, arrive, emanate, issue. ANT.—disappear, vanish, withdraw.

emergency, SYN.—crisis, exigency, juncture, pass, pinch, strait, urgency.

eminence, SYN.—acclaim, credit, distinction, fame, glory, honor, notoriety, renown, reputation. ANT.—disrepute, ignominy, infamy, obscurity.

eminent, SYN.—conspicuous, distinguished, elevated, famous, glorious, illustrious, noted, prominent, renowned. ANT.—common, obscure, ordinary, unimportant, unknown.

emit, SYN.—belch, breathe, discharge, eject, emanate, expel, hurl, shed, shoot, spurt, vent.

emotion, SYN.—affection, agitation, feeling, passion, perturbation, sentiment, trepidation, turmoil. ANT.—calm, dispassion, indifference, restraint, tranquility.

employ, SYN.—apply, avail, busy, devote, occupy, use, utilize. ANT.—banish, discard, discharge, reject.

employment, SYN.—business, engagement, function, occupation, service, vocation, work. ANT.—idleness, leisure, slothfulness.

empty, SYN.—barren, devoid, hollow, senseless, unfilled, unfurnished, unoccupied, vacant, vacuous, vain, void, worthless. ANT.—full, inhabited, occupied, replete, supplied.

enclose, SYN.—bound, circumscribe, confine, encompass, envelop, fence, limit, surround. ANT.—develop, distend, enlarge, expand, expose, open.

encounter, SYN.—battle, collision, combat, conflict, duel, fight, struggle; contention, controversy, discord, inconsistency, interference, opposition, variance. ANT.—amity, concord, consonance, harmony.

encounter, SYN.—collide, confront, engage, find, greet, intersect, meet; experience, suffer, undergo. ANT.—cleave, disperse, part, scatter, separate.

encourage, SYN.—animate, cheer, countenance, embolden, exhilarate, favor, hearten, impel, incite, inspirit, urge; foster, promote, sanction, stimulate, support. ANT.—deject, deter, discourage, dispirit, dissuade.

encroach, SYN.—attack, infringe, intrude, invade, penetrate, trespass, violate. ANT.—abandon, evacuate, relinquish, vacate.

end, SYN.—aim, cessation, close, completion, conclusion, expiration, extremity, finish, object, purpose, result, termination, terminus, tip. ANT.—beginning, commencement, inception, introduction.

endanger, SYN.—expose, hazard, jeopardize, peril, risk. ANT.—insure, protect, secure.

endeavor, SYN.—attempt, effort, essay, exertion, trial; labor, pains, strain, strife, struggle, toil trouble.

endless, SYN.—boundless, eternal, illimitable, immeasurable, immense, infinite, interminable, unbounded, unlimited, vast. ANT.—bounded, circumscribed, confined, finite, limited.

endorsement, SYN.—approbation, approval, assent, commendation, consent, praise, sanction, support. ANT.—censure, reprimand, reproach, stricture.

endurance, SYN.—composure, forbearance, fortitude, long-suffering, patience, perseverance, resignation. ANT.—impatience, nervousness, restlessness, unquiet.

endure, SYN.—bear, brook, experience, suffer, sustain, tolerate, undergo; abide, continue, last, persist, remain. ANT.—fail, falter, succumb; disperse, wane.

enduring, SYN.—abiding, ceaseless, constant, continual, faithful, fixed, immutable, invariant, permanent, perpetual, persistent, unalterable, unchanging, unwavering. ANT.—fickle, mutable, vacillating, wavering.

enemy, SYN.—adversary, antagonist, competitor, foe, opponent, rival. ANT.—accomplice, ally, comrade, confederate, friend.

energetic, SYN.—active, animated, blithe, brisk,

frolicsome, lively, spirited, sprightly, supple, vigorous, vivacious. ANT.—dull, insipid, listless, stale, vapid.

energy, SYN.—dint, emphasis, force, intensity, might, potency, power, strength, vigor, coercion, compulsion, constraint, violence. ANT.—feebleness, frailty, impotence, weakness; persuasion.

enervation, SYN.—exhaustion, fatigue, languor, lassitude, tiredness, weariness. ANT.—freshness, rejuvenation, restoration, vigor, vivacity.

engage, SYN.—attach, bind, fasten, fetter, join, link, oblige, restrain, restrict, tie. ANT.—free, loose, unfasten, untie.

engender, SYN.—cause, create, fashion, form, formulate, generate, invent, make, originate, produce. ANT.—annihilate, demolish, destroy.

engross, SYN.—absorb, assimilate, consume, engulf, imbibe, swallow up; engage, occupy. ANT.—discharge, dispense, emit, expel, exude.

engulf, SYN.—absorb, assimilate, consume, imbibe, swallow up; engage, engross, occupy. ANT.—discharge, dispense, emit, expel, exude.

enigma, SYN.—conundrum, mystery, problem, puzzle, riddle. ANT.—answer, clue, key, resolution, solution.

enjoyment, SYN.—bliss, ecstasy, gladness, happiness, joy, pleasure, rapture, transport. ANT.—annoyance, dejection, melancholy, misery, sorrow.

enlarge, SYN.—amplify, augment, broaden, dilate, distend, expand, increase, magnify, widen. ANT.—abridge, contract, diminish, restrict, shrink.

enlargement, SYN.—amplification, augmentation, broadening, dilation, distension, expansion, increase, magnification, widening. ANT.—abridgement, contraction, diminish, restriction, shrinkage.

enlighten, SYN.—brighten, clarify, elucidate, illumine, illustrate, irradiate. ANT.—complicate, confuse, darken, obfuscate, obscure.

enmity, SYN.—animosity, antagonism, antipathy, hatred, hostility, ill will, invidiousness, malignity. ANT.—affection, cordiality, friendliness, good will, love.

ennoble, SYN.—aggrandize, consecrate, dignify, elevate, erect, exalt, extol, glorify, hallow, raise. ANT.—debase, degrade, dishonor, humble, humiliate.

enormous, SYN.—colossal, elephantine, gargantuan, gigantic, huge, immense, large, prodigious, vast. ANT.—diminutive, little, minute, small, tiny.

enough, SYN.—adequate, ample, capable, commensurate, fitting, satisfactory, sufficient, suitable. ANT.—deficient, lacking, scant.

ensue, SYN.—follow, succeed, come next; accompany, attend; result. ANT.—precede; guide, lead; avoid, elude, flee; cause.

entangle, SYN.—embrace, embroil, envelop, implicate, include, incriminate, involve. ANT.—disconnect, disengage, extricate, separate.

entente, SYN.—alliance, association, coalition, combination, confederacy, federation, league, partnership, union; compact, covenant, treaty. ANT.—divorce, schism, separation.

enterprise, SYN.—art, business, commerce, employment, engagement, job, occupation, profession, trade, trading, vocation, work. ANT.—avocation, hobby, pastime.

enterprising, SYN.—adventurous, bold, chivalrous, daring, foolhardy, precipitate, rash. ANT.—cautious, hesitating, timid.

entertain, SYN.—consider, contemplate, harbor, hold; amuse, beguile, cheer, delight, divert, gladden, please, regale. ANT.—annoy, bore, disgust, disturb, repulse.

entertainment, SYN.—amusement, diversion, fun, game, pastime, play, recreation, sport. ANT.—boredom, labor, toil, work.

enthusiasm, SYN.—ardor, devotion, earnestness, excitement, fanaticism, fervency, fervor, inspiration, intensity, vehemence, warmth, zeal. ANT.—apathy, detachment, ennui, indifference, unconcern.

enthusiastic, SYN.—anxious, ardent, avid, eager, fervent, hot, impassioned, impatient, keen, yearning. ANT.—apathetic, indifferent, unconcerned, uninterested.

entice, SYN.—allure, attract, captivate, charm, enchant, fascinate, lure. ANT.—alienate, deter, repel, repulse.

entire, SYN.—all, complete, intact, integral, perfect, total, undivided, unimpaired, whole. ANT.—defective, deficient, incomplete, partial.

entrance, SYN.—doorway, entry, inlet, opening, portal. ANT.—departure, exit.

entreat, SYN.—adjure, ask, beg, beseech, crave, implore, importune, petition, pray, request, solicit, supplicate. ANT.—bestow, cede, favor, give, grant.

entrust, SYN.—commend,

commit, consign, rele-
gate, trust; bind, obli-
gate, pledge. ANT.—
mistrust, release, re-
nounce; free, loose.

envy, SYN.—covetousness,
jealousy, spitefulness.
ANT.—generosity, geni-
ality, indifference.

episode, SYN.—circum-
stance, event, happen-
ing, incident, issue; oc-
currence.

epoch, SYN.—age, antiquity, date, era, generation,
period, time.

equal, SYN.—alike, commensurate, equitable,
equivalent, even, identi-
cal, like, same, uniform,
unvarying. ANT.—
different, disparate, dissimilar, diverse.

equilibrium, SYN.—
balance, composure,
poise, stability, steadi-
ness; proportion, sym-
metry. ANT.—fall, imbal-
ance, instability, un-
steadiness.

equip, SYN.—endow, fit, fit
out, furnish, provide,
supply. ANT.—denude,
despoil, divest, strip.

equitable, SYN.—fair, honest, impartial, just, reasonable, unbiased.
ANT — dishonorable,
fraudulent, partial.

equity, SYN.—fairness, impartiality, justice, justness, law, rectitude,
right. ANT.—inequity,
partiality, unfairness,
wrong.

equivalent, SYN.—coincident, equal, identical,
indistinguishable, like,

same. ANT.—contrary,
disparate, dissimilar, distinct, opposed.

era, SYN.—age, antiquity,
date, epoch, generation,
period, time.

eradicate, SYN.—eliminate,
erase, exclude, expel,
extirpate, oust, remove.
ANT.—accept, admit, in-
clude, involve.

erase, SYN.—cancel, cross
out, delete, eliminate,
expunge, obliterate;
abolish, abrogate, annul,
invalidate, nullify,
quash, repeal, rescind,
revoke. ANT.—confirm,
enact, enforce, perpetu-
ate.

erect, SYN.—unbent, upright; straight, vertical.
ANT.—circuitous, wind-
ing; bent, crooked.

erroneous, SYN.—amiss,
askew, awry, fallacious,
false, faulty, inaccurate,
incorrect, mistaken, un-
precise, untrue, wrong;
improper, inappropriate,
unsuitable; aberrant,
bad, criminal, evil, im-
moral, iniquitous, repre-
hensible. ANT.—correct,
right, true; suitable,
proper.

error, SYN.—blunder, fallacy, fault, inaccuracy,
mistake, slip. ANT.—
accuracy, precision,
truth.

erudition, SYN.—information, insight, intelli-
gence, judgment, know-
ledge, learning, reason,
sagacity, sageness,
sense, wisdom. ANT.—
foolishness, ignorance,

nonsense, stupidity.

escape, SYN.—abscond, decamp, flee, fly; avert, avoid, elude, evade, shun. ANT.—catch, confront, face, invite, meet.

eschew, SYN.—avert, avoid, dodge, escape, elude, forbear, forestall, free, shun, ward. ANT.—confront, encounter, meet, oppose.

escort, SYN.—accompany, attend, follow, guard, lackey, protect, serve, tend, watch; be present, frequent.

essay, SYN.—composition, motive, subject, text, theme, thesis, topic.

essential, SYN.—basic, fundamental, important, indispensable, intrinsic, necessary, requisite, vital. ANT.—expendable, extrinsic, optional, peripheral.

establish, SYN.—form, found, institute, organize, raise; confirm, fix, ordain, sanction, settle, strengthen; prove, substantiate, verify. ANT.—abolish, demolish, overthrow, unsettle, upset; dislike, scorn.

estate, SYN.—belongings, commodities, effects, goods, merchandise, possessions, property, stock, wares, wealth. ANT.—deprivation, destitution, poverty, privation, want.

esteemed, SYN.—beloved, dear, precious, valued. ANT.—despised, unwanted.

estimate, SYN.—appraise, access, assign, calculate, compute, evaluate, fix, levy, reckon, tax.

eternal, SYN.—ceaseless, deathless, endless, everlasting, immortal, infinite, perpetual, timeless, undying. ANT.—ephemeral, finite, mortal, temporal, transient.

eternally, SYN.—always, constantly, continually, ever, evermore, forever, incessantly, perpetually, unceasingly. ANT.—fitfully, never, occasionally, rarely, sometimes.

ethereal, SYN.—divine, ghostly, holy, immaterial, incorporeal, religious, sacred, spiritual, supernatural, unearthly, unworldly. ANT.—carnal, corporeal, material, mundane, physical.

ethical, SYN.—chaste, decent, good, honorable, just, moral, pure, right, righteous, scrupulous, virtuous. ANT.—amoral, libertine, licentious, sinful, unethical.

evade, SYN.—avert, avoid, escape, shun. ANT.—catch, confront, face, invite, meet.

evaluate, SYN.—appraise, assess, assign, calculate, compute, estimate, fix, levy, reckon, tax.

event, SYN.—circumstance, episode, happening, incident, issue; consequence, end, occurrence, outcome, result.

ever, SYN.—always, constantly, continually, eternally, evermore, forever, incessantly, perpetually, unceasingly. ANT.—fitfully, never, occasionally, rarely, sometimes.

everlasting, SYN.—ceaseless, deathless, endless, eternal, immortal, infinite, perpetual, timeless, undying. ANT.—ephemeral, finite, mortal, temporal, transient.

evidence, SYN.—confirmation, corroboration, demonstration, experiment, proof, test, testimony, trial, verification. ANT.—failure, fallacy, invalidity.

evident, SYN.—apparent, clear, conspicuous, indubitable, manifest, obvious, open, overt, patent, unmistakable. ANT.—concealed, covert, hidden, obscure.

evil, SYN.—bad, baleful, base, deleterious, immoral, iniquitous, noxious, pernicious, sinful, unsound, unwholesome, villainous, wicked. ANT.—excellent, good, honorable, moral, reputable.

evil, SYN.—crime, guilt, iniquity, offense, sin, transgression, ungodliness, vice, wickedness, wrong. ANT.—goodness, innocence, purity, righteousness, virtue.

evolve, SYN.—amplify, create, develop, elaborate, enlarge, expand, mature, unfold. ANT.—compress, contract, restrict, stunt,

wither.

exact, SYN.—accurate, correct, definite, distinct, precise, strict, unequivocal. ANT.—erroneous, loose, rough, vague; careless, easy, informal.

exactness, SYN.—accuracy, fidelity, precision.

exaggerate, SYN.—amplify, caricature, embroider, enlarge, expand, heighten, magnify, overstate, stretch. ANT.—belittle, depreciate, minimize, understate.

exalt, SYN.—aggrandize, consecrate, dignify, elevate, ennoble, erect, extol, glorify, hallow, raise. ANT.—debase, degrade, dishonor, humble, humiliate.

exalted, SYN.—dignified, elevated, eminent, grand, illustrious, lofty, majestic, noble, stately. ANT.—base, low, mean, plebian, vile.

examination, SYN.—exploration, inquiry, interrogation, investigation, query, quest, question, research, scrutiny. ANT.—disregard, inactivity, inattention, negligence.

examine, SYN.—analyze, assess, audit, check, contemplate, dissect, inquire, interrogate, notice, question, quiz, review, scan, scrutinize, survey, view, watch. ANT.—disregard, neglect, omit, overlook.

example, SYN.—archetype, illustration, instance,

model, pattern, prototype, sample, specimen. ANT.—concept, precept, principle, rule.

exasperate, SYN.—aggravate, annoy, chafe, embitter, inflame, irritate, nettle, provoke, vex. ANT.—appease, mitigate, palliate, soften.

exasperation, SYN.—annoyance, chagrin, irritation, mortification, pique, vexation. ANT.—appeasement, comfort, gratification, pleasure.

excellent, SYN.—conscientious, exemplary, honest, moral, pure, reliable, virtuous, worthy; admirable, commendable, ɟ genuine, good, precious, safe, sound, valid; fair, honorable, immaculate; auspicious, beneficial, favorable, profitable, useful; able, capable, efficient, expert, proficient, skillful.

exception, SYN.—exclusion, omission, preclusion; anomaly, deviation, unusual case; affront, objection, offense. ANT.—inclusion, rule, standard.

exceptional, SYN.—infrequent, occasional, strange, unusual; choice, incomparable, precious, rare, scarce, singular, uncommon, unique. ANT.—customary, frequent, ordinary, usual; abundant, commonplace, numerous, worthless.

excess, SYN.—extrava-gance, immoderation, intemperance, profusion, superabundance, superfluity, surplus. ANT.—dearth, deficiency, lack, paucity, want.

excessive, SYN.—abundant, copious, extravagant, exuberant, immoderate, improvident, lavish, luxuriant, overflowing, plentiful, prodigal, profuse, wasteful. ANT.—economical, meager, poor, skimpy, sparse.

exchange, SYN.—change, substitute; convert, modify, shift, transfigure, transform, vary, veer. ANT.—retain; continue, establish, preserve, settle, stabilize.

excite, SYN.—agitate, arouse, awaken, disquiet, disturb, incite, irritate, provoke, rouse, stimulate, stir up. ANT.—allay, calm, pacify, quell, quiet.

exclaim, SYN.—call out, cry, cry out, ejaculate, shout, vociferate. ANT.—intimate, whisper, write.

exclude, SYN.—bar, blackball, except, expel, hinder, omit, ostracize, prevent, prohibit, restrain, shut out. ANT.—accept, admit, include, welcome.

exculpation, SYN.—absolution, acquittal, amnesty, forgiveness, pardon, remission. ANT.—conviction, penalty, punishment, sentence.

excuse, SYN.—absolve, acquit, condone, exculpate, exempt, forgive, free, justify, overlook, pardon, remit. ANT.—convict, prosecute, punish, retaliate, revenge.

execrable, SYN.—abominable, detestable, foul, hateful, loathsome, odious, revolting, vile. ANT.—agreeable, commendable, delightful, pleasant.

execute, SYN.—accomplish, achieve, attain, complete, consummate, do, effect, finish, fulfill, perfect, perform. ANT.—block, defeat, fail, frustrate, spoil.

execution, SYN.—accomplishment, act, action, deed, doing, feat, operation, performance, transaction. ANT.—cessation, deliberation, inactivity, inhibition, intention.

exemplar, SYN.—copy, duplicate, facsimile, imitation, replica, reproduction, transcript. ANT.—original, prototype.

exemplary, SYN.—fancied, faultless, ideal, imaginary, perfect, supreme, unreal, utopian, visionary. ANT.—actual, faulty, imperfect, material, real.

exercise, SYN.—activity, application, drill, employment, exertion, lesson, operation, performance, practice, task, training, use. ANT.—idleness, indolence, relaxation, repose, rest.

exhaust, SYN.—fatigue, tire, tucker, wear out, weary. ANT.—amuse, invigorate, refresh, restore, revive.

exhausted, SYN.—faint, fatigued, spent, tired, wearied, weary, worn. ANT.—fresh, hearty, invigorated, rested.

exhaustion, SYN.—enervation, fatigue, languor, lassitude, tiredness, weariness. ANT.—freshness, rejuvenation, restoration, vigor, vivacity.

exhibit, SYN.—display, expose, flaunt, parade, reveal, show, spread out. ANT.—conceal, cover, disguise, hide.

exhibition, SYN.—array, display, exposition, show; demonstration, flourish, ostentation, parade, spectacle, splurge; entertainment, movie, performance, production.

exile, SYN.—banishment, deportation, expatriation, expulsion, extradition, ostracism, proscription. ANT.—admittance, recall, reinstatement, retrieval, welcome.

existence, SYN.—animation, being, buoyancy, life, liveliness, spirit, vigor, vitality, vivacity. ANT.—death, demise, dullness, languor, lethargy.

exoneration, SYN.—absolution, acquittal, amnesty, forgiveness, pardon, remission.

ANT.—conviction, penalty, punishment, sentence.

expand, SYN.—advance, develop, distend, enlarge, extend, germinate, grow, increase, mature, swell. ANT.—atrophy, contract, decay, diminish, shrink, wane.

expanse, SYN.—amount, area, compass, degree, extent, length, magnitude, measure, range, reach, scope, size, stretch.

expansion, SYN.—development, elaboration, unfolding, unraveling; evolution, growth, maturing, progress. ANT.—abbreviation, compression, curtailment.

expatriation, SYN.—banishment, deportation, exile, expulsion, extradition, ostracism, proscription. ANT.—admittance, recall, reinstatement, retrieval, welcome.

expect, SYN.—anticipate, awaite, contemplate, hope for. ANT.—despair of.

expectation, SYN.—anticipation, contemplation, foresight, forethought, hope, preconception, prescience, presentiment. ANT.—doubt, dread, fear, worry.

expedite, SYN.—accelerate, dispatch, facilitate, forward, hasten, hurry, push, quickness, rush, speed. ANT.—block, hinder, impede, retard, slow.

expedition, SYN.—cruise, jaunt, journey, passage, pilgrimage, tour, travel, trip, voyage.

expel, SYN.—banish, discharge, dismiss, disown, excommunicate, exile, expatriate, ostracize, oust, proscribe; dislodge, eject, eliminate, void. ANT.—admit, favor, include, recall.

expend, SYN.—avail, employ, exploit, manipulate, operate, utilize; exercise, exert, practice; consume, exhaust, use. ANT.—ignore, neglect, overlook, waste.

expense, SYN.—charge, cost, price, value, worth.

expensive, SYN.—costly, precious, valuable; profitable, useful. ANT.—cheap, mean, poor; trashy, worthless.

expert, SYN.—able, accomplished, adept, clever, competent, cunning, ingenious, practiced, proficient, skilled, skillful, versed. ANT.—awkward, bungling, clumsy, inexpert, untrained.

expire, SYN.—cease, decay, decease, decline, depart, die, fade, languish, perish, sink, wane, wither. ANT.—begin, flourish, grow, live, survive.

explain, SYN.—clarify, decipher, elucidate, expound, illustrate, interpret, resolve, unfold, unravel. ANT.—baffle, confuse, darken, obscure.

explanation, SYN.—alibi, apology, confession, defense, excuse, justification. ANT.—accusation, complaint, denial, dissimulation.

explicit, SYN.—clear, definitive, express, lucid, manifest, specific. ANT. — ambiguous, equivocal, implicit, obscure, vague.

exploit, SYN.—deed, feat; accomplishment, achievement, attainment, performance, realization. ANT.—neglect, omission; defeat, failure.

exploit, SYN.—avail, employ, manipulate, operate, use, utilize; exercise, exert, consume, exhaust, expend; handle, manage, treat. ANT.—ignore, neglect, overlook, waste.

exposed, SYN.—agape, ajar, open, unclosed, uncovered, unlocked; clear, passable, unobstructed; accessible, public, unrestricted.

expound, SYN.—clarify, elucidate, explain, illustrate, interpret, unfold, unravel. ANT.—baffle, confuse, darken, obscure.

express, SYN.—clear, definitive, explicit, lucid, manifest, specific. ANT. — ambiguous, equivocal, implicit, obscure, vague.

express, SYN.—affirm, assert, avow, claim, declare, explain, propound, recite, recount, say, specify, state, tell, utter.

ANT.—conceal, deny, imply, retract.

expressive, SYN.— animated, clear, fresh, graphic, lively, lucid, vivid. ANT.—dull, vague.

exquisite, SYN.—choice, dainty, delicate, elegant, fine, nice, pure, refined, splendid, subtle; beautiful, handsome, pretty; small, thin. ANT.—blunt, coarse, large, rough, thick.

extend, SYN.—distend, distort, elongate, expand, lengthen, protract, spread, strain, stretch. ANT.—contract, loosen, shrink, slacken, tighten.

extended, SYN.—drawn out, elongated, lasting, lengthy, lingering, long, prolix, prolonged, protracted, tedious, wordy. ANT.—abridged, brief, concise, short, terse.

extension, SYN.—amount, area, compass, degree, expanse, extent, length, magnitude, measure, range, reach, scope, size, stretch.

extensive, SYN.—broad, expanded, large, sweeping, vast, wide. ANT.— confined, narrow, restricted.

extent, SYN.—amount, area, compass, degree, expanse, length, magnitude, measure, range, reach, scope, size, stretch.

exterior, SYN.—countenance, mug, visage; cover, face, front, surface. ANT.—timidity; back, interior, rear.

extol, SYN.—celebrate, commend, glorify, honor, laud, praise. ANT.—disregard, overlook; decry, disgrace, dishonor, profane.

extract, SYN.—abandon, depart, desert, forsake, give up, go, quit, relinquish, renounce, retire, withdraw. ANT.—abide, remain, stay, tarry.

extradition, SYN.—banishment, deportation, exile, expatriation, expulsion, ostracism, proscription. ANT.—admittance, recall, reinstatement, retrieval, welcome.

extraneous, SYN.—adverse, alien, contrasted, foreign, irrelevant, remote, strange, unconnected. ANT.—akin, germane, kindred, relevant.

extraordinary, SYN.—exceptional, marvelous, peculiar, rare, remarkable, singular, uncommon, unusual, wonderful. ANT.—common, frequent, ordinary, usual.

extravagant, SYN.—abundant, copious, excessive, exuberant, immoderate, improvident, lavish, luxuriant, overflowing, plentiful, prodigal, profuse, wasteful. ANT.—economical, meager, poor, skimpy, sparse.

extreme, SYN.—acute, arduous, distressing, exacting, hard, harsh, intense, relentless, rigid, rigorous, severe, sharp, stern, stringent, unmitigated, unyielding.

exude, SYN.—discharge, dislodge, eject, eliminate, expel, void.

F

fabrication, SYN.—allegory, fable, falsehood, fiction, invention, narrative, novel, romance, story, tale. ANT.—fact, history, reality, truth, verify.

face, SYN.—countenance, mug, visage; assurance, audacity; cover, exterior, front, surface. ANT.—timidity; back, interior, rear.

facetiousness, SYN.—humor, irony, jocularity, joke, sarcasm, satire, waggery, wit. ANT.—gravity, seriousness, sorrow.

facilitate, SYN.—allay, alleviate, assuage, calm, comfort, ease, lighten, mitigate, pacify, relieve, soothe. ANT.—confound, distress, disturb, trouble, worry.

fact, SYN.—actuality, certainty, reality, truth; act, circumstance, deed, event, incident, occurrence. ANT.—fiction, supposition, theory, delusion, falsehood.

faculty, SYN.—ability, capability, capacity, power, skill, talent; magnitude, size, volume. ANT.—impotence, inability, incapacity, stupidity.

fail, SYN.—defeat, disappoint, foil, frustrate, hinder, thwart. ANT.—accomplish, fulfill, further, promote.

failure, SYN.—fiasco, miscarriage, default, dereliction, omission; decay, decline; deficiency, lack, loss, want. ANT.—achievement, success, victory; sufficiency.

faint, SYN.—dim, faded, indistinct, pale; feeble, languid, wearied; irresolute, timid, weak. ANT.—conspicuous, glaring; strong, vigorous; brave, forceful.

fair, SYN.—bright, clear, light; attractive, blond, comely, lovely; equitable, honest, impartial, just, reasonable, unbiased; average, mediocre, passable. ANT.—foul, ugly; dishonorable, fraudulent, partial; excellent, first-rate, worst.

faith, SYN.—confidence, credence, dependence, reliance, trust; belief, creed, doctrine, dogma, persuasion, religion, tenet; constancy, fidelity, loyalty. ANT.—doubt, incredulity, mistrust, skepticism; infidelity.

faithful, SYN.—constant, devoted, loyal, staunch, steadfast, true; accurate, reliable, trusty. ANT.—disloyal, false, fickle, treacherous, untrustworthy.

fall, SYN.—collapse, decline, decrease, descend, diminish, drop, sink, subside; stumble, topple, tumble; droop, extend downward, hang. ANT.—arise, ascend, climb, mount, soar; steady.

fame, SYN.—acclaim, credit, distinction, eminence, glory, honor, notoriety, renown, reputation. ANT.—disrepute, ignominy, infamy, obscurity.

familiar, SYN.—acquainted, aware, cognizant, conversant, intimate, knowing, versed; affable, amicable, close, courteous, friendly, informal, sociable, unreserved. ANT.—affected, cold, distant, reserved, unfamiliar.

familiarity, SYN.—acquaintance, fellowship, friendship, sociability; frankness, informality, intimacy, liberty, unreserve. ANT.—constraint, distance, haughtiness, presumption, reserve.

famous, SYN.—celebrated, distinguished, eminent, glorious, illustrious, noted, renowned; wellknown. ANT.—hidden, ignominious, infamous, obscure, unknown.

fanatical, SYN.—bigoted, dogmatic, illiberal, intolerant, narrowminded, prejudiced. ANT.—liberal, progressive, radical, tolerant.

fantasy, SYN.—caprice, dream, fancy, hallucination, illusion, imagination, whim.

farewell, SYN.—departure, good-by, leave-taking, valediction. ANT.—greeting, salutation, welcome.

fast, SYN.—expeditious, fleet, quick, rapid, speedy, swift; constant, firm, inflexible, secure, solid, stable, steadfast, steady, unswerving, unyielding. ANT.—slow, sluggish; insecure, loose, unstable, unsteady.

fasting, SYN.—abstention, continence, forbearance. ANT.—excess, gluttony, greed, intoxication, self-indulgence.

fat SYN.—chubby, corpulent, obese, paunchy, plump, portly, pudgy, rotund, stocky, stout, thickset. ANT.—gaunt, lean, slender, slim, thin.

fate, SYN.—consequence, doom, fortune, lot, portion; destiny, issue, necessity, outcome, result.

fatigue, SYN.—enervation, exhaustion, languor, lassitude, tiredness, weariness. ANT.—freshness, rejuvenation, restoration, vigor, vivacity.

fault, SYN.—blemish, defect, error, failure, flaw, imperfection, mistake, omission, shortcoming, vice. ANT.—completeness, correctness, perfection.

fear, SYN.—alarm, apprehension, consternation, cowardice, dismay, dread, fright, horror, panic, scare, terror, timidity, trepidation. ANT.—assurance, boldness, bravery, courage, fearlessness.

feat, SYN.—accomplishment, act, action, deed, doing, execution, operation, performance, transaction. ANT.—cessation, deliberation, inactivity, intention.

feeble, SYN.—decrepit, delicate, enervated, exhausted, faint, forceless, impaired, infirm, languid, powerless, puny, weak. ANT.—forceful, lusty, stout, strong, vigorous.

feeling, SYN.—sensation; affection, emotion, passion, sensibility, sentiment, tenderness; impression, opinion. ANT.—anesthesia; coldness, imperturbability, insensibility; fact.

fellowship, SYN.—brotherhood, brotherliness, kindness, solidarity; association, clan, fraternity, society. ANT.—acrimony, discord, opposition, strife.

feminine, SYN.—female, girlish, ladylike, maidenly, womanish, womanly. ANT.—male, manly, mannish, masculine, virile.

fertile, SYN.—bountiful, fecund, fruitful, luxuriant, plenteous, productive, prolific, rich, teeming. ANT.—barren, impotent, sterile, unproductive.

festival, SYN.—banquet, celebration, entertainment, feast, regalement.

fickle, SYN.—capricious,

changeable, fitful, inconstant, restless, unstable, variable. ANT.—constant, reliable, stable, steady, trustworthy.

fiction, SYN.—allegory, fable, fabrication, falsehood, invention, narrative, novel, romance, story, tale. ANT.—fact, history, reality, truth, verity.

fidelity, SYN.—allegiance, constancy, devotion, faithfulness, fealty, loyalty; accuracy, exactness, precision. ANT.—disloyalty, faithlessness, perfidy, treachery.

fight, SYN.—battle, brawl, combat, conflict, contend, dispute, encounter, quarrel, scuffle, skirmish, squabble, struggle, wrangle.

fill, SYN.—fill up, occupy, pervade; furnish, replenish, stock, store, supply; content, glut, gorge, sate, satiate, satisfy, stuff. ANT.—deplete, drain, empty, exhaust, void.

final, SYN.—concluding, conclusive, decisive, ending, eventual, last, latest, terminal, ultimate. ANT.—first, inaugural, incipient, original, rudimentary.

fine, SYN.—choice, dainty, delicate, elegant, exquisite, nice, pure, refined, splendid, small, thin. ANT.—blunt, coarse, large, rough, thick.

finish, SYN.—accomplish, achieve, close, complete, conclude, consummate, do, end, execute, fulfill, get done, perfect, perform, terminate.

fire, SYN.—blaze, burning, combustion, conflagration, flame, glow, heat, warmth; ardor, fervor, intensity, passion, vigor. ANT.—cold; apathy, quiescence.

first, SYN.—beginning, earliest, initial, original, primary, prime, primeval, primitive, pristine; chief, foremost. ANT.—hindmost, last, latest, least, subordinate.

fit, SYN.—accommodate, adapt, adjust, conform, suit. ANT.—disturb, misapply, misfit.

fitful, SYN.—capricious, changeable, fickle, inconstant, restless, unstable, variable. ANT.—constant, reliable, stable, steady, trustworthy.

fix, SYN.—affix, attach, bind, fasten, link, place, set, stick, tie; define, determine, establish, limit, set, settle; adjust, mend, rectify, regulate, repair. ANT.—displace, remove, unfasten; alter, change, disturb, modify; damage, mistreat.

flat, SYN.—even, horizontal, level, plane, smooth; dull, insipid, stale, tasteless, vapid. ANT.—broken, hilly, irregular, sloping; exciting, racy, savory, tasty.

flee, SYN.—abscond, decamp, escape, fly, hasten, run away. ANT.—appear, arrive, remain, stay.

flexible, SYN.—compliant, ductile, elastic, lithe, pliable, pliant, resilient, supple, tractable. ANT.—brittle, hard, rigid, stiff, unbending.

flow, SYN.—gush, run, spout, spurt, stream; come, emanate, issue, originate, proceed, result; abound, be copious.

fluctuate, SYN.—change, hesitate, oscillate, undulate, vacillate, vary, waver. ANT.—adhere, decide, persist, resolve, stick.

fly, SYN.—flit, float, flutter, glide, hover, mount, sail, soar; dart, rush, shoot, spring; abscond, decamp, escape, flee, run away. ANT.—descend, fall, plummet, sink.

follow, SYN.—succeed, come next; comply, heed, obey, observe; adopt, copy, imitate; accompany, attend; chase, pursue, trail; ensue, result. ANT.—precede; guide, lead; avoid, elude, flee; cause.

follower, SYN.—adherent, attendant, devotee, disciple, henchman, partisan, successor, supporter, votary. ANT.—chief, head, leader, master.

folly, SYN.—foolishness, imbecility, silliness; absurdity, extravagance, imprudence, indiscretion. ANT.—sense, wisdom; judgment, prudence, reasonableness.

food, SYN.—diet, edibles, fare, feed, meal, nutriment, provisions, rations, repast, sustenance, viands, victuals. ANT.—drink, hunger, starvation, want.

fool, SYN.—buffoon, clown, harlequin, jester; blockhead, dolt, dunce, idiot, imbecile, nincompoop, numbskull, oak, simpleton. ANT.—genius, philosopher, sage, scholar.

foolish. SYN.—absurd, asinine, brainless, crazy, idiotic, irrational, nonsensical, preposterous, ridiculous, senseless, silly, simple. ANT.—judicious, prudent, sagacious, sane, wise.

forbearance, SYN.—abstention, abstinence, continence, moderation, self-denial. ANT.—excess, gluttony, greed, intoxication, self-indulgence.

force, SYN.—dint, emphasis, energy, intensity, might, potency, power, strength, vigor; coercion, compulsion, constraint, violence. ANT.—feebleness, frailty, impotence, weakness; persuasion.

form, SYN.—construct, create, fashion, forge, make, mold, produce, shape; compose, constitute, make up; arrange, combine, organize; devise, frame, invent. ANT.—destroy, disfigure, dismantle, misshape, wreck.

formal, SYN.—affected, ceremonious, correct, decorous, exact, methodical, precise, proper, regular, solemn, stiff; external, outward, perfunctory. ANT.—easy, natural, unconstrained, unconventional; heartfelt.

fortuitous, SYN.—advantageous, auspicious, benign, favored, felicitous, fortunate, happy, lucky, propitious, successful. ANT.—cheerless, condemned, ill-fated, persecuted, unlucky.

fortunate, SYN.—advantageous, auspicious, benign, favored, felicitous, fortunate, happy, lucky, propitious, successful. ANT.—cheerless, condemned, ill-fated, persecuted, unlucky.

forward, SYN.—advance, aggrandize, elevate, further, promote; bring forward. ANT.—hinder, oppose, retard, retreat, withhold.

foul, SYN.—dirty, filthy, grimy, muddy, soiled, squalid; indecent, nasty, obscene; base, contemptible, despicable, low, mean, pitiful, shabby. ANT.—clean, neat, presentable; pure, wholesome.

foundation, SYN.—base, basis, bottom, ground, groundwork, root, substructure, support, underpinning. ANT.—building, cover, superstructure, top.

fragile, SYN.—breakable, brittle, delicate, feeble, frail, infirm, weak. ANT.—durable, hardy, strong, sturdy, tough.

fraud, SYN.—artifice, cheat, chicanery, deceit, deception, duplicity, guile, imposition, imposture, swindle, trick. ANT.—fairness, honesty, integrity, sincerity.

fray, SYN.—battle, combat, conflict, contest, fight, skirmish, strife, struggle. ANT.—agreement, concord, peace, truce.

free, SYN.—autonomous, emancipated, exempt, freed, independent, liberated, unconfined, unrestricted; clear, loose, open, unfastened, unobstructed; immune; careless, easy, familiar, frank; artless, bounteous, bountiful, generous, liberal, munificent. ANT.—confined, restrained, restricted; blocked, clogged, impeded; subject; illiberal, parsimonious, stingy.

freedom, SYN.—exemption, familiarity, immunity, independence, liberation, liberty, license, privilege, unrestraint. ANT.—bondage, compulsion, constraint, necessity, servitude.

frequent, SYN.—common, general, habitual, often, persistent, usual. ANT.—exceptional, rare, scanty, solitary, unique.

fresh, SYN.—modern, new, novel, recent; additional,

further; brisk, cool, refreshing; artless, green, inexperienced, natural, raw. ANT.—decayed, faded, hackneyed, musty, stagnant.

friend, SYN.—companion, comrade, crony, intimate; advocate, defender, patron, supporter, well-wisher; ally, associate. ANT.—adversary, enemy, stranger.

friendly, SYN.—affable, amicable, companionable, genial, kindly, neighborly, sociable, social. ANT.—antagonistic, cool, distant, hostile, reserved.

friendship, SYN.—acquaintance, cognizance, companionship, familiarity, fellowship, intimacy, knowledge. ANT.—ignorance, inexperience, unfamiliarity.

frighten, SYN.—affright, alarm, appal, astound, daunt, dismay, horrify, intimidate, scare, startle, terrify, terrorize. ANT.—allay, compose, embolden, reassure, soothe.

frugal, SYN.—economical, parsimonious, provident, saving, sparing, stingy, temperate, thrifty. ANT.—extravagant, intemperate, self-indulgent, wasteful.

fruitful, SYN.—bountiful, fecund, fertile, luxuriant, plenteous, productive, prolific, rich, teeming. ANT.—barren, impotent, sterile, unproductive.

frustrate, SYN.—baffle, balk, circumvent, defeat, disappoint, foil, hinder, outwit, prevent, thwart. ANT.—accomplish, fulfill, further, promote.

full, SYN.—crammed, filled, gorged, packed, replete, satiated, soaked; ample, complete, copious, entire, extensive, perfect, plentiful, sufficient; baggy, flowing, loose, voluminous; circumstantial, detailed, exhaustive. ANT.—depleted, devoid, empty, vacant; insufficient, lacking, partial.

funny, SYN.—amusing, comical, droll, farcical, humorous, laughable, ludicrous, ridiculous, witty; curious, odd, queer. ANT.—melancholy, sad, serious, sober, solemn.

furnish, SYN.—endow, equip, fit, fit out, provide, supply; afford, give, produce, yield. ANT.—denude, despoil, divest, strip.

G

gain, SYN.—account, advantage, avail, behalf, benefit, favor, good, interest, profit, service. ANT.—calamity, distress, handicap, trouble.

gain, SYN.—achieve, acquire, attain, earn, get, obtain, procure, reach, secure, win; benefit, net, profit. ANT.—forfeit, lose, surrender.

game, SYN.—amusement,

contest, diversion, fun, match, merriment, pastime, play, recreation, sport. ANT.—business.

gap, SYN.—abyss, aperture, cavity, chasm, gulf, hole, opening, pore, void.

garb, SYN.—apparel, array, attire, clothes, clothing, drapery, dress, garments, raiment, vestments, vesture. ANT.—nakedness, nudity.

garments, SYN.—apparel, array, attire, clothes, clothing, drapery, dress, garb, raiment, vestments, vesture. ANT.—nakedness, nudity.

garnish, SYN.—adorn, beautify, deck, decorate, embellish, enrich, ornament, trim. ANT.—debase, defame, expose, strip, uncover.

garrulous, SYN.—chattering, chatty, communicative, glib, loquacious, talkative, verbose, voluble. ANT.—laconic, reticent, silent, taciturn, uncommunicative.

gather, SYN.—accumulate, amass, assemble, collect, congregate, convene, muster; cull, garner, glean, harvest, pick, reap, conclude, deduce, infer, judge. ANT.—disband, disperse, distribute, scatter, separate.

gaunt, SYN.—attenuated, diaphanous, diluted, emaciated, fine, flimsy, gauzy, gossamer, lank, lean, meager, narrow, rare, scanty, scrawny, skinny, slender, slight, slim, spare, tenuous, thin. ANT.—broad, bulky, fat, thick, wide.

gay, SYN.—cheerful, glad, happy, jolly, joyful, lighthearted, merry, sprightly. ANT.—depressed, glum, mournful, sad, sullen.

gaze, SYN.—behold, discern, eye, glance, look, see, stare, survey, view, watch, witness; appear, seem; examine, inspect, observe, regard. ANT.—avert, hide, miss, overlook.

general, SYN.—common, customary, ordinary, popular, prevalent, regular, universal, usual; indefinite, inexact, vague. ANT.—exceptional, rare, singular; definite, particular, specific.

generate, SYN.—afford, bear, bestow, breed, impart, pay, produce, supply; accord, allow, concede, grant, permit; abdicate, accede, acquiesce, capitulate, cede, quit, relent, relinquish, resign, submit, succumb, surrender, waive, yield. ANT.—deny, dissent, oppose, refuse; assert, resist, strive, struggle.

generation, SYN.—age, dotage, senescence, senility, seniority; antiquity, date, epoch, era, period, time. ANT.—childhood, infancy, youth.

generosity, SYN.—altruism, beneficence, benevolence, charity, humanity, kindness, liberality, magnanimity, philanthropy, tenderness. ANT.—cruelty, inhumanity, malevolence, selfishness, unkindness.

generous, SYN.—beneficent, bountiful, giving, liberal, magnanimous, munificent, openhanded, unselfish. ANT.—covetous, greedy, miserly, selfish, stingy.

genius, SYN.—ability, aptitude, creativity, faculty, gift, inspiration, intellect, originality, sagacity, talent; adept, intellectual, master, proficient. ANT.—ineptitude, obtuseness, shallowness, stupidity; dolt, dullard, moron.

genre, SYN.—caste, category, class, denomination, kind; grade, order, rank, set; elegance, excellence.

gentle, SYN.—benign, calm, docile, mild, peaceful, placid, relaxed, serene, soft, soothing, tame, tractable. ANT.—fierce, harsh, rough, savage, violent.

genuine, SYN.—authentic, bona fide, legitimate, proven, real, sincere, true, unadulterated, unaffected, veritable. ANT.—artificial, bogus, counterfeit, false, sham.

genus, SYN.—breed, character, family, kind, race, sort, species, stock, strain, type, variety.

germ, SYN.—contagion, infection, pest, virus; ailment, contamination, disease, poison, pollution, taint.

gesture, SYN.—emblem, indication, mark, note, omen, portent, proof, sign, signal, symbol, symptom, token.

get, SYN.—achieve, acquire, attain, earn, gain, obtain, procure, receive, secure. ANT.—forfeit, leave, lose, renounce, surrender.

ghost, SYN.—apparition, phantom, shade, spectre, spirit, spook.

gift, SYN.—benefaction, bequest, boon, charity, donation, endowment, favor, grant, gratuity, largess, present; aptitude, faculty, genius, talent. ANT.—deprivation, earnings, loss, purchase; incapacity, ineptitude, stupidity.

gigantic, SYN.—colossal, elephantine, enormous, gargantuan, huge, immense, large, prodigious, vast. ANT.—diminutive, little, minute, small, tiny.

giggle, SYN.—cackle, chuckle, guffaw, jeer, laugh, mock, roar, scoff; snicker, titter.

gist, SYN.—acceptation, connotation, drift, explanation, implication, import, intent, interpretation, meaning, purport, purpose, sense, significance, signification.

give, SYN.—bestow, confer, contribute, deliver, donate, furnish, grant, impart, present, provide, supply. ANT.—keep, retain, seize, withdraw.

glad, SYN.—cheerful, delighted, exulting, gratified, happy, joyous, lighthearted, merry, pleased. ANT.—dejected, depressed, despondent, melancholy, sad.

gladness, SYN.—beatitude, blessedness, bliss, contentment, delight, felicity, happiness, pleasure, satisfaction, wellbeing, ANT.—despair, grief, misery, sadness, sorrow.

glance, SYN.—behold, discern, eye, gaze, look, scan, see, stare, survey, view, watch, witness, appear, seem; examine, inspect, observe, regard. ANT.—avert, hide, miss, overlook.

gleam, SYN.—beam, blaze, flash, flicker, glare, glimmer, glisten, glitter, glow, radiate, scintillate, shimmer, shine, sparkle, twinkle.

glib, SYN.—flat, level, plain, polished, sleek, stick; diplomatic, smooth, suave, urbane. ANT.—bluff; blunt, harsh, rough, rugged.

gloom, SYN.—blackness, bleakness, darkness, obscurity, shadow; dejection, depression, despondency, melancholy, misery, sadness, woe. ANT.—exultation, frivolity, joy, light, mirth.

gloomy, SYN.—dejected, depressed, despondent, disconsolate, dismal, dispirited, doleful, glum,

melancholy, moody, sad, somber, sorrowful; grave, pensive. ANT.—cheerful, happy, joyous, merry.

glorify, SYN.—adore, consecrate, dignify, enshrine, enthrone, exalt, extol, hallow, honor, revere, venerate. ANT.—abuse, debase, degrade, dishonor, mock.

glorious, SYN.—elevated, exalted, grand, high, lofty, majestic, noble, raised, splendid, sublime, supreme. ANT.—base, ignoble, low, ordinary, ridiculous.

glory, SYN.—admiration, adoration, deference, dignity, esteem, fame, homage, honor, praise, renown, respect, reverence, worship. ANT.—contempt, derision, disgrace, dishonor, reproach.

glow, SYN.—beam, blaze, flash, flicker, glare, glimmer, glisten, glitter, radiate, scintillate, shimmer, shine, sparkle, twinkle.

glowing, SYN.—ardent, eager, enthusiastic, fervent, fervid, fiery, hot, impassioned, intense, keen, passionate, vehement, zealous. ANT.—apathetic, cool, indifferent, nonchalant.

glum, SYN.—crabbed, dour, fretful, gloomy, moody, morose, sulky, surly. ANT.—amiable, gay, joyous, merry, pleasant.

glut, SYN.—fill, fill up, occupy, pervade; furnish, replenish, stock, store, supply; content, gorge, sate, satiate, satisfy, stuff. ANT.—deplete, drain, empty, exhaust, void.

gluttony, SYN.—devouring, insatiability, ravenousness, voraciousness. ANT.—fullness, satisfaction.

go, SYN.—depart, exit, fade, flee, leave, move, proceed, quit, retire, vanish, walk, withdraw. ANT.—arrive, come, enter, stand, stay.

goal, SYN.—aim, ambition, aspiration, craving, desire, hope, longing, objective, passion.

godlike, SYN.—celestial, divine, heavenly, holy, superhuman, supernatural, transcendent. ANT.—blasphemous, diabolical, mundane, profane, wicked.

good, SYN.—conscientious, exemplary, honest, moral, pure, reliable, virtuous, worthy; admirable, commendable, excellent, genuine, precious, safe, sound, valid; benevolent, gracious, humane, kind; agreeable, cheerful, friendly, genial, pleasant; fair, honorable, immaculate; auspicious, beneficial, favorable, profitable, useful; able, capable, efficient, expert, proficient, skillful; adequate, ample, sufficient.

govern, SYN.—administer, command, control, direct, manage, oversee, regulate, reign, rule, supervise, sway. ANT.—acquiesce, assent, obey, submit, yield.

grace, SYN.—attractiveness, beauty, charm, comeliness, elegance, fairness, handsomeness, loveliness, pulchritude. ANT.—deformity, disfigurement, eyesore, homeliness, ugliness.

graceful, SYN.—beautiful, comely, elegant, flowing, fluid, lithe, natural, supple. ANT.—awkward, clumsy, deformed, gawky, ungainly.

gracious, SYN.—agreeable, amiable, engaging, friendly, good-natured, pleasing. ANT.—churlish, disagreeable, hateful, ill-natured, surly.

grade, SYN.—caste, category, denomination, genre, kind; order, rank, set; elegance, excellence.

gradual, SYN.—dawdling, delaying, deliberate, dull, laggard, leisurely, sluggish, slow, tired. ANT.—fast, quick, rapid, speedy, swift.

grandiose, SYN.—august, dignified, grand, high, imposing, lofty, magnificent, majestic, noble, pompous, stately, sublime. ANT.—common, humble, lowly, ordinary, undignified.

grant, SYN.—allot, apportion, deal, dispense, distribute, divide, mete; allocate, appropriate, assign, give, measure. ANT.—confiscate, keep, refuse, retain, withhold.

graph, SYN.—cabal, conspiracy, design, intrigue, machination, plan, plot, scheme, stratagem; chart, diagram, sketch.

grasp, SYN.—apprehend, arrest, capture, clutch, catch, grip, lay hold of, seize, snare, trap. ANT.—liberate, lose, release, throw.

grateful, SYN.—appreciative, beholden, indebted, obliged, thankful. ANT.—thankless, unappreciative.

gratifying, SYN.—comfort, consolation, contentment, ease, enjoyment, relief, solace, succor. ANT.—affliction, discomfort, misery, suffering, torment, torture.

grating, SYN.—coarse, gruff, harsh, jarring, rigorous, rough, rugged, severe, strict, stringent. ANT.—gentle, melodious, mild, smooth, soft.

grave, SYN.—consequential, important, momentous, serious, weighty; dignified, sedate, sober, solemn, staid, thoughtful. ANT.—insignificant, trifling, trivial; flighty, frivolous, light, merry.

great, SYN.—big, enormous, gigantic, huge, immense, large, vast; numerous, countless; celebrated, eminent, famed, illustrious, prominent, renowned; critical, important, momentous, serious, vital, weighty; august, dignified, elevated, grand, majestic, noble; excellent, fine, magnificent. ANT.—diminutive, little, minute, small; common, obscure, ordinary, unknown; menial, paltry.

greedy, SYN.—avaricious, covetous, grasping, rapacious, selfish; devouring, gluttonous, insatiable, ravenous, voracious. ANT.—generous, munificent; full, satisfied.

green, SYN.—modern, new, novel, recent; additional, further; brisk, cool, fresh, refreshing; artless, inexperienced, natural, raw. ANT.—decayed, faded, hackneyed, musty, stagnant.

greet, SYN.—accost, approach, hail, speak to. ANT.—avoid, pass by.

gregarious, SYN.—affable, civil, communicative, friendly, hospitable, outgoing, sociable. ANT.—antisocial, disagreeable, hermitic, inhospitable.

grief, SYN.—affliction, anguish, distress, heartache, lamentation, misery, mourning, sadness, sorrow, trial, tribulation, woe. ANT.—comfort, consolation, happiness, joy, solace.

grievance, SYN.—damage, detriment, harm, injury, mischief; injustice, prejudice, wrong. ANT.—benefit, improvement, repair.

grieve, SYN.—bemoan, bewail, deplore, lament, mourn, suffer, weep. ANT.—carouse, celebrate, rejoice, revel.

grieved, SYN.—afflicted, hurt, pained, sad, sorrowful, vexed; contrite, penitent, remorseful, repentant, sorry; beggarly, contemptible, mean, paltry, pitiable, pitiful, poor, shabby, vile, worthless, wretched. ANT.—cheerful, delighted, impenitent, splendid, unrepentant.

grip, SYN.—apprehend, arrest, capture, catch, clutch, grip, lay hold of, seize, snare, trap. ANT.—liberate, lose, release, throw.

gross, SYN.—aggregate, entire, total, whole; brutal, enormous, glaring, grievous, manifest, plain; coarse, crass, earthy, indelicate, obscene; rough, rude, vulgar, big, bulky, fat, great, large. ANT.—proper, refined; appealing, comely, delicate.

grouch, SYN.—complain, grumble, lament, murmur, protest, regret, remonstrate, repine, whine. ANT.—applaud, approve, praise, rejoice.

ground, SYN.—base, basis, bottom, foundation, groundwork, support, underpinning; assumption, postulate, premise, presumption, presupposition, principle. ANT.—derivative, implication, superstructure, trimming.

groundwork, SYN.—base, basis, bottom, foundation, ground, support, underpinning; assumption, postulate, premise, presumption, presupposition, principle. ANT.—derivative, implication, superstructure, trimming.

group, SYN.—aggregation, assembly, band, brood, bunch, class, cluster, collection, crowd, flock, herd, horde, lot, mob, pack, party, set swarm, throng, troupe.

groveling, SYN.—abject, contemptible, despicable, dishonorable, base, ignoble, ignominious, low, lowly, mean, menial, servile, sordid, vile, vulgar. ANT.—esteemed, exalted, honored, lofty, noble, righteous.

grow, SYN.—advance, develop, distend, enlarge, expand, extend, germinate, increase, mature, swell. ANT.—atrophy, contract, decay, diminish, shrink, wane.

growth, SYN.—development, elaboration, expansion, unfolding, unraveling; evolution, maturing, progress. ANT. —abbreviation, compression, curtailment.

grudge, SYN.—animosity, enmity, ill will, malevolence, malice, malignity, rancor, spite. ANT.—affection, kindness, love, toleration.

gruff, SYN.—craggy, irregular, jagged, rugged, scabrous, scratchy, uneven; approximate, coarse, crude, cursory, imperfect, incomplete, unfinished, unpolished; harsh, severe, stormy, tempestuous, turbulent, violent; blunt, brusque, churlish, rough, rude, uncivil. ANT.—even, level, sleek, slippery, smooth; fine, finished, polished, refined; calm, placid, tranquil, unruffled; civil, courteous, gentle, mild.

guarantee, SYN.—bail, bond, earnest, guaranty, pawn, pledge, security, surety, token, warrant.

guard, SYN.—bulwark, fence, protection, refuge, safeguard, shelter, shield; defense, security.

guard, SYN.—cloak, clothe, conceal, cover, curtain, disguise, envelop, hide, mask, protect, screen, shield, shroud, veil. ANT.—bare, divulge, expose, reveal, unveil.

guess, SYN.—assume, believe, conjecture, estimate, reason, reckon, speculate, suppose, surmise, think.

guide, SYN.—conduct, direct, escort, lead, steer; control, manage, regulate, supervise.

guile, SYN.—beguilement, cheat, chicanery, cunning, deceitfulness, deception, duplicity, fraud, sham, trick, wiliness.

ANT.—candor, honesty, openness, sincerity, truthfulness.

guise, SYN.—advent, apparition, appearance, arrival; air, aspect, demeanor, look, manner, mien; fashion, pretense, semblance.

H

habit, SYN.—custom, fashion, practice, routine, usage, use, wont.

habitual, SYN.—common, frequent, general, often, persistent, usual. ANT.—exceptional, rare, scanty, solitary, unique.

hackneyed, SYN.—banal, common, ordinary, stale, stereotyped, trite. ANT.—fresh, modern, momentous, novel, stimulating.

hail, SYN.—accost, approach, greet, speak to. ANT.—avoid, pass by.

hale, SYN.—healthy, hearty, robust, sound, strong, well; hygienic, salubrious, salutary, wholesome. ANT.—delicate, diseased, frail, infirm; injurious, noxious.

hallow, SYN.—aggrandize, consecrate, dignify, elevate, ennoble, erect, exalt, extol, glorify, raise. ANT.—debase, degrade, dishonor, humble, humiliate.

hallucination, SYN.—aberration, fantasy, illusion, phantasm, vision.

halt, SYN.—abstain, arrest, bar, cease, check, close, cork, desist, discontinue, end, hinder, impede, interrupt, obstruct, plug, seal, stop, terminate. ANT.—begin, proceed, promote, speed, start.

handicap, SYN.—chastisement, fine, forfeiture, punishment, retribution; disadvantage, penalty. ANT.—compensation, pardon, remuneration, reward.

handsome, SYN.—beauteous, beautiful, charming, comely, elegant, fair, fine, lovely, pretty. ANT.—foul, hideous, homely, repulsive, unsightly.

handy, SYN.—accessible, adapted, advantageous, appropriate, commodious, convenient, favorable, fitting, suitable, timely. ANT.—awkward, inconvenient, inopportune, troublesome.

happen, SYN.—bechance, befall, betide, chance, occur, take place, transpire.

happiness, SYN.—beatitude, blessedness, bliss, contentment, delight, felicity, gladness, pleasure, satisfaction, wellbeing. ANT.—despair, grief, misery, sadness, sorrow.

happy, SYN.—blessed, cheerful, contented, delighted, fortunate, gay, glad, joyful, joyous, lucky, merry, opportune, propitious. ANT.—blue, depressed, gloomy, morose.

harass, SYN.—aggravate, annoy, badger, bother, disturb, harry, irritate, molest, nag, pester, plague, provoke, tantalize, taunt, torment, vex, worry. ANT.—comfort, delight, gratify, please, soothe.

hard, SYN.—compact, firm, impenetrable, rigid, solid; arduous, burdensome, difficult, onerous, tough; intricate, perplexing, puzzling; cruel, harsh, rigorous, severe, stern, strict, unfeeling. ANT.—brittle, elastic, flabby, fluid, plastic, soft; easy, effortless, facile; simple; gentle, lenient, tender.

hardship, SYN.—examination, experiment, ordeal, proof, test; attempt, effort, endeavor, essay, affliction, misery, misfortune, suffering, tribulation, trouble. ANT.—alleviation, consolation.

harm, SYN.—damage, detriment, evil, hurt, ill, infliction, injury, mischief, misfortune, mishap, wrong. ANT.—benefit, boon, favor, kindness.

harmful, SYN.—detrimental, damaging, deleterious, hurtful, injurious, mischievous. ANT.—advantageous, beneficial, helpful, profitable, salutary.

harmless, SYN.—certain, dependable, protected, reliable, secure, snug,

trustworthy. ANT.—
dangerous, hazardous,
insecure, perilous, un-
safe.

harmony, SYN.—accord-
ance, coincidence, con-
cord, concurrence, un-
derstanding, unison; bar-
gain, compact, contract,
covenant, pact, stipula-
tion. ANT.—difference,
disagreement, discord,
dissension, variance.

harsh, SYN.—blunt, coarse,
grating, gruff, jarring,
rigorous, rough, rugged,
severe, strict, stringent.
ANT.—gentle, melodi-
ous, mild, smooth, soft.

harvest, SYN.—crop, fruit,
proceeds, produce, prod-
uct, reaping, result,
store, yield.

harvest, SYN.—acquire,
gain, garner, gather,
glean, reap. ANT.—lose,
plant, sow, squander.

hasten, SYN.—acclerate,
expedite, hurry, precipi-
tate, quicken, rush,
speed. ANT.—delay, de-
tain, hinder, retard,
tarry.

hasty, SYN.—active, brisk,
fast, lively, nimble, precipitate, quick, rapid,
speedy, swift; excitable,
impatient, irascible,
sharp, testy, touchy.
ANT.—slow, sluggish;
dull.

hate, SYN.—abhor, abomi-
nate, despise, detest, dislike, loathe. ANT.—
admire, approve, cher-
ish, like, love.

hatred, SYN.—abhorrence,
animosity, detestation,

dislike, enmity, hostility;
ill will, malevolence, rancor. ANT.—affection, at-
traction, friendship,
love.

haughty, SYN.—arrogant,
disdainful, overbearing,
proud, stately, supercilious, vain, vainglorious.
ANT.—ashamed, humble,
lowly, meek.

have, SYN.—control, hold,
occupy, own; affect, ob-
tain, possess, seize.
ANT.—abandon, lose, re-
nounce, surrender.

hazard, SYN.—danger,
jeopardy, peril, risk.
ANT.—defense, immuni-
ty, protection, safety.

hazardous, SYN.—critical,
dangerous, insecure,
menacing, perilous, pre-
carious, risky, threaten-
ing, unsafe. ANT.—firm,
protected, safe, secure.

hazy, SYN.—ambiguous,
dim, indefinite, indis-
tinct, obscure, uncertain,
unclear, undetermined,
unsettled, vague.
ANT.—clear, explicit, lu-
cid, precise, specific.

head, SYN.—chief, com-
mander, director, leader,
master, principal, acme,
crest, pinnacle, summit,
top; crisis, culmination.
ANT.—follower, subordi-
nate, underling, base,
bottom, foot.

healthy, SYN.—hale,
hearty, robust, sound,
strong, well; hygienic,
salubrious, salutary,
wholesome. ANT.—
delicate, diseased, frail,
infirm; injurious, nox-

ious.

heap, SYN.—accrue, accumulate, amass, collect, gather, hoard, increase, store. ANT.—diminish, disperse, dissipate, scatter, waste.

hear, SYN.—harken, heed, listen, regard.

heart, SYN.—center, core, middle, midpoint, midst, nucleus. ANT.—border, boundary, outskirts, periphery, rim.

heartache, SYN.—affliction, anguish, distress, grief, lamentation, misery, mourning, sadness, sorrow, trial, tribulation, woe. ANT.—comfort, consolation, happiness, joy, solace.

heartbroken, SYN.—comfortless, disconsolate, distressed, forlorn, miserable, pitiable, wretched; abject, contemptible, despicable, low, mean, paltry, worthless. ANT.—contented, fortunate, happy; noble, significant.

hearten, SYN.—animate, cheer, countenance, embolden, encourage, exhilarate, favor, impel, incite, inspire, urge; foster, promote, sanction, stimulate, support. ANT.—deject, deter, discourage, dispirit, dissuade.

hearty, SYN.—ardent, cordial, earnest, gracious, sincere, sociable, warm. ANT.—aloof, cool, reserved, taciturn.

heavenly, SYN.—celestial, divine, god-like, holy, superhuman, supernatural, transcendant. ANT.—blasphemous, diabolical, mundane, profane, wicked.

heavy, SYN.—massive, ponderous, weighty; burdensome, cumbersome, grievous, trying; gloomy, grave, serious, dull, sluggish. ANT.—animated, brisk, light.

heed, SYN.—alertness, attention, care, circumspection, consideration, mindfulness, notice, observance, watchfulness; application, contemplation, reflection, study. ANT.—disregard, indifference, negligence, omission, oversight.

heed, SYN.—consider, contemplate, deliberate, examine, meditate, ponder, reflect, study, weigh; esteem, regard, respect. ANT.—ignore, neglect, overlook.

heedless, SYN.—ignorant, blind, oblivious, sightless, unmindful, unseeing; headlong, rash. ANT.—aware, calculated, discerning, perceiving, sensible.

height, SYN.—acme, apex, culmination, peak, summit, zenith. ANT.—anticlimax, base, depth, floor.

heighten, SYN.—aggravate, increase, intensify, magnify; annoy, chafe, embitter, exasperate, inflame, irritate, nettle, provoke, vex. ANT.—

appease, mitigate, palliate, soften, soothe.

help, SYN.—abet, aid, assist, succor, support, uphold, facilitate, further, promote; mitigate, relieve, remedy. ANT.—impede, resist, thwart; hinder; afflict.

helpful, SYN.—advantageous, beneficial, good, profitable, salutary, serviceable, useful, wholesome. ANT.—deleterious, destructive, detrimental, harmful, injurious.

hence, SYN.—accordingly, consequently, so, thence, therefore.

heretic, SYN.—apostate, dissenter, nonconformist, schismatic, sectarian, sectary, unbeliever.

heroic, SYN.—adventurous, audacious, bold, brave, chivalrous, courageous, daring, dauntless, fearless, gallant, intrepid, magnanimous, valiant, valorous. ANT.—cowardly, cringing, fearful, timid, weak.

hesitant, SYN.—averse, disinclined, loath, reluctant, slow, unwilling. ANT.—disposed, eager, inclined, ready, willing.

hesitate, SYN.—delay, demur, doubt, falter, pause, scruple, stammer, stutter, vacillate, waver. ANT.—continue, decide, persevere, proceed, resolve.

hesitation, SYN.—ambiguity, distrust, doubt, incredulity, scruple, skepticism, suspense, suspicion, unbelief, uncertainty. ANT.—belief, certainty, conviction, determination, faith.

hidden, SYN.—concealed, dormant, inactive, latent, potential, quiescent, secret, undeveloped, unseen. ANT.—conspicuous, evident, explicit, manifest, visible.

hide, SYN.—cloak, conceal, cover, disguise, mask, screen, secrete, suppress, veil, withhold. ANT.—disclose, divulge, expose, reveal, show, uncover.

high, SYN.—lofty, tall, towering; elevated, eminent, exalted, proud. ANT.—small, stunted, tiny; base, low, mean.

hinder, SYN.—block, check, hamper, impede, obstruct, prevent, resist, restrain, retard, stop, thwart. ANT.—assist, expedite, facilitate, further, promote.

hint, SYN.—allusion, implication, insinuation, intimate, reminder. ANT.—affirmation, declaration, statement.

hire, SYN.—apply, avail, busy, devote, employ, occupy, use, utilize. ANT.—banish, discard, discharge, reject.

history, SYN.—account, chronicle, description, detail, narration, narrative, recital, relation; computation, reckoning, record. ANT.—caricature, confusion, distortion, misrepresentation.

hit, SYN.—beat, hurt, knock, pound, pummel, smite, strike.

hoard, SYN.—accrue, accumulate, amass, collect, gather, heap, increase, store. ANT.—diminish, disperse, dissipate, scatter, waste.

hoax, SYN.—antic, artifice, cheat, deception, device, fraud, guile, imposture, ploy, ruse, stratagem, stunt, subterfuge, wile. ANT.—candor, exposure, honesty, openness, sincerity.

hobbling, SYN.—crippled, defective, deformed, disabled, feeble, halt, lame, limping, maimed, unconvincing, unsatisfactory, weak. ANT.—agile, athletic, robust, sound, vigorous.

hold, SYN.—adhere, clasp, clutch, grasp, grip; have, keep, maintain, occupy, possess, retain, support; check, confine, curb, detain, restrain; accommodate, carry, contain, receive, stow. ANT.—abandon, relinquish, surrender, vacate.

hole, SYN.—abyss, aperture, cavity, chasm, gap, gulf; opening, pore, void.

hollow, SYN.—depressed, empty, unfilled, vacant, void; hypocritical, insincere, vain. ANT.—full, solid, sound; genuine, sincere.

holy, SYN.—blessed, consecrated, devout, divine, hallowed, pious, religious, sacred, saintly, spiritual. ANT.—evil, profane, sacrilegious, secular, worldly.

home, SYN.—abode, domicile, dwelling, habitat, hearth, quarters, residence, seat.

homely, SYN.—deformed, hideous, plain, repellent, repulsive, uncomely; disagreeable, illnatured, spiteful, surly, ugly, vicious. ANT.—attractive, beautiful, fair, handsome, pretty.

honest, SYN.—candid, conscientious, fair, honorable, ingenuous, just, scrupulous, sincere, trustworthy, truthful, upright. ANT.—deceitful, dishonest, fraudulent; lying, tricky.

honesty, SYN.—candor, fairness, frankness, integrity, justice, openness, rectitude, responsibility, sincerity, trustworthiness, uprightness. ANT.—cheating, deceit, dishonesty, fraud, trickery.

honor, SYN.—admiration, adoration, deference, dignity, esteem, fame, glory, homage, praise, renown, respect, reverence, worship. ANT.—contempt, derision, disgrace, dishonor, reproach.

honor, SYN.—admire, consider, heed, respect, revere, reverence, value, venerate. ANT.—abuse, despise, disdain, neglect, scorn.

honorable, SYN.—admirable, eminent, fair, honest, noble, respectable, true, trusty, upright, virtuous; creditable, esteemed, proper, reputable. ANT.—disgraceful, ignominious, infamous, shameful.

hope, SYN.—anticipation, expectancy, expectation; confidence, faith, optimism, trust. ANT.—despair, despondency, pessimism.

hopelessness, SYN.—depression, desperation, despondency, discouragement, gloom, pessimism. ANT.—confidence, elation, hope, optimism.

horde, SYN.—bevy, crowd, crush, host, masses, mob, multitude, populace, press, rabble, swarm, throng.

horrible, SYN.—appalling, awful, dire, dreadful, fearful, frightful, ghastly, hideous, horrid, repulsive, terrible. ANT.—beautiful, enchanting, enjoyable, fascinating, lovely.

horrid, SYN.—appalling, awful, dire, dreadful, fearful, frightful, ghastly, hideous, horrible, repulsive, terrible. ANT.—beautiful, enchanting, enjoyable, fascinating, lovely.

horror, SYN.—alarm, apprehension, awe, dread, fear, foreboding, reverence, terror. ANT.—

assurance, boldness, confidence, courage.

hostile, SYN.—adverse, antagonistic, inimical, opposed, unfriendly, warlike. ANT.—amicable, cordial, favorable.

hostility, SYN.—bitterness, enmity, grudge, hatred, malevolence, rancor, spite. ANT.—friendliness, good will, love.

hot, SYN.—burning, scalding, scorching, torrid, warm; ardent, fervent, fiery, hot-blooded, impetuous, intense, passionate; peppery, pungent. ANT.—cold, cool, freezing, frigid; apathetic, impassive, indifferent, passionless, phlegmatic; bland.

however, SYN.—but, nevertheless, notwithstanding, still, yet.

hue, SYN.—complexion, dye, paint, pigment, shade, stain, tincture, tinge, tint. ANT.—achromatism, paleness, transparency.

hug, SYN.—caress, coddle, cuddle, embrace, fondle, kiss, pet. ANT.—annoy, buffet, spurn, tease, vex.

huge, SYN.—ample, big, capacious, colossal, extensive, great, immense, large, vast, wide. ANT.—little, mean, short, small, tiny.

humane, SYN.—clement, compassionate, forbearing, forgiving, kind, lenient, merciful, tender, tolerant. ANT.—brutal, cruel, pitiless, remorseless, unfeeling.

humanity, SYN.—altruism, beneficence, benevolence, charity, generosity, humanity, kindness, liberality, magnanimity, philanthropy, tenderness. ANT.—cruelty, inhumanity, malevolence, selfishness, unkindness.

humble, SYN.—compliant, lowly, meek, modest, plain, simple, submissive, unassuming, unostentatious, unpretentious. ANT.—arrogant, boastful, haughty, proud, vain.

humble, SYN.—abase, abash, break, crush, degrade, humiliate, mortify, shame, subdue. ANT.—elevate, exalt, honor, praise.

humiliate, SYN.—abase, adulterate, alloy, corrupt, debase, defile, degrade, deprave, depress, impair, lower, pervert, vitiate. ANT.—enhance, improve, raise, restore, vitalize.

humilation, SYN.—abashment, chagrin, mortification; disgrace, dishonor, disrepute, ignominy, odium, opprobrium, scandal, shame. ANT.—dignity, glory, honor, praise, renown.

humor, SYN.—facetiousness, irony, jocularity, joke, sarcasm, satire, waggery, wit; disposition, mood, temper, temperament. ANT.—gravity, seriousness, sorrow.

humorous, SYN.—amusing, comical, droll, farcical, funny, laughable, ludicrous, ridiculous, witty; curious, odd, queer. ANT.—melancholy, sad, serious, sober, solemn.

hunger, SYN.—relish, stomach, thirst, zest; craving, desire, inclination, liking, longing, passion. ANT.—disgust, distaste, renunciation, repugnance, satiety.

hunt, SYN.—examination, exploration, inquiry, investigation, pursuit, quest, search. ANT.—abandonment, cession, resignation.

hurl, SYN.—cast, fling, pitch, propel, throw, thrust, toss. ANT.—draw, haul, hold, pull, retain.

hurry, SYN.—accelerate, expedite, hasten, precipitate, quicken, rush, speed. ANT.—delay, detain, hinder, retard, tarry.

hurt, SYN.—damage, detriment, harm, mischief; grievance, injustice, prejudice, wrong. ANT.—benefit, improvement, repair.

hurt, SYN.—damage, disfigure, harm, impair, injure, mar, spoil, wound; abuse, affront, dishonor, insult, wrong. ANT.—ameliorate, benefit, help, preserve; compliment, praise.

hygienic, SYN.—hale, healthy, hearty, robust, sound, strong, well; salubrious, salutary, wholesome. ANT.—delicate, diseased, frail, infirm; injurious, noxious.

hypothesis, SYN.—conjecture, law, supposition, theory. ANT.—certainty, fact, proof.

I

idea, SYN.—abstraction, concept, conception, fancy, image, impression, notion, opinion, sentiment, thought. ANT.—entity, matter, object, substance, thing.

ideal, SYN.—exemplary, fancied, faultless, imaginary, perfect, supreme, unreal, utopian, visionary. ANT.—actual, faulty, imperfect, material, real.

identical, SYN.—coincident, equal, equivalent, indistinguishable, like, same. ANT.—contrary, disparate, dissimilar, distinct, opposed.

idiom, SYN.—dialect, diction, jargon, language, lingo, phraseology, slang, speech, tongue, vernacular. ANT.—babble, drivel, gibberish, nonsense.

idle, SYN.—dormant, inactive, indolent, inert, lazy, slothful, unemployed, unoccupied. ANT.—active, employed, industrious, occupied, working.

ignoble, SYN.—abject, base, contemptible, despicable, dishonorable, groveling, ignominious,

low, lowly, mean, menial, servile, sordid, vile, vulgar. ANT.—esteemed, exalted, honored, lofty, noble, righteous.

ignorant, SYN.—illiterate, uncultured, uneducated, uninformed, unlearned, unlettered, untaught. ANT.—cultured, educated, erudite, informed, literate.

ignore, SYN.—disregard, neglect, omit, overlook, skip, slight. ANT.—include, notice, regard.

ill-use, SYN.—abuse, asperse, defame, disparage, malign, revile, scandalize, traduce, vilify; misapply, misemploy, misuse. ANT.—cherish, honor, praise, protect, respect.

illegal, SYN.—criminal, illegitimate, illicit, outlawed, prohibited, unlawful. ANT.—honest, lawful, legal, permitted.

illiberal, SYN.—bigoted, dogmatic, fanatical, intolerant, narrow-minded, prejudiced. ANT.—liberal, progressive, radical, tolerant.

illuminate, SYN.—brighten, clarify, elucidate, enlighten, illumine, illustrate, irradiate. ANT.—complicate, confuse, darken, obfuscate, obscure.

illusion, SYN.—delusion, dream, fantasy, hallucination, mirage, phantom, vision. ANT.—actuality, reality, substance.

illusive, SYN.—deceitful,

deceptive, delusive, delusory, fallacious, false, misleading, specious. ANT.—authentic, genuine, honest, real, truthful.

illustration, SYN.—drawing, engraving, etching, image, likeness, painting, panorama, photograph, picture, portrait, portrayal, print, representation, scene, sketch, view.

illustrious, SYN.—celebrated, eminent, famed, great, prominent, renowned; critical, important, momentous, serious, vital, weighty; august, dignified, elevated, grand, majestic, noble; excellent, fine, magnificent. ANT.—diminutive, little, minute, small; common, obscure, ordinary, unknown; menial, paltry.

imagination, SYN.—conception, creation, fancy, fantasy, idea, invention, notion.

imaginative, SYN.—clever, creative, fanciful, inventive, mystical, poetical, visionary. ANT.—dull, literal, prosaic, unromantic.

imagine, SYN.—conceive, dream, fancy, picture, pretend; assume, believe, conjecture, guess, opine, suppose, surmise, think.

imbecile, SYN.—blockhead, dolt, dunce, fool, idiot, nincompoop, numbskull, oaf, simpleton. ANT.—

genius, philosopher, sage, scholar.

imitate, SYN.—ape, copy, counterfeit, duplicate, impersonate, mimic, mock, simulate. ANT.—alter, distort, diverge.

imitation, SYN.—copy, duplicate, exemplar, facsimile, replica, reproduction, transcript. ANT.—original, prototype.

immature, SYN.—boyish, callow, childish, childlike, girlish, juvenile, puerile, young, youthful. ANT.—aged, elderly, mature, old, senile.

immeasurable, SYN.—boundless, endless, eternal, illimitable, immense, infinite, interminable, unbounded, unlimited, vast. ANT.—bounded, circumscribed, confined, finite, limited.

immediately, SYN.—directly, forthwith, instantaneously, instantly, now, presently, promptly, straightaway. ANT.—distantly, hereafter, later, shortly, sometime.

immense, SYN.—colossal, elephantine, enormous, gargantuan, gigantic, huge, large, prodigious, vast. ANT.—diminutive, little, minute, small, tiny.

immerse, SYN.—dip, douse, dunk, plunge, sink, submerge; absorb, engage, engross. ANT.—elevate, recover, uplift.

immigration, SYN.—colonization, settlement. ANT.—emigration, exodus.

imminent, SYN.—approaching, impending, menacing, nigh, threatening. ANT.—afar, distant, improbable, remote, retreating.

immoderation, SYN.—excess, extravagance, intemperance, profusion, superabundance, superfluity, surplus. ANT.—dearth, deficiency, lack, paucity, want.

immoral, SYN.—antisocial, bad, corrupt, dissolute, indecent, licentious, profligate, sinful, unprincipled, vicious, wicked. ANT.—chaste, highminded, noble, pure, virtuous.

immortal, SYN.—ceaseless, deathless, endless, eternal, everlasting, infinite, perpetual, timeless, undying. ANT.—ephemeral, finite, mortal, temporal, transient.

immune, SYN.—exempt, free, freed; clear, loose, open, unfastened, unobstructed. ANT.—subject.

immutable, SYN.—abiding, ceaseless, constant, continual, enduring, faithful, fixed, invariant, permanent, perpetual, persistent, unalterable, unchanging, unwavering. ANT.—fickle, mutable, vacillating, wavering.

impair, SYN.—damage, deface, harm, hurt, injure, mar, spoil. ANT.—ameliorate, benefit, enhance, mend, repair.

impart, SYN.—communicate, convey, disclose, divulge, inform, notify, relate, reveal, tell, transmit. ANT.—conceal, hide, withhold.

impartial, SYN.—equitable, fair, honest, just, reasonable, unbiased. ANT.—dishonorable, fraudulent, partial.

impartiality, SYN.—disinterestedness, indifference, insensibility, neutrality, unconcern. ANT.—affection, ardor, fervor, passion.

impede, SYN.—bar, block, check, clog, delay, encumber, frustrate, hamper, hinder, interrupt, obstruct, restrain, retard, stop, thwart. ANT.—advance, assist, further, help, promote.

impel, SYN.—coerce, compel, constrain, drive, force, oblige. ANT.—convince, induce, persuade, prevent.

impending, SYN.—approaching, imminent, menacing, nigh, overhanging, threatening. ANT.—afar, distant, improbable, remote, retreating.

impenetrable, SYN.—compact, firm, hard, impenetrable, rigid, solid; arduous, burdensome, difficult, onerous, tough; intricate, perplexing, puzzling; cruel, harsh, rigorous, severe, stern, strict, unfeeling. ANT.—brittle, elastic, flabby, fluid, plastic, soft; easy, effortless, facile; simple; gentle, lenient, tender.

imperative, SYN.—cogent, compelling, critical, exigent, impelling, important, importunate, insistent, instant, necessary, pressing, serious, urgent. ANT.—insignificant, petty, trifling, trivial, unimportant.

imperceptible, SYN.— indistinguishable, invisible, undiscernible, unseen. ANT.—evident, perceptible, seen, visible.

imperfection, SYN.— blemish, defect, error, failure, fault, flaw, mistake, omission, shortcoming, vice. ANT.— completeness, correctness, perfection.

imperil, SYN.—endanger, hazard, jeopardize, peril, risk. ANT.—guard, insure.

impersonate, SYN.—ape, copy, duplicate, imitate, mimic, mock, simulate. ANT.—alter, distort, diverge, invent.

impertinence, SYN.— audacity, boldness, effrontery, impudence, insolence, presumption, rudeness, sauciness. ANT.—diffidence, politeness, subserviency, truckling.

impertinent, SYN.— abusive, arrogant, brazen, contemptuous, impudent, insolent, insulting, offensive, rude. ANT. — considerate, courteous, polite, respectful.

impetuous, SYN.—careless, hasty, heedless, impulsive, passionate, quick, rash. ANT.—calculating, cautious, reasoning.

implicate, SYN.—accuse, blame, censure, condemn, rebuke, reproach, upbraid. ANT.—absolve, acquit, exonerate.

implore, SYN.—adjure, ask, beg, beseech, crave, entreat, importune, petition, pray, request, solicit, supplicate. ANT.— bestow, cede, favor, give, grant.

imply, SYN.—connote, insinuate, involve, mean, signify, suggest. ANT.— assert, express, state.

impolite, SYN.—blunt, boorish, discourteous, impudent, insolent, rough, rude, saucy, surly, uncivil, vulgar; coarse, savage, unpolished, untaught. ANT.— civil, genteel, polished; courtly, dignified, noble, stately.

import, SYN.—emphasis, importance, influence, significance, stress, value, weight. ANT.— insignificance, triviality.

important, SYN.—consequential, critical, decisive, grave, influential, material, momentous, pressing, prominent, relevant, significant, weighty. ANT.—insignificant, irrelevant, mean, petty, trivial.

imposing, SYN.—august, dignified, grand, grandiose, high, lofty, magnificent, majestic, noble, pompous, stately, sublime. ANT.—common, humble, lowly, ordinary, undignified.

impression, SYN.—sensibility; feeling, opinion. ANT.—insensibility; fact.

impressive, SYN.—affecting, arresting, august, commanding, exciting. forcible, grandiose, imposing, majestic, moving, overpowering, remarkable, splendid, stirring, striking, thrilling, touching. ANT.—commonplace, ordinary, regular, unimpressive.

improve, SYN.—ameliorate, amend, better, help, rectify, reform. ANT.—corrupt, damage, debase, impair, vitiate.

improvement, SYN.—advance, advancement, betterment, development, growth, progress, progression. ANT.—decline, delay, regression, relapse, retrogression.

imprudent, SYN.—careless, heedless, inattentive, inconsiderate, indiscreet, reckless, thoughtless, unconcerned; desultory, inaccurate, lax, neglectful, negligent, remiss. ANT.—accurate, careful, meticulous.

impudence. SYN.—assurance, audacity, boldness, effrontery, impertinence, insolence, presumption, rudeness, sauciness. ANT.—diffidence, politeness, sub-

serviency, truckling.

impudent, SYN.—bold, brazen, forward, insolent, pushy, rude; abrupt, conspicuous, prominent, striking. ANT.—cowardly, flinching, timid; bashful, retiring.

impulsive, SYN.—careless, hasty, heedless, impetuous, passionate, quick, rash. ANT.—calculating, cautious, reasoning.

impure, SYN.—contaminated, corrupt, corrupted, crooked, debased, depraved, dishonest, profligate, putrid, spoiled, tainted, unsound, venal, vitiated.

imputation, SYN.—arraignment, diary, incrimination, indictment. ANT.—exculpation, exoneration, pardon.

inability, SYN.—disability, handicap, impotence, incapacity, incompetence, weakness. ANT.—ability, capability, power, strength.

inaccurate, SYN.—amiss, askew, awry, erroneous, fallacious, false, faulty, incorrect, mistaken, unprecise, untrue. ANT.—correct, right, true.

inactive, SYN.—dormant, idle, indolent, inert, lazy, slothful, unemployed, unoccupied. ANT.—active, employed, industrious, occupied, working.

inadequate, SYN.—defective, deficient, incomplete, insufficient, lack-

ing, scanty, short.
ANT.—adequate, ample,
enough, satisfactory,
sufficient.

inane, SYN.—banal, commonplace, hackneyed,
insipid, trite, vapid.
ANT.—fresh, novel, orig-
inal, stimulating, strik-
ing.

inanimate, SYN.—dead, deceased, defunct, depart-
ed, dull, gone, insensible,
lifeless, spiritless, un-
conscious. ANT.—alive,
animate, living, stirring.

inattentive, SYN.—absent-
minded, abstracted, dis-
tracted, preoccupied.
ANT.—attending, atten-
tive, watchful.

inaugurate, SYN.—arise,
begin, commence, enter,
initiate, institute, open,
originate, start. ANT.—
close, complete, end, finish, terminate.

inception, SYN.—beginning, commencement,
opening, origin, outset,
source, start. ANT.—
close, completion, con-
summation, end, termi-
nation.

incessant, SYN.—ceaseless,
constant, continual, con-
tinuous, endless, ever-
lasting, perennial, per-
petual, unceasing, unin-
terrupted, unremitting.
ANT.—interrupted, occa-
sional, periodic, rare.

incident, SYN.—
circumstance, condition,
event, fact, happening,
occurrence, position, situation.

incidental, SYN.—accidental, casual, chance, con-
tingent, fortuitous, undesigned, unintended.
ANT.—calculated, de-
creed, intended, planned,
willed.

incinerate, SYN.—blaze,
burn, char, consume,
scald, scorch, sear,
singe. ANT.—extinguish,
put out, quench.

incisive, SYN.—brief, compact, concise, con-
densed, neat, pithy, suc-
cinct, summary, terse.
ANT.—lengthy, prolix,
verbose, wordy.

incite, SYN.—arouse,
cause, encourage, fo-
ment, goad, induce,
instigate, provoke, stim-
ulate, urge. ANT.—bore,
pacify, quiet, soothe.

inclination, SYN.—bending,
incline, leaning, slope;
affection, attachment,
bent, bias, desire, disposition, penchant, predi-
lection, preference.
ANT.—apathy, aversion,
distaste, nonchalance,
repugnance.

include, SYN.—accommodate, comprise, contain,
embody, embrace, hold.
ANT.—discharge, omit,
exclude.

incompetency, SYN.—
disability, handicap, im-
potence, inability, inca-
pacity, weakness.
ANT.—ability, capability,
power, strength.

incongruous, SYN.—
contradictory, contrary,
discrepant, illogical, incompatible, inconsistent,
irreconcilable, paradoxi-

cal. ANT.—compatible, congruous, consistent, correspondent.

inconsistency, SYN.—conflict, contention, controversy, discord, interference, opposition, variance. ANT.—amity, concord, consonance, harmony.

inconsistent, SYN.—changeable, fickle, fitful, shifting, unstable, vacillating, variable, wavering. ANT.—constant, stable, steady, unchanging, uniform.

increase, SYN.—accrue, amplify, augment, enhance, enlarge, expand, extend, grow, heighten, intensify, magnify, multiply, raise, wax. ANT.—atrophy, contract, decrease, diminish, reduce.

incriminate, SYN.—accuse, arraign, censure, charge, indict. ANT.—absolve, acquit, exonerate, release, vindicate.

incrimination, SYN.—accusation, arraignment, charge, imputation, indictment. ANT.—exculpation, exoneration, pardon.

indebted, SYN.—appreciative, beholden, grateful, obliged, thankful. ANT.—thankless, unappreciative.

indecent, SYN.—coarse, dirty, disgusting, filthy, gross, impure, lewd, obscene, offensive, pornographic, smutty. ANT.—decent, modest, pure, refined.

independence, SYN.—exemption, freedom, immunity, liberation, liberty, license, privilege, unrestraint. ANT.—bondage, compulsion, constraint, necessity, servitude.

independent, SYN.—autonomous, free, self-reliant, uncontrolled, unrestrained, unrestricted, voluntary. ANT.—contingent, dependent, enslaved, restricted.

indestructible, SYN.—abiding, changeless, constant, durable, enduring, fixed, lasting, permanent, stable, unchangeable. ANT.—ephemeral, temporary, transient, transitory, unstable.

indicate, SYN.—denote, designate, disclose, imply, intimate, manifest, reveal, show, signify, specify. ANT.—conceal, distract, divert, falsify, mislead.

indication, SYN.—emblem, gesture, mark, note, omen, portent, proof, sign, signal, symbol, symptom, token.

indict, SYN.—accuse, arraign, censure, charge, incriminate. ANT.—absolve, acquit, exonerate, release, vindicate.

indifference, SYN.—apathy, disinterestedness, impartiality, insensibility, neutrality, unconcern. ANT.—affection, ardor, fervor, passion.

indigence, SYN.—destitution, necessity, need,

penury, poverty, priva-
tion, want. ANT.—
abundance, affluence,
plenty, riches, wealth.

indigenous, SYN.—
aboriginal, domestic, en-
demic, inborn, inherent,
innate, native, natural.

indigent, SYN.—claiming,
covetous, craving, de-
manding, desiring, lack-
ing, needy, requiring,
wanting, wishing.

indignation, SYN.—anger,
animosity, choler, exas-
peration, fury, ire, irritation, passion, petulance,
rage, resentment, tem-
per, wrath. ANT.—
conciliation, forbear-
ance, patience, peace,
self-control.

indignity, SYN.—abuse, affront, insolence, insult,
offense. ANT.—apology,
homage, salutation.

indirect, SYN.—circuitous,
crooked, devious, dis-
torted, erratic, round-
about, swerving, tortu-
ous, wandering, winding;
crooked, cunning, tricky.
ANT.—direct, straight;
honest, straightforward.

indiscretion, SYN.—
absurdity, extravagance,
folly, imprudence.
ANT.—sense, wisdom,
judgment, prudence, rea-
sonableness.

indispensable, SYN.—basic,
essential, fundamental,
important, intrinsic, necessary, requisite, vital.
ANT.—expendable, ex-
trinsic, optional, peripheral.

indistinct, SYN.—abstruse,

ambiguous, cloudy,
cryptic, dark, dim,
dusky, enigmatic, mys-
terious, obscure, unintelligible, vague. ANT.—
bright, clear, distinct, lucid.

indistinguishable, SYN.—
coincident, equal, equiv-
alent, identical, like,
same. ANT.—contrary,
disparate, dissimilar, distinct, opposed.

individual, SYN.—
distinctive, marked, par-
ticular, separate, singu-
lar, special, specific,
unique. ANT.—common,
general, ordinary, uni-
versal.

individuality, SYN.—
character, mark, sign,
symbol.

indolent, SYN.—idle, inactive, inert, lazy, slothful,
sluggish, supine, torpid.
ANT.—active, alert, as-
siduous, diligent.

indomitable, SYN.—
impregnable, insur-
mountable, invincible,
invulnerable unassaila-
ble, unconquerable.
ANT.—powerless, puny,
vulnerable, weak.

induce, SYN.—cause, create, effect, evoke, incite,
make, occasion, origi-
nate, prompt.

inducement, SYN.—cause,
impulse, incentive, in-
citement, motive, princi-
ple, purpose, reason,
spur, stimulus. ANT.—
action, attempt, deed, effort, result.

indurate, SYN.—callous,
hard, impenitent, insen-

sible, insensitive, obdurate, tough, unfeeling. ANT. — compassionate, sensitive, soft, tender.

industrious, SYN.—active, assiduous, busy, careful, diligent, hard-working, patient, perseverant. ANT.—apathetic, careless, indifferent, lethargic, unconcerned.

inebriated, SYN.—drunk, drunken, high, intoxicated, tight, tipsy. ANT.—clear-headed, sober, temperate.

ineffective, SYN.—bending, fragile, frail, pliant, tender, yielding; debilitated, decrepit, delicate, feeble, impotent, infirm, illogical, inadequate, lame, poor, vague; irresolute, pliable, vacillating, wavering; assailable, defenseless, exposed, vulnerable, weak. ANT.—potent, powerful, robust, strong, sturdy.

inequity, SYN.—grievance, injury, injustice, unfairness, wrong. ANT.—equity, justice, lawfulness, righteousness.

inert, SYN.—dormant, idle, inactive, indolent, lazy, slothful. ANT.—active, industrious, occupied, working.

inertia, SYN.—idleness, inactivity, indolence, slothfulness, sluggishness, supineness, torpidity. ANT.—activity, alertness, assiduousness, diligence.

inevitable, SYN.—assured, certain, definite, fixed, indubitable, positive, secure, sure, undeniable, unquestionable. ANT.—doubtful, probable, questionable, uncertain.

inexpensive, SYN.—cheap, low-priced, poor; beggarly, common, inferior, mean, shabby. ANT.—costly, dear, expensive.

inexplicable, SYN.—cabalistic, cryptic, dark, dim, enigmatical, hidden, incomprehensible, inscrutable, mysterious, mystical, obscure, occult, recondite, secret. ANT.—clear, explained, obvious, plain, simple.

infect, SYN.—befoul, contaminate, corrupt, defile, poison, pollute, sully, taint. ANT.—disinfect, purify.

infection, SYN.—contagion, germ, pest, virus; ailment, contamination, disease, poison, pollution, taint.

infectious, SYN.—catching, communicable, contagious, pestilential, virulent. ANT.—healthful, hygienic, noncommunicable.

inference, SYN.—conclusion, consequence, corollary, deduction, judgment, result. ANT.—assumption, foreknowledge, preconception, presupposition.

inferior, SYN.—lower, minor, poorer, secondary, subordinate. ANT.—better, greater, higher, superior.

infinite, SYN.—boundless,

endless, eternal, illimitable, immeasurable, immense, interminable, unbounded, unlimited, vast. ANT.—bounded, circumscribed, confined, finite, limited.

infirm, SYN.—decrepit, delicate, enervated, exhausted, faint, feeble, forceless, impaired, languid, powerless, puny, weak. ANT.—forceful, lusty, stout, strong, vigorous.

infirmity, SYN.—ailment, complaint, disease, disorder, illness, malady, sickness. ANT.—health, healthiness, soundness, vigor.

inflexible, SYN.—contumacious, determined, dogged, firm, headstrong, immovable, intractable, obdurate, obstinate, pertinacious, stubborn, uncompromising, unyielding. ANT.—amenable, compliant, docile, submissive, yielding.

influenced, SYN.—actuate, affect, bias, control, impel, incite, stir, sway.

influential, SYN.—consequential, critical, decisive, grave, important, material, momentous, pressing, prominent, relevant, significant, weighty. ANT.—insignificant, irrelevant, mean, petty, trivial.

inform, SYN.—acquaint, advise, apprise, enlighten, impart, instruct, notify, teach, tell, warn. ANT.—conceal, delude, distract, mislead.

informal, SYN.—easy, familiar, natural, simple, unofficial. ANT.—conceal, delude, distract, mislead.

informality, SYN.—acquaintance, familiarity, fellowship, friendship, sociability; frankness, intimacy, liberty, unreserve. ANT.—constraint, distance, haughtiness, presumption, reserve.

infrequent. SYN.—occasional, rare, strange, unusual. ANT.—customary, frequent, ordinary, usual; abundant, commonplace, numerous.

ingenious, SYN.—adroit, apt, clever, dexterous, quick, quick-witted, skillful, talented, witty; bright, sharp, smart. ANT.—awkward, bungling, clumsy, slow, unskilled; dull, foolish, stupid.

ingenuity, SYN.—aptitude, cleverness, cunning, faculty, ingeniousness, inventiveness, resourcefulness, skill. ANT.—clumsiness, dullness, ineptitude, stupidity.

ingenuous, SYN.—candid, frank, free, honest, open, plain, sincere, straightforward, truthful. ANT.—contrived, scheming, sly, wily.

inhabit, SYN.—absorb, dwell, fill, occupy, possess. ANT.—abandon, release, relinquish.

inherent, SYN.—congenital, inborn, inbred, innate, intrinsic, native, natural, real. ANT.—acquired, external, extraneous, extrinsic.

inhibit, SYN.—bridle, check, constrain, curb, hinder, hold back, limit, repress, restrain, stop, suppress. ANT.—aid, encourage, incite, loosen.

inhuman, SYN.—cruel; barbarous, brutal, ferocious, malignant, merciless, ruthless, savage. ANT.—benevolent, compassionate, forbearing, gentle, humane, kind, merciful.

inimical, SYN.—adverse, antagonistic, hostile, opposed, unfriendly, warlike. ANT.—amicable, cordial, favorable.

iniquitous, SYN.—bad, baleful, base, deleterious, evil, immoral, noxious, pernicious, sinful, unsound, unwholesome, villainous, wicked. ANT.—excellent, good, honorable, moral, reputable.

iniquity, SYN.—grievance, injury, injustice, unfairness, wrong. ANT.—equity, justice, lawfulness, righteousness.

initial, SYN.—beginning, earliest, first, original, primary, prime, primeval, primitive, pristine; chief, foremost. ANT.—hindmost, last, latest; least, subordinate.

initiate, SYN.—arise, begin, commence, enter, inaugurate, institute, open, originate, start. ANT.—close, complete, end, finish, terminate.

injure, SYN.—damage, disfigure, harm, hurt, impair, mar, spoil, wound; abuse, affront, dishonor, insult, wrong. ANT.—ameliorate, benefit, help, preserve; compliment, praise.

injurious, SYN.—damaging, deleterious, detrimental, harmful, hurtful, mischievous. ANT.—advantageous, beneficial, helpful, profitable, salutary.

injury, SYN.—damage, detriment, harm, mischief; grievance, injustice, prejudice, wrong. ANT.—benefit, improvement, repair.

injustice, SYN.—grievance, iniquity, injury, unfairness, wrong. ANT.—equity, justice, lawfulness, righteousness.

innate, SYN.—congenital, inborn, inbred, inherent, intrinsic, native, natural, real. ANT.—acquired, external, extraneous, extrinsic.

innocent, SYN.—blameless, faultless, innocuous, lawful, naive, pure, sinless, virtuous. ANT.—corrupt, culpable, guilty, sinful, unrighteous.

innocuous, SYN.—blameless, faultless, innocent, lawful, naive, pure, sinless, virtuous. ANT —corrupt, culpable, guilty, sinful, unrighteous.

inquire, SYN.—ask, beg, claim, demand, entreat, invite, request, solicit; inquire, interrogate, query, question. ANT.—command, dictate, insist, order, reply.

inquiring, SYN.—curious, inquisitive, interrogative, meddling, nosy, peeping, peering, prying, searching, snoopy. ANT.—incurious, indifferent, unconcerned, uninterested.

inquiry, SYN.—examination, exploration, interrogation, investigation, query, quest, question, research, scrutiny. ANT.—disregard, inactivity, inattention, negligence.

inquisitive, SYN.—curious, inquiring, interrogative, meddling, nosy, peeping, peering, prying, searching, snoopy. ANT.—incurious, indifferent, unconcerned, uninterested.

insane, SYN.—crazy, delirious, demented, deranged, foolish, idiotic, imbecilic, mad, maniacal. ANT.—rational, reasonable, sane, sensible, sound.

insanity, SYN.—aberration, craziness, delirium, dementia, derangement, frenzy, lunacy, madness, mania.

insensitive, SYN.—callous, hard, impenitent, indurate, insensible, obdurate, tough, unfeeling. ANT. — compassionate, sensitive, soft, tender.

insight, SYN.—acumen, discernment, intuition, penetration, perspicuity. ANT.—obtuseness.

insignificant, SYN.—frivolous, paltry, petty, small, trifling, trivial, unimportant. ANT.—important, momentous, serious, weighty.

insinuate, SYN.—connote, imply, involve, mean, signify, suggest. ANT.—assert, express, state.

insipid, SYN.—dull, flat, stale, tasteless, vapid. ANT.—exciting, racy, savory, tasty.

insolence, SYN.—assurance, audacity, boldness, effrontery, impertinence, impudence, presumption, rudeness, sauciness. ANT.—diffidence, politeness, subserviency, truckling.

insolent, SYN.—abusive, arrogant, brazen, contemptuous, impertinent, impudent, insulting, offensive, rude. ANT.—considerate, courteous, polite, respectful.

inspect, SYN.—behold, discern, eye, gaze, glance, look, scan, see, stare, survey, view, watch, witness; examine, observe, regard. ANT.—avert, hide, miss, overlook.

inspection, SYN.—criticism, critique, examination, reconsideration, retrospect, retrospection, revision, review, survey.

inspiration, SYN.—ability, aptitude, creativity, faculty, **genius**, gift, intellect, originality, sagacity, talent; adept, intellectual, master, proficient. ANT.—ineptitude, obtuseness, shallowness, stupidity; dolt, dullard, moron.

instantaneous, SYN.—abrupt, hasty, immediate, rapid, sudden, unexpected. ANT.—anticipated, gradual, slowly.

instantly, SYN.—directly, forthwith, immediately, instantaneously, now, presently, promptly, straightaway. ANT.—distantly, hereafter, later, shortly, sometime.

instinctive, SYN.—automatic, extemporaneous, impulsive, offhand, spontaneous, voluntary, willing. ANT.—compulsory, forced, planned, prepared, rehearsed.

institute, SYN.—establish, form, found, organize, raise; fix, ordain, sanction. ANT.—abolish, demolish, overthrow, unsettle, upset.

instruct, SYN.—educate, inculcate, inform, instill, school, teach, train, tutor. ANT.—misguide, misinform.

instruction, SYN.—admonition, advice, caution, counsel, exhortation, recommendation, suggestion, warning; information, intelligence, notification.

instrument, SYN.—agent, apparatus, channel, device, means, medium, tool, utensil vehicle. ANT.—hindrance, impediment, obstruction, preventive.

insubordinate, SYN.—defiant, disobedient, forward, rebellious, refractory, undutiful, unruly. ANT.—compliant, dutiful, obedient, submissive.

insufficient, SYN.—deficient, inadequate, lacking, limited, short. ANT.—abundant, ample, big, extended, protracted.

insulation, SYN.—alienation, isolation, loneliness, quarantine, retirement, seclusion, segregation, solitude, withdrawal. ANT.—association, communion, connection, fellowship, union.

insult, SYN.—abuse, affront, indignity, insolence, offense. ANT.—apology, homage, salutation.

insult, SYN.—abuse, affront, dishonor, injure, wrong. ANT.—compliment, praise.

integrity, SYN.—candor, fairness, frankness, honesty, justice, openness, rectitude, responsibility, sincerity, trustworthiness, uprightness. ANT.—cheating, deceit, dishonesty, fraud, trickery.

intelligence, SYN.—ability, intellect, mind, reason, sense, understanding. ANT.—emotion, feeling, passion.

intelligent, SYN.—alert, astute, bright, clever, discerning, quick, smart; enlightened, intellectual, knowledgeable, well-informed. ANT.—dull, foolish, insipid, obtuse, slow, stupid.

intend, SYN.—contrive, delineate, design, devise, outline, plan, plot, prepare, project, scheme, sketch.

intense, SYN.—bright, brilliant, striking; animated, clear, expressive, fresh, graphic, lively, lucid, vivid. ANT.—dull, vague; dim, dreary, dusky.

intent, SYN.—design, intention, objective, purpose. ANT.—result; accidental, chance.

intensity, SYN.—activity, durability, force, fortitude, might, potency, power, stamina, toughness, vigor. ANT.—feebleness, frailty, infirmity, weakness.

intention, SYN.—design, intent, objective, purpose. ANT.—result; accident, chance.

intentional, SYN.—contemplated, deliberate, designed, intended, premeditated, studied, voluntary, willful. ANT.—accidental, fortuitous.

interfere, SYN.—interpose, interrupt, meddle, monkey, tamper.

interior, SYN.—inmost, inner, internal, inward. ANT.—adjacent, exterior, external, outer.

interject, SYN.—inject, insert, interpose, introduce, intrude. ANT.—avoid, disregard, overlook.

interminable, SYN.—boundless, endless, eternal, illimitable, immeasurable, immense, infinite, unbounded, unlimited, vast. ANT.—bounded, circumscribed, confined, finite, limited.

interpose, SYN.—inject, insert, interject, introduce, intrude; arbitrate, intercede, interfere, intervene, meddle, mediate. ANT.—avoid, disregard, overlook.

interpret, SYN.—construe, decipher, decode, elucidate, explain, explicate, render, solve, translate, unravel. ANT.—confuse, distort, falsify, misconstrue, misinterpret.

interrogate, SYN.—examine, inquire, question, quiz. ANT.—disregard, neglect, omit, overlook.

interrupt, SYN.—adjourn, defer, delay, discontinue, postpone, suspend, stay. ANT.—continue, maintain, persist, proceed, prolong.

intervene, SYN.—inject, insert, interject, introduce, intrude; arbitrate, intercede, interfere, interpose, meddle, mediate. ANT.—avoid, disregard, overlook.

intimacy, SYN.—acquaintance, familiarity, fellowship, friendship, sociability; frankness, informality, liberty, unreserve. ANT.—constraint, distance, haughtiness, presumption, reserve.

intimate, SYN.—affectionate, chummy, close, confidential, familiar, friendly, loving, near. ANT.—ceremonious, conventional, distant, formal.

intimation, SYN.—allusion, hint, implication, insinuation, reminder. ANT.—affirmation, declaration, statement.

intolerant, SYN.—bigoted, dogmatic, fanatical, illiberal, narrow-minded, prejudiced. ANT.—liberal, progressive, radical, tolerant.

intoxicated, SYN.—drunk, drunken, high, inebriated, tight, tipsy. ANT.—clear-headed, sober, temperate.

intrepid, SYN.—adventurous, audacious, bold, brave, courageous, daring, dauntless, fearless, brazen, forward, impudent, insolent, pushy, rude; abrupt, conspicuous, prominent, striking. ANT.—cowardly, flinching, timid; bashful, retiring.

intricate, SYN.—complex, complicated, compound, involved, perplexing. ANT.—plain, simple, uncompounded.

intrigue, SYN.—cabal, conspiracy, design, machination, plan, plot, scheme, stratagem.

intrinsic, SYN.—congenital, inborn, inbred, inherent, innate, native, natural, real. ANT.—acquired, external, extraneous, extrinsic.

introduction, SYN.—beginning, forward, overture, preamble, preface, prelude, prologue, start. ANT.—completion, conclusion, end, epilogue, finale.

intrude, SYN.—attack, encroach, infringe, invade, penetrate, trespass, violate. ANT.—abandon, evacuate, relinquish, vacate.

intuition, SYN.—acumen, discernment, insight, penetration, perspicuity. ANT.—obtuseness.

invade, SYN.—attack, encroach, infringe, intrude, penetrate, trespass, violate. ANT.—abandon, evacuate, relinquish, vacate.

invalidate, SYN.—abolish, abrogate, annul, cancel, revoke. ANT.—continue, establish, promote, restore, sustain.

invasion, SYN.—aggression, assault, attack, onslaught. ANT.—defense, opposition, resistance, surrender.

invective, SYN.—abuse, aspersion, defamation, disparagement, insult, reproach, upbraiding. ANT. — commendation, laudation, plaudit.

invent, SYN.—conceive, concoct, contrive, design, devise, fabricate, frame. ANT.—copy, imitate, reproduce.

inventive, SYN.—clever, creative, fanciful, imaginative, mystical, poetical, visionary. ANT.—dull, literal, prosaic, unromantic.

inventiveness, SYN.—aptitude, cleverness, cunning, faculty, ingeniousness, ingenuity, resourcefulness, skill. ANT.—clumsiness, dullness, ineptitude, stupidity.

invert, SYN.—reverse, transpose, turn about; overturn, upset; countermand, repeal, rescind, revoke. ANT.—endorse, maintain, stabilize.

investigate, SYN.—examine, explore, ferret (out), hunt, look, probe, ransack, rummage, search, scour, scrutinize, seek.

investigation, SYN.—examination, exploration, inquiry, interrogation, query, quest, question, research, scrutiny. ANT.—disregard, inactivity, inattention, negligence.

invincible, SYN.—impregnable, indomitable, insurmountable, invulnerable, unassailable, unconquerable. ANT.—powerless, puny, vulnerable, weak.

invisible, SYN.—imperceptible, indistinguishable, undiscernible, unseen. ANT.—evident, perceptible, seen, visible.

involve, SYN.—embrace, embroil, entangle, envelop, implicate, include, incriminate. ANT.—disconnect, disengage, extricate, separate.

involved, SYN.—complex, complicated, compound, intricate, perplexing. ANT.—plain, simple, uncompounded.

invulnerable, SYN.—impregnable, indomitable, insurmountable, invincible, unassailable, unconquerable. ANT.—powerless, puny, vulnerable, weak.

ire, SYN.—anger, animosity, choler, exasperation, fury, indignation, irritation, passion, petulance, rage, resentment, temper, wrath. ANT.—conciliation, forbearance, patience, peace, self-control.

irk, SYN.—annoy, bother, chafe, disturb, inconvenience, irritate, molest, pester, tease, trouble, vex. ANT.—accommodate, console, gratify, soothe.

irrational, SYN.—absurd, foolish, inconsistent, nonsensical, preposterous, ridiculous, selfcontradictory, silly, unreasonable. ANT.—consistent, rational, reasonable, sensible, sound.

irregular, SYN.—aberrant, abnormal, capricious, devious, eccentric, unnatural, unusual, variable. ANT.—fixed, methodical, ordinary, regular, usual.

irrelevant, SYN.—alien, extraneous, foreign, remote, strange, unconnected. ANT.—akin, germane, kindred, relevant.

irresolute, SYN.—bending, fragile, frail, pliant, yielding; ineffective, pliable, vacillating, wavering. ANT.—potent, powerful, robust, strong, sturdy.

irritable, SYN.—choleric, excitable, fiery, hasty, hot, irascible, peevish, petulant, snappish, testy, touchy. ANT.—agreeable, calm, composed, tranquil.

irritate, SYN.—annoy, bother, chafe, disturb, inconvenience, irk, molest, pester, tease, trouble, vex. ANT.—accommodate, console, gratify.

irritation, SYN.—annoyance, chagrin, exasperation, mortification, pique, vexation. ANT.—appeasement, comfort, gratification, pleasure.

isolated, SYN.—alone, deserted, desolate, lonely, secluded, unaided; lone, only, single, sole, solitary. ANT.—accompanied, attended, surrounded.

isolation, SYN.—alienation, insulation, loneliness, quarantine, retirement, seclusion, segregation, separation, solitude, withdrawal. ANT.— association, communion, connection, fellowship, union.

issue, SYN.—come, emanate, flow, originate, proceed, result; abound, be copious.

J

jargon, SYN.—dialect, diction, idiom, language, lingo, phraseology, slang, speech, tongue, vernacular. ANT.— babble, drivel, gibberish, nonsense.

jealousy, SYN.— covetousness, envy, invidiousness, resentfulness, suspicion. ANT.— geniality, indifference, liberality, tolerance.

jeer, SYN.—deride, fleer, flout, gibe, mock, scoff, sneer, taunt. ANT.— compliment, flatter, laud, praise.

jeering, SYN.—derision, gibe, irony, mockery, raillery, ridicule, sarcasm, satire, sneering.

jeopardize, SYN.—chance, conjecture, dare, endanger, hazard, imperil, peril, risk, venture. ANT.—determine, guard, insure, know.

jester, SYN.—buffoon, clown, fool, harlequin. ANT.—genius, philosopher, sage, scholar.

job, SYN.—chore, labor, stint, task, toil, work, undertaking; business, employment, occupation, position, post, situation.

jocularity, SYN.—facetiousness, humor, joke, waggery, wit. ANT.—gravity, seriousness, sorrow.

join, SYN.—accompany, adjoin, associate, attach, combine, conjoin, connect, couple, go with, link, unite. ANT.—detach, disconnect, disjoin, separate.

jolly, SYN.—cheerful, gay, glad, happy, joyful, lighthearted, merry, sprightly. ANT.—depressed, glum, mournful, sad, sullen.

jolt, SYN.—jar, quake, rock, shake, sway, totter, waver.

journey, SYN.—cruise, expedition, jaunt, passage, pilgrimage, tour, travel. ANT.—stay, stop.

joy, SYN.—bliss, delight, ecstasy, felicity, happiness, pleasure, rapture, transport; elation, exultation, festivity, glee, merriment, mirth. ANT.—affliction, depression, despair, grief, sorrow.

joyful, SYN.—cheerful, contented, delighted, fortunate, gay, glad, happy, joyous, lucky, merry, opportune. ANT.—blue, depressed, gloomy, morose.

joyous, SYN.—blithe, cheerful, festive, gay, gleeful, hilarious, jolly, jovial, lively, merry, mirthful, sprightly. ANT.—gloomy, melancholy, morose, sad, sorrowful.

judge, SYN.—adjudicator, arbitrator, critic, justice, magistrate, referee, umpire.

judge, SYN.—decide, decree, determine; adjudicate, arbitrate, condemn, try, umpire; appreciate, consider, estimate, evaluate, measure, think.

judgment, SYN.—discernment, discrimination, intelligence, perspicacity, sagacity, understanding, wisdom. ANT.—arbitrariness, senselessness, stupidity, thoughtlessness.

jumble, SYN.—agitation, chaos, commotion, confusion, disarrangement, disarray, disorder, ferment, stir, tumult, turmoil. ANT.—certainty, order, peace, tranquility.

jumble, SYN.—amalgamate, blend, combine, commingle, compound, concoct, confound, fuse, mingle, mix. ANT.—divide, segregate, separate, sort.

jump, SYN.—bound, caper, hop, jerk, leap, skip, spring, start, vault.

just, SYN.—candid, conscientious, fair, honest, honorable, scrupulous, sincere, trustworthy, truthful, upright. ANT.—deceitful, dishonest, fraudulent, lying, tricky.

justice, SYN.—equity, fairness, impartiality, justness, law, rectitude, right. ANT.—inequity, partiality, unfairness, wrong.

justifiable, SYN.—admissible, allowable, fair, permissible, tolerable, warranted. ANT.—inadmissible, irrelevant, unsuitable.

justify, SYN.—absolve, defend, excuse, exonerate, support, uphold, vindicate. ANT.—blame, convict.

K

keen, SYN.—acute, cutting, penetrating, piercing, severe; astute, clever, cunning, quick, sharp, shrewd, wily, witty. ANT.—bland, blunt, gentle, shallow, stupid.

keep, SYN.—conserve, continue, maintain, preserve, save; confine, detain, hold, reserve, restrain, retain; execute, obey; celebrate, commemorate, honor, observe; guard, protect; support, sustain. ANT.—discard, reject; dismiss, relinquish; disobey, ignore; abandon, forsake, neglect.

kill, SYN.—assassinate, butcher, execute, massacre, murder, put to death, slaughter, slay. ANT.—animate, protect, resuscitate, save, vivify.

kind, SYN.—affable, benevolent, benign, compassionate, forbearing, gentle, good, humane, indulgent, kindly, merciful, sympathetic, tender, thoughtful. ANT.—cruel, inhuman, merciless, severe, unkind.

kind, SYN.—breed, character, family, genus, race, sort, species, stock, strain, type, variety.

kindred, SYN.—affinity, consanguinity, family, kinsfolk, relations, relationship, relatives. ANT.—disconnection, foreigners, strangers.

kiss, SYN.—caress, cuddle, embrace, fondle, pet. ANT.—annoy, buffet, spurn, tease, vex.

knack, SYN.—ability, adroitness, cleverness, deftness, dexterity, facility, ingenuity, readiness, skill, skillfullness. ANT.—awkwardness, clumsiness, inability, ineptitude.

know, SYN.—apprehend, ascertain, cognize, comprehend, discern, distinguish, perceive, recognize, understand. ANT.—dispute, doubt, ignore, suspect.

knowledge, SYN.—apprehension, cognizance, erudition, information, learning, lore, scholarship, science, understanding, wisdom. ANT.—ignorance, illiteracy, misunderstanding, stupidity.

L

labor, SYN.—drudgery, effort, endeavor, exertion, striving, task, toil, travail, work; childbirth, parturition. ANT.—

idleness, indolence, leisure, recreation.

lacking, SYN.—defective, deficient, inadequate, incomplete, insufficient, scanty, short. ANT.—adequate, ample, enough, satisfactory, sufficient.

ladylike, SYN.—female, feminine, girlish, maidenly, womanish, womanly. ANT.—male, manly, mannish, masculine, virile.

lame, SYN.—crippled, defective, deformed, disabled, feeble, halt, hobbling, limping, maimed, unconvincing, unsatisfactory, weak. ANT.—agile, athletic, robust, sound, vigorous.

lament, SYN.—bemoan, bewail, deplore, grieve, mourn, repine, wail, weep.

lamp, SYN.—beam, gleam, illumination, incandescence, light, luminosity, radiance, shine; enlightenment, insight, knowledge, understanding. ANT.—darkness, gloom, obscurity, shadow.

land, SYN.—continent, country, earth, field, ground, island, plain, region, soil, tract; domain, estate, farm, realm.

language, SYN.—cant, dialect, diction, idiom, jargon, lingo, phraseology, slang, speech, tongue, vernacular. SYN.—babble, drivel, gibberish, nonsense.

languid, SYN.—faint, feeble, wearied; irresolute, weak. ANT.—strong, vigorous; forceful.

languish, SYN.—droop, waste, wilt, wither, wizen; decline, fail, sink, weaken. ANT.—refresh, rejuvenate, renew, revive.

larceny, SYN.—burglary, larceny, pillage, plunder, robbery, theft.

large, SYN.—ample, big, capacious, colossal, extensive, great, huge, immense, vast, wide. ANT.—little, mean, short, small, tiny.

last, SYN.—concluding, extreme, final, hindmost, latest, terminal, ultimate, utmost. ANT.—beginning, first, foremost, initial, opening.

late, SYN.—delayed, overdue, slow, tardy; advanced, new, recent. ANT.—early, timely.

latent, SYN.—concealed, dormant, hidden, inactive, potential, quiescent, secret, undeveloped, unseen. ANT.—conspicuous, evident, explicit, manifest, visible.

laudation, SYN.—acclaim, applause, commendation, compliment, eulogy, extolling, flattery, glorification, praise. ANT.—censure, condemnation, criticizing, disparagement, reproach.

laugh, SYN.—cackle, chuckle, giggle, guffaw, jeer, mock, roar, scoff, snicker, titter.

lavish, SYN.—dissipate,

misuse, scatter, spend, squander, waste, wear out. ANT.—accumulate, conserve, economize, preserve, save.

law, SYN.—act, decree, edict, statute.

lawful, SYN.—allowable, authorized, constitutional, legal, legitimate, permissible, rightful. ANT.—criminal, illegal, illegitimate, illicit, prohibited.

lay, SYN.—earthly, laic, mundane, profane, secular, temporal, worldly. ANT.—ecclesiastical, religious, spiritual, unworldly.

lay, SYN.—arrange, deposit, dispose, place, put, set. ANT.—disarrange, disturb, mislay, misplace, remove.

lax, SYN.—careless, desultory, inaccurate, neglectful, negligent, remiss. ANT.—accurate, careful, meticulous.

lazy, SYN.—idle, inactive, indolent, inert, slothful, sluggish, supine, torpid. ANT.—active, alert, assiduous, diligent.

lead, SYN.—conduct, direct, escort, guide, steer; control, manage, regulate, supervise.

leader, SYN.—captain, chief, chieftain, commander, head, master, principal, ruler. ANT.—attendant, follower, servant, subordinate.

league, SYN.—alliance, association, coalition, combination, confedera-cy, entente, federation, partnership, union. ANT.—schism, separation.

lean, SYN.—bend, incline, sag, slant, slope, tend; depend, rely, trust. ANT.—erect, raise, rise, straighten.

leaning, SYN.—bent, bias, drift, inclination, predisposition, proclivity, proneness, propensity, tendency, trend. ANT.—aversion, deviation, disinclination.

leap, SYN.—bound, caper, hop, jerk, jump, skip, spring, start, vault.

learned, SYN.—deep, discerning, enlightened, intelligent, penetrating, profound, sagacious, sound; erudite, informed, knowing, scholarly, wise. ANT.—foolish, shallow, simple.

learning, SYN.—apprehension, cognizance, erudition, information, knowledge, lore, scholarship, science, understanding, wisdom. ANT.—ignorance, illiteracy, misunderstanding, stupidity.

leave, SYN.—abandon, depart, desert, forsake, give up, go, quit, relinquish, renounce, retire, withdraw. ANT.—abide, remain, stay, tarry.

lecture, SYN.—conference, discourse, discussion, report, speech, talk. ANT. — correspondence, meditation, silence, writing.

legal, SYN.—allowable, authorized, constitutional, lawful, legitimate, permissible, rightful. ANT.—criminal, illegal, illegitimate, illicit, prohibited.

legend, SYN.—allegory, chronicle, fable, fiction, myth, parable, saga. ANT.—fact, history.

legitimate, SYN.—authentic, bona fide, genuine, proven, real, sincere, true, unadulterated, veritable. ANT.—artificial, bogus, counterfeit, false, sham.

leisure, SYN.—calm, ease, peace, quiet, relaxation, repose, rest, tranquility; cessation, intermission, pause, respite. ANT.—agitation, commotion, disturbance, motion, tumult.

leisurely, SYN.—dawdling, delaying, deliberate, gradual, laggard, slow, sluggish. ANT.—fast, quick, rapid, speedy, swift.

lengthen, SYN.—draw, extend, prolong, protract, stretch. ANT.—contract, shorten.

leniency, SYN.—charity, clemency, compassion, forgiveness, grace, mercy, mildness, pity. ANT.—cruelty, punishment, retribution, vengeance.

lenient, SYN.—clement, compassionate, forbearing, forgiving, humane, kind, merciful, tender, tolerant. ANT.—brutal, cruel, pitiless, remorseless, unfeeling.

lessen, SYN.—curtail, decrease, deduct, diminish, reduce, remove, shorten, subtract. ANT.—amplify, enlarge, expand, grow, increase.

lethargy, SYN.—daze, drowsiness, insensibility, languor, numbness, stupefaction, stupor, torpor. ANT.—activity, alertness, liveliness, readiness, wakefulness.

letter, SYN.—mark, sign, symbol; letter, memorandum, message, note.

level, SYN.—even, flat, horizontal, plane, smooth. ANT.—broken, hilly, irregular, sloping.

levy, SYN.—assessment, custom, duty, exaction, excise, impost, rate, tax, toll, tribute. ANT.—gift, remuneration, reward, wages.

lewd, SYN.—coarse, dirty, disgusting, filthy, gross, impure, indecent, obscene, offensive, pornographic, smutty. ANT.—decent, modest, pure, refined.

liable, SYN.—accountable, amenable, answerable, exposed to, responsible, subject to. ANT.—exempt, free, immune, independent.

libel, SYN.—aspersion, backbiting, calumny, defamation, slander, vilification. ANT.—applause, commendation, defense, flattery, praise.

liberal, SYN.—broad, extensive, large, tolerant. ANT.—confined, narrow, restricted.

liberality, SYN.—altruism, beneficience, benevolence, charity, generosity, humanity, kindness, magnanimity, philanthropy. ANT.—cruelty, inhumanity, malevolence, selfishness.

liberate, SYN.—deliver, discharge, emancipate, free, let go, release, set free. ANT.—confine, imprison, oppress, restrict, subjugate.

liberated, SYN.—autonomous, emancipated, exempt, free, freed, independent, unconfined, unrestricted; loose, unfastened, unobstructed; immune; careless, easy, familiar, frank; liberal. ANT.—confined, restrained, restricted; blocked, clogged, impeded; subject.

liberty, SYN.—autonomy, freedom, independence, self-government; license, permission, privilege. ANT.—captivity, imprisonment, submission, constraint.

license, SYN.—exemption, familiarity, freedom, immunity, independence, liberation, liberty, privilege, unrestraint. ANT.—bondage, compulsion, constraint, necessity, servitude.

lie, SYN.—delusion, equivocation, falsehood, fib, fiction, illusion, untruth.

ANT.—axiom, canon, fact, truism.

life, SYN.—animation, being, buoyancy, existence, liveliness, spirit, vigor, vitality, vivacity. ANT.—death, demise, dullness, languor, lethargy.

lifeless, SYN.—dead, deceased, defunct, departed, dull, gone, inanimate, insensible, spiritless, unconscious. ANT.—alive, animate, living, stirring.

lift, SYN.—elevate, erect, exalt, heave, heighten, hoist, lift, raise, uplift. ANT.—abase, depreciate, depress, destroy, hover.

light, SYN.—buoyant, effervescent, resilient; animated, blithe, cheerful, elated, hopeful, jocund, lively, spirited, sprightly, vivacious. ANT.—dejected, depressed, despondent, hopeless, sullen.

light, SYN.—beam, brightness, dawn, flame, gleam, illumination, incandescence, lamp, luminosity, radiance, shine; enlightenment, insight, knowledge, understanding. ANT.—darkness, gloom, obscurity, shadow.

like, SYN.—coincident, equal, equivalent, identical, indistinguishable, same. ANT.—contrary, disparate, dissimilar, distinct, opposed.

likeness, SYN.—analogy, correspondence, parity, resemblance, similarity, similitude. ANT.—difference, distinction, variance.

limit, SYN.—border, bound, boundary, confine, edge, extent, limitation, restraint, restriction, terminus. ANT.—boundlessness, endlessness, extension, infinity, vastness.

limpid, SYN.—clear, transparent; open, unobstructed. ANT.— foul.

lineage, SYN.—ancestry, clan, folk, nation, people, race, stock, strain, tribe.

linger, SYN.—abide, bide, delay, remain, rest, stay, tarry, wait. ANT.—expedite, hasten, leave.

link, SYN.—bond, connection, connective, coupler, juncture, tie, union. ANT.—break, gap, interval, opening, split.

link, SYN.—attach, conjoin, connect, couple, go with, join, unite. ANT.—detach, disconnect, disjoin, separate.

liquid, SYN.—flowing, fluent, juicy, watery. ANT.—congealed, gaseous, solid.

listen, SYN.—attend to, hear, hearken, heed, list, overhear. ANT.—be deaf to, disregard, ignore, reject, scorn.

little, SYN.—diminutive, insignificant, miniature, minute, petty, puny, slight, small, tiny, trivial, wee. ANT.—big, enormous, huge, immense, large.

lively, SYN.—active, animated, blithe, brisk, energetic, frolicsome, spirited, sprightly, supple, vigorous, vivaciousness; bright, clear, fresh, glowing, vivid. ANT.—dull, insipid, listless, stale, vapid.

liveliness, SYN.—activity, agility, briskness, energy, intensity, movement, quickness, rapidity, vigor. ANT.—dullness; idleness, inactivity, inertia, sloth.

load, SYN.—afflict, burden, encumber, oppress, overload, tax, trouble, weigh. ANT.—alleviate, console, ease, lighten, mitigate.

loathe, SYN.—abhor, abominate, despise, detest, dislike, hate. ANT.—admire, approve, cherish, like, love.

loathsome, SYN.—abominable, detestable, execrable, foul, hateful, odious, revolting, vile. ANT.—agreeable, commendable, delightful, pleasant.

locality, SYN.—district, environs, neighborhood; adjacency, nearness, vicinity. ANT.—distance, remoteness.

location, SYN.—area, locale, locality, place, region, site, situation, spot, station, vicinity.

lock, SYN.—bar, bolt, clasp, fastening, hook, latch, padlock; curl, ringlet, tress, tuft.

lofty, SYN.—grand, grandiose, high, imposing, magnificent, majestic, noble, pompous, stately, sublime. ANT.—common, humble, lowly, ordinary, undignified.

logical, SYN.—cogent, convincing, effective, efficacious, sound, strong, telling, valid, weighty. ANT.—spurious, weak.

lone, SYN.—deserted, desolate, isolated, lonely, secluded, unaided; alone, only, single, sole, solitary. ANT.—accompanied, attended, surrounded.

loneliness, SYN.—alienation, isolation, privacy, seclusion, solitude.

lonely, SYN.—deserted, desolate, isolated, secluded, unaided; alone, lone, only, single, sole, solitary. ANT.—accompanied, attended, surrounded.

long, SYN.—drawn out, elongated, extended, lasting, lengthy, lingering, prolix, prolonged, protracted, tedious, wordy. ANT.—abridged, brief, concise, short, terse.

look, SYN.—behold, discern, eye, gaze, glance, scan, see, stare, survey, view, watch, witness; appear, seem; examine, inspect, observe, regard. ANT.—avert, hide, miss, overlook.

loose, SYN.—disengaged, free, indefinite, lax, limp, slack, unbound, unfastened, untied, vague; careless, dissolute, heedless, unrestrained, wanton. ANT.—fast, tied, tight; inhibited, restrained.

loss, SYN.—deficiency, failure, lack, want. ANT.—sufficiency.

lost, SYN.—adrift, astray, missing, consumed, destroyed, forefeited, misspent, used, wasted; absorbed, bewildered, confused, dazed, distracted, perplexed, preoccupied. ANT.—anchored, found, located.

lot, SYN.—doom, fate, fortune, portion; destiny, issue, outcome, result.

loud, SYN.—clamorous, deafening, noisy, resounding, sonorous, stentorian, vociferous. ANT.—dulcet, inaudible, quiet, soft, subdued.

love, SYN.—adoration, affection, attachment, devotion, endearment, fondness. ANT.—aversion, dislike, enmity, hatred, indifference.

loveliness, SYN.—attractiveness, beauty, charm, comeliness, elegance, fairness, grace, handsomeness, pulchritude. ANT.—deformity, disfigurement, eyesore, homeliness, ugliness.

lovely, SYN.—beauteous, beautiful, charming, comely, elegant, fair, fine, handsome, pretty. ANT.—foul, hideous, homely, repulsive, unsightly.

loving, SYN.—affectionate,

chummy, close, confidential, familiar, friendly, intimate, near. ANT. — ceremonious, conventional, distant, formal.

low, SYN.—abject, contemptible, despicable, dishonorable, groveling, ignoble, ignominious, lowly, mean, menial, servile, sordid, vile, vulgar. ANT.—esteemed, exalted, honored, lofty, noble, righteous.

lower, SYN.—inferior, minor, poorer, secondary, subordinate. ANT.— better, greater, higher, superior.

lower, SYN.—abase, adulterate, alloy, corrupt, debase, defile, degrade, deprave, depress, humiliate, impair, pervert, vitiate. ANT.—enhance, improve, raise, restore, vitalize.

loyal, SYN.—addicted, affectionate, ardent, attached, dedicated, devoted, earnest, faithful, fond, given up to, inclined, prone, true. ANT.—detached, disinclined, indisposed, untrammeled.

loyalty, SYN.—allegiance, constancy, devotion, faithfulness, fealty, fidelty. ANT.—disloyalty, falseness, perfidy, treachery.

lucid, SYN.—clear, limpid, transparent, distinct; evident, intelligible, manifest, obvious, plain, unmistakable, visible; open, unobstructed. ANT.—ambiguous, obscure, unclear, vague.

lucky, SYN.—advantageous, auspicious, benign, favored, felicitous, fortuitous, fortunate, happy, propitious, successful. ANT.—cheerless, condemned, ill-fated, persecuted, unlucky.

luminous, SYN.—bright, brilliant, clear, gleaming, lucid, lustrous, radiant, shining. ANT.—dark, dull, gloomy, murky.

lunacy, SYN.—aberration, craziness, delirium, dementia, derangement, frenzy, insanity, madness, mania, psychosis. ANT.—rationality, sanity, stability.

lure, SYN.—drag, haul, pull, tow, tug; allure, attract, draw, entice, induce, persuade. ANT.—alienate, contract, drive, propel.

luscious, SYN.—delectable, delicious, delightful, palatable, savory, sweet, tasty. ANT.—acrid, distasteful, nauseous, unpalatable, unsavory.

lust, SYN.—appetite, aspiration, craving, desire, hungering, longing, urge, wish, yearning. ANT.—abomination, aversion, distaste, hate, loathing.

luster, SYN.—brightness, brilliance, brilliancy, effulgence, radiance, splendor. ANT.—darkness, dullness, gloom, obscurity.

M

mad, SYN.—angry, enraged, exasperated, furious, incensed, provoked, wrathful; crazy, delirious, demented, insane, lunatic, maniacal. ANT.—calm, happy, pleased; healthy, sane, sensible.

madness, SYN.—aberration, craziness, delirium, dementia, derangement, frenzy, insanity, lunacy, mania, psychosis. ANT.—rationality, sanity, stability.

magic, SYN.—black art, charm, conjuring, enchantment, legerdemain, necromancy, sorcery, voodoo, witchcraft, wizardry.

magistrate, SYN.—adjudicator, arbitrator, judge.

magnanimous, SYN.—beneficent, bountiful, generous, giving, liberal, munificent, openhanded, unselfish. ANT.—covetous, greedy, miserly, selfish, stingy.

magnify, SYN.—amplify, caricature, embroider, enlarge, exaggerate, expand, heighten, overstate, stretch. ANT.—belittle, depreciate, minimize, understate.

magnitude, SYN.—amplitude, area, bigness, bulk, dimensions, expanse, extent, greatness, largeness, mass, size, volume.

main, SYN.—cardinal, chief, essential, first, foremost, highest, leading, paramount, predominant, principal, supreme. ANT.—auxiliary, minor, subordinate, subsidiary, supplemental.

maintain, SYN.—continue, keep, preserve, support, sustain, uphold; affirm, allege, assert, claim, contend, declare, defend, justify, vindicate. ANT.—discontinue, neglect; deny, oppose, resist.

majestic, SYN.—august, dignified, grand, grandiose, high, imposing, lofty, magnificent, noble, pompous, stately, sublime. ANT.—common, humble, lowly, ordinary, undignified.

make, SYN.—assemble, build, cause, compel, construct, create, establish, execute, fashion, form, gain, manufacture, mold, produce, shape. ANT.—break, demolish, destroy, undo, unmake.

makeshift, SYN.—agent, alternate, deputy, lieutenant, proxy, representative, substitute, understudy; equivalent, expedient. ANT.—head, master, principal, sovereign.

malady, SYN.—ailment, complaint, disease, disorder, illness, infirmity, sickness. ANT.—health, healthiness, soundness, vigor.

malevolence, SYN.—animosity, enmity, grudge, ill will, malice, malignity, rancor, spite. ANT.—

affection, kindness, love, toleration.

malice, SYN.—animosity, enmity, grudge, ill will, malevolence, malignity, rancor, spite. ANT.—affection, kindness, love, toleration.

malicious, SYN.—bitter, evil-minded, hostile, malevolent, malignant, rancorous, spiteful, virulent, wicked. ANT.—affectionate, benevolent, benign, kind.

malign, SYN.—abuse, asperse, defame, disparage, ill-use, revile, scandalize, traduce, vilify; misapply, misemploy, misuse. ANT.—cherish, honor, praise, protect, respect.

malleable, SYN.—compassionate, flexible, gentle, lenient, meek, mellow, mild, soft, subdued, supple, tender, yielding. ANT.—hard, rigid, rough, tough, unyielding.

maltreatment, SYN.—abuse, aspersion, defamation, desecration, dishonor, disparagement, insult, invective, misuse, outrage, perversion, profanation, reproach, reviling, upbraiding. ANT.—approval, commendation, laudation, plaudit, respect.

manage, SYN.—command, control, direct, dominate, govern, regulate, rule, superintend; bridle, check, curb, repress, restrain. ANT.—abandon,

follow, forsake, ignore, submit.

maneuver, SYN.—action, agency, effort, enterprise, execution, instrumentality, operation, performance, proceeding, working. ANT.—cessation, inaction, inactivity, rest.

manifest, SYN.—clear, cloudless, fair, sunny; limpid, transparent; apparent, distinct, evident, intelligible, lucid, obvious, plain, unmistakable, visible; open, unobstructed. ANT.—cloudy, foul, overcast; ambiguous, obscure, unclear, vague.

manifest, SYN.—denote, designate, disclose, imply, indicate, intimate, reveal, show, signify, specify. ANT.—conceal, distract, divert, falsify, mislead.

manner, SYN.—custom, fashion, habit, method, mode, practice, style, way; air, behavior, conduct, demeanor, deportment.

many, SYN.—divers, manifold, multifarious, multitudinous, numerous, several, sundry, various. ANT.—few, infrequent, meager, scanty, scarce.

mar, SYN.—damage, deface, harm, hurt, impair, injure, spoil. ANT.—ameliorate, benefit, enhance, mend, repair.

marine, SYN.—maritime, nautical, naval, ocean, oceanic.

mark, SYN.—brand, scar, stain, stigma, trace, vestige; badge, label, sign; characteristic, feature, indication, property, symptoms, trait.

mark, SYN.—attend to, behold, descry, heed, note, notice, observe, perceive, recognize, regard, remark, see. ANT.—disregard, ignore, overlook, skip.

marriage, SYN.—espousal, matrimony, nuptials, union, wedding, wedlock. ANT.—celibacy, divorce, virginity.

marvelous, SYN.—exceptional, extraordinary, peculiar, rare, remarkable, singular, uncommon, unusual, wonderful. ANT.—common, frequent, ordinary, usual.

masculine, SYN.—bold, hardy, lusty, male, manly, mannish, robust, strong, vigorous, virile. ANT.—effeminate, emasculated, feminine, unmanly, weak, womanish.

mask, SYN.—cloak, conceal, cover, disguise, hide, screen, secrete, suppress, veil, withhold. ANT.—disclose, divulge, expose, reveal, show, uncover.

mass, SYN.—body, carcass, corpse, remains; form, frame, torso; bulk, corpus; aggregate, association, company, society. ANT.—intellect, mind, soul, spirit.

massacre, SYN.—butchery, carnage, pogrom, slaughter.

massacre, SYN.—assassinate, butcher, execute, kill, murder, put to death, slaughter, slay. ANT.—animate, protect, resuscitate, save, vivify.

massive, SYN.—heavy, ponderous, weighty; burdensome, cumbersome, grievous, trying; gloomy, grave, serious, dull, sluggish. ANT.—animated, brisk, light.

master, SYN.—chief; commander, employer, head, leader, lord, manager, overseer, ruler, teacher, holder, owner, proprietor; adept, expert. ANT.—servant, slave; amateur.

mastery, SYN.—ascendancy, domination, predominance, sovereignty, supremacy, sway, transcendence. ANT.—inferiority.

mate, SYN.—associate, attendant, colleague, companion, comrade, consort, crony, friend, partner. ANT.—adversary, enemy, stranger.

material, SYN.—bodily, corporeal, palpable, physical, sensible, tangible; essential, germane, important, momentous, relevant. ANT.—mental, metaphysical, spiritual; immaterial, insignificant.

material, SYN.—stuff, substance; cause, concern, matter, occasion, subject, theme, thing, topic; consequence, importance, moment. ANT.—

immateriality, phantom, spirit.

matrimony, SYN.—espousal, marriage, nuptials, union, wedding, wedlock. ANT.—celibacy, divorce, virginity.

matter, SYN.—material, stuff, substance; cause, concern, occasion, subject, theme, thing, topic; consequence, importance, moment. ANT.—immateriality, phantom, spirit.

mature, SYN.—complete, consummate, finished, full-grown, matured, mellow, ready, ripe, seasonable. ANT.—crude, green, immature, raw, undeveloped.

mature, SYN.—age, develop, perfect, ripen, season.

mean, SYN.—average, medium, middle; base, contemptible, despicable, low, sordid, vile, vulgar; malicious, nasty, offensive, selfish. ANT.—admirable, dignified, exalted, generous, noble.

meaning, SYN.—acceptation, connotation, drift, explanation, gist, implication, import; intent, interpretation, purport, purpose, sense, significance, signification.

means, SYN.—agent, apparatus, channel, device, instrument, medium, tool, utensil, vehicle. ANT.—hindrance, impediment, obstruction, preventive.

measure, SYN.—criterion, gauge, law, principle, proof, rule, standard, test, touchstone. ANT.—chance, fancy, guess, supposition.

meddle, SYN.—interfere, interpose, interrupt, mix in, monkey, tamper.

mediocre, SYN.—average, fair, intermediate, mean, median, medium, middling, moderate, ordinary. ANT.—exceptional, extraordinary, outstanding.

meditate, SYN.—conceive, imagine, picture, recall, recollect, remember; cogitate, contemplate, deliberate, muse, ponder, reason, reflect, speculate, think; apprehend, believe, consider, deem, esteem, judge, opine, reckon, regard, suppose; devise, intend, mean, plan, purpose. ANT.—conjecture, forget, guess.

meek, SYN.—docile, domestic, domesticated, gentle, subdued, submissive, tame; dull, flat, insipid, tedious. ANT.—fierce, savage, spirited, wild; animated, exciting, lively, spirited.

meet, SYN.—collide, confront, encounter, engage, find, greet, intersect; answer; fulfill, gratify, satisfy; experience, suffer, undergo. ANT.—cleave, disperse, part, scatter, separate.

melancholy, SYN.—dejected, depressed, despondent, disconsolate, dismal, dispirited, doleful, gloomy, glum, moody, sad, somber, sorrowful; grave, pensive. ANT.— cheerful, happy, joyous, merry.

melodramatic, SYN.— affected, artificial, ceremonious, dramatic, histrionic, showy, stagy, theatrical. ANT.— modest, subdued, unaffected, unemotional.

melody, SYN.—air, concord, harmony, strain, tune.

mellow, SYN.—complete, consummate, finished, full-grown, mature, matured, ready, seasonable, ANT.—crude, green, immature, raw, undeveloped.

member, SYN.—allotment, apportionment, division, fragment, moiety, piece, portion, scrap, section, segment, share; component, element, ingredient, organ, part; concern, faction, interest, party, side; character, lines, role. ANT.—entirety, whole.

memorandum, SYN.— indication, mark, sign, symbol, token; annotation, comment, letter, message, note, observation, remark.

memorial, SYN.—commemoration, memento, monument, remembrance, souvenir.

memory, SYN.—recollection, remembrance, reminiscence, retrospection; fame, renown, reputation. ANT.— forgetfulness, oblivion.

mend, SYN.—fix, patch, refit, repair, restore, sew; ameliorate, better, correct, improve, rectify, reform, remedy. ANT.— deface, destroy, hurt, injure, rend.

mendicant, SYN.—beggar, pauper, ragamuffin, scrub, starveling, tatterdemalion, vagabond, wretch.

mentality, SYN.—brain, faculties, intellect, intelligence, judgment, mind, psyche, reason, soul, spirit, understanding, wit; disposition, inclination, intention, liking, purpose, will, wish. ANT.—body, corporeality, materiality, matter.

mercenary, SYN.— avaricious, corrupt, greedy, sordid, venal. ANT.—generous, honorable, liberal.

merciful, SYN.—clement, compassionate, forbearing, forgiving, humane, kind, lenient, tender, tolerant. ANT.—brutal, cruel, pitiless, remorseless, unfeeling.

merciless, SYN.—barbarous, bestial, brute, brutish, carnal, coarse, cruel, ferocious, gross, inhuman, remorseless, rough, rude, ruthless, savage, sensual. ANT.— civilized, courteous, gentle, humane, kind.

mercy, SYN.—charity, clemency, compassion, forgiveness, grace, le-

niency, mildness, pity.
ANT.—cruelty, punishment, retribution, vengeance.

merge, SYN.—amalgamate, blend, coalesce, combine, commingle, conjoin, consolidate, fuse, mingle, mix, unify, unite. ANT.—analyze, decompose, disintegrate, separate.

merit, SYN.—chastity, goodness, integrity, morality, probity, purity, rectitude, virginity; effectiveness, efficacy, force, power, strength; excellence, virtue, worth. ANT.—corruption, lewdness, sin, vice; fault.

merit, SYN.—achieve, acquire, attain, deserve, earn, gain, get, obtain, win. ANT.—consume, forfeit, lose, spend, waste.

merited, SYN.—adequate, condign, deserved, earned, proper, suitable. ANT.—improper, undeserved, unmerited.

merry, SYN.—blithe, cheerful, festive, gay, gleeful, hilarious, jolly, jovial, joyous, lively, mirthful, sprightly. ANT.—gloomy, melancholy, morose, sad, sorrowful.

message, SYN.—indication, mark, sign, symbol, token; annotation, comment, letter, memorandum, observation, remark.

mete, SYN.—allot, apportion, deal, dispense, distribute, divide; allocate, appropriate, assign, give, grant, measure. ANT.—confiscate, keep, refuse, retain, withhold.

method, SYN.—design, fashion, manner, mode, order, plan, procedure, system, way. ANT.—confusion, disorder.

methodical, SYN.—accurate, correct, definite, distinct, exact, precise, strict, unequivocal; ceremonious, formal, prim, rigid, stiff. ANT.—erroneous, loose, rough, vague; careless, easy, informal.

mettle, SYN.—boldness, bravery, chivalry, courage, fearlessness, fortitude, intrepidity, prowess, resolution. ANT.—cowardice, fear, pusillanimity, timidity.

microscopic, SYN.—fine, minute, tiny; detailed, exact, particular, precise. ANT.—enormous, huge, large; general.

middle, SYN.—center, core, heart, midpoint, midst, nucleus. ANT.—border, boundary, outskirts, periphery, rim.

might, SYN.—ability, force, potency, power, strength, vigor. ANT.—inability, weakness.

mighty, SYN.—athletic, cogent, concentrated, enduring, firm, forceful, forcible, fortified, hale, hardy, impregnable, potent, powerful, robust, sinewy, strong, sturdy, tough. ANT.—brittle, delicate, feeble, fragile, insipid.

mild, SYN.—bland, gentle, kind, meek, moderate, soft, soothing, tender. ANT.—bitter, fierce, harsh, rough, severe.

mimic, SYN.—ape, copy, counterfeit, duplicate, imitate, impersonate, mock, simulate. ANT.—alter, distort, diverge, invent.

mind, SYN.—brain, faculties, intellect, intelligence, judgment, mentality, psyche, reason, soul, spirit, understanding, wit; disposition, inclination, intention, liking, purpose, will, wish. ANT.—body, corporeality, materiality, matter.

mingle, SYN.—amalgamate, blend, coalesce, combine, commingle, conjoin, consolidate, fuse, mix, merge, unify, unite. ANT.—analyze, decompose, disintegrate, separate.

minimize, SYN.—belittle, curtail, deduct, diminish, lessen, reduce, shorten, subtract. ANT.—amplify, enlarge, expand, increase.

minor, SYN.—inferior, lower, poorer, secondary, subordinate. ANT.—better, greater, higher, superior.

minute, SYN.—fine, microscopic, tiny, detailed, exact, particular, precise. ANT.—enormous, huge, large; general.

miraculous, SYN.—marvelous, metaphysical, other-worldly, preternatural, spiritual, superhuman, supernatural, unearthly. ANT.—common, human, natural, physical, plain.

mirage, SYN.—delusion, dream, fantasy, hallucination, illusion, phantom, vision. ANT.—actuality, reality, substance.

miscarriage, SYN.—fiasco, failure; default, dereliction, omission; decay, decline; deficiency, lack, loss, want. ANT.—achievement, success, victory; sufficiency.

miscellaneous, SYN.—assorted, diverse, heterogeneous, indiscriminate, mixed, motley, sundry, varied. ANT.—alike, classified, homogeneous, ordered, selected.

mischief, SYN.—damage, detriment, evil, harm, hurt, ill, infliction, injury, misfortune, mishap, wrong. ANT.—benefit, boon, favor, kindness.

miserable, SYN.—comfortless, disconsolate, distressed, forlorn, heartbroken, pitiable, wretched; abject, contemptible, despicable, low, mean, paltry, worthless. ANT.—contented, fortunate, happy, noble, significant.

miserly, SYN.—acquisitive, avaricious, greedy, niggardly, parsimonious, penurious, stingy, tight. ANT.—altruistic, bountiful, extravagant, generous, munificent.

misery, SYN.—agony, anguish, distress, grief, sorrow, suffering, torment, tribulation, woe; calamity, disaster, evil, misfortune, trouble. ANT.—delight, elation, fun, joy, pleasure.

misfortune, SYN.—accident, adversity, affliction, calamity, catastrophe, disaster, distress, hardship, mishap, ruin. ANT.—blessing, comfort, prosperity, success.

mishap, SYN.—accident, calamity, casualty, disaster, misfortune. ANT.—calculation, design, intention, purpose.

misleading, SYN.—deceitful, deceptive, delusive, delusory, fallacious, false, illusive, specious. ANT.—authentic, genuine, honest, real, truthful.

miss, SYN.—fail, default, lack, lose, omit, want. ANT.—achieve, have, include, succeed, suffice.

mistake, SYN.—blunder, error, fallacy, fault, inaccuracy, slip. ANT.—accuracy, precision, truth.

mistaken, SYN.—amiss, askew, awry, erroneous, fallacious, false, faulty, inaccurate, incorrect, unprecise, untrue, wrong; improper, inappropriate, unsuitable; aberrant, bad, criminal, evil, immoral, iniquitous, reprehensible. ANT.—correct, right, true; suit-

able; proper.

misuse, SYN.—abuse, asperse, defame, disparage, ill-use, malign, revile, scandalize, traduce, vilify; misapply, misemploy. ANT.—cherish, honor, praise, protect, respect.

misuse, SYN.—despoil, destroy, devastate, pillage, plunder, ravage, ruin, sack, strip; consume, corrode, dissipate, lavish, scatter, spend, squander, waste, wear out; decay, diminish, dwindle, pine, wither. ANT.—accumulate, conserve, economize, preserve, save.

mitigate, SYN.—abate, allay, alleviate, assuage, diminish, extenuate, relieve, soften, solace, soothe. ANT.—aggravate, agitate, augment, increase, irritate.

mix, SYN.—alloy, amalgamate, blend, combine, commingle, compound, concoct, confound, fuse, jumble, mingle; associate, consort, fraternize, join. ANT.—dissociate, divide, segregate, separate, sort.

mixture, SYN.—assortment, change, difference, dissimilarity, diversity, heterogeneity, medley, miscellany, multifariousness, variety, variousness; breed, kind, sort, stock, strain, subspecies. ANT.—homogeneity, likeness, monotony, sameness, uniformity.

mob, SYN.—bevy, crowd, crush, horde, host, masses, multitude, populace, press, rabble, swarm, throng.

mock, SYN.—deride, fleer, flout, gibe, jeer, scoff, sneer, taunt. ANT.—compliment, flatter, laud, praise.

mockery, SYN.—banter, derision, gibe, irony, jeering, raillery, ridicule, sarcasm, satire, sneering.

mode, SYN.—design, fashion, manner, method, order, plan, procedure, system, way. ANT.—confusion, disorder.

model, SYN.—archetype, copy, example, mold, pattern, prototype, specimen, standard, type. ANT.—imitation, production, reproduction.

moderate, SYN.—abate, assuage, decrease, diminish, lessen, lower, reduce, suppress. ANT.—amplify, enlarge, increase, intensify.

moderation, SYN.—forbearance, self-denial, sobriety. ANT.—excess, gluttony, greed, intoxication, self-indulgence.

modern, SYN.—contemporary, current, new, novel, present, recent. ANT.—ancient, antiquated, bygone, old, past.

modest, SYN.—bashful, humble, meek, reserved, shy, unassuming, unpretentious, virtuous. ANT.—arrogant, bold, conceited, forward, immodest, ostentatious, proud.

modification, SYN.—alteration, alternation, change, mutation, substitution, variation, variety, vicissitude. ANT.—monotony, stability, uniformity.

modify, SYN.—change, exchange, substitute; alter, convert, shift, transfigure, transform, vary, veer. ANT.—retain; continue, establish, preserve, settle, stabilize.

moiety, SYN.—allotment, apportionment, division, fragment, part, piece, portion, scrap, section, segment, share. ANT.—entirety, whole.

mold, SYN.—construct, create, fashion, forge, form, make, produce, shape; compose, constitute, make up; arrange, combine, organize; devise, frame, invent. ANT.—destroy, disfigure, dismantle, misshape, wreck.

molest, SYN.—annoy, bother, chafe, disturb, inconvenience, irk, irritate, pester, tease, trouble, vex. ANT.—accommodate, console, gratify, soothe.

momentary, SYN.—brief, compendious, concise, curt, laconic, pithy, short, succinct, terse; fleeting, passing, transient. ANT.—extended, lengthy, long, prolonged, protracted.

momentous, SYN.—consequential, critical, decisive, grave, important, influential, material, pressing, prominent, relevant, significant, weighty. ANT.—insignificant, irrelevant, mean, petty, trivial.

monastery, SYN.—abbey, cloister, convent, hermitage, nunnery, priory.

monkey, SYN.—interfere, interpose, interrupt, meddle, mix in, tamper.

monotonous, SYN.—boring, burdensome, dilatory, dreary, dull, humdrum, irksome, slow, sluggish, tardy, tedious, tiresome, uninteresting, wearisome. ANT.—amusing, entertaining, exciting, interesting, quick.

monument, SYN.—commemoration, memento, memorial, remembrance, souvenir.

mood, SYN.—disposition, temper, temperament; facetiousness, irony, jocularity, joke, sarcasm, satire, waggery, wit. ANT.—gravity, seriousness, sorrow.

moody, SYN.—crabbed, dour, fretful, gloomy, glum, morose, sulky, surly. ANT.—amiable, gay, joyous, merry, pleasant.

moody, SYN.—dejected, depressed, despondent, disconsolate, dismal, dispirited, doleful, gloomy, glum, melancholy, sad, somber, sorrowful; grave, pensive. ANT.— cheerful, happy, joyous, merry.

moral, SYN.—chaste, decent, ethical, good, honorable, just, pure, right, righteous, scrupulous, virtuous. ANT.—amoral, libertine, licentious, sinful, unethical.

morality, SYN.—chastity, goodness, integrity, probity, purity, rectitude, virginity, virtue; effectiveness, efficacy, force, power, strength; excellence merit, worth. ANT.—corruption, lewdness, sin, vice; fault.

morose, SYN.—crabbed, dour, fretful, gloomy, glum, moody, sulky, surly. ANT.—amiable, gay, joyous, merry, pleasant.

morsel, SYN.—amount, bit, fraction, fragment, part, piece, portion, scrap. ANT.—all, entirety, sum, total, whole.

mortal, SYN.—deadly, destructive, fatal, final; human. ANT.—life-giving; divine, immortal.

mortify, SYN.—abase, abash, break, crush, degrade, humiliate, humble, shame, subdue. ANT.—elevate, exalt, honor, praise.

motion, SYN.—action, activity, change, gesture, move, movement; proposal, proposition. ANT.—equilibrium, immobility, stability, stillness.

motive, SYN.—cause, impulse, incentive, incitement, inducement, principle, purpose, reason, spur, stimulus. ANT.—

action, attempt, deed, effort, result.

motley, SYN.—assorted, diverse, heterogeneous, indiscriminate, miscellaneous, mixed, sundry, varied. ANT.—alike, classified, homogeneous, ordered.

motto, SYN.—adage, aphorism, apothegm, byword, maxim, proverb, saw, saying.

mount, SYN.—ascend, climb, rise, scale, soar, tower. ANT.—descend, fall, sink.

mourn, SYN.—bemoan, bewail, deplore, grieve, lament, suffer, weep. ANT.—carouse, celebrate, rejoice, revel.

mourning, SYN.—affliction, anguish, distress, heartache, lamentation, grief, misery, sadness, sorrow, trial, tribulation, woe. ANT.—comfort, consolation, happiness, joy, solace.

move, SYN.—actuate, agitate, drive, impel, induce, instigate, persuade, propel, push, shift, stir, transfer. ANT.—deter, halt, rest, stay, stop.

movement, SYN.—action, activity, change, gesture, motion, move, proposal, proposition. ANT.—equilibrium, immobility, stability, stillness.

muddled, SYN.—bewildered, confused, deranged, disconcerted, disordered, disorganized, indistinct, mixed,

perplexed. ANT.—clear, lucid, obvious, organized, plain.

multifarious, SYN.—divers, manifold, many, multitudinous, numerous, several, sundry, various. ANT.—few, infrequent, meager, scanty, scarce.

multitude, SYN.—army, crowd, host, legion, mob. ANT.—few, handful, paucity, scarcity.

mundane, SYN.—earthly, laic, lay, profane, secular, temporal, worldly. ANT.—ecclesiastical, religious, spiritual, unworldly.

munificent, SYN.—generous; full, satisfied. ANT.—avaricious, covetous, grasping, rapacious, selfish; devouring, gluttonous, insatiable, ravenous, voracious.

murder, SYN.—assassinate, butcher, execute, kill, massacre, put to death, slaughter, slay. ANT.—animate, protect, resuscitate, save, vivify.

murmur, SYN.—complain, grumble, lament, protest, regret, remonstrate, repine, whine. ANT.—applaud, approve, praise, rejoice.

music, SYN.—consonance, harmony, melody, symphony.

muster, SYN.—accumulate, amass, assemble, collect, congregate, convene, gather; cull, garner, glean, harvest, pick, reap; conclude, deduce, infer, judge. ANT.—disband, disperse, distribute, scatter, separate.

mute, SYN.—calm, dumb, hushed, noiseless, peaceful, quiet, silent, still, taciturn, tranquil. ANT.—clamorous, loud, noisy, raucous.

mutiny, SYN.—coup, insurrection, overthrow, rebellion, revolt, revolution, uprising.

mutual, SYN.—common, correlative, interchangeable, joint, reciprocal, shared. ANT.—dissociated, separate, unrequited, unshared.

mysterious, SYN.—cabalistic, cryptic, dark, dim, enigmatical, hidden, incomprehensible, inexplicable, inscrutable, mystical, obscure, occult, recondite, secret. ANT.—clear, explained, obvious, plain, simple.

mystery, SYN.—conundrum, enigma, problem, puzzle, riddle. ANT.—answer, clue, key, resolution, solution.

mystical, SYN.—cabalistic, cryptic, dark, dim, enigmatical, hidden, incomprehensible, inexplicable, inscruhable, mysterious, obscure, occult, recondite, secret. ANT.—clear, explained, obvious, plain, simple.

myth, SYN.—allegory, chronicle, fable, fiction, legend, parable, saga. ANT.—fact, history.

N

nag, SYN.—aggravate, annoy, badger, bother, disturb, harass, harry, irritate, molest, pester, plague, provoke, tantalize, taunt, tease, torment, vex, worry. ANT.—comfort, delight, gratify, please, soothe.

naive, SYN.—artless, candid, frank, ingenuous, innocent, natural, open, simple, unsophisticated. ANT.—crafty, cunning, sophisticated, worldly.

naked, SYN.—bare, exposed, nude, stripped, unclad, uncovered; bald, barren, unfurnished; mere, plain, simple; defenseless, open, unprotected. ANT.—clothed, covered, dressed; concealed; protected.

name, SYN.—appellation, denomination, designation, epithet, style, surname, title; character, reputation, repute; distinction, eminence, fame, renown. ANT.—misnomer, namelessness; anonymity.

name, SYN.—appoint, call, christen, denominate, entitle, mention, specify. ANT.—hint, miscall, misname.

nap, SYN.—catnap, doze, drowse, nod, repose, rest, sleep, slumber, snooze.

narrate, SYN.—declaim, deliver, describe, detail, mention, recite, recapitulate, rehearse, relate, repeat, tell.

narrative, SYN.—account, chronicle, description, detail, history, narration, recital, relation; record. ANT.—caricature, confusion, distortion, misrepresentation.

narrow, SYN.—bigoted, dogmatic, fanatical, illiberal, intolerant, narrow-minded, prejudiced. ANT.—liberal, progressive, radical, tolerant.

nasty, SYN.—malicious, mean, offensive, selfish. ANT.—admirable, dignified, exalted, generous, noble.

nation, SYN.—commonwealth, community, kingdom, nationality, people, realm, state.

native, SYN.—aboriginal, domestic, endemic, inborn, indigenous, inherent, innate, natural.

natural, SYN.—characteristic, inherent, innate, native, original; normal, regular; genuine, ingenuous, real, simple, spontaneous, unaffected. ANT.—abnormal, artificial, irregular; forced, formal.

nature, SYN.—character, disposition, individuality, kind, reputation, repute, sort.

nautical, SYN.—marine, maritime, naval, ocean, oceanic.

naval, SYN.—marine, maritime, nautical, ocean, oceanic.

near, SYN.—adjacent, bordering, close, neighboring, nigh, proximate; approaching, imminent, impending; dear, familiar, intimate. ANT.—distant, far, removed.

neat, SYN.—clear, nice, orderly, precise, spruce, tidy, trim. ANT.—dirty, disheveled, sloppy, slovenly, unkempt.

necessary, SYN.—inevitable, unavoidable, essential, expedient, indispensable, needed, requisite. ANT.—accidental, casual; contingent, nonessential, optional.

necessity, SYN.—compulsion, constraint, destiny, fate; requirement, requisite; exigency, indigence, need, poverty, want. ANT.—choice, freedom, luxury, option, uncertainty.

necromancy, SYN.—black art, charm, conjuring, enchantment, legerdemain, magic, sorcery, voodoo, witchcraft, wizardy.

need, SYN.—claim, covet, crave, demand, desire, lack, require, want, wish.

needed, SYN.—essential, expedient, indispensable, necessary, requisite. ANT.—contingent, nonessential, optional.

neglect, SYN.—carelessness, default, disregard, failure, heedlessness, negligence, omission, oversight, slight, thoughtlessness. ANT.—attention, care, diligence, watchfulness.

neglect, SYN.—disregard,

ignore, omit, overlook, slight, ANT.—do, guard, perform, protect, satisfy.

negligent, SYN.—careless, heedless, imprudent, inattentive, inconsiderate, reckless, thoughtless, unconcerned; desultory, inaccurate, lax, neglectful, remiss. ANT.—accurate, careful, meticulous, nice.

neighborhood, SYN.—district, environs, locality; adjacency, nearness, vicinity. ANT.—distance, remoteness.

neighborly, SYN.—affable, amicable, companionable, friendly, genial, kindly, sociable, social. ANT.—antagonistic, cool, distant, hostile, reserved.

new, SYN.—fresh, late, modern, newfangled, novel, original, recent. ANT.—ancient, antiquated, archaic, obsolete, old.

news, SYN.—advice, copy, information, intelligence, message, report, tidings.

niggardly, SYN.—acquisitive, avaricious, greedy, miserly, parsimonious, penurious, stingy, tight. ANT.—altruistic, bountiful, extravagant, generous, munificent.

nigh, SYN.—adjacent, bordering, close, near, neighboring, proximate; approaching, imminent, impending. ANT.—distant, far, removed.

nimble, SYN.—active, agile, alert, brisk, flexible, lively, quick, spry, supple. ANT.—clumsy, heavy, inert, slow, sluggish.

noble, SYN.—dignified, elevated, eminent, exalted, grand, illustrious, lofty, majestic, stately. ANT.—base, low, mean, plebian, vile.

noise, SYN.—babel, clamor, cry, din, outcry, racket, row, sound, tumult, uproar. ANT.—hush, quiet, silence, stillness.

noisy, SYN.—clamorous, deafening, loud, resounding, sonorous, stentorian, vociferous. ANT.—dulcet, inaudible, quiet, soft, subdued.

nonplus, SYN.—bewilder, confound, confuse, dumfound, mystify, perplex, puzzle. ANT.—clarify, explain, illumine, instruct, solve.

nonsensical, SYN.—absurd, foolish, inconsistent, irrational, preposterous, ridiculous, self-contradictory, silly, unreasonable. ANT.—consistent, rational, reasonable, sensible, sound.

normal, SYN.—customary, natural, ordinary, regular, steady, uniform, unvaried. ANT.—abnormal, erratic, exceptional, rare, unusual.

nosy, SYN.—curious, inquiring, inquisitive, interrogative, meddling, peeping, peering, prying, searching, snoopy. ANT.—incurious, indifferent, unconcerned, uninterested.

note, SYN.—indication, mark, sign, symbol, token; annotation, comment, letter, memorandum, message, observation, remark.

noted, SYN.—celebrated, distinguished, eminent, famous, glorious, illustrious, renowned, well-known. ANT.—hidden, ignominious, infamous, obscure, unknown.

notice, SYN.—attend to, behold, descry, heed, mark, note, observe, perceive, recognize, regard, remark, see. ANT.—disregard, ignore, overlook, skip.

notify, SYN.—acquaint, advise, apprise, enlighten, impart, inform, instruct, teach, tell, warn. ANT.—conceal, delude, distract, mislead.

notion, SYN.—abstraction, concept, conception, fancy, idea, image, impression, opinion, sentiment, thought. ANT.—entity, matter, object, substance, thing.

novel, SYN.—allegory, fable, fabrication, fiction, invention, narrative, romance, story, tale. ANT.—fact, history, reality, truth, verity.

novice, SYN.—amateur, apprentice, beginner, dabbler, dilettante, learner, neophyte. ANT.—adept, authority, expert, master, professional.

now, SYN.—present, today.

nude, SYN.—bare, exposed, naked, stripped, unclad, uncovered; mere, plain, simple; defenseless, open, unprotected. ANT.—clothed, covered, dressed; concealed; protected.

nullify, SYN.—cancel, cross out, delete, eliminate, erase, expunge, obliterate; abolish, abrogate, annul, invalidate, quash, repeal, rescind, revoke. ANT.—confirm, enact, enforce, perpetuate.

number, SYN.—aggregate, amount, quantity, sum, volume. ANT.—nothing, nothingness, zero.

numerous, SYN.—divers, manifold, many, multifarious, multitudinous, several, sundry, various. ANT.—few, infrequent, meager, scanty, scarce.

nuptials, SYN.—espousal, marriage, matrimony, union, wedding, wedlock. ANT.—celibacy, divorce, virginity.

nurture, SYN.—appreciate, cherish, hold dear, prize, treasure, value; foster, sustain. ANT.—dislike, disregard, neglect; abandon, reject.

nutriment, SYN.—diet, edibles, fare, feed, food, meal, provisions, rations, repast, sustenance, viands, victuals. ANT.—drink, hunger, starvation, want.

O

obdurate, SYN.—callous, hard, impenitent, indurate, insensible, insensitive, tough, unfeeling. ANT.— compassionate, sensitive, soft, tender.

obedient, SYN.—compliant, deferential, dutiful, submissive, tractable, yielding. ANT.—insubordinate, intractable, obstinate, rebellious.

obese, SYN.—chubby, corpulent, fat, paunchy, plump, portly, pudgy, rotund, stocky, stout, thickset. ANT.—gaunt, lean, slender, slim, thin.

object, SYN.—article, particular, thing; aim, design, end, goal, intention, mark, objective, purpose. ANT.—acquiesce, approve, assent, comply, concur.

objection, SYN.—challenge, difference, disagreement, dissent, dissentience, noncompliance, nonconformity, protest, recusancy, rejection, remonstrance, variance. ANT.— acceptance, agreement, assent, compliance.

objective, SYN.—aim, ambition, aspiration, craving, desire, goal, hope, longing, passion.

obligate, SYN.—commit, pledge. ANT.—free, loose.

obligation, SYN.—accountability, bond, compulsion, contract, duty, engagement, responsibility. ANT.—choice, exemption, freedom.

oblige, SYN.—coerce, compel, constrain, drive, enforce, force, impel.

ANT.—allure, convince, induce, persuade, prevent.

obliterate, SYN.—annihilate, demolish, destroy, devastate, eradicate, exterminate, extinguish, ravage, raze, ruin, wreck. ANT.—construct, establish, make, preserve, save.

oblivious, SYN.—blind, ignorant, sightless, undiscerning, unmindful, unseeing; headlong, heedless, rash. ANT.—aware, calculated, discerning, perceiving, sensible.

obscene, SYN.—coarse, dirty, disgusting, filthy, gross, impure, indecent, lewd, offensive, pornographic, smutty. ANT.—decent, modest, pure, refined.

obscure, SYN.—abstruse, ambiguous, cloudy, cryptic, dark, dim, dusky, enigmatic, indistinct, mysterious, unintelligible, vague. ANT.—bright, clear, distinct, lucid.

observance, SYN.—ceremony, formality, parade, pomp, protocol, rite, ritual, solemnity.

observant, SYN.—alert, alive, attentive, awake, aware, careful, considerate, heedful, mindful, thoughtful, wary, watchful. ANT.—indifferent, oblivious, unaware.

observe, SYN.—behold, detect, discover, examine, eye, inspect, mark, note, notice, perceive, see, view, watch; keep, celebrate, commemorate; express, mention, remark, utter. ANT.—disregard, ignore, neglect, overlook.

obsolete, SYN.—ancient, antiquated, archaic, obsolescent, old, out-of-date, venerable. ANT.—current, extant, fashionable, modern, recent.

obstacle, SYN.—bar, barrier, block, check, difficulty, hindrance, impediment, obstruction, snag. ANT.—aid, assistance, encouragement, help.

obstinate, SYN.—contumacious, determined, dogged, firm, headstrong, immovable, inflexible, intractable, obdurate, pertinacious, stubborn, uncompromising, unyielding. ANT.—amenable, compliant, docile, submissive, yielding.

obstruct, SYN.—bar, barricade, block, clog, close, stop; delay, impede, hinder. ANT.—clear, open; aid, further, promote.

obtain, SYN.—acquire, assimilate, attain, earn, get, procure, secure, win. ANT.—forego, forfeit, lose, miss, surrender.

obtuse, SYN.—dense, dull, slow, stupid; blunt. ANT.—animated, lively, sharp; clear, interesting.

obvious, SYN.—apparent, clear, distinct, evident, manifest, palpable, patent, plain, self-evident, unmistakable. ANT.—

abstruse, concealed, hidden, obscure.

occupation, SYN.—art, business, commerce, employment, engagement, enterprise, job, profession, trade, trading, vocation, work. ANT.—avocation, hobby, pastime.

occupy, SYN.— absorb, busy, dwell, fill, have, hold, inhabit, keep, possess. ANT.—abandon, release, relinquish.

occur, SYN.—bechance, befall, betide, chance, happen, take place, transpire.

occurrence, SYN.—circumstance, episode, event, happening, incident, issue; consequence, end, outcome, result.

odd, SYN.—bizarre, curious, eccentric, peculiar, quaint, queer, singular, strange, unique, unusual; remaining, single, uneven, unmatched. ANT.—common, familiar, normal, regular, typical; even, matched.

odious, SYN.—base, debased, depraved, foul, loathsome, obscene, revolting, sordid, vicious, vile, vulgar, wicked; abject, despicable, innoble, low, mean, worthless, wretched. ANT.—attractive, decent, laudable; honorable, upright.

odor, SYN.—aroma, fetidness, fragrance, fume, incense, perfume, redolence, scent, smell, stench, stink.

offense, SYN.—affront, atrocity, indignity, insult, outrage; aggression, crime, injustice, misdeed, sin, transgression, trespass, vice, wrong. ANT.—gentleness, innocence, morality, right.

offer, SYN.—overture, proposal, proposition, suggestion, tender. ANT.—acceptance, denial, rejection, withdrawal.

offer, SYN.—advance, exhibit, extend, present, proffer, propose, sacrifice, tender, volunteer. ANT.—accept, receive, reject, retain, spurn.

office, SYN.—berth, incumbency, job, position, post, situation.

often, SYN.—commonly, frequently, generally, recurrently, repeatedly. ANT.—infrequently, occasionally, rarely, seldom, sporadically.

old, SYN.—aged, ancient, antiquated, antique, archaic, elderly, obsolete, old-fashioned, senile, superannuated, venerable. ANT.—modern, new, young, youthful.

omen, SYN.—emblem, gesture, indication, mark, note, portent, proof, sign, signal, symbol, symptom, token.

omission, SYN.—default, deletion, failure, neglect, oversight. ANT.—attention, inclusion, insertion, notice.

omit, SYN.—cancel, delete, disregard, drop, eliminate, exclude, ignore, miss, neglect, overlook, skip. ANT.—enter, include, insert, introduce, notice.

onerous, SYN.—arduous, burdensome, difficult, hard, tough; intricate, perplexing, puzzling. ANT.—easy, effortless, facile; simple.

onslaught, SYN.—aggression, assault, attack, criticism, denunciation, invasion, offense. ANT.—defense, opposition, resistance, surrender, vindication.

opaque, SYN.—dark, dim, gloomy, murky, obscure, shadowy, unilluminated. ANT.—light; bright, clear.

open, SYN.—agape, ajar, unclosed, uncovered, unlocked; clear, passable, unobstructed; available, disengaged, free, unoccupied; accessible, exposed, public, unrestricted; candid, frank, honest, overt, plain.

open, SYN.—exhibit, expand, spread, unbar, unfasten, unfold, unlock, unseal. ANT.—close, conceal, hide, shut.

opening, SYN.—abyss, aperture, cavity, chasm, gap, gulf, hole, pore, void.

operate, SYN.—act, behave, comport, conduct, demean, deport, interact, manage.

operation, SYN.—action, agency, effort, enterprise, execution, instrumentality, maneuver, performance, proceeding, working. ANT.—cessation, inaction, inactivity, rest.

operative, SYN.—active, working; busy, industrious. ANT.—dormant, inactive.

opinion, SYN.—belief, conviction, decision, feeling, idea, impression, judgment, notion, persuasion, sentiment, view. ANT.—fact, skepticism, misgiving, knowledge.

opinionated, SYN.—arrogant, authoritarian, dictatorial, doctrinaire, dogmatic, domineering, magisterial, overbearing, positive. ANT.—fluctuating, indecisive, open-minded, questioning, skeptical.

opponent, SYN.—adversary, antagonist, competitor, contestant, enemy, foe, rival. ANT.—ally, comrade, confederate, team.

opportunity, SYN.—chance, contingency, occasion, opening, possibility. ANT.—disadvantage, hindrance, obstacle.

oppose, SYN.—bar, combat, confront, contradict, counteract, defy, hinder, obstruct, resist, thwart, withstand. ANT.—agree, cooperate, submit, succumb, support.

opposed, SYN.—adverse, antagonistic, contrary, hostile, opposite; counteractive, disastrous, unfavorable, unlucky.

ANT.—benign, favorable, fortunate, lucky, propitious.

opposition, SYN.—battle, collision, combat, conflict, encounter, fight, struggle; contention, controversy, discord, inconsistency, interference, variance. ANT.—amity, concord, consonance, harmony.

oppress, SYN.—afflict, annoy, badger, harass, harry, hound, persecute, pester, plague, torment, torture, vex, worry. ANT.—aid, assist, comfort, encourage, support.

optimism, SYN.—confidence, faith, hope, trust. ANT.—despair, despondency, pessimism.

option, SYN.—alternative, choice, election, preference, selection.

opulence, SYN.—abundance, affluence, fortune, luxury, money, plenty, possessions, riches, wealth. ANT.—indigence, need, poverty, want.

oral, SYN.—spoken, verbal, vocal. ANT.—documentary, recorded, written.

ordain, SYN.—appoint, create, constitute. ANT.—disband, terminate.

ordeal, SYN.—examination, proof, test; affliction, hardship, misery, misfortune, suffering, trial, tribulation, trouble. ANT.—alleviation, consolation.

order, SYN.—arrangement,

class, method, plan, rank, regularity, sequence, series, succession, system; bidding, command, decree, dictate, injuction, instruction, mandate, requirement. ANT.—confusion, disarray, disorder, irregularity; consent, license, permission.

order, SYN.—conduct, direct, govern, guide, manage, regulate, rule; bid, command, instruct. ANT.—deceive, distract, misdirect, misguide.

ordinary, SYN.—accustomed, common, conventional, customary, familiar, habitual, normal, plain, regular, typical, usual, vulgar. ANT.—extraordinary, marvelous, remarkable, strange, uncommon.

organization, SYN.—arrangement, method, mode, order, plan, process, regularity, rule, scheme, system. ANT.—chance, chaos, confusion, disarrangement, disorder, irregularity.

organize, SYN.—adjust, arrange, assort, classify, dispose, regulate; devise, plan, prepare. ANT.—confuse, disorder, disturb, jumble, scatter.

origin, SYN.—beginning, birth, commencement, cradle, derivation, foundation, inception, source, spring, start. ANT.—end, harvest, issue, outcome, product.

original, SYN.—first, initial; primary, primeval, primordial, pristine; creative, fresh, inventive, new, novel. ANT.—derivative, later, modern, subsequent, terminal; banal, plagiarized, trite.

originate, SYN.—cause, create, engender, fashion, form, formulate, generate, invent, make, produce. ANT.—annihilate, demolish, destroy; disband, terminate.

ornament, SYN.—adornment, decoration, embellishment, garnish, ornamentation.

oscillate, SYN.—change, fluctuate, hesitate, undulate, vacillate, vary, waver. ANT.—adhere, decide, persist, resolve, stick.

ostentation, SYN.—boasting, display, flourish, pageantry, parade, pomp, show, vaunting. ANT.—humility, modesty, reserve, unobtrusiveness.

ostracize, SYN.—bar, blackball, except, exclude, expel, hinder, omit, prevent, prohibit, restrain, shut out. ANT.—accept, admit, include, welcome.

oust, SYN.—banish, deport, dismiss, dispel, eject, exclude, exile, expatriate, expel, ostracize. ANT.—accept, admit, harbor, receive, shelter.

outcome, SYN.—consequence, doom, fate, fortune, lot, portion; destiny, issue, necessity, result.

outline, SYN.—brief, contour, delineation, draft, figure, form, plan, profile, silhouette, sketch.

outrage, SYN.—affront, atrocity, indignity, insult, offense; aggression, crime, injustice, misdeed, sin, transgression, trespass, vice, wrong. ANT.—gentleness, innocence, morality, right.

outset, SYN.—beginning, commencement, inception, opening, origin, source, start. ANT.—close, completion, consummation, end, termination.

outsider, SYN.—alien, foreigner, immigrant, newcomer, stranger. ANT.—acquaintance, associate, countryman, friend, neighbor.

outspoken, SYN.—bluff, blunt, brusque, impolite, plain, rough, rude, unceremonious. ANT.—polished, polite, suave, subtle, tactful.

overcast, SYN.—cloudy, dark, dim, indistinct, murky, shadowy. ANT.—bright, clear, distinct, limpid, sunny.

overcome, SYN.—beat, conquer, crush, defeat, humble, master, quell, rout, subdue, subjugate, surmount, vanquish. ANT.—capitulate, cede, lose, retreat, surrender.

overdue, SYN.—delayed, late, slow, tardy; advanced, new, recent. ANT.—early, timely.

overflowing, SYN.—abundant, ample, bountiful, copious, plenteous, plentiful, profuse, teeming. ANT.—deficient, insufficient, scant, scarce.

overload, SYN.—afflict, burden, encumber, load, oppress, tax, trouble, weigh. ANT.—alleviate, console, ease, lighten, mitigate.

overlook, SYN.—disregard, drop, eliminate, exclude, ignore, miss, neglect, omit, skip. ANT.—enter, include, insert, introduce, notice.

overseer, SYN.—chief, commander, employer, head, leader, lord, manager, master, ruler, teacher. ANT.—servant, slave.

oversight, SYN.—error, inadvertence, inattention, mistake, neglect, omission; charge, control, inspection, management, superintendence, supervision, surveilance. ANT.—attention, care, observation, scrutiny.

overt, SYN.—candid, frank, honest, open, plain.

overturn, SYN.—demolish, destroy, overcome, overthrow, rout, ruin, supplant, upset, vanquish. ANT.—build, conserve, construct, preserve, uphold.

overthrow, SYN.—demolish, destroy, overcome, overturn, rout, ruin, supplant, upset, vanquish. ANT.—build, conserve, construct, preserve, up-hold.

P

pacific, SYN.—calm, composed, dispassionate, imperturbable, peaceful, placid, quiet, serene, still, tranquil, undisturbed, unruffled. ANT.—excited, frantic, stormy, turbulent, wild.

pacify, SYN.—allay, alleviate, appease, assuage, calm, compose, lull, placate, quell, quiet, relieve, satisfy, soothe, still, tranquilize. ANT.—arouse, excite, incense, inflame.

packed, SYN.—crammed, filled, full, gorged, replete, satiated, soaked; ample, complete, copious, entire, extensive, perfect, plentiful, sufficient. ANT.—depleted, devoid, empty, vacant; insufficient, lacking, partial.

pact, SYN.—agreement, bargain, compact, contract, covenant, stipulation. ANT.—difference, disagreement, discord, dissension, variance.

pain, SYN.—ache, pang, paroxysm, throe, twinge; agony, anguish, distress, grief, suffering. ANT.—comfort, ease, relief; happiness, pleasure, solace.

painful, SYN.—bitter, galling, grievous, poignant. ANT.—pleasant, sweet.

painting, SYN.—drawing, illustration, image, likeness, panorama, picture, portrait, portrayal, print, representation, scene, sketch, view.

palpable, SYN.—apparent, clear, distinct, evident, manifest, obvious, patent, plain, self-evident, unmistakable. ANT.—abstruse, concealed, hidden, obscure.

palpable, SYN.—bodily, corporeal, material, physical, sensible, tangible. ANT.—mental, metaphysical, spiritual.

paltry, SYN.—abject, contemptible, despicable, low, mean, miserable, worthless. ANT.—noble, significant.

panic, SYN.—alarm, apprehension, dread, fear, fright, horror, terror, trembling. ANT.—calmness, composure, serenity, tranquility.

parable, SYN.— allegory, chronicle, fable, fiction, legend, myth, saga. ANT.—fact, history.

parade, SYN.—cavalcade, cortege, file, procession, retinue, sequence, succession, train.

paradoxical, SYN.—contradictory, contrary, discrepant, illogical, incompatible, incongruous, inconsistent, irreconcilable, unsteady, vacillating, wavering. ANT.—compatible, congruous, consistent, correspondent.

parallel, SYN.—akin, alike, allied, analogous, comparable, correlative, correspondent, corresponding, like, similar. ANT.—different, incongruous, opposed.

parched, SYN.—arid, dehydrated, desiccated, drained, dry, thirsty. ANT.—damp, moist.

pardon, SYN.—absolution, acquittal, amnesty, forgiveness, remission. ANT.—conviction, penalty, punishment, sentence.

pardon, SYN.—absolve, acquit, condone, excuse, forgive, overlook, release, remit. ANT.—accuse, chastise, condemn, convict, punish.

parley, SYN.—chat, colloquy, conference, conversation, dialogue, interview, talk.

paroxism, SYN.—ache, pain, pang, throe, twinge. ANT.—comfort, ease, relief.

parsimonious, SYN.—acquisitive, avaricious, greedy, miserly, niggardly, penurious, stingy, tight. ANT.—altruistic, bountiful, extravagant, generous, munificent.

part, SYN.—allotment, apportionment, division, fragment, moiety, piece, portion, scrap, section, segment, share; component, element, ingredient, member, organ; concern, faction, interest, party, side; character, lines, role. ANT.—entirety, whole.

part, SYN.—divide, separate, sever, sunder. ANT.—combine, convene, gather, join, unite.

partake, SYN.—allot, apportion, appropriate, assign, dispense, distribute, divide, parcel, partition, portion, share. ANT.—aggregate, amass, combine, condense.

partiality, SYN.—bias, bigotry, preconception, predisposition, prejudice. ANT.—fairness, impartiality, proof, reason.

participation, SYN.—association, communion, fellowship, intercourse, sacrament, union. ANT.—alienation, nonparticipation.

particle, SYN.—atom, bit, corpuscle, crumb, grain, iota, jot, mite, scrap, shred, smidgen, speck. ANT.—aggregate, bulk, mass, quantity.

particular, SYN.—characteristic, distinctive, individual, peculiar, specific; singular, unusual; circumstantial, detailed, exact, minute, specific; careful, fastidious, squeamish. ANT.—comprehensive, general, universal; ordinary; general, rough; undiscriminating.

particular, SYN.—circumstance, detail, item, minutia, part. ANT.—generality.

partisan, SYN.—adherent, attendant, devotee, disciple, follower, henchman, successor, supporter, votary. ANT.—chief, head, leader, master.

partner, SYN.—associate, attendant, colleague, companion, comrade, consort, crony, friend, mate. ANT.—adversary, enemy, stranger.

pass by, SYN.—avert, avoid, dodge, escape, eschew, elude, forbear, forestall, free, shun, ward. ANT.—confront, encounter, meet, oppose.

passable, SYN.—average, fair, mediocre. ANT.—excellent, first-rate, worst.

passion, SYN.—affection, agitation, emotion, feeling, perturbation, sentiment, trepidation, turmoil. ANT.—calm, dispassion, indifference, restraint, tranquility.

passionate, SYN.—ardent, burning, excitable, fervent, fervid, fiery, glowing, hot, impetuous, irascible, vehement. ANT.—apathetic, calm, cool, deliberate, quiet.

passive, SYN.—idle, inactive, inert, quiet, relaxed; enduring, patient, stoical, submissive. ANT.—active, aggressive, dynamic.

pastime, SYN.—amusement, contest, diversion, fun, game, match, merriment, play, recreation, sport. ANT.—business, cold; apathy, quiescence.

patch, SYN.—fix, mend, refit, repair, restore, sew; ameliorate, better, correct, improve, rectify, reform, remedy. ANT.—deface, destroy, hurt, injure, rend.

patent, SYN.—apparent, clear, conspicuous, evident, indubitable, manifest, obvious, open, overt, unmistakable. ANT.—concealed, covert, hidden, obscure.

path, SYN.—avenue, channel, course, passage, road, route, street, thoroughfare, track, trail, walk, way.

pathetic, SYN.—affecting, moving, piteous, pitiable, poignant, sad, touching. ANT.—comical, funny, ludicrous.

patience, SYN.—composure, endurance, forbearance, fortitude, long-suffering, perseverance, resignation. ANT.—impatience, nervousness, restlessness, unquiet.

patient, SYN.—assiduous, composed, forbearing, indulgent, long-suffering, passive, resigned, stoical, uncomplaining. ANT.—chafing, clamorous, high-strung, hysterical, turbulent.

paunchy, SYN.—chubby, corpulent, fat, obese, plump, portly, pudgy, rotund, stocky, stout, thickset. ANT.—gaunt, lean, slender, slim, thin.

pause, SYN.—delay, demur, doubt, falter, hesitate, scruple, vacillate, waver. ANT.—continue, decide, persevere, proceed, resolve.

pay, SYN.—allowance,

compensation, earnings, fee, payment, recompense, salary, stipend, wages. ANT.—gift, gratuity, present.

peace, SYN.—calm, calmness, hush, quiescence, quiet, quietude, repose, rest, serenity, silence, stillness, tranquility. ANT.—agitation, disturbance, excitement, noise, tumult.

peaceful, SYN.—calm, gentle, mild, pacific, placid, quiet, serene, still, tranquil, undisturbed. ANT.—agitated, disturbed, noisy, turbulent, violent.

peak, SYN.—acme, apex, climax, consummation, culmination, height, summit, zenith. ANT.—anticlimax, base, depth, floor.

peculiar, SYN.—eccentric, exceptional, extraordinary, odd, rare, singular, strange, striking, unusual; characteristic, distinctive, individual, particular, special. ANT.—common, general, normal, ordinary.

peculiarity, SYN.—attribute, characteristic, feature, mark, property, quality, trait.

pedantic, SYN.—academic, bookish, erudite, formal, learned, scholarly, scholastic, theoretical. ANT.— common-sense, ignorant, practical, simple.

peevish, SYN.—fractious, fretful, ill-natured, ill-tempered, irritable, petulant, snappish, testy, touchy, waspish. ANT.—affable, genial, good-natured, good-tempered, pleasant.

penalty, ANT.—chastisement, fine, forfeiture, punishment, retribution; disadvantage, handicap. ANT.— compensation, pardon, remuneration, reward.

penchant, SYN.—bias, bent, disposition, inclination, leaning. partiality, predilection, predisposition, proclivity, propensity, slant, tendency, turn. ANT.—equity, fairness, impartiality, justice.

penetrating, SYN.—abstruse, deep, profound, recondite, solemn. ANT.—shallow, slight, superficial, trivial.

penitent, SYN.—contrite, regretful, remorseful, repentant, sorrowful, sorry. ANT.—objurate, remorseless.

penniless, SYN.—destitute, impecunious, indigent, needy, poor, poverty-stricken. ANT.—affluent, opulent, rich, wealthy.

pensive, SYN.—comtemplative, dreamy, introspective, meditative, reflective, thoughtful. ANT.—heedless, inconsiderate, precipitous, rash, thoughtless.

penurious, SYN.—acquisitive, avaricious, greedy, miserly, niggardly, parsimonious, stingy, tight. ANT.—altruistic, bountiful, extravagant, generous, munificent.

penury, SYN.—destitution, indigence, necessity, need, poverty, privation, want. ANT.—abundance, affluence, plenty, riches, wealth.

perceive, SYN.—conceive, discern, note, notice, observe, recognize, see; apprehend, comprehend, understand. ANT.—ignore, miss, overlook.

perceptible, SYN.—appreciable, apprehensible, sensible. ANT.—absurd, impalpable, imperceptible.

perception, SYN.—apprehension, cognizance, comprehension, conception, discernment, insight, understanding. ANT.—ignorance, insensibility, misapprehension, misconception.

perceptive, SYN.—apprised, aware, cognizant, conscious, informed, mindful, observant, sensible. ANT.—ignorant, insensible, oblivious, unaware.

perfect, SYN.—complete, entire, finished, full, utter, whole; blameless faultless, holy, immaculate, pure, sinless; complete, consummate, excellent, ideal, superlative, supreme; absolute, downright, unqualified, utter. ANT.—deficient, incomplete, lacking; blemished, defective, faulty, imperfect.

perform, SYN.—act, imper-

sonate, play, pretend.

performance, SYN.—demonstration, flourish, ostentation, parade, spectacle, entertainment, movie, production, show.

perfunctory, SYN.—affected, ceremonious, correct, decorous, exact, methodical, precise, proper, regular, solemn, stiff; external, formal, outward. ANT.—easy, natural, unconstrained, unconventional; heartfelt.

peril, SYN.—danger, hazard, jeopardy, risk. ANT.—defense, immunity, protection, safety.

perilous, SYN.—critical, dangerous, hazardous, insecure, menacing, precarious, risky, threatening, unsafe. ANT.—firm, protected, safe, secure.

period, SYN.—age, date, duration, epoch, era, interim, season, span, spell, tempo, term, time.

periodical, SYN.—customary, methodical, orderly, regular, steady, systematic, uniform, unvaried. ANT.—abnormal, erratic, exceptional, rare, unusual.

perish, SYN.—cease, decay, decease, decline, depart, die, expire, fade, languish, sink, wane, wither. ANT.—begin, flourish, grow, live, survive.

permanent, SYN.—abiding, changeless, constant, durable, enduring, fixed, indestructible, lasting, stable, unchangeable. ANT.—ephemeral, temporary, transient, transitory, unstable.

permeate, SYN.—diffuse, fill, infiltrate, penetrate, pervade, run through, saturate.

permissible, SYN.—admissible, allowable, fair, justifiable, probable, tolerable, warranted. ANT.—inadmissible, irrelevant, unsuitable.

permission, SYN.—authority, authorization, consent, leave, liberty, license, permit. ANT.—denial, opposition, prohibition, refusal.

permit, SYN.—allow, let, sanction, suffer, tolerate; authorize, give, grant, yield. ANT.—forbid, object, protest, refuse, resist.

perpetrate, SYN.—do, commit, perform. ANT.—fail, miscarry, neglect.

perpetual, SYN.—ceaseless, deathless, endless, eternal, everlasting, immortal, infinite, timeless, undying. ANT.—ephemeral, finite, mortal, temporal, transient.

perpetually, SYN.—always, constantly, continually, eternally, ever, evermore, forever, incessantly, unceasingly. ANT.—fitfully, never, occasionally, rarely, sometimes.

perplex, SYN.—bewilder, confound, confuse, dumfound, mystify, nonplus,

puzzle. ANT.—clarify, explain, illumine, instruct, solve.

perplexed, SYN.—bewildered, confused, deranged, disconcerted, disordered, disorganized, indistinct, mixed, muddled. ANT.—clear, lucid, obvious, organized, plain.

perplexing, SYN.—complex, complicated, compound, intricate, involved. ANT.—plain, simple, uncompounded.

persecute, SYN.—afflict, annoy, badger, harass, harry, hound, oppress, pester, plague, torment, torture, vex, worry. ANT.—aid, assist, comfort, encourage, support.

persevere, SYN.—abide, continue, endure, last, persist, remain. ANT.—cease, desist, discontinue, vacillate, waver.

perseverance, SYN.—constancy, industry, persistence, persistency; pertinacity, steadfastness, tenacity. ANT.—cessation, idleness, laziness, rest, sloth.

persist, SYN.—abide, continue, endure, last, persevere, remain. ANT.—cease, desist, discontinue, vacillate, waver.

persistence, SYN.—constancy, industry, perseverance, persistency, pertinacity, steadfastness, tenacity. ANT.—cessation, idleness, laziness, rest, sloth.

persistent, SYN.—constant,

enduring, fixed, immovable, indefatigable, lasting, persevering, steady; dogged, obstinate, perverse, stubborn. ANT.—hesitant, unsure, vacillating, wavering.

perspicacity, SYN.—discernment, discrimination, intelligence, judgment, sagacity, understanding, wisdom. ANT.— arbitrariness, senselessness, stupidity, thoughtlessness.

persuade, SYN.—allure, coax, convince, entice, exhort, incite, induce, influence, prevail upon, urge, win over. ANT.— coerce, compel, deter, dissuade, restrain.

persuasion, SYN.—belief, conviction, decision, feeling, idea, impression, judgment, notion, opinion, sentiment, view. ANT.—fact, skepticism, misgiving, knowledge.

pertain, SYN.—apply, refer, relate.

pertinacious, SYN.—contumacious, determined, dogged, firm, headstrong, immovable, inflexible, intractable, obdurate, obstinate, stubborn, uncompromising, unyielding. ANT.—amenable, compliant, docile, submissive, yielding.

pertinent, SYN.—applicable, apposite, appropriate, apropos, apt, fit, germane, material, related, relating, relevant, to the point. ANT.—alien, extraneous, foreign, unrelated.

pervade, SYN.—diffuse, fill, infiltrate, penetrate, permeate, run through, saturate.

perverse, SYN.—contrary, disobedient, fractious, peevish, petulant; forward, intractable, obstinate, stubborn, ungovernable, untoward; perverted, sinful, wicked. ANT.—aggreeable, obliging; docile, tractable.

perversion, SYN.—abuse, desecration, maltreatment, misuse, outrage, profanation, reviling. ANT.—respect.

pervert, SYN.—abase, corrupt, defile, debase, degrade, deprave, humiliate, impair, lower vitiate. ANT.—enhance, improve, raise.

perverted, SYN.—perverse, sinful, wicked.

pester, SYN.—annoy, bother, chafe, disturb, inconvenience, irk, irritate, molest, tease, trouble, vex. ANT.—accommodate, console, gratify, soothe.

petition, SYN.—appeal, entreaty, invocation, plea, prayer, request, suit, supplication.

petty, SYN.—frivolous, insignificant, paltry, small, trifling, trivial, unimportant. ANT.—important, momentous, serious, weighty.

petulant, SYN.—fracious, fretful, ill-natured, ill-tempered, irritable, peevish, snappish,

testy, touchy, waspish.
ANT.—affable, genial,
good-natured, good-
tempered, pleasant.

philanthropy, SYN.—altruism, beneficence, benev-
olence, charity, generos-
ity, humanity, kindness,
liberality, magnanimity,
tenderness. ANT.—cruel-
ty, inhumanity, malevo-
lence, selfishness, un-
kindness.

phlegmatic, SYN.—cold,
passionless, stoical, un-
feeling. ANT.—ardent,
passionate.

phony, SYN.—affected,
assumed, artificial, bo-
gus, counterfeit, ersatz,
fake, feigned, fictitious,
sham, spurious, synthet-
ic, unreal. ANT.—gen-
uine, natural, real, true.

phrase, SYN.—expression,
name, term, word.

physical, SYN.—bodily,
carnal, corporal, corpo-
real, somatic; material,
natural. ANT.—mental,
spiritual.

pick, SYN.—choose, cull,
elect, opt, select.
ANT.—refuse, reject.

picture, SYN.—appearance,
cinema, drawing, effigy,
engraving, etching, film,
illustration, image, likeness, painting, pano-
rama, photograph, por-
trait, portrayal, print,
representation, resem-
blance, scene, sketch,
view.

piece, SYN.—amount, bit,
fraction, fragment, mor-
sel, part, portion, scrap.
ANT.—all, entirety, sum,
total, whole.

pigment, SYN.—color,
complexion, dye, hue,
paint, shade, stain, tincture, tinge, tint. ANT.—
achromatism, paleness,
transparency.

pinnacle, SYN.—apex,
chief, crest, crown, head,
summit, top, zenith.
ANT.—base, bottom,
foot, foundation.

pious, SYN.—blessed, consecrated, devout, divine,
hallowed, holy, religious,
sacred, saintly, spiritual.
ANT.—evil, profane, sac-
rilegious, secular, worldly.

pitch, SYN.—cast, fling,
hurl, propel, throw,
thrust, toss. ANT.—draw,
haul, hold, pull, retain.

piteous, SYN.—affecting,
moving, pathetic, pitia-
ble, poignant, sad, touching. ANT.—comical, fun-
ny, ludicrous.

pitfall, SYN.—ambush, artifice, bait, intrigue, lure,
net, ruse, snare, strata-
gem, trap, trick, wile.

pitiable, SYN.—affecting,
moving, piteous, poign-
ant, sad, touching.
ANT.—comical, funny,
ludicrous.

pity, SYN.—commisera-
tion, compassion, condo-
lence, mercy, sympathy.
ANT.—brutality, cruelty,
hardness, inhumanity,
ruthlessness.

place, SYN.—arrange, deposit, dispose, lay, put,
set. ANT.—disarrange,
disturb, mislay, mis-
place, remove.

placid, SYN.—calm, composed, dispassionate, imperturbable, pacific, peaceful, quiet, serene, still, tranquil, undisturbed, unruffled. ANT.—excited, frantic, stormy, turbulent, wild.

plagiarize, SYN.—adduce, cite, extract, paraphrase, quote, recite, repeat. ANT.—contradict, misquote, refute, retort.

plague, SYN.—afflict, annoy, badger, harass, harry, hound, oppress, persecute, pester, torment, torture, vex, worry. ANT.—aid, assist, comfort, encourage, support.

plain, SYN.—even, flat, level, smooth; apparent, clear, distinct, evident, manifest, obvious, palpable, visible; candid, frank, open, simple, sincere, unpretentious; absolute, unqualified. ANT.—abrupt, broken, rough, undulatory, uneven; abstruse, ambiguous, enigmatical, obscure; adorned, embellished, feigned, insincere.

plan, SYN.—contrive, create, design, devise, invent, scheme; intend, mean, purpose; draw, sketch.

plausible, SYN.—credible, feasible, likely, possible, practicable, practical, probable. ANT.—impossible, impracticable, visionary.

play, SYN.—amusement, diversion, entertainment, fun, game, pastime, recreation, sport. ANT.—boredom, labor, toil, work.

play, SYN.—caper, frolic, gamble, gambol, revel, romp, sport, stake, toy, wager; execute, perform; act, impersonate, pretend.

plea, SYN.—appeal, entreaty, invocation, petition, prayer, request, suit, supplication.

plead, SYN.—appeal, ask, beg, beseech, entreat, implore, petition, supplicate; argue, defend, discuss, rejoin. ANT.—deny, deprecate, refuse.

pleasant, SYN.—acceptable, agreeable, amiable, charming, gratifying, pleasing, pleasurable, suitable, welcome. ANT.—disagreeable, obnoxious, offensive, unpleasant.

please, SYN.—appease, compensate, content, fulfill, gratify, remunerate, satiate, satisfy, suffice. ANT.—annoy, displease, dissatisfy, frustrate, tantalize.

pleasing, SYN.—agreeable, delightful, engaging, gentle, honeyed, luscious, mellifluous, melodious, saccharine, sugary, winning. ANT.—acrid, bitter, offensive, repulsive, sour.

pleasure, SYN.—amusement, comfort, delight, enjoyment, felicity, gladness, gratification, happiness, joy. ANT.—affliction, pain, suffering, trouble, vexation.

pledge, SYN.—assurance, promise, word; assertion, declaration, statement.

pledge, SYN.—bind, commit, obligate. ANT.—neglect; mistrust, release, renounce.

plentiful, SYN.—abundant, ample, bounteous, bountiful, copious, luxurious, plenteous, profuse, replete. ANT.—deficient, insufficient, rare, scanty, scarce.

pliable, SYN.—compliant, ductile, elastic, flexible, pliant, resilient, supple, tractable. ANT.—brittle, hard, rigid, stiff, unbending.

plight, SYN.—condition, difficulty, dilemma, fix, predicament, scrape, situation, strait. ANT.—calmness, comfort, ease, satisfaction.

plot, SYN.—cabal, conspiracy, design, intrigue, machination, plan, scheme, stratagem; chart, diagram, graph, sketch.

plotting, SYN.—artfulness, contrivance, cunning, design, scheming; intent, intention, objective, purpose. ANT.—result; candor, sincerity; accident, chance.

ploy, SYN.—antic, artifice, cheat, deception, device, fraud, guile, hoax, imposture, ruse, stratagem, stunt, subterfuge, trick, wile. ANT.—candor, ex-

posure, honesty, openness, sincerity.

plump, SYN.—chubby, corpulent, fat, obese, paunchy, portly, pudgy, rotund, stocky, stout, thickset. ANT.—gaunt, lean, slender, slim, thin.

pogrom, SYN.—butchery, carnage, massacre, slaughter.

poignant, SYN.—affecting, heart-rending, impressive, moving, pitiable, sad, tender, touching.

point, SYN.—aim, direct, level, train. ANT.—deceive, distract, misdirect, misguide.

pointed, SYN.—acute, cutting, keen; sharp; penetrating, piercing, severe; astute, clever, cunning, quick, shrewd, wily, witty. ANT.—bland, blunt, gentle, shallow, stupid.

poise, SYN.—balance, calmness, carriage, composure, equanimity, equilibrium, self-possession. ANT.—agitation, anger, excitement, rage, turbulence.

poise, SYN.—adjourn, defer, delay, discontinue, interrupt, postpone, stay; balance, dangle, hang, suspend, swing. ANT.—continue, maintain, persist, proceed, prolong.

poison, SYN.—befoul, contaminate, corrupt, defile, infect, pollute, sully, taint. ANT.—disinfect, purify.

polished, SYN.—refined, sleek, slick; glib, diplo-

matic, suave, urbane.
ANT.—bluff, blunt,
harsh, rough, rugged.

polite, SYN.—accomplished, civil, considerate, courteous, cultivated, genteel, refined, urbane, well-bred, well-mannered. ANT.—boorish, impertinent, rude, uncivil, uncouth.

pollute, SYN.—befoul, contaminate, corrupt, defile, infect, poison, sully, taint. ANT.—disinfect, purify.

pomp, SYN.—boasting, display, flourish, ostentation, pageantry, parade, show, vaunting. ANT.—humility, modesty, reserve, unobstrusiveness.

pompous, SYN.—august, dignified, grand, grandiose, high, imposing, lofty, magnificent, majestic, noble, stately, sublime. ANT.—common, humble, lowly, ordinary, undignified.

ponder, SYN.—contemplate, examine, investigate, scrutinize, study, weigh; cogitate, meditate, muse, reflect.

ponderous, SYN.—heavy, massive, weighty; burdensome, cumbersome, grievous, trying; gloomy, grave, serious; dull, sluggish. ANT.—animated, brisk, light.

poor, SYN.—destitute, impecunious, indigent, needy, penniless, poverty-stricken; bad, deficient, inferior,

scanty, shabby, unfavorable, wrong. ANT.—affluent, opulent, rich, wealthy; ample, good, right, sufficient.

popular, SYN.—common, familiar, favorite, general, prevailing, prevalent. ANT.—esoteric, exclusive, restricted, unpopular.

pornographic, SYN.—coarse, dirty, disgusting, filthy, gross, impure, indecent, lewd, obscene, offensive, smutty. ANT.—decent, modest, pure, refined.

portal, SYN.—doorway, entrance, entry, inlet, opening. ANT.—departure, exit.

portion, SYN.—bit, division, fragment, parcel, part, piece, section, segment, share. ANT.—bulk, whole.

portray, SYN.—delineate, depict, describe, draw, paint, picture, represent, sketch. ANT.—caricature, misrepresent, suggest.

position, SYN.—locality, place, site, situation, station; caste, condition, place, rank, standing, status; berth, incumbency, job, office, post, situation; attitude, bearing, pose, posture.

positive, SYN.—assured, certain, definite, fixed, indubitable, inevitable, secure, sure, undeniable, unquestionable. ANT.—doubtful, probably, questionable, uncertain.

possess, SYN.—control, have, hold, occupy, own, affect, obtain, seize. ANT.—abandon, lose, renounce, surrender.

possessions, SYN.—belongings, commodities, effects, estate, goods, merchandise, property, stock, wares, wealth.

possible, SYN.—credible, feasible, likely, plausible, practicable, practical, probable. ANT.—impossible, impracticable, visionary.

possibility, SYN.—chance, contingency, occasion, opening, opportunity. ANT.— disadvantage, hindrance, obstacle.

post, SYN.—berth, incumbency, job, office, position, situation.

postpone, SYN.—adjourn, defer, delay, discontinue, interrupt, stay, suspend. ANT.—continue, maintain, persist, proceed, prolong.

postulate, SYN.—adage, aphorism, apothegm, axiom, byword, fundamental, maxim, principle, proverb, saw, saying, theorem, truism.

potency, SYN.—ability, capability, competency, effectiveness, efficacy, efficiency, skillfullness. ANT.—inability, ineptitude, wastefulness.

pound, SYN.—beat, belabor, buffet, dash, hit, knock, pummel, punch, smite, strike, thrash, thump; conquer, defeat, overpower, overthrow, rout, subdue, vanquish; palpitate, pulsate, pulse, throb. ANT.—defend, shield, stroke; fail, surrender.

poverty, SYN.—destitution, indigence, necessity, need, penury, privation, want. ANT.—abundance, affluence, plenty, riches, wealth.

power, SYN.—ability, capability, competency, faculty, potency, talent, validity; cogency, energy, force, might, strength, vigor; authority, command, control, dominion, influence, predominance, sovereignty, sway. ANT.—disablement, impotence, incapacity, ineptitude; debility, fatigue, weakness.

powerful, SYN.—athletic, cogent, concentrated, enduring, firm, forceful, forcible, fortified, hale, hardy, impregnable, mighty, potent, robust, sinewy, strong, sturdy, tough. ANT.—brittle, delicate, feeble, fragile, insipid.

practical, SYN.—prudent, reasonable, sagacious, sage, sensible, sober, sound, wise. ANT.—absurd, impalpable, imperceptible, stupid, unaware.

practice, SYN.—custom, drill, exercise, habit, manner, training, usage, use, wont. ANT.—disuse, idleness, inexperience, speculation, theory.

praise, SYN.—acclaim, applaud, commend, compliment, eulogize, extol, flatter, glorify, laud. ANT.—censure, condemn, criticize, disparage, reprove.

prayer, SYN.—appeal, entreaty, invocation, petition, plea, request, suit, supplication.

preamble, SYN.—beginning, foreword, introduction, overture, preface, prelude, prologue, start. ANT.—completion, conclusion, end, epilogue, finale.

precarious, SYN.—critical, dangerous, hazardous, insecure, menacing, perilous, risky, threatening, unsafe. ANT.—firm, protected, safe, secure.

precept, SYN.—belief, creed, doctrine, dogma, teaching, tenet. ANT.—conduct, deed, performance, practice.

precious, SYN.—costly, expensive, dear, esteemed; profitable, useful, valuable. ANT.—cheap, mean, poor; trashy, worthless.

precipitous, SYN.—abrupt, hasty, precipitate, sudden, unannounced, unexpected, craggy, harsh, rough, rugged, sharp, steep. ANT.—anticipated, expected, gradual, smooth.

precise, SYN.—accurate, correct, definite, distinct, exact, strict, unequivocal; ceremonious, formal, prim, rigid, stiff. ANT.—erroneous, loose, rough, vague; careless, easy, informal.

preclude, SYN.—forstall, hinder, impede, obstruct, obviate, prevent, thwart. ANT.—aid, encourage, expedite, permit, promote.

preclusion, SYN.—exception, exclusion, omission. ANT.—inclusion, rule, standard.

predicament, SYN.—condition, difficulty, dilemma, fix, plight, scrape, situation, strait. ANT.—calmness, comfort, ease, satisfaction.

predilection, SYN.—affection, attachment, bent, bias, desire, disposition, inclination, penchant, preference. ANT.—apathy, aversion, distaste, nonchalance, repugnance.

predominant, SYN.—cardinal, chief, essential, first, foremost, highest, leading, main, paramount, principal, supreme. ANT.—auxiliary, minor, subordinate, subsidiary, supplemental.

preference, SYN.—alternative, choice, election, option, selection.

prejudiced, SYN.—bigoted, dogmatic, fanatical, illiberal, intolerant, narrow-minded. ANT.—liberal, progressive, radical, tolerant.

premeditated, SYN.—contemplated, deliberate, designed, intended, intentional, studied, voluntary, wilful. ANT.—accidental, fortuitous.

premeditation, SYN.—deliberation, forecast, forethought, intention. ANT.—accident, extemporization, hazard, impromptu.

premise, SYN.—assumption, basis, postulate, presumption, presupposition, principle. ANT.—derivative, implication, superstructure, trimming.

preoccupied, SYN.—absent, absent-minded, abstracted, distracted, inattentive. ANT.—attending, present; attentive, watchful.

prepare, SYN.—concoct, condition, contrive, equip, fit, furnish, get ready, make ready, predispose, provide, qualify, ready.

preposterous, SYN.—absurd, foolish, inconsistent, irrational, nonsensical, ridiculous, self-contradictory, silly, unreasonable. ANT.—consistent, rational, reasonable, sensible, sound.

prerogative, SYN.— authority, grant, liberty, license, privilege, right. ANT.— encroachment, injustice, violation, wrong.

present, SYN.—boon, donation, gift, grant, gratuity, largess; now, today.

present, SYN.—advance, exhibit, extend, offer, proffer, propose, sacrifice, tender. ANT.—accept, receive, reject, retain, spurn.

preserve, SYN.—conserve, defend, guard, keep, maintain, protect, rescue, safeguard, save, secure, spare, uphold. ANT.—abandon, abolish, destroy, impair, injure.

press, SYN.—crowd, drive, force, impel, jostle, propel, push, shove; hasten, promote, urge. ANT.—drag, falter, halt, pull, retreat; ignore, oppose.

pressing, SYN.—cogent, compelling, critical, crucial, exigent, impelling, imperative, important, importunate, insistent, instant, necessary, serious, urgent. ANT.—insignificant, petty, trifling, trivial, unimportant.

pressure, SYN.—compression, force; constraint, influence; compulsion, exigency, hurry, press, stress, urgency. ANT.—ease, leniency, recreation, relaxation.

presume, SYN.—apprehend, assume, believe, conjecture, deduce, guess, imagine, speculate, suppose, surmise, think. ANT.—ascertain, conclude, demonstrate, know, prove.

presumption, SYN.—assurance, audacity, boldness, effrontery, impertinence, impudence, insolence, rudeness, sauciness. ANT.—diffidence, politeness, subserviency, truckling.

presupposition, SYN.—assumption, basis, postulate, premise, presumption, principle. ANT.—derivative, implication, superstructure.

pretend, SYN.—act, affect, assume, feign, profess, sham, stimulate. ANT.—display, exhibit, expose, reveal.

pretense, SYN.—affection, cloak, disguise, excuse, garb, mask, pretension, pretext, semblance, show, simulation, subterfuge. ANT.—actuality, fact, reality, sincerity, truth.

pretty, SYN.—beauteous, beautiful, charming, comely, elegant, fair, fine, handsome, lovely. ANT.—foul, hideous, homely, repulsive, unsightly.

prevalent, SYN.—common, familiar, frequent, general, ordinary, popular, universal, usual. ANT.—exceptional, extraordinary, odd, scarce.

prevent, SYN.—forstall, hinder, impede, obstruct, obviate, preclude, thwart. ANT.—aid, encourage, expedite, permit, promote.

previous, SYN.—aforesaid, antecedent, anterior, foregoing, former, preceeding, prior. ANT.—consequent, following, later, subsequent, succeeding.

price, SYN.—charge, cost, expense, value, worth.

pride, SYN.—arrogance, conceit, haughtiness, self-esteem, self-respect, superciliousness, vainglory, vanity. ANT.—humility, lowliness, meekness, modesty, shame.

primary, SYN.—beginning, earliest, first, initial, original, prime, primeval, primitive, pristine; chief, foremost. ANT.—hindmost, last, latest; least, subordinate.

primeval, SYN.—first, initial, original, primary, primordial, pristine; creative, fresh, inventive, new, novel. ANT.—derivative, later, modern, subsequent, terminal; banal, plagiarized, trite.

primitive, SYN.—aboriginal, ancient, antiquated, early, old, primary, primeval, primordial, pristine. ANT.—civilized, late, modern, modish, sophisticated.

primordial, SYN.—first, initial, original, primary, primeval, pristine; creative, fresh, inventive, new, novel. ANT.—derivative, later, modern, subsequent, terminal; banal, plagiarized, trite.

principal, SYN.—cardinal, chief, essential, first, foremost, highest, leading, main, paramount, predominant, supreme. ANT.—auxiliary, minor, subordinate, subsidiary, supplemental.

principal, SYN.—chief, commander, director, head, leader, master. ANT.—follower, subordinate, underling.

principle, SYN.—axiom,

canon, formula, guide, law, maxim, method, order, precept, propriety, regulation, rule, statute, system. ANT.—chance, deviation, exception, hazard.

prior, SYN.—aforesaid, antecedent, anterior, foregoing, former, preceeding, previous. ANT.—consequent, following, later, subsequent, succeeding.

pristine, SYN.—first, initial, original, primary, primeval, primordial, creative, fresh, inventive, new, novel. ANT.—derivative, later, modern, subsequent, terminal; banal, plagiarized, trite.

private, SYN.—clandestine, concealed, covert, hidden, latent, secret, surreptitious, unknown. ANT.—conspicuous, disclosed, exposed, known, obvious.

privation, SYN.—destitution, indigence, necessity, need, penury, poverty, want. ANT.—abundance, affluence, plenty, riches, wealth.

privilege, SYN.—advantage, exemption, favor, immunity, liberty, license, prerogative, right, sanction. ANT.—disallowance, inhibition, prohibition, restriction.

prize, SYN.—award, bonus, bounty, compensation, premium, recompense, remuneration, requital, reward. ANT.—assessment, charge, earnings, punishment, wages.

probe, SYN.—extend, reach, stretch. ANT.—short, miss.

procedure, SYN.—fashion, form, habit, manner, method, mode, plan, practice, process, style, system, way.

proceed, SYN.—advance, improve, progress, rise, thrive. ANT.—hinder, oppose, retard, retreat, withhold.

proceeding, SYN.—affair, business, deal, deed, negotiation, occurrence, transaction.

proceeds, SYN.—crop, fruit, harvest, produce, product, reaping, result, store, yield.

procession, SYN.—cavalcade, cortege, file, parade, retinue, sequence, succession, train.

proclaim, SYN.—affirm, announce, assert, aver, broadcast, declare, express, make known, profess, promulgate, protest, state, tell. ANT.—conceal, repress, suppress, withhold.

procreate, SYN.—beget, breed, create, engender, father, generate, originate, produce, propagate, sire. ANT.—abort, destroy, extinguish, kill, murder.

procure, SYN.—acquire, attain, earn, gain, get, obtain, secure, win. ANT.—lose.

prodigious, SYN.—amazing, astonishing, astounding, enormous, huge, immense, marvelous, monstrous, monumental, remarkable, stupendous, vast. ANT.—commonplace, insignificant, small.

produce, SYN.—crop, fruit, harvest, proceeds, product, reaping, result, store, yield.

produce, SYN.—bear, breed, conceive, generate, hatch, procreate, yield; fabricate, fashion, make, manufacture, supply; bring forward, exhibit, show; accomplish, cause, effect, occasion, originate. ANT.—consume, destroy, reduce, waste; conceal, hide.

productive, SYN.—bountiful, fecund, fertile, fruitful, luxuriant, plenteous, prolific, rich, teeming. ANT.—barren, impotent, sterile, unproductive.

profanation, SYN.—abuse, aspersion, defamation, desecration, dishonor, disparagement, insult, invective, maltreatment, misuse, outrage, perversion, reproach, reviling, upbraiding. ANT.—approval, commendation, laudation, plaudit, respect.

profane, SYN.—desecrate, dishonor, pollute, debauch, deflower, ravish, violate.

profess, SYN.—affirm, announce, assert, aver, broadcast, declare, express, make known, proclaim, promulgate, protest, state, tell.

ANT.—conceal, repress, suppress, withhold.

proffer, SYN.—advance, extend, present, propose, tender, volunteer. ANT.—accept, receive, reject, retain, spurn.

proficient, SYN.—able, accomplished, adept, clever, competent, cunning, expert, ingenious, practiced, skillful, skilled, versed. ANT.—awkward, bungling, clumsy, inexpert, untrained.

profit, SYN.—advantage, avail, benefit, emolument, gain, improvement, service, use. ANT.—damage, detriment, loss, ruin, waste.

profitable, SYN.—advantageous, beneficial, good, helpful, salutary, serviceable, useful, wholesome. ANT.—deleterious, destructive, detrimental, harmful, injurious.

profligate, SYN.—contaminated, corrupt, corrupted, crooked, debased, depraved, dishonest, impure, tainted, unsound, venal, vitiated.

profound, SYN.—abstruse, deep, penetrating, recondite, solemn. ANT.—shallow, slight, superficial, trivial.

profuse, SYN.—abundant, copious, excessive, extravagant, exuberant, immoderate, improvident, lavish, luxuriant, overflowing, plentiful, prodigal, wasteful. ANT.—economical, meager, poor, skimpy, sparse.

profusion, SYN.—extravagance, immoderation, intemperance, superabundance, superfluity, surplus. ANT.—dearth, deficiency, lack, paucity, want.

progress, SYN.—advance, advancement, betterment, development, growth, improvement, progression. ANT.—decline, delay, regression, relapse, retrogression.

progress, SYN.—advance, improve, proceed, rise, thrive. ANT.—hinder, oppose, retard, retreat, withhold.

progression, SYN.—arrangement, chain, following, gradation, order, sequence, series, string, succession, train.

prohibit, SYN.—ban, debar, forbid, hinder, inhibit, interdict, prevent. ANT.—allow, permit, sanction, tolerate.

project, SYN.—contrivance, design, device, plan, scheme. ANT.—accomplishment, performance, production.

prolific, SYN.—bountiful, fecund, fertile, fruitful, luxuriant, plenteous, productive, rich, teeming. ANT.—barren, impotent, sterile, unproductive.

prolong, SYN. —draw, extend, lengthen, protract, stretch. ANT.—shorten.

prominent, SYN.—celebrated, conspicuous, distinguished, eminent, famous, illustrious, influential, noteworthy, outstanding, remarkable, renowned. ANT.—common, humble, low, ordinary, vulgar.

promise, SYN.—agreement, assurance, bestowal, contract, engagement, fulfillment, guarantee, oath, pledge, undertaking, vox.

promote, SYN.—advance, aid, assist, encourage, facilitate, forward, foster, ANT.—demote, discourage, hinder, impede, obstruct.

prompt, SYN.—exact, precise, punctual, ready, timely. ANT.—dilatory, late, slow, tardy.

prompt, SYN.—cause, effect, evoke, incite, induce, make, occasion, originate.

promptly, SYN.—directly, forthwith, immediately, instantaneously, instantly, now, presently, straightaway. ANT.—distantly, hereafter, later, shortly, sometime.

promulgate, SYN.—affirm, announce, assert, aver, broadcast, declare, express, make known, proclaim, profess, protest, state, tell. ANT.—conceal, repress, suppress, withhold.

proof, SYN.—confirmation, corroboration, demonstration, evidence, experiment, test, testimony, trial, verification. ANT.—failure, fallacy, invalidity.

propagate, SYN.—beget, breed, create, engender, father, generate, originate, procreate, produce, sire. ANT.—abort, destroy, extinguish, kill, murder.

propel, SYN.—actuate, agitate, drive, impel, induce, instigate, move, persuade, push, shift, stir, transfer. ANT.—deter, halt, rest, stay, stop.

propensity, SYN.—aim, bent, bias, drift, inclination, leaning, predisposition, proclivity, proneness, tendency, trend. ANT.—aversion, deviation, disinclination.

proper, SYN.—appropriate, befitting, correct, fit, legitimate, meet, right, seemly, suitable; conventional, correct, decent, formal, respectable; individual, peculiar, special.

property, SYN.—belongings, commodities, effects, estate, goods, merchandise, possessions, stock, wares, wealth; attribute, characteristic, peculiarity, quality, trait. ANT.—deprvation, destitution, poverty, privation, want.

propitious, SYN.—fortunate, happy, lucky, opportune.

proportion, SYN.—balance, composure, equilibrium, poise, stability, steadiness; symmetry. ANT.—fall, imbalance, instability, unsteadiness.

proposal, SYN.—offer, overture, proposition, suggestion, tender. ANT.—acceptance, denial, rejection, withdrawal.

propose, SYN.—design, intend, move, offer, present, proffer, propound, purpose, suggest. ANT.—effect, fulfill, perform.

proposition, SYN.—motion, proposal.

propound, SYN.—advance, allege, assign, bring forward, offer, propose. ANT.—hinder, oppose, retard, retreat, withhold.

proprietor, SYN.—master, owner. ANT.—servant, slave.

prosper, SYN.—achieve, flourish, gain, prevail, succeed, thrive, win. ANT.—fail, miscarry, miss.

prosperous, SYN.—affluent, luxurious, opulent, rich, sumptuous, wealthy, well-to-do. ANT.—beggarly, destitute, indigent, needy, poor.

protect, SYN.—conserve, defend, guard, keep, maintain, preserve, safeguard, save, secure. ANT.—abandon, abolish, destroy, impair, injure.

protection, SYN.—bulwark, fence, refuge, safeguard, shelter, shield; defense, guard, security.

protest, SYN.—challenge, difference, disagreement, dissent, dissentience, noncompliance, nonconformity, objection, recusancy, rejection, remonstrance, variance. ANT.—acceptance, agreement, assent, compliance.

protest, SYN.—abominate, disagree, disapprove, object, oppose, reject, remonstrate. ANT.—acquiesce, approve, assent, comply, concur.

prototype, SYN.—archetype, example, illustration, instance, model, pattern, sample, specimen. ANT.—concept, precept, principle, rule.

protract, SYN.—distend, distort, elongate, expand, extend, lengthen, spread, strain, stretch. ANT.—contract, loosen, shrink, slacken, tighten.

proud, SYN.—arrogant, disdainful, haughty, overbearing, stately, supercilious, vain, vainglorious. ANT.—ashamed, humble, lowly, meek.

prove, SYN.—confirm, corroborate, demonstrate, establish, manifest, test, try, verify. ANT.—contradict, disprove, refute.

proverb, SYN.—adage, aphorism, apothegm, byword, maxim, motto, saw, saying.

provide, SYN.—endow, equip, fit, fit out, supply; afford, give, produce, yield. ANT.—denude, despoil, divest, strip.

provident, SYN.—economical, frugal, niggardly, saving, sparing, thrifty. ANT.—extravagant, improvident, lavish, prodigal, wasteful.

provision, SYN.—accumulation, fund, hoard, reserve, stock, store, supply.

provoke, SYN.—agitate, arouse, awaken, disquiet, disturb, excite, incite, irritate, rouse, stimulate, stir up. ANT.—allay, calm, pacify, quell, quiet.

prowess, SYN.—boldness, bravery, chivalry, courage, fearlessness, fortitude, intrepidity, mettle, resolution. ANT.—cowardice, fear, pusillanimity, timidity.

proximate, SYN.—adjacent, bordering, close, near, neighboring, nigh; approaching, imminent, impending. ANT.—distant, far, removed.

proxy, SYN.—agent, alternate, deputy, lieutenant, representative, substitute, understudy; equivalent, expedient, makeshift. ANT.—head, master, principal, sovereign.

prudence, SYN.—care, caution, heed, vigilance, wariness, watchfullness. ANT.—abandon, carelessness, recklessness.

prudent, SYN.—discreet, intelligent, judicious, practical, reasonable, sagacious, sage, sensible, sober, sound, wise. ANT.—absurd, stupid, unaware.

prying, SYN.—curious, inquiring, inquisitive, interrogative, meddling, nosy, peeping, peering, searching, snoopy. ANT.—incurious, indifferent, unconcerned, uninterested.

psyche, SYN.—brain, faculties, intellect, intelligence, judgment, mentality, mind, reason, soul, spirit, understanding, wit. ANT.—body, corporeality, materiality, matter.

psychosis, SYN.—aberration, craziness, delirium, dementia, derangement, frenzy, insanity, lunacy, madness, mania. ANT.—rationality, sanity, stability.

public, SYN.—open, unrestricted.

pulchritude, SYN.—attractiveness, beauty, charm, comeliness, elegance, fairness, grace, handsomeness, loveliness. ANT.—deformity, disfigurement, eyesore, homeliness, ugliness.

pull, SYN.—drag, draw, haul, tow, tug; extract, remove, take out, unsheathe; allure, attract, entice, induce, lure, persuade; lengthen, prolong, protract, stretch. ANT.—alienate, contract, drive, propel, shorten.

pulsate, SYN.—beat, palpitate, pulse, throb.

pummel, SYN.—castigate, chastise, correct, discipline, punish, strike. ANT.—acquit, exonerate, free, pardon, release.

pump, SYN.—ask, examine, inquire, interrogate, query, question, quiz. ANT.—answer, reply, respond, state.

punctual, SYN.—exact, nice, precise, prompt, ready, timely. ANT.—dilatory, late, slow, tardy.

punish, SYN.—castigate, chastise, correct, discipline, pummel, strike. ANT.—acquit, exonerate, free, pardon, release.

punishment, SYN.—correction, discipline. ANT.—chaos, confusion, turbulence.

puny, SYN.—decrepit, delicate, enervated, exhausted, faint, feeble, forceless, impaired, infirm, languid, powerless, weak. ANT.—forceful, lusty, stout, strong, vigorous.

purchase, SYN.—acquire, buy, get, obtain, procure. ANT.—dispose of, sell, vend.

pure, SYN.—clean, clear, genuine, immaculate, spotless, unadulterated, untainted; chaste, guiltless, innocent, modest, sincere, undefiled, virgin; absolute, bare, sheer. ANT.—foul, polluted, sullied, tainted, tarnished; corrupt, defiled.

purify, SYN.—clean, cleanse, mop, scrub, sweep, wash. ANT.—dirty, pollute, soil, stain, sully.

purloin, SYN.—burglarize, embezzle, loot, pilfer, pillage, plagiarize, plunder, rob, snitch, steal, swipe. ANT.—buy, refund, repay, restore, return.

purport, SYN.—acceptation, connotation, drift, explanation, gist, implication, import, intent, interpretation, meaning, purpose, sense, significance, signification.

purpose, SYN.—aim, design, drift, end, goal, intent, intention, object, objective. ANT.—accident, fate, hazard.

pursue, SYN.—chase, follow, hunt, persist, track, trail. ANT.—abandon, elude, escape, evade, flee.

push, SYN.—crowd, drive, force, impel, jostle, press, propel, shove; hasten, promote, urge. ANT.—drag, falter, halt, pull, retreat; ignore, oppose.

pushy, SYN.—bold, brazen, forward, impudent, insolent, rude; abrupt, conspicuous, prominent, striking. ANT.—cowardly, flinching, timid; bashful, retiring.

putrefy, SYN.—decay, decompose, disintegrate, rot, spoil, waste. ANT.—flourish, grow, increase, luxuriate.

puzzle, SYN.—conundrum, enigma, mystery, problem, riddle. ANT.—answer, clue, key, resolution, solution.

puzzle, SYN.—bewilder, confound, confuse, dumfound, mystify, nonplus, perplex. ANT.—clarify, explain, illumine, instruct, solve.

Q

quaint, SYN.—curious, droll, eccentric, odd, peculiar, queer, singular, strange, unusual, whimsical. ANT.—common, familiar, normal, ordinary, usual.

qualification, SYN.—ability, aptitude, aptness, capability, capacity, dexterity, efficiency, faculty, power, skill, talent. ANT.—disability, incapacity, incompetency, unreadiness.

qualified, SYN.—able, clever, competent, efficient, fitted, skillful. ANT.—inadequate, incapable, incompetent, unfitted.

quality, SYN.—attribute, characteristic, distinction, feature, peculiarity, property, trait; caliber, grade, value. ANT.—being, essence, nature, substance.

quantity, SYN.—content, extent, measure, portion; aggregate, amount, number, sum, volume. ANT.—nothing, nothingness, zero.

quarrel, SYN.—affray, altercation, argument, bickering, contention, disagreement, dispute, feud, spat, squabble, wrangle. ANT.—agreement, friendliness, harmony, peace, reconciliation.

queer, SYN.—curious,

droll, eccentric, odd, peculiar, quaint, singular, strange, unusual, whimsical. ANT.—common, familiar, normal, ordinary, usual.

quest, SYN.—examination, exploration, interrogation, investigation, query, question, research, scrutiny. ANT.—disregard, inactivity, inattention, negligence.

question, SYN.—ask, examine, inquire, interrogate, pump, query, quiz; challenge, dispute, doubt. ANT.—answer, reply, respond, state; accept.

quick, SYN.—active, brisk, fast, hasty, lively, nimble, precipitate, rapid, speedy, swift; excitable, impatient, irascible, sharp, testy, touchy; acute, clever, discerning, keen, sensitive, shrewd. ANT.—slow, sluggish; dull, inattentive, unaware.

quicken, SYN.—accelerate, dispatch, expedite, facilitate, forward, hasten, hurry, push, rush, speed. ANT.—block, hinder, impede, retard, slow.

quickness, SYN.—action, activity, agility, briskness, energy, enterprise, exercise, intensity, liveliness, motion, movement, rapidity, vigor. ANT.—dullness, idleness, inactivity, inertia, sloth.

quiescent, SYN.—concealed, dormant, hidden, inactive, latent, potential, secret, undeveloped, unseen. ANT.—conspicuous, evident, explicit, manifest, visible.

quiet, SYN.—hushed, motionless, peaceful, placid, quiescent, still, tranquil, undisturbed; calm, gentle, meek, mild, modest, passive, patient, silent. ANT.—loud, strident; agitated, disturbed, perturbed.

quiet, SYN.—calm, calmness, hush, peace, quiescence, quietude, repose, rest, serenity, silence, stillness, tranquility. ANT.—agitation, disturbance, excitement, noise, tumult.

quiet, SYN.—allay, alleviate, appease, assuage, calm, compose, lull, pacify, placate, quell, relieve, satisfy, soothe, still, tranquilize. ANT.—arouse, excite, incense, inflame.

quit, SYN.— abandon, cease, desist, discontinue, stop; give up, relinquish, resign, surrender; abandon, depart, leave, withdraw. ANT.—continue, endure, occupy, persist, stay.

quiz, SYN.—ask, examine, inquire, interrogate, pump, query, question, challenge, dispute, doubt. ANT.—answer, reply, respond, state; accept.

quote, SYN.—adduce, cite, extract, paraphrase, plagiarize, recite, repeat. ANT.—contradict, misquote, refute, retort.

R

race, SYN.—ancestry, clan, folk, lineage, nation, people, stock, strain, tribe.

racket, SYN.—babel, clamor, cry, din, noise, outcry, row, sound, tumult, uproar. ANT.—hush, quiet, silence, stillness.

radiance, SYN.—brightness, brilliance, brilliancy, effulgence, luster, splendor. ANT.—darkness, dullness, gloom, obscurity.

radiant, SYN.—brilliant, bright, dazzling, effulgent, glorious, gorgeous, grand, illustrious, magnificent, resplendent, shining, showy, splendid, sumptuous, supurb. ANT.—dull, mediocre, modest, ordinary, unimpressive.

radical, SYN.—complete, extreme, insurgent, total, thorough, ultra, uncompromising; basic, constitutional, fundamental, inherent, innate, intrinsic, natural, organic, original. ANT.—conservative, moderate, superficial; extraneous.

ragamuffin, SYN.—beggar, mendicant, pauper, scrub, starveling, tatterdemalion, vagabond, wretch.

rage, SYN.—anger, animosity, choler, exasperation, fury, indignation, ire, irritation, passion, petulance, resentment, temper, wrath. ANT.—conciliation, forbearance, patience, peace, self-control.

raging, SYN.—boisterous, fierce, forceful, furious, impetuous, passionate, powerful, raving, turbulent, vehement, violent, wild; acute, extreme, intense, severe. ANT.—calm, feeble, gentle, quiet, soft.

raise, SYN.—elevate, erect, exalt, heave, heighten, hoist, lift, uplift; breed, cultivate, grow, produce; gather, levy, muster. ANT.—abase, depreciate, depress, destroy, lower.

ramble, SYN.—deviate, digress, err, range, roam, rove, saunter, stray, stroll, traipse, wander. ANT.—halt, linger, settle, stay, stop.

rancor, SYN.—animosity, enmity, grudge, ill will, malevolence, malice, malignity, spite. ANT.—affection, kindness, love, toleration.

rank, SYN.—hue, range, row, series; blood, class, degree, estate, grade, quality, standing, station, status; dignity, distinction, eminence. ANT.—disrepute, humiliation, shame, stigma.

rapid, SYN.—fast, quick, speedy, swift. ANT.—slow, sluggish.

rapidity, SYN.—action, activity, agility, briskness, energy, enterprise, exercise, intensity, liveliness, motion, movement, quickness, vigor.

ANT.—dullness, idleness, inactivity, inertia, sloth.

rapture, SYN.—bliss, ecstasy, exaltation, gladness, happiness, joy, transport. ANT.—depression, grief, melancholy, misery, sorrow, woe, wretch.

rare, SYN.—infrequent, occasional, strange, unusual; choice, exceptional, incomparable, precious, scarce, singular, uncommon, unique. ANT.—customary, frequent, ordinary, usual; abundant, commonplace, numerous, worthless.

rash, SYN.—careless, hasty, heedless, impetuous, passionate, quick. ANT.—calculating, cautious, reasoning.

rate, SYN.—decide, decree, determine; adjudicate, arbitrate, condemn, judge, try, umpire; appreciate, consider, estimate, evaluate, measure, think.

rational, SYN.—intelligent, judicious, reasonable, sensible, wise; sane, sober, sound. ANT.—absurd, foolish; irrational, insane.

rationality, SYN.—argument, basis, cause, ground, motive; aim, design, purpose, intelligence, mind, reason, sense, understanding.

ravage, SYN.—despoil, destroy, devastate, pillage, plunder, ruin, sack, strip, waste. ANT.—accumulate, conserve, economize, preserve, save.

ravenous, SYN.—craving, famished, hungry, starved, thirsting, voracious; ANT.—full, gorged, sated, satiated.

ravish, SYN.—debauch, deflower, violate.

raw, SYN.—coarse, crude, green, harsh, ill-prepared, rough, unfinished, unpolished, unrefined. ANT.—finished, well-prepared.

raze, SYN.—annihilate, demolish, destroy, devastate, eradicate, exterminate, extinguish, obliterate, ravage, ruin, wreck. ANT.—construct, establish, make, preserve, save.

reach, SYN.—extend, stretch; arrive at, attain, come to, overtake. ANT.—fail, fall short, miss.

react, SYN.—answer, rejoin, reply, respond. ANT.—disregard, ignore, overlook.

ready, SYN.—complete, consummate, finished, full-grown, mature, matured, mellow, ripe, seasonable. ANT.—crude, green, immature, raw, undeveloped.

ready, SYN.—concoct, condition, contrive, equip, fit, furnish, get ready, make ready, predispose, prepare, provide, qualify.

real, SYN.—actual, authentic, certain, genuine, positive, substantial, true, veritable. ANT.—apparent, fictitious, imaginary, supposed, unreal.

realization, SYN.—accomplishment, achievement, attainment, completion, performance. ANT.—defeat, failure.

realize, SYN.—appreciate, apprehend, comprehend, conceive, discern, grasp, know, learn, perceive, see, understand. ANT.—ignore, misapprehend, mistake, misunderstand.

realm, SYN.—domain, estate, farm, land.

reap, SYN.—acquire, gain, garner, gather, glean, harvest. ANT.—lose, plant, sow, squander.

reaping, SYN.—crop, fruit, harvest, proceeds, produce, product, result, store, yield.

rear, SYN.—foster, nurture, raise, train.

reason, SYN.—argument, basis, cause, ground, motive, sake; aim, design, purpose, intelligence, mind, rationality, sense, understanding.

reason, SYN.—argue, conclude, deduce, deliberate, discuss, infer, judge, reflect. ANT.—bewilder, confuse, guess.

reasonable, SYN.—discreet, intelligent, judicious, practical, prudent, sagacious, sage, sensible, sober, sound, wise. ANT.—absurd, impalpable, imperceptible, stupid, unaware.

rebel, SYN.—mutiny, revolt, strike.

rebellion, SYN.—coup, insurrection, mutiny, overthrow, revolt, revolution, uprising.

rebellious, SYN.—defiant, disobedient, forward, insubordinate, refractory, undutiful, unruly. ANT.—compliant, dutiful, obedient, submissive.

rebuild, SYN.—reconstruct, reestablish, refresh, rehabilitate, renew, renovate, repair, restore.

rebuke, SYN.—accuse, censure, condemn, implicate, reproach, upbraid. ANT.—absolve, acquit, exonerate.

rebuttal, SYN.—answer, defense. ANT.—argument.

recall, SYN.—mind, recollect, remember, remind, reminisce. ANT.—disregard, forget, ignore, overlook.

receive, SYN.—accept, gain, get, take; admit, shelter; entertain, welcome. ANT.—bestow, give, impart, reject; discharge, turn away.

recent, SYN.—fresh, late, modern, newfangled, novel, original. ANT.—ancient, antiquated, archaic, obsolete, old.

recital, SYN.—account, chronicle, description, detail, history, narration, narrative, relation. ANT.—caricature, confusion, distortion, misrepresentation.

recite, SYN.—declaim, deliver, describe, detail,

mention, narrate, recapitulate, rehearse, relate, repeat, tell.

reckless, SYN.—careless, heedless, imprudent, inattentive, inconsiderate, indiscreet, thoughtless, unconcerned. ANT.—accurate, careful, meticulous, nice.

recognize, SYN.—apprehend, identify, perceive, recollect, remember; acknowledge, avow, concede, confess, own. ANT.—forget, ignore, overlook; disown, renounce, repudiate.

recollection, SYN.—memory, remembrance, reminiscence, retrospection. ANT.— forgetfulness, oblivion.

recommend, SYN.—advise, allude, counsel, hint, imply, insinuate, intimate, offer, propose, refer, suggest. ANT.—declare, demand, dictate, insist.

recommendation, SYN.— admonition, advice, caution, counsel, exhortation, instruction, honesty, integrity, justice, openness, responsibility, sincerity, trustworthiness, uprightness. ANT.— cheating, deceit, dishonesty, fraud, trickery.

recuperate, SYN.—cure, rally, recover, restore, revive, recapture, recoup, redeem, regain, repossess, retrieve. ANT.—regress, relapse, revert, weaken; forfeit, lose.

reduce, SYN.—abate, assuage, decrease, diminish, lessen, lower, moderate, suppress. ANT.—amplify, enlarge, increase, intensify, revive.

reduction, SYN.—abbreviation, abridgement, contraction, shortening. ANT.—amplification, enlargement, expansion, extension.

refined, SYN.—courtly, cultivated, cultured, genteel, polished, polite, well-bred; clarified, purified. ANT.—boorish, coarse, crude, rude, vulgar.

refinement, SYN.—breeding, civilization, cultivation, culture, education, enlightenment. ANT.— boorishness, ignorance, illiteracy, vulgarity.

reflect, SYN.—cogitate, contemplate, deliberate, meditate, muse, ponder, reason, speculate, think.

reflection, SYN.—cogitation, conception, suggestion, warning; information, intelligence, notification.

reckon, SYN.—account, believe, consider, deem, esteem, estimate, hold, judge, rate, regard, think, view.

reckoning, SYN.—account, computation, record.

reconsider, SYN.—consider, examine, inspect, review, revise, survey. ANT.—ignore, reject.

record, SYN.—account, archive, chronicle, document, memorandum, minute, note, report, register; mark, memorial, trace, vestige; achievement, career, history.

recount, SYN.—describe, narrate, recite, rehearse, relate, report, tell.

recover, SYN.—cure, rally, recuperate, restore, revive, recapture, recoup, redeem, regain, repossess, retrieve. ANT.—regress, relapse, revert, weaken; forfeit, lose.

recreation, SYN.—amusement, diversion, entertainment, fun, game, pastime, play, sport. ANT.—boredom, labor, toil, work.

rectify, SYN.—amend, correct, mend, reform, right. ANT.—aggravate, ignore, spoil.

rectitude, SYN.—candor, fairness, frankness, consideration, contemplation, deliberation, fancy, idea, imagination, impression, judgment, meditation, memory, notion, opinion, recollection, regard, retrospection, sentiment, thought, view.

reform, SYN.—amend, correct, improve, rectify, right. ANT.—aggravate, corrupt, damage, debase, impair, spoil, vitiate.

refrain, SYN.—abstain, desist, forbear, withhold. ANT.—continue, indulge, persist.

refreshing, SYN.—brisk, cool, fresh.

refuge, SYN.—asylum, harbor, haven, retreat, sanc-

tuary, shelter. ANT.—danger, exposure, hazard, jeopardy, peril.

refuse, SYN.—decline, deny, rebuff, reject, repudiate, spurn, withhold. ANT.—accept, grant, welcome.

refute, SYN.—confute, controvert, disprove, falsify, rebut. ANT.—accept, affirm, confirm, establish, prove.

regain, SYN.—recapture, recoup, recover, redeem, repossess, retrieve. ANT.—forfeit, lose.

regal, SYN.—courtly, dignified, grand, imperial, kingly, lordly, majestic, monarchial, noble, princely, royal, ruling, sovereign, stately, supreme. ANT.—common, humble, low, plebian, proletarian, servile, vulgar.

regalement, SYN.—celebration, dinner, entertainment, feast, festival.

regard, SYN.—attention, care, concern, consideration, notice, observation; affection, esteem, liking. ANT.—antipathy, disgust, disaffection, neglect.

regard, SYN.—esteem, honor, respect, value; behold, contemplate, look, mark, notice, observe, see, view, watch; account, believe, deem, hold, imagine, reckon, suppose, think. ANT.—insult, mock; ignore, neglect, overlook.

region, SYN.—area, belt,

climate, locale, locality, location, place, sector, site, situation, spot, station, vicinity, zone.

regressive, SYN.—backward, retrograde, revisionary. ANT.—advanced, civilized, progressive.

regret, SYN.—compunction, contrition, grief, penitence, qualm, remorse, repentance, self-reproach, sorrow. ANT.—complacency, impenitence, obduracy, self-satisfaction.

regular, SYN.—customary, methodical, natural, normal, orderly, ordinary, periodical, steady, systematic, uniform, unvaried. ANT.—abnormal, erratic, exceptional, rare, unusual.

regulation, SYN.—axiom, canon, control, discipline, formula, guide, law, maxim, method, order, precept, principle, propriety, restraint, rule, self-control, standard, statute, system. ANT.—chance, chaos, confusion, deviation, exception, hazard, irregularity, turbulence.

rehabilitate, SYN.—rebuild, reconstruct, reestablish, refresh, renew, renovate, repair, restore.

reiterate, SYN.—duplicate, iterate, recapitulate, repeat, reproduce.

reject, SYN.—decline, deny, rebuff, refuse, repudiate, spurn, withhold. ANT.—accept, grant,

welcome.

rejection, SYN.—challenge, difference, disagreement, dissent, dissentience, noncompliance, nonconformity, objection, protest, recusancy, remonstrance, variance. ANT.— acceptance, agreement, assent, compliance.

relate, SYN.—describe, narrate, recite, recount, rehearse, report, tell; apply, beat, connect, correlate, pertain, refer.

relation, SYN.—alliance, association, coalition, combination, confederacy, entente, federation, league, partnership, union; compact, covenant, marriage, treaty. ANT.—divorce, schism, separation.

relationship, SYN.—affinity, alliance, association, bond, conjunction, connection, link, relationship, tie, union. ANT.—disunion, isolation, separation.

relatives, SYN.—affinity, consanguinity, family, kindred, kinsfolk, relations, relationship. ANT.— disconnection, foreigners, strangers.

relaxed, SYN.—acceptable, agreeable, casual, comfortable, convenient, cozy, gratifying, incidental, informal, nonchalant, offhand, pleasing, pleasurable, restful, unconcerned, unpremeditated, welcome. ANT.—distressing, formal, miserable, planned, pretentious, troubling, uncomfortable, wretched.

release, SYN.—deliver, discharge, emancipate, free, let go, liberate, set free. ANT.—confine, imprison, oppress, restrict, subjugate.

relent, SYN.—abdicate, accede, acquiesce, capitulate, cede, quit, relinquish, resign, submit, succumb, surrender, waive, yield. ANT.—assert, resist, strive, struggle.

relevant, SYN.—applicable, apposite, appropriate, apropos, apt, fit, germane, material, pertinent, related, relating, to the point. ANT.—alien, extraneous, foreign, unrelated.

reliable, SYN.—certain, dependable, safe, secure, sure, tried, trustworthy, trusty. ANT.—dubious, fallible, questionable, uncertain, unreliable.

reliance, SYN.—confidence, credence, dependence, faith, trust. ANT.—doubt, incredulity, mistrust, skepticism.

relief, SYN.—aid, alms, assistance, backing, furtherance, help, patronage, succor, support. ANT.— antagonism, counteraction, defiance, hostility, resistance.

relieve, SYN.—abate, allay, alleviate, assuage, calm, comfort, diminish, ease, extenuate, facilitate, lighten, mitigate, pacify, soften, solace, soothe. ANT.—aggravate, agitate, augment, confound, distress, disturb, increase, irritate, trouble, worry.

religion, SYN.—belief, creed, doctrine, dogma, persuasion, tenet. ANT.—infidelity.

religious, SYN.—devout, divine, godly, holy, pietistic, pious, reverent, sacred, santimonious, spiritual, theological. ANT.—atheistic, impious, profane, secular, skeptical.

religiousness, SYN.—affection, ardor, attachment, consecration, dedication, devotion, devoutness, fidelity, love, loyalty, piety, zeal. ANT.—alienation, apathy, aversion, indifference, unfaithfulness.

relinquish, SYN.—abandon, acquiesce, capitulate, cede, renounce, resign, sacrifice, submit, surrender, yield. ANT.—conquer, overcome, resist, rout.

reluctance, SYN.—abhorrence, antipathy, aversion, disgust, disinclination, dislike, distaste, dread, hatred, loathing, repugnance, repulsion. ANT.—affection, attachment, devotion, enthusiasm.

reluctant, SYN.—averse, disinclined, hesitant, loath, slow, unwilling. ANT.—disposed, eager, inclined, ready, willing.

rely, SYN.—depend, lean, trust.

remain, SYN.—abide, dwell, halt, rest, stay, tarry, wait; continue, endure, last, survive. ANT.—depart, go, leave; dissipate, finish, terminate.

remains, SYN.—balance, remainder, residue, rest, surplus.

remark, SYN.—annotation, assertion, comment, declaration, observation, statement, utterance,

remark, SYN.—express, mention, observe, utter.

remarkable, SYN.—affecting, arresting, august, commanding, exciting, forcible, grandiose, imposing, impressive, majestic, moving, overpowering, splendid, stirring, striking, thrilling, touching. ANT.—commonplace, ordinary, regular, unimpressive.

remedy, SYN.—antidote, cure, help, medicant, restorative; redress, relief, reparation.

remedy, SYN.—ameliorate, better, correct, improve, mend, rectify, reform.

remember, SYN.—mind, recall, recollect, remind, reminisce. ANT.—disregard, forget, ignore, overlook.

remembrance, SYN.—commemoration, memento, memorial, monument, souvenir.

remonstrate, SYN.—complain, grouch, grumble, lament, murmur, protest, regret, repine, whine. ANT.—applaud, approve, praise, rejoice.

remorse, SYN.—compunction, contrition, grief, penitence, qualm, regret, repentance, self-reproach, sorrow. ANT.—complacency, impenitence, obduracy, self-satisfaction.

remorseless, SYN.—barbarian, barbaric, barbarous, brutal, crude, cruel, inhuman, merciless, rude, ruthless, savage, uncivilized, uncultured, unrelenting. ANT.—civilized, humane, kind, polite, refined.

remote, SYN.—distant, far, faraway, removed. ANT.—close, near, nigh.

remove, SYN.—dislodge, displace, move, shift, transfer, transport; discharge, dismiss, eject, oust, vacate; extract, withdraw. ANT.—leave, remain, stay; retain.

renounce, SYN.—abandon, forego, forsake, quit, relinquish, resign, sacrifice; deny, disavow, disclaim, disown, reject, retract, revoke. ANT.—defend, maintain, uphold; acknowledge, assert, recognize.

renovate, SYN.—rebuild, reconstruct, reestablish, refresh, rehabilitate, renew, repair, restore.

renown, SYN.—acclaim, distinction, eminence, fame, honor, luster, notability, reputation. ANT.—disgrace, disrepute, obscurity.

renowned, SYN.—celebrated, distinguished, eminent, famous, glorious, illustrious, noted, well-known. ANT.—hidden, ignominious, infamous, obscure, unknown.

repair, SYN.—correct, darn, fix, mend, patch, refit, renew, renovate, restore, tinker with; amend, redress, remedy, retrieve. ANT.—break, destroy, harm.

repeal, SYN.—abolish, abrogate, annul, cancel, invalidate, nullify, quash, rescind, revoke.

repeat, SYN.—quote, recite, rehearse, relate; duplicate, iterate, recapitulate, reiterate, reproduce.

repentance, SYN.—compunction, contrition, grief, penitence, qualm, regret, remorse, self-reproach, sorrow. ANT.—complacency, impenitence, obduracy, self-satisfaction.

repentant, SYN.—contrite, penitent, regretful, remorseful, sorrowful, sorry. ANT.—obdurate, remorseless.

repine, SYN.—complain, grouch, grumble, lament, murmur, protest, regret, remonstrate, whine. ANT.—applaud, approve, praise, rejoice.

replace, SYN.—reinstate, restore, return.

replenish, SYN.—fill, fill up, occupy, pervade; furnish, stock, store, sup-

ply. ANT.—deplete, drain, empty, exhaust, void.

replica, SYN.—copy, duplicate, exemplar, facsimile, imitation, reproduction, transcript. ANT.—original, prototype.

reply, SYN.—answer, rejoinder, response, retort. ANT.—inquiry, questioning, summoning.

reply, SYN.—answer, react, rejoin, respond. ANT.—disregard, ignore, overlook.

report, SYN.—advertise, announce, declare, give out, herald, make known, notify, proclaim, promulgate, publish. ANT.—bury, conceal, stifle, suppress, withhold.

repose, SYN.—calm, calmness, hush, peace, quiescence, quiet, quietude, rest, serenity, silence, stillness, tranquility. ANT.—agitation, disturbance, excitement, noise, tumult.

represent, SYN.—delineate, depict, describe, draw, paint, picture, portray, sketch. ANT.—caricature, misrepresent, suggest.

representation, SYN.—appearance, cinema, drawing, effigy, engraving, etching, film, illustration, image, likeness, painting, panorama, photograph, picture, portrait, portrayal, print, resemblance, scene, sketch, view.

repress, SYN.—bridle,

check, constrain, curb, hinder, hold back, inhibit, limit, restrain, stop, suppress. ANT.—aid, encourage, incite, loosen.

reprimand, SYN.—admonish, berate, blame, censure, lecture, rate, rebuke, reprehend, scold, upbraid, vituperate. ANT.—approve, commend, praise.

reproach, SYN.—abuse, aspersion, defamation, desecration, dishonor, disparagement, insult, invective, maltreatment, misuse, outrate, perversion, profanation, reviling, upbraiding. ANT.—approval, commendation, laudation, plaudit, respect.

reproduction, SYN.—copy, duplicate, exemplar, facsimile, imitation, replica, transcript. ANT.—original, prototype.

repugnance, SYN.—abhorrence, antipathy, aversion, disgust, disinclination, dislike, distaste, dread, hatred, loathing, repulsion, reluctance. ANT.—affection, attachment, devotion, enthusiasm.

repulsive, SYN.—deformed, hideous, homely, plain, repellent, ugly, uncomely. ANT.—attractive, beautiful, fair, handsome, pretty.

reputation, SYN.—character, class, description, disposition, individuality, kind, nature, repute, sort, standing.

repute, SYN.—character, class, description, disposition, individuality, kind, nature, reputation, sort, standing.

request, SYN.—appeal, ask, beg, beseech, desire, entreat, implore, importune, petition, pray, seek, sue, supplicate. ANT.—demand, require.

require, SYN.—call for, claim, command, demand, exact, order, prescribe; lack, necessitate, need, want.

requisite, SYN.—basic, essential, fundamental, important, indispensable, intrinsic, necessary, needed, vital. ANT.—accidental, casual, contingent, expendable, extrinsic, nonessential, optional, peripheral.

rescind, SYN.—abolish, abrogate, annul, invalidate, nullify, quash, repeal, revoke.

research, SYN.—examination, exploration, inquiry, interrogation, investigation, query, quest, question, scrutiny. ANT.—disregard, inactivity, inattention, negligence.

resemblance, SYN.—analogy, correspondence, likeness, parity, similarity, similitude. ANT.—difference, distinction, variance.

resentfulness, SYN.—covetousness, envy, invidiousness, jealousy, suspicion. ANT.—geniality, indifference, liberality, tolerance.

reserve, SYN.—accumulation, fund, hoard, provision, stock, store, supply.

reserved, SYN.—aloof, bashful, cautious, chary, demure, diffident, distant, fearful, modest, retiring, sheepish, shrinking, stiff, timorous, unfriendly, wary. ANT.—audacious, bold, brazen, cordial, forward, friendly, immodest.

residence, SYN.—abode, domicile, dwelling, habitat, hearth, home, quarters, seat.

resign, SYN.—give up, quit, relinquish, surrender.

resignation, SYN.—composure, endurance, forbearance, fortitude, long-suffering, perseverance. ANT.—impatience, nervousness, restlessness, unquiet.

resigned, SYN.—assiduous, composed, forbearing, indulgent, long-suffering, passive, patient, stoical, uncomplaining. ANT.—chafing, clamorous, high-strung, hysterical, turbulent.

resist, SYN.—attack, confront, defy, hinder, impede, obstruct, oppose, thwart, withstand. ANT.—accede, allow, cooperate, relent, yield.

resolution, SYN.—courage, decision, determination, firmness, fortitude, persistence, resolve, steadfastness. ANT.—inconstancy, indecision, vacil-

lation.

resolve, SYN.—courage, decision, determination, firmness, fortitude, persistence, resolution, steadfastness. ANT.—inconstancy, indecision, vacillation.

resolve, SYN.—adjudicate, close, conclude, decide, determine, end, fix, settle, terminate. ANT.—doubt, hesitate, suspend, vacillate, waver.

respect, SYN.—admire, consider, heed, honor, regard, revere, reverence, value, venerate. ANT.—abuse, despise, disdain, neglect, scorn.

respectable, SYN.—adequate, becoming, befitting, comely, decorous, fit, proper, seemly, suitable, tolerable. ANT.—coarse, gross, indecent, reprehensible, vulgar.

respond, SYN.—answer, react, rejoin, reply. ANT.—disregard, ignore, overlook.

response, SYN.—answer, rejoinder, reply, retort. ANT.—inquiry, questioning, summoning.

responsibility, SYN.—accountability, amenability, liability, obligation, trustworthiness; duty, trust.

responsbile, SYN.—accountable, amenable, liable; reliable, trustworthy. ANT.—exempt, free, immune; careless, negligent.

rest, SYN.—sleep, slumber; calm, ease, leisure,

peace, quiet, relaxation, repose, tranquillity; cessation, intermission, pause, respite; balance, remainder, surplus. ANT.—agitation, commotion, disturbance, motion, tumult.

restless, SYN.—agitated, disquieted, disturbed, irresolute, sleepless, uneasy, unquiet; active, roving, transient, wandering. ANT.—at ease, peaceable, quiet, tractable.

restore, SYN.—rebuild, reconstruct, reestablish, refresh, rehabilitate, renew, renovate, repair; cure, heal, recover, rejuvenate, revive; reinstate, replace, return.

restrain, SYN.—bridle, check, constrain, curb, hinder, hold back, inhibit, limit, repress, stop, suppress. ANT.—aid, encourage, incite, loosen.

restraint, SYN.—control, discipline, order, regulation, self-control. ANT.—chaos, confusion, turbulence.

restrict, SYN.—attach, bind, connect, engage, fasten, fetter, join, link, oblige, restrain, tie. ANT.—free, loose, unfasten, untie.

result, SYN.—conclusion, consequence, determination, effect, end, eventuality, issue, resolution, resolve.

retaliation, SYN.—reparation, reprisal, requital, retribution, revenge,

vengeance, vindictiveness. ANT.—mercy, pardon, reconciliation, remission, forgiveness.

retard, SYN.—arrest, detain, hinder, impede, stay.

retire, SYN.—abandon, depart, desert, forsake, give up, go, leave, quit, relinquish, renounce, withdraw. ANT.—abide, remain, stay, tarry.

retort, SYN.—answer, rejoinder, reply, response. ANT.—inquiry, questioning, summoning.

retrograde, SYN.—backward, regressive, revisionary. ANT.—advanced, civilized, progressive.

retribution, SYN.—reparation, reprisal, requital, retaliation, revenge, vengeance, vindictiveness. ANT.—mercy, pardon, reconciliation, remission, forgiveness.

return, SYN.—go back, recur, retreat, revert; repay, replace, requite, restore. ANT.—appropriate, keep, retain, take.

reveal, SYN.—betray, disclose, discover, divulge, expose, impart, show, uncover. ANT.—cloak, conceal, cover, hide, obscure.

revelation, SYN.—apparition, daydream, dream, ghost, hallucination, mirage, phantoms, prophecy, specter, vision. ANT.—reality, substance, verity.

revenge, SYN.—reparation,

reprisal, requital, retaliation, retribution, vengeance, vindictiveness. ANT.—mercy, pardon, reconciliation, remission, forgiveness.

revenge, SYN.—avenge, requite, retaliate, vindicate. ANT.—forgive, pardon, pity, reconcile.

revere, SYN.—adore, esteem, honor, venerate, worship. ANT.—despise, hate, ignore.

reverence, SYN.—admiration, adoration, deference, dignity, esteem, fame, glory, homage, honor, praise, renown, respect, worship. ANT.—contempt, derision, disgrace, dishonor, reproach.

reverse, SYN.—invert, transpose, turn about; overthrow, overturn, subvert, unmake, upset; annual, countermand, repeal, rescind, revoke. ANT.—endorse, maintain, stabilize; affirm, confirm, vouch.

revert, SYN.—go back, recur, retreat, return. ANT—appropriate, keep, retain, take.

review, SYN.—commentary, criticism, critique, examination, inspection, reconsideration, retrospect, retrospection, revision, survey, synopsis; digest, journal, periodical.

review, SYN.—consider, examine, inspect, reconsider, revise, survey; analyze, criticize, discuss,

edit. ANT.—ignore, reject.

revile, SYN.—abuse, asperse, defame, disparage, ill-use, malign, scandalize, traduce, vilify. ANT.—cherish, honor, praise, protect, respect.

revision, SYN.—commentary, criticism, critique, examination, inspection, reconsideration, retrospect, retrospection, review, survey, synopsis.

revive, SYN.—abate, assuage, decrease, diminish, lessen, lower, moderate, reduce, suppress. ANT.—amplify, enlarge, increase, intensify.

revoke, SYN.—abolish, abrogate, annul, cancel, invalidate, nullify, quash, repeal, rescind.

revolting, SYN.—abominable, detestable, execrable, foul, hateful, loathsome, odious, vile. ANT.—agreeable, commendable, delightful, pleasant.

revolution, SYN.—coup, insurrection, mutiny, overthrow, rebellion, revolt, uprising.

revolve, SYN.—circle, gyrate, rotate, spin, turn, twirl, wheel, whirl. ANT.—proceed, stop, stray, travel, wander.

reward, SYN.—award, bonus, bounty, compensation, premium, prize, recompense, remuneration, requital. ANT.—assessment, charge, earnings, punishment, wages.

rich, SYN.—abundant, affluent, ample, bountiful, copious, costly, exorbitant, luxurious, opulent, plentiful, prosperous, sumptuous, wealthy, well-to-do; fecund, fertile, fruitful, luxuriant, prolific. ANT.—beggarly, destitute, indigent, needy, poor; barren, sterile, unfruitful, unproductive.

riddle, SYN.—conundrum, enigma, mystery, problem, puzzle. ANT.—answer, clue, key, resolution, solution.

ridicule, SYN.—banter, derision, gibe, irony, jeering, mockery, raillery, sarcasm, satire, sneering.

ridiculous, SYN.—absurd, foolish, inconsistent, irrational, nonsensical, preposterous, self-contradictory, silly, unreasonable. ANT.—consistent, rational, reasonable, sensible, sound.

right, SYN.—ethical, fair, just, lawful, legitimate; accurate, correct, real, true; appropriate, fit, proper, seemly, suitable; direct, erect, straight, upright. ANT.—bad, false, improper, wrong.

right, SYN.—authority, grant, liberty, license, prerogative, privilege; equity, honor, justice, propriety, virtue ANT.— encroachment, injustice, violation, wrong.

righteous, SYN.—chaste, decent, ethical, good, honorable, just, pure, right, scrupulous, virtuous. ANT.—amoral, libertine, licentious, sinful, unethical.

rigid, SYN.—austere, harsh, rigorous, severe, stern, strict, stringent, unyielding; inflexible, stiff, unbending. ANT.— compassionate, lax, lenient, mild, yielding; elastic, flexible, resilient, supple.

rigorous, SYN.—blunt, coarse, cruel, grating, gruff, hard, harsh, jarring, rough, severe, stern, strict, stringent, unfeeling. ANT.—gentle, lenient, melodious, mild, smooth, soft, tender.

rim, SYN.—border, boundary, brim, brink, edge, fringe, frontier, limit, margin, outskirts, termination, verge. ANT.—center, core, interior, mainland.

rip, SYN.—cleave, disunite, lacerate, rend, rive, sever, shred, slit, split, sunder, tear, wound. ANT.—join, mend, repair, sew, unite.

ripe, SYN.—complete, consummate, finished, full-grown, mature, matured, mellow, ready, seasonable. ANT.—crude, green, immature, raw, undeveloped.

rise, SYN.—climb, mount, proceed, progress, scale, soar, thrive, tower. ANT.—descend, fall, sink.

risk, SYN.—danger, hazard,

jeopardy, peril. ANT.—defense, immunity, protection, safety.

risk, SYN.—endanger, expose, hazard, jeopardize, peril, speculate, venture. ANT.—insure, protect, secure.

risky, SYN.—critical, dangerous, hazardous, insecure, menacing, perilous, precarious, threatening, unsafe. ANT.—firm, protected, safe, secure.

rite, SYN.—ceremony, formality, observance, parade, pomp, protocol, ritual, solemnity.

ritual, SYN.—ceremony, formality, observance, parade, pomp, protocol, rite, solemnity.

rival, SYN.—adversary, antagonist, competitor, contestant, enemy, foe, opponent. ANT.—allay, comrade, confederate, teammate.

roam, SYN.—deviate, digress, err, ramble, range, rove, saunter, stray, stroll, traipse, wander. ANT.—halt, linger, settle, stay, stop.

rob, SYN.—despoil, fleece, loot, pilfer, pillage, plunder, sack, steal, strip.

robbery, SYN.—burglary, depredation, larceny, pillage, plunder, theft.

robust, SYN.—hale, healthy, hearty, sound, strong, well. ANT.—delicate, diseased, frail, infirm.

rock, SYN.—boulder, gravel, jewel, pebble, stone.

role, SYN.—character, lines, part.

romantic, SYN.—dreamy, extravagant, fanciful, fantastic, fictitious, ideal, idealistic, imaginative, maudlin, mawkish, picturesque, poetic, sentimental. ANT.—factual, literal, matter-of-fact, practical, prosaic.

roomy, SYN.—ample, broad, capacious, extensive, large, spacious, vast, wide. ANT.—confined, cramped, limited, narrow.

root, SYN.—base, basis, bottom, foundation, ground, groundwork, substructure, support, underpinning. ANT.—building, cover, superstructure, top.

rot, SYN.—decay, decline, decompose, decrease, disintegrate, dwindle, ebb, putrefy, spoil, wane, waste. ANT.—flourish, grow, increase, luxuriate, rise.

rotate, SYN.—circle, circulate, invert, revolve, spin, twirl, twist, wheel, whirl. ANT.—arrest, fix, stand, stop.

rotund, SYN.—bulbous, chubby, circular, complete, curved, cylindrical, entire, globular, plump, round, spherical.

rough, SYN.—craggy, irregular, jagged, rugged, scabrous, scratchy, uneven; approximate, coarse, crude, cursory, imperfect, incomplete, unfinished, unpolished; harsh, severe, stormy, tempestuous, turbulent, violent; blunt, brusque, churlish, gruff, rude, uncivil. ANT.—even, level, sleek, slippery, smooth; fine, finished, polished, refined; calm, placid, tranquil, unruffled; civil, courteous, gentle, mild.

round, SYN.—bulbous, chubby, circular, complete, curved, cylindrical, entire, globular, plump, rotund, spherical.

roundabout, SYN.—circuitous, crooked, distorted, erratic, indirect, swerving, tortuous, wandering, winding. ANT.—direct, straight.

rout, SYN.—beat. conquer, crush, defeat, humble, master, overcome, quell, subdue, subjugate, surmount, vanquish. ANT.—capitulate, cede, lose, retreat, surrender.

route, SYN.—avenue, channel, course, passage, road, street, thoroughfare, track, trail, walk, way.

routine, SYN.—custom, fashion, habit, practice, usage, use, wont.

royal, SYN.—courtly, dignified, grand, imperial, kingly, lordly, majestic, monarchial, noble, princely, regal, ruling, sovereign, stately, supreme. ANT.—common, humble, low, plebian, proletarian, servile, vulgar.

rude, SYN.—blunt, boorish, discourteous, gruff, impolite, impudent, inso-lent, rough, saucy, surly, uncivil, vulgar; coarse, crude, ignorant, illiterate, primitive, raw, rough, savage, unpolished, untaught; fierce, harsh, inclement, tumultuous, violent. ANT.—civil, genteel, polished; courtly, dignified, noble, stately; calm, mild, peaceful.

rugged, SYN.—craggy, irregular, jagged, rough, scabrous, scratchy, uneven. ANT.—even, level, sleek, slippery, smooth.

ruin, SYN.—annihilate, demolish, devastate, eradicate, exterminate, extinguish, obliterate, ravage, raze, wreck. ANT.—construct, establish, make, preserve, save.

ruinous, SYN.—baneful, deadly, deleterious, destructive, detrimental, devastating, fatal, injurious, noxious, pernicious. ANT.—beneficial, constructive, creative, profitable, salutary.

rule, SYN.—axiom, canon, formula, guide, law, maxim, method, order, precept, principle, propriety, regulation, standard, statute, system; authority, control, direction, dominion, government, jurisdiction, mastery, reign, sovereignty, sway. ANT.—chance, deviation, exception, hazard, irregularity; anarchy, chaos, misrule.

rule, SYN.—command,

control, direct, dominate, govern, manage, regulate, superintend. ANT.—abandon, follow, forsake, ignore, submit.

rupture, SYN.—break, burst, crack, crush, demolish, destroy, fracture, infringe, pound, rack, rend, shatter, smash, squeeze. ANT.—join, mend, renovate, repair, restore.

rural, SYN.—country, pastoral, rustic. ANT.—cultured, elegant, polished, refined, urbane.

ruse, SYN.—antic, artifice, cheat, deception, device, fraud, guile, hoax, imposture, ploy, stratagem, stunt, subterfuge, trick, wile. ANT.—candor, exposure, honesty, openness, sincerity.

rush, SYN.—accelerate, expedite, hasten, hurry, precipitate, quicken, speed. ANT.—delay, detain, hinder, retard, tarry.

rustic, SYN.—country, pastoral, rural; coarse, homely, plain, simple; boorish, bucolic, uncouth, unsophisticated. ANT.—cultured, elegant, polished, refined, urbane.

ruthless, SYN.—barbarous, bestial, brutal, brute, brutish, carnal, coarse, cruel, ferocious, gross, inhuman, merciless, remorseless, rough, rude, savage, sensual. ANT.—civilized, courteous, gentle, humane, kind.

S

sacrament, SYN.—association, communion, fellowship, intercourse, participation, union. ANT.—alienation, nonparticipation.

sacred, SYN.—blessed, consecrated, devout, divine, hallowed, holy, pious, religious, saintly, spiritual. ANT.—evil, profane, sacrilegious, secular, worldly.

sad, SYN.—cheerless, dejected, depressed, despondent, disconsolate, dismal, doleful, downcast, gloomy, lugubrious, melancholy, mournful, somber, sorrowful. ANT.—cheerful, glad, happy, joyous, merry.

safe, SYN.—certain, dependable, harmless, protected, reliable, secure, snug, trustworthy. ANT.—dagerous, hazardous, insecure, perilous, unsafe.

safeguard, SYN.—bulwark, fence, protection, refuge, shelter, shield; defense, guard, security.

sag, SYN.—bend, incline, lean, slant, slope, tend; depend, rely, trust. ANT.—erect, raise, rise, straighten.

sagacity, SYN.—discretion, erudition, foresight, information, insight, intelligence, judgment, knowledge, learning, prudence, reason, sageness, sense, wisdom.

ANT.—foolishness, ignorance, imprudence, nonsense, stupidity.

sage, SYN.—disciple, intellectual, learner, pupil, savant, scholar, student. ANT.—dolt, dunce, fool, idiot, ignoramus.

salary, SYN.—allowance, compensation, earnings, fee, pay, payment, recompense, stipend, wages. ANT.—gift, gratuity, present.

salient, SYN.—clear, distinguished, manifest, noticeable, obvious, prominent, striking, visible. ANT.—common, hidden, inconspicuous, obscure.

salubrious, SYN.—hale, healthy, robust, sound, strong, well; hygienic, salutary, wholesome. ANT.—delicate, diseased, frail, infirm; injurious, noxious.

salutary, SYN.—advantageous, beneficial, good, helpful, profitable, serviceable, useful, wholesome. ANT.—deleterious, destructive, detrimental, harmful, injurious.

same, SYN.—coincident, equal, equivalent, indistinguishable, like. ANT.—contrary, disparate, dissimilar, distinct, opposed.

sample, SYN.—case, example, illustration, instance, model, pattern, prototype, specimen.

sanction, SYN.—approbation, approval, assent, commendation, consent, endorsement, praise, support. ANT.—censure, reprimand, reproach, stricture.

sanction, SYN.—allow, let, permit, suffer, tolerate. ANT.—forbid, object, protest, refuse, resist.

sanctuary, SYN.—asylum, harbor, haven, refuge, retreat, shelter. ANT.—danger, exposure, hazard, jeopardy, peril.

sarcastic, SYN.—acrimonious, biting, caustic, cutting, derisive, ironic, sardonic, satirical, sneering, taunting. ANT.—affable, agreeable, amiable, pleasant.

sardonic, SYN.—acrimonious, bitter, caustic, harsh, severe. ANT.—delicious, mellow, pleasant, sweet.

sate, SYN.—fill, fill up, occupy, pervade; furnish, replenish, stock, store, supply; content, glut, gorge, satiate, satisfy, stuff. ANT.—deplete, drain, empty, exhaust, void.

satiate, SYN.—appease, compensate, content, fulfill, gratify, please, remunerate, satisfy, suffice. ANT.—annoy, displease, dissatisfy, frustrate, tantalize.

satire, SYN.—banter, cleverness, fun, humor, irony, pleasantry, raillery, sarcasm, wit, witticism. ANT.— commonplace, platitude, sobriety, solemnity, stupidity.

satirical, SYN.—acrimonious, biting, caustic, cutting, derisive, ironic, sarcastic, sardonic, sneering, taunting. ANT.—affable, agreeable, amiable, pleasant.

satisfaction, SYN.—beatitude, blessedness, bliss, contentment, delight, felicity, gladness, pleasure, well-being. ANT.—despair, grief, misery, sadness, sorrow.

satisfactory, SYN.—adequate, ample, capable, commensurate, enough, fitting, sufficient, suitable. ANT.—deficient, lacking, scant.

satisfy, SYN.—appease, compensate, content, fulfill, gratify, please, remunerate, satiate, suffice. ANT.—annoy, displease, dissatisfy, frustrate, tantalize.

saturate, SYN.—diffuse, fill, infiltrate, penetrate, permeate, pervade, run through.

savage, SYN.—barbarous, brutal, cruel, ferocious, inhuman, malignant, merciless, ruthless. ANT.—benevolent, compassionate, forbearing, gentle, humane, kind, merciful.

save, SYN.—conserve, defend, guard, keep, maintain, protect, preserve, rescue, safeguard, secure, spare, uphold. ANT.—abandon, abolish, destroy, impair, injure.

savory, SYN.—delectable, delicious, delightful, luscious, palatable, sweet, tasty. ANT.—acrid, distasteful, nauseous, unpalatable, unsavory.

say, SYN.—articulate, converse, declare, discourse, express, harangue, speak, talk, tell, utter. ANT.—be silent, hush, refrain.

saying, SYN.—adage, aphorism, apothegm, byword, maxim, motto, proverb, saw.

scalding, SYN.—burning, hot, scorching, torrid, warm; ardent, fervent, fiery, hot-blooded, impetuous, intense, passionate; peppery, pungent. ANT.—cold, cool, freezing, frigid; passionless, phlegmatic; bland.

scandal, SYN.—abashment, chagrin, humiliation, mortification; disgrace, dishonor, disrepute, ignominy, odium, opprobrium, shame. ANT.—dignity, glory, honor, praise, renown.

scandalize, SYN.—abuse, asperse, defame, disparage, ill-use, malign, revile, traduce, vilify. ANT.—cherish, honor, praise, respect.

scandalous, SYN.—discreditable, disgraceful, dishonorable, disreputable, ignominious, shameful. ANT.—esteemed, honorable, renowned, respectable.

scant, SYN.—concise, succinct, summary, terse;

deficient, inadequate, insufficient, lacking, limited. ANT.—abundant, ample, big, extended, protracted.

scarce, SYN.—infrequent, occasional; choice, exceptional, incomparable, precious, rare, singular, uncommon, unique. ANT.—customary, frequent, ordinary, usual; abundant, commonplace, numerous, worthless.

scare, SYN.—affright, alarm, appal, astound, daunt, dismay, frighten, horrify, intimidate, startle, terrify, terrorize. ANT.—allay, compose, embolden, reassure, soothe.

scared, SYN.—afraid, apprehensive, fainthearted, fearful, frightened, timid, timorous. ANT.—assured, bold, composed, courageous, sanguine.

scatter, SYN.—diffuse, dispel, disperse, disseminate, dissipate, separate. ANT.—accumulate, amass, assemble, collect, gather.

scent, SYN.—aroma, fetidness, fragrance, fume, incense, odor, perfume, redolence, smell, stench, stink.

scheme, SYN.—cabal, conspiracy, design, intrigue, machination, plan, plot, stratagem; chart, diagram, graph, sketch.

scheme, SYN.—contrive, delineate, design, devise, intend, outline, plan, plot, prepare, project, sketch.

scheming, SYN.—contrive, create, design, devise, invent, plan, intend, mean, purpose; draw, sketch.

scholar, SYN.—disciple, intellectual, learner, pupil, sage, savant, student. ANT.—dolt, dunce, fool, idiot, ignoramus.

scholarly, SYN.—academic, bookish, erudite, formal, learned, pedantic, scholastic, theoretical. ANT.— common-sense, ignorant, practical, simple.

scholarship, SYN.—apprehension, cognizance, erudition, information, knowledge, learning, lore, science, understanding, wisdom. ANT.—ignorance, illiteracy, misunderstanding, stupidity.

science, SYN.—discipline, enlightenment, knowledge, learning, scholarship. ANT.—ignorance, nescience, superstition.

scold, SYN.—admonish, berate, blame, censure, lecture, rate, rebuke, reprehend, reprimand, upbraid, vituperate. ANT.—approve, commend, praise.

scope, SYN.—amount, area, compass, degree, expanse, extent, length, magnitude, measure, range, reach, size, stretch.

scorch, SYN.—blaze, burn, char, consume, incinerate, scald, sear, singe. ANT.—extinguish, put out, quench.

scorn, SYN.—contempt, contumely, derision, detestation, disdain, hatred. ANT.—awe, esteem, regard, respect, reverence.

scrap, SYN.—apportionment, fragment, moiety, part, piece, portion, section, segment, share. ANT.—entirety, whole.

scrape, SYN.—condition, difficulty, dilemma, fix, plight, predicament, situation, strait. ANT.—calmness, comfort, ease, satisfaction.

scrub, SYN.—clean, cleanse, mop, purify, sweep, wash. ANT.—dirty, pollute, soil, stain, sully.

scrupulous, SYN.—candid, conscientious, fair, honest, honorable, just, sincere, trustworthy, truthful, upright. ANT.—deceitful, dishonest, fraudulent, lying, tricky.

scrutinize, SYN.—analyze, appraise, criticize, evaluate, examine, inspect. ANT.—approve, neglect, overlook.

search, SYN.—examination, exploration, inquiry, investigation, pursuit, quest. ANT.—abandonment, cession, resignation.

search, SYN.—examine, explore, ferret (out), hunt, investigate, look, probe, ransack, rummage, scour, scrutinize, seek.

searching, SYN.—curious, inquiring, inquisitive, interrogative, meddling, nosy, peeping, peering, prying, snoopy. ANT.—incurious, indifferent, unconcerned, uninterested.

season, SYN.—age, develop, mature, perfect, ripen.

secluded, SYN.—alone, deserted, desolate, isolated, lonely, unaided; lone, only, single, sole, solitary. ANT.—accompanied, attended, surrounded.

seclusion, SYN.—alienation, insulation, isolation, loneliness, quarantine, retirement, segregation, separation, solitude, withdrawal. ANT.—association, communion, connection, fellowship, union.

secondary, SYN.—inferior, lower, minor, poorer, subordinate. ANT.—better, greater, higher, superior.

secret, SYN.—clandestine, concealed, covert, hidden, latent, private, surreptitious, unknown. ANT.—conspicuous, disclosed, exposed, known, obvious.

secrete, SYN.—cloak, clothe, conceal, cover, curtain, disguise, envelop, guard, hide, mask, protect, screen, shield, shroud, veil. ANT.—bare, divulge, expose, reveal, unveil.

section, SYN.—country,

district, division, domain, dominion, land, place, province, quarter, region, territory.

secular, SYN.—earthly, laic, lay, mundane, profane, temporal, worldly. ANT.—ecclesiastical, religious, spiritual, unworldly.

secure, SYN.—assured, certain, definite, fixed, indubitable, inevitable, positive, sure, undeniable, unquestionable. ANT.—doubtful, probable, questionable, uncertain.

secure, SYN.—achieve, acquire, attain, earn, gain, get, obtain, procure, receive. ANT.—forfeit, leave, lose, renounce, surrender.

security, SYN.—bail, bond, earnest, guaranty, pawn, pledge, surety, token, warrant.

see, SYN.—behold, contemplate, descry, discern, distinguish, espy, glimpse, inspect, look at, notice, observe, perceive, scan, scrutinize, view, watch, witness.

seek, SYN.—examine, explore, ferret (out), hunt, investigate, look, probe, ransack, rummage, search, scour, scrutinize.

seem, SYN.—appeal, look. ANT.—be, exist; disappear, vanish, withdraw.

segment, SYN.—allotment, apportionment, division, fragment, piece, moiety, part, piece, portion, scrap, section, share; element, ingredient, faction, inter-est, side. ANT.—entirety, whole.

seize, SYN.—apprehend, arrest, check, detain, hinder, interrupt, obstruct, restrain, stop, withhold. ANT.—activate, discharge, free, liberate, release.

select, SYN.—choose, cull, elect, opt, pick. ANT.—refuse, reject.

selection, SYN.—alternative, choice, election, option, preference.

self-contradictory, SYN.—absurd, foolish, inconsistent, irrational, nonsensical, preposterous, ridiculous, silly, unreasonable. ANT.—consistent, rational, reasonable, sensible, sound.

self-denial, SYN.—abstention, abstinence, continence, fasting, forbearance, moderation, sobriety, temperance. ANT.—excess, gluttony, greed, intoxication, self-indulgence.

self-indulgence, SYN.—egotism, illiberality, mercenariness, narrowness, parsimoniousness, self-centeredness, self-seeking, selfishness, stinginess, ungenerousness. ANT.—altruism, charity, liberality, magnanimity.

selfish, SYN.—egoistic, illiberal, mercenary, narrow, parsimonious, self-centered, self-seeking, stingy, ungenerous. ANT.—altruistic, charitable, liberal, magnanimous.

send, SYN.—cast, discharge, dispatch, emit, impel, propel, throw, transmit. ANT.—bring, get, hold, receive, retain.

senescence, SYN.—age, dotage, senility, seniority. ANT.—childhood, infancy, youth.

senile, SYN.—aged, ancient, antiquated, antique, archaic, elderly, obsolete, old, old-fashioned, superannuated, venerable. ANT.—modern, new, young, youthful.

sensation, SYN.—apprehension, feeling, image, impression, perception, sense, sensibility. ANT.—apathy, insensibility, stupor, torpor.

sense, SYN.—acceptation, connotation, drift, explanation, gist, implication, import, intent, interpretation, meaning, purport, purpose, significance, signification.

senseless, SYN.—brainless, crass, dense, dull, dumb, foolish, obtuse, stupid, witless. ANT.—alert, bright, clever, discerning, intelligent.

sensibility, SYN.—feeling, sensation; emotion, passion, sentiment, tenderness. ANT.—anesthesia; coldness, imperturbability, insensibility; fact.

sensible, SYN.—appreciable, apprehensible, perceptible; alive, awake, aware, cognizant, comprehending, conscious, perceiving, sentient; discreet, intelli-

gent, judicious, practical, prudent, reasonable, sagacious, sage, sober, sound, wise. ANT.—absurd, impalpable, imperceptible, stupid, unaware.

sensitive, SYN.—impressionable, perceptive, prone, responsive, sentient, susceptible, tender. ANT.—callous, dull, hard, indifferent, insensitive.

sensual, SYN.—carnal, earthy, lascivious, lecherous, lewd, licentious, sensory, voluptuous, wanton. ANT.—abstemious, ascetic, chaste, continent, virtuous.

sentence, SYN.—condemn, convict. ANT.—absolve, acquit, exonerate, pardon.

sentiment, SYN.—sensation; affection, emotion, feeling, passion, sensibility, tenderness; impression, opinion. ANT.—anesthesia; coldness, imperturbability, insensibility; fact.

sentimental, SYN.—dreamy, extravagant, fanciful, fantastic, fictitious, ideal, idealistic, imaginative, maudlin, mawkish, picturesque, poetic, romantic. ANT.—factual, literal, matter-of-fact, practical, prosaic.

separate, SYN.—divide, part, sever, sunder; allot, deal out, dispense, distribute, share. ANT.—combine, convene, gather, join, unite.

separation, SYN.—alienation, insulation, isolation, loneliness, quarantine, retirement, seclusion, segregation, solitude, withdrawal. ANT.—association, communion, connection, fellowship, union.

sequence, SYN.—arrangement, chain, following, graduation, order, progression, series, string, succession, train.

serene, SYN.—calm, composed, dispassionate, imperturbable, pacific, peaceful, placid, quiet, still, tranquil, undisturbed, unruffled. ANT.—excited, frantic, stormy, turbulent, wild.

serenity, SYN.—calm, calmness, hush, peace, quiescence, quiet, quietude, repose, rest, silence, stillness, tranquility. ANT.—agitation, disturbance, excitement, noise, tumult.

series, SYN.—arrangement, chain, following, graduation, order, progression, sequence, string, succession, train.

serious, SYN.—great, important, momentous, weighty, earnest, grave, sedate, sober, solemn, staid; alarming, critical, dangerous, risky. ANT.—small, trifling, trivial; informal, relaxed.

serve, SYN.—aid, assist, attend, help, oblige, succor; advance, benefit, forward, promote; answer, content, satisfy, suffice; distribute, supply, wait on. ANT.—command, dictate, direct, rule.

service, SYN.—account, advantage, avail, behalf, benefit, favor, gain, good, interest, profit. ANT.—calamity, distress, handicap, trouble.

serviceable, SYN.—advantageous, beneficial, good, helpful, profitable, salutary, useful, wholesome. ANT.—deleterious, destructive, detrimental, harmful, injurious.

servile, SYN.—abject, base, contemptible, despicable, dishonorable, groveling, ignoble, ignominious, low, lowly, mean, menial, sordid, vile, vulgar. ANT.—esteemed, exalted, honored, lofty, noble, righteous.

servitude, SYN.—bondage, captivity, confinement, imprisonment, serfdom, slavery, thralldom, vassalage. ANT.—freedom, liberation.

set, SYN.—arrange, deposit, dispose, lay, place, put. ANT.—disarrange, disturb, mislay, misplace, remove.

settle, SYN.—adjudicate, close, conclude, decide, determine, end, resolve, terminate. ANT.—doubt, hesitate, suspend, vacillate, waver.

settlement, SYN.—close, completion, conclusion, end, finale, issue, termination; decision, deduction, inference, judgment. ANT.—beginning, commencement, inception, prelude, start.

sever, SYN.—divide, part, separate, sunder. ANT.—combine, convene, gather, join, unite.

severe, SYN.—acute, arduous, distressing, exacting, extreme, hard, harsh, intense, relentless, rigid, rigorous, sharp, stern, stringent, unmitigated, unyielding, violent. ANT.—considerate, genial, indulgent, merciful, yielding.

sew, SYN.—fix, mend, patch, refit, repair, restore. ANT.—deface, destroy, hurt, injure, rend.

shabby, SYN.—destitute, impecunious, indigent, needy, penniless, poor, poverty-stricken; deficient, inferior, scanty. ANT.—affluent, opulent, rich, wealthy; ample, good, right, sufficient.

shade, SYN.—color, complexion, dye, hue, paint, pigment, stain, tincture, tinge, tint. ANT.—achromatism, paleness, transparency.

shadowy, SYN.—black, dark, dim, gloomy, murky, obscure, unilluminated; dusky; dismal, gloomy; evil, sinister, wicked; hidden, mystic, occult, secret. ANT.—light; bright, clear; pleasant; lucid.

shake, SYN.—agitate, flutter, jar, jolt, quake, quiver, rock, shiver, shudder, sway, totter, tremble, vibrate, waver.

shallow, SYN.—cursory, exterior, flimsy, frivolous, imperfect, slight, superficial. ANT.—abstruse, complete, deep, profound, thorough.

sham, SYN.—act, affect, assume, feign, pretend, profess, simulate. ANT.—display, exhibit, expose, reveal.

shame, SYN.—abashment, chagrin, humiliation, mortification; disgrace, dishonor, disrepute, ignominy, odium, opprobrium, scandal. ANT.—dignity, glory, honor, praise, renown.

shameful, SYN.—discreditable, disgraceful, dishonorable, disreputable, ignominious, scandalous. ANT.—esteemed, honorable, renowned, respectable.

shape, SYN.—appearance, build, cast, configuration, contour, cut, figure, form, frame, guise, image, mould, outline, pattern. ANT.—contortion, deformity, distortion, mutilation.

shape, SYN.—construct, create, fashion, forge, form, make, mold, produce, compose, constitute, make up; arrange, combine, organize; devise, frame, invent. ANT.—destroy, disfigure, dismantle, misshape, wreck.

share, SYN.—bit, division, fragment, parcel, part,

piece, portion, section, segment. ANT.—bulk, whole.

share, SYN.—allot, apportion, appropriate, assign, dispense, distribute, divide, parcel, partake, partition, portion. ANT.—aggregate, amass, combine, condense.

shared, SYN.—common, correlative, interchangeable, joint, mutual, reciprocal. ANT.—dissociated, separate, unrequited, unshared.

sharp, SYN.—acute, cutting, keen, pointed; acrid, biting, bitter, pungent; penetrating, piercing, severe, shrill; astute, clever, cunning, quick, shrewd, wily, witty; blunt, brusque, curt, rude; craggy, harsh, precipitous, rough, rugged, steep. ANT.—bland, blunt, gentle, shallow, stupid; courteous, gradual, smooth.

shatter, SYN.—break, burst, crack, crush, demolish, destroy, fracture, infringe, pound, rack, rend, rupture, smash. ANT.—join, mend, renovate, repair, restore.

shattered, SYN.—broken, crushed, destroyed, flattened, fractured, interrupted, reduced, rent, ruptured, separated, smashed, wrecked. ANT.—integral, repaired, united, whole.

sheepish, SYN.—abashed, bashful, coy, diffident, embarrassed, humble, modest, recoiling, shamefaced, shy, timid, timorous. ANT.—adventurous, daring, fearless, gregarious, outgoing.

shelter, SYN.—asylum, harbor, haven, refuge, retreat, sanctuary; cover, protection, safety, security. ANT.—danger, exposure, hazard, jeopardy, peril.

shelter, SYN.—cloak, clothe, conceal, cover, curtain, disguise, envelop, guard, hide, mask, protect, screen, shield, shroud, veil. SYN.—bare, divulge, expose, reveal, unveil.

shield, SYN.—cloak, clothe, conceal, cover, curtain, disguise, envelop, guard, hide, mask, protect, screen, shroud, veil. ANT.—bare, divulge, expose, reveal, unveil.

shift, SYN.—change, exchange, substitute; alter, convert, modify, transfigure, transform, vary, veer. ANT.—retoain, continue, establish, preserve, settle, stablize. ˙

shifting, SYN.—changeable, fickle. fitful, inconstant, unstable, vacillating, variable, wavering. ANT.—constant, stable, steady, unchanging, uniform.

shine, SYN.—beam, blaze, flash, flicker, glare, gleam, glimmer, glisten, glitter, glow, radiate, scintillate, shimmer, sparkle, twinkle.

shining, SYN.—brilliant, bright, dazzling, effulgent, glorious, gorgeous, grand, illustrious, magnificent, radiant, resplendent, showy, splendid, sumptuous, superb. ANT.—dull, mediocre, modest, ordinary, unimpressive.

shock, SYN.—alarm, amaze, astonish, astound, disconcert, dumbfound, flabbergast, startle, stun, surprise, take aback. ANT.—admonish, caution, forewarn, prepare.

shocking, SYN.—appalling, awful, dire, dreadful, fearful, frightful, gruesome, hideous, horrible, horrid, severe, terrible. ANT.—happy, joyous, pleasing, safe, secure.

short, SYN.—dumpy, dwarfed, little, low, pudgy, small, squat, undersized; abrupt, brief, compendious, concise, curt, laconic, succinct, summary, terse; deficient, inadequate, insufficient, lacking, limited. ANT.—abundant, ample, big, extended, protracted.

shortcoming, SYN.—blemish, defect, error, failure, fault, flaw, imperfection, mistake, omission, vice. ANT.— completeness, correctness, perfection.

shorten, SYN.—abbreviate, abridge, condense, contract, curtail, diminish, lessen, limit, reduce, restrict. ANT.—elongate, extend, lengthen.

shortening, SYN.—abbreviation, abridgement, contraction, reduction. ANT.—amplification, enlargement, expansion, extension.

shout, SYN.—call out, cry, cry out, ejaculate, exclaim, vociferate. ANT.—intimate, whisper, write.

shove, SYN.—crowd, drive, force, impel, jostle, press, propel, push; hasten, promote, urge. ANT.—drag, falter, halt, pull, retreat; ignore, oppose.

show, SYN.—array, display, exhibition, exposition; demonstration, flourish, ostentation, parade, spectacle, splurge; entertainment, movie, performance, production.

show, SYN.—disclose, display, exhibit, expose, indicate, manifest, parade, present, reveal, unfold; demonstrate, evidence, manifest, prove, verify; conduct, direct, guide, usher; inform, instruct, teach. ANT.—conceal, confuse, hide.

showy, SYN.—affected, artificial, ceremonious, dramatic, histrionic, melodramatic, stagy, theatrical. ANT.—modest, subdued, unaffected, unemotional.

shred, SYN.—bit, iota, jot, mite, particle, scrap, smidgen, speck. ANT.—aggregate, bulk, mass, quantity.

shred, SYN.—cleave, disunite, lacerate, rend, rip, rive, sever, slit, split, sunder, tear, wound. ANT.—join, mend, repair, sew, unite.

shrewd, SYN.—artful, astute, clandestine, covert, crafty, cunning, foxy, furtive, guileful, insidious, shy, stealthy, subtle, surreptitious, tricky, underhand, wily. ANT.—candid, frank, ingenuous, open, sincere.

shrill, SYN.—acute, cutting, keen, pointed; penetrating, piercing, severe, sharp. ANT.—bland, blunt, gentle, shallow.

shrivel, SYN.—droop, dry, sear, shrink, waste, wilt, wither, wizen; decline, fail, languish, sink, weaken. ANT.—refresh, rejuvenate, renew, revive.

shun, SYN.—avert, avoid, dodge, escape, eschew, elude, forbear, forestall, free, ward. ANT.—confront, encounter, meet, oppose.

shut, SYN.—close, seal; clog, obstruct, stop; cease, complete, conclude, end, finish, terminate. ANT.—open, unbar, unlock; begin, commence, inaugurate, start.

shy, SYN.—bashful, cautious, chary, demure, diffident, fearful, modest, reserved, retiring, sheepish, shrinking, timorous, wary. ANT.—audacious, bold, brazen, forward, immodest.

sick, SYN.—ailing, diseased, ill, indisposed, infirm, morbid, unhealthy, unwell. ANT.—healthy, robust, sound, strong, well.

sickness, SYN.—ailment, complaint, disease, disorder, illness. infirmity, malady. ANT.—health, healthiness, soundness, vigor.

sightless, SYN.—blind, ignorant, oblivious, undiscerning, unmindful, unseeing; headlong, heedless, rash. ANT.—aware, calculated, discerning, perceiving, sensible.

sign, SYN.—emblem, gesture, indication, mark, note, omen, portent, proof, signal, symbol, symptom, token.

signal, SYN.—alarm, warning. ANT.—quiet, security, tranquility.

significance, SYN.—acceptation, connotation, drift, explanation, gist, implication, import, intent, interpretation, meaning, purport, purpose, sense, signification.

significant, SYN.—critical, grave, important, indicative, material, momentous, telling, weighty. ANT.—insignificant, irrelevant, meaningless, negligible, unimportant.

signify, SYN.—denote, designate, disclose, imply, intimate, indicate, manifest, reveal, show, specify. ANT.—conceal, distract, divert, falsify, mislead.

silence, SYN.—hushed, motionless, peaceful, placid, quiescent, quiet, still, tranquil, undisturbed. ANT.—loud, strident; agitated, disturbed, perturbed.

silent, SYN.—calm, dumb, hushed, mute, noiseless, peaceful, quiet, still, taciturn, tranquil. ANT.—clamorous, loud, noisy, raucous.

silhouette, SYN.—brief, contour, delineation, draft, figure, form, outline, plan, profile, sketch.

silly, SYN.—absurd, asinine, brainless, crazy, foolish, idiotic, irrational, nonsensical, preposterous, ridiculous, senseless, simple. ANT.—judicious, prudent, sagacious, sane, wise.

similar, SYN.—akin, alike, allied, analogous, comparable, correlative, correspondent, corresponding, like, parallel. ANT.—different, dissimilar, divergent, incongruous, opposed.

similarity, SYN.—analogy, correspondence, likeness, parity, resemblance, similtude. ANT.—difference, distinction, variance.

simple, SYN.—easy, effortless, elementary, facile, mere, pure, single, uncompounded, unmixed; homely, humble, plain; artless, frank, naive, natural, open, unsophisticated; asinine, credulous, foolish, silly.

ANT.— adorned, artful, complex, intricate, wise.

simulate, SYN.—ape, copy, counterfeit, duplicate, imitate, impersonate, mimic, mock. ANT.—alter, distort, diverge, invent.

sin, SYN.—crime, evil, guilt, iniquity, offense, transgression, ungodliness, vice, wickedness, wrong. ANT.—goodness, innocence, purity, righteousness, virtue.

sincere, SYN.—candid, earnest, frank, genuine, heartfelt, honest, open, straightforward, true, truthful, unfeigned, upright. ANT.—affected, dishonest, hypocritical, insincere, untruthful.

sincerity, SYN.—candor, fairness, frankness, honesty, integrity, justice, openness, rectitude, responsibility, trustworthiness, uprightness. ANT.—cheating, deceit, dishonesty, fraud, trickery.

sinful, SYN.—antisocial, bad, corrupt, dissolute, immoral, indecent, licentious, profligate, unprincipled, vicious, wicked. ANT.—chaste, highminded, noble, pure, virtuous.

sing, SYN.—carol, chant, croon, hum, intone, lilt, warble.

singe, SYN.—blaze, burn, char, consume, incinerate, scald, scorch, sear. ANT.— extinguish, put out, quench.

single, SYN.—distinctive, individual, marked, particular, separate, singular, special, specific, unique. ANT.—common, general, ordinary, universal.

singular, SYN.—eccentric, exceptional, extraordinary, odd, peculiar, rare, strange, striking, unusual; characteristic, distinctive, individual, particular, special. ANT.—common, general, normal, ordinary.

sinless, SYN.—blameless, faultless, holy, immaculate, perfect, pure; consummate, excellent, ideal, superlative, supreme. ANT.—blemished, defective, faulty, imperfect.

sink, SYN.—collapse, decline, decrease, descend, diminish, drop, fall, subside; droop, extend, downward, hang. ANT.—arise, ascend, climb, mount, soar; steady.

sire, SYN.—beget, breed, create, engender, father, generate, originate, procreate, produce, propagate. ANT.—abort, destroy, extinguish, kill, murder.

site, SYN.—locality, place, position, situation, station.

situation, SYN.—case, circumstance, condition, plight, predicament, state.

size, SYN.—amplitude, area, bigness, bulk, dimensions, expanse, extent, greatness, largeness, magnitude, mass, volume.

skeptic, SYN.—agnostic, deist, doubter, freethinker, infidel, questioner, unbeliever. ANT.—adorer, believer, follower, worshiper.

skepticism, SYN.—doubting, hesitation, questioning, wavering; distrust, mistrust, suspicion. ANT.—belief, confidence, decision, reliance, trust.

sketch, SYN.—contour, delineation, draft, figure, form, outline, plan, profile, silhouette.

sketch, SYN.—delineate, depict, draw, trace; compose, draft, formulate, write.

skill, SYN.—ability, adroitness, cleverness, cunning, deftness, dexterity, facility, ingenuity, knack, readiness, skillfulness. ANT.—awkwardness, clumsiness, inability, ineptitude.

skillful, SYN.—able, accomplished, adept, clever, competent, cunning, expert, ingenious, practiced, proficient, skilled, versed. ANT.—awkward, bungling, clumsy, inexpert, untrained.

skip, SYN.—cancel, delete, disregard, drop, eliminate, exclude, ignore, miss, neglect, omit, overlook. ANT.—enter, include, insert, introduce, notice.

skirmish, SYN.—battle,

brawl, combat, conflict, contend, dispute, encounter, fight, quarrel, scuffle, squabble, struggle, wrangle.

slack, SYN.—disengaged, free, indefinite, lax, limp, loose, unbound, unfastened, untied, vague; careless, dissolute, heedless, unrestrained, wanton. ANT.—fast, tied, right; inhibited, restrained.

slander, SYN.—aspersion, backbiting, calumny, defamation, libel, scandal, vilification. ANT.—applause, commendation, defense, flattery, praise.

slant, SYN.—bent, bias, disposition, inclination, leaning, partiality, penchant, predilection, predisposition, prejudice, proclivity, proneness, propensity, tendency, turn. ANT.—equity, fairness, impartiality, justice.

slavery, SYN.—bondage, captivity, confinement, imprisonment, serfdom, servitude, thralldom, vassalage. ANT.—freedom, liberation.

slaughter, SYN.—butchery, carnage, massacre, pogrom.

slaughter, SYN.—assassinate, butcher, execute, kill, massacre, murder, put to death, slay. ANT.—animate, protect, resuscitate, save, vivify.

sleek, SYN.—polished, slick, smooth. ANT.—bluff, blunt, harsh, rough, rugged.

sleep, SYN.—catnap, doze, drowse, nap, nod, repose, rest, slumber, snooze.

slender, SYN.—emaciated, gaunt, lank, lean, meager, narrow, rare, scanty, scrawny, skinny, slight, slim, spare, tenuous, thin. ANT.—broad, bulky, fat, thick, wide.

slight, SYN.—emaciated, fine, gaunt, lank, lean, meager, narrow, rare, scanty, scrawny, skinny, slender, slim, spare, tenuous, thin. ANT.—broad, bulky, fat, thick, wide.

slight, SYN.—disregard, neglect, ignore, omit, overlook, skip. ANT.—include, notice, regard.

slip, SYN.—blunder, error, fallacy, fault, inaccuracy, mistake. ANT.—accuracy, precision, truth.

slope, SYN.—bending, incline, inclination, leaning.

sloth, SYN.—idleness, inactivity, indolence, inertia, sluggishness, supineness, torpidity. ANT.—activity, alertness, assiduousness, diligence.

slothful, SYN.—idle, inactive, indolent, inert, lazy, sluggish, supine, torpid. ANT.—active, alert, assiduous, diligent.

slow, SYN.—dawdling, delaying, deliberate, dull, gradual, laggard, leisurely, sluggish, tired. ANT.—fast, quick, rapid, speedy, swift.

sluggish, SYN.—dawdling, delaying, deliberate, dull, gradual, laggard, leisurely, slow, tired. ANT.—fast, quick, rapid, speedy, swift.

slumber, SYN.—catnap, doze, drowse, nap, nod, repose, rest, sleep, snooze.

sly, SYN.—artful, astute, clandestine, covert, crafty, cunning, foxy, furtive, guileful, insidious, shrewd, stealthy, subtle, surreptitious, tricky, underhand, wily. ANT.—candid, frank, ingenuous, open, sincere.

small, SYN.—diminutive, insignificant, little, miniature, minute, petty, puny, slight, tiny, trivial, wee. ANT.—big, enormous, huge, immense, large.

smart, SYN.—adroit, apt, clever, dexterous, quick, quick-witted, skillful, talented, witty; bright, ingenious, sharp. ANT.—awkward, bungling, clumsy, slow, unskilled; dull, foolish, stupid.

smash, SYN.—break, burst, crack, crush, demolish, destroy, fracture, infringe, pound, rack, rend, rupture, shatter. ANT.—join, mend, renovate, repair, restore.

smell, SYN.—aroma, fetidness, fragrance, fume, incense, odor, perfume, redolence, scent, stench, stink.

smidgen, SYN.—bit, crumb, grain, iota, jot, mite, particle, scrap, shred, speck. ANT.—aggregate, bulk, mass, quantity.

smite, SYN.—beat, belabor, buffet, dash, hit, knock, pound, pummel, punch, strike, thrash, thump; conquer, defeat, overpower, overthrow, rout, subdue, vanquish. ANT.—defend, shield, stroke; fail, surrender.

smooth, SYN.—flat, level, plain, polished, sleek, slick; glib, diplomatic, suave, urbane. ANT.—bluff, blunt, harsh, rough, rugged.

smutty, SYN.—coarse, dirty, disgusting, filthy, gross, impure, indecent, lewd, obscene, offensive, pornographic. ANT.—decent, modest, pure, refined.

snag, SYN.—bar, barrier, block, check, difficulty, hindrance, impediment, obstacle, obstruction. ANT.—aid, assistance, encouragement, help.

snappish, SYN.—fractious, fretful, ill-natured, ill-tempered, irritable, peevish, petulant, testy, touchy, waspish. ANT.—affable, genial, good-natured, good-tempered, pleasant.

snare, SYN.—apprehend, arrest, capture, catch, clutch, grasp, grip, lay hold of, seize, trap. ANT.—liberate, lose, release, throw.

sneer, SYN.—deride, fleer, flout, gibe, jeer, mock,

scoff, taunt. ANT.—compliment, flatter, laud, praise.

sneering, SYN.—banter, derision, gibe, irony, jeering, mockery, raillery, ridicule, sarcasm, satire.

snoopy, SYN.—curious, inquiring, inquisitive, interrogative, meddling, nosy, peeping, peering, prying, searching. ANT.—incurious, indifferent, unconcerned, uninterested.

snug, SYN.—close, compact, constricted, contracted, firm, narrow, stretched, taut, tense, tight. ANT.—lax, loose, open, relaxed, slack.

soar, SYN.—flit, float, flutter, fly, glide, hover, mount, sail. ANT.—descend, fall, plummet, sink.

sober, SYN.—earnest, grave, sedate, serious, solemn, staid. ANT.—boisterous, informal, joyful, ordinary.

sobriety, SYN.—abstinence, abstention, forbearance, moderation, self-denial, temperance. ANT.—excess, intoxication, self-indulgence.

social, SYN.—affable, civil, communicative, friendly, gregarious, hospitable, out-going, sociable. ANT.—antisocial, disagreeable, hermitic, inhospitable.

soft, SYN.—compassionate, flexible, gentle, lenient, malleable, meek, mellow, mild, subdued, supple, tender, yielding. ANT.—hard, rigid, rough, tough, unyielding.

soften, SYN.—abate, allay, alleviate, assuage, diminish, extenuate, mitigate, relieve, solace, soothe. ANT.—aggravate, agitate, augment, increase, irritate.

soil, SYN.—continent, country, earth, field, ground, island, land, plain, region, tract.

soil, SYN.—befoul, blemish, blight, defile, discolor, disgrace, spot, stain, sully, tarnish. ANT.—bleach, cleanse, decorate, honor, purify.

solace, SYN.—comfort, consolation, contentment, ease, enjoyment, relief, succor. ANT.—affliction, discomfort, misery, suffering, torment, torture.

sole, SYN.—alone, deserted, desolate, isolated, lonely, secluded, unaided; lone, only, single, solitary. ANT.—accompanied, attended, surrounded.

solemn, SYN.—august, awe-inspiring, ceremonious, formal, imposing, impressive, majestic, reverential, ritualistic; earnest, grave, sedate, serious, sober, staid. ANT.—boisterous, informal, joyful, ordinary.

solicitude, SYN.—anxiety, care, concern, worry; attention, caution, regard, vigilance, wariness. ANT.—disregard, indifference, neglect, negligence.

solitary, SYN.—alone, deserted, desolate, isolated, lonely, secluded, unaided; lone, only, single, sole. ANT.—accompanied, attended, surrounded.

solitude, SYN.—alienation, asylum, concealment, isolation, loneliness, privacy, refuge, retirement, retreat, seclusion. ANT.—exposure, notoriety, publicity.

somatic, SYN.—bodily, carnal, corporal, corporeal, material, natural, physical. ANT.—mental, spiritual.

somber, SYN.—bleak, cheerless, dark, dismal, doleful, dreary, dull, funereal, gloomy, lonesome, melancholy, sad. ANT.—cheerful, gay, joyous, lively.

soon, SYN.—beforehand, betimes, early, shortly. ANT.—belated, late, overdue, tardy.

soothe, SYN.—cheer, comfort, console, encourage, gladden, solace, sympathize. ANT.—antagonize, aggravate, depress, dishearten.

soothing, SYN.—benign, calm, docile, gentle, mild, peaceful, placid, relaxed, serene, soft, tame, tractable. ANT.—fierce, harsh, rough, savage, violent.

sophisticated, ANT.—blase, cultivated, cultured, worldly, worldly-wise.

ANT.—crude, ingenuous, naive, simple, uncouth.

sorcery, SYN.—black art, charm, conjuring, enchantment, legerdemain, magic, necromancy, voodoo, witchcraft, wizardry.

sordid, SYN.—base, debased, depraved, foul, loathsome, obscene, odious, revolting, vicious, vile, vulgar, wicked; abject, despicable, ignoble, low, mean, worthless, wretched. ANT.—attractive, decent, laudable; honorable, upright.

sorrow, SYN.—affliction, anguish, distress, grief, heartache, lamentation, misery, mourning, sadness, trial, tribulation, woe. ANT.—comfort, consolation, happiness, joy, solace.

sorrowful, SYN.—dejected, depressed, despondent, disconsolate, dismal, dispirited, doleful, gloomy, glum, melancholy, moody, sad, somber; grave, pensive. ANT.—cheerful, happy, joyous, merry.

sorry, SYN.—afflicted, grieved, hurt, pained, sad, sorrowful, vexed; contrite, penitent, remorseful, repentant; beggarly, contemptible, mean, paltry, pitiable, pitiful, poor, shabby, vile, worthless, wretched. ANT.—cheerful, delighted, impenitent, splendid, unrepentant.

sort, SYN.—category, character, class, description, kind, nature, stamp, type. ANT.—deviation, eccentricity, monstrosity, peculiarity.

sound, SYN.—binding, cogent, conclusive, convincing, effective, efficacious, legal, logical, powerful, strong, telling, valid, weighty. ANT.—counterfeit, null, spurious, void, weak.

sound, SYN.—din, noise, note, tone. ANT.—hush, quiet, silence, stillness.

sour, SYN.—acid, acrimonious, bitter, glum, morose, peevish, rancid, sharp, sullen, tart. ANT.—genial, kindly, sweet, wholesome.

source, SYN.—agent, cause, determinant, incentive, inducement, motive, origin, principle, reason; beginning, birth, commencement, cradle, derivation, foundation, inception, origin, spring, start. ANT.—consequence, effect, end, result; end, harvest, issue, outcome, product.

souvenir, SYN.—commemoration, memento, memorial, monument, remembrance.

sovereignty, ANT.—authority, command, control, dominion, influence, predominance, sway. ANT.—disablement, impotence, incapacity, ineptitude; debility, fatigue, weakness.

spacious, SYN.—ample, broad, capacious, extensive, large, roomy, vast, wide. ANT.—confined, cramped, limited, narrow.

spare, SYN.—conserve, defend, guard, keep, maintain, preserve, protect, rescue, safeguard, save, secure, uphold. ANT.—abandon, abolish, destroy, impair, injure.

sparkle, SYN.—beam, blaze, flash, flicker, glare, gleam, glimmer, glisten, glitter, glow, radiate, scintillate, shimmer, shine, twinkle.

spat, SYN.—affray, altercation, argument, bickering, contention, disagreement, dispute, feud, quarrel, squabble, wrangle. ANT.—agreement, friendliness, harmony, peace, reconciliation.

spawn, SYN.—bear, produce, yield.

speak, SYN.—articulate, converse, declare, discourse, express, harangue, say, talk, tell, utter. ANT.—be silent, hush, refrain.

special, SYN.—distinctive, exceptional, extraordinary, individual, particular, peculiar, uncommon, unusual. ANT.—broad, comprehensive, general, prevailing, widespread.

specific, SYN.—definite, explicit, limited, precise; categorical, characteristic, especial, peculiar. ANT.—general, generic, vague.

specify, SYN.—appoint,

call, denominate, entitle, mention, name. ANT.—hint, miscall, misname.

specimen, SYN.—example, instance, prototype, sample.

speck, SYN.—bit, crumb, grain, iota, jot, mite, particle, scrap, shred, smidgen. ANT.—aggregate, bulk, mass, quantity.

spectacle, SYN.—array, display, exhibition, exposition; demonstration, flourish, ostentation, parade, show, splurge; entertainment, movie, performance, production.

speculate, SYN.—apprehend, assume, believe, conjecture, deduce, guess, imagine, presume, suppose, surmise, think. ANT.—ascertain, conclude, demonstrate, know, prove.

speech, SYN.—chatter, conference, conversation, dialogue, discourse, discussion, gossip, lecture, report, rumor, talk. ANT. — correspondence, meditation, silence, writing.

speed, SYN.—accelerate, dispatch, expedite, facilitate, forward, hasten, hurry, push, quicken, rush. ANT.—block, hinder, impede, retard, slow.

spherical, SYN.—circular, curved, globular, round.

spirit, SYN.—apparition, ghost, phantom, soul, specter; courage, enthusiasm, fortitude, liveliness, temper, verve, vig-

or, vitality, zeal. ANT.—body, flesh, substance; languor, listlessness.

spiritless, SYN.—dead, deceased, defunct, departed, dull, gone, inanimate, insensible, lifeless, unconscious. ANT.—alive, animate, living, stirring.

spiritual, SYN.—divine, ethereal, ghostly, holy, immaterial, incorporeal, religious, sacred, supernatural, unearthly, unworldly. ANT.—carnal, corporeal, material, mundane, physical.

spite, SYN.—animosity, enmity, grudge, ill will, malevolence, malice, malignity, rancor. ANT.—affection, kindness, love, toleration.

spiteful, SYN.—disagreeable, ill-natured, surly, ugly, vicious. ANT.—attractive, beautiful, fair, handsome, pretty.

splendid, SYN.—brilliant, bright, dazzling, effulgent, glorious, gorgeous, grand, illustrious, magnificent, radiant, resplendent, shining, showy, sumptuous, superb. ANT.—dull, mediocre, modest, ordinary, unimpressive.

splendor, SYN.—brightness, brilliance, brilliancy, effulgence, luster, radiance. ANT.—darkness, dullness, gloom, obscurity.

split, SYN.—cleave, disunite, lacerate, rend, rip, rive, sever, shred, slit, tear, wound. ANT.—join, mend, repair, sew, unite.

spoil, SYN.—decay, decompose, disintegrate, putrefy, rot, waste. ANT.—flourish, grow, increase, luxuriate.

spoken, SYN.—oral, verbal, vocal. ANT.—documentary, recorded, written.

spontaneous, SYN.—automatic, extemporaneous, impulsive, instinctive, offhand, voluntary, willing. ANT.—compulsory, forced, planned, prepared, rehearsed.

sport, SYN.—amusement, contest, diversion, fun, game, match, merriment, pastime, play, recreation. ANT.—business.

sport, SYN.—caper, frolic, gamble, gambol, play, revel, romp, stake, toy, wager.

spread, SYN.—exhibit, expand, open, unfold, unseal. ANT.—close, conceal, hide, shut.

sprightly, SYN.—buoyant, effervescent, light, resilient; animated, blithe, cheerful, elated, hopeful, jocund, lively, spirited, vivacious. ANT.—dejected, depressed, despondent, hopeless, sullen.

spring, SYN.—beginning, birth, commencement, cradle, derivation, foundation, inception, origin, source, start. ANT.—end, harvest, issue, outcome, product.

spruce, SYN.—clear, neat, nice, orderly, precise, tidy, trim. ANT.—dirty,

disheveled, sloppy, slovenly, unkempt.

spry, SYN.—active, agile, alert, brisk, flexible, lively, nimble, quick, supple. ANT.—clumsy, heavy, inert, slow, sluggish.

spur, SYN.—cause, impulse, incentive, incitement, inducement, motive, principle, purpose, reason, stimulus. ANT.—action, attempt, deed, effort, result.

squabble, SYN.—altercate, argue, bicker, contend, contest, debate, discuss, dispute, quarrel, wrangle. ANT.—agree, allow, assent, concede.

squalid, SYN.—dirty, filthy, foul, grimy, muddy, soiled, indecent, nasty, obscene; base, contemptible, despicable, low, mean, pitiful, shabby. ANT.—clean, neat, presentable, pure, wholesome.

squander, SYN.—consume, corrode, dissipate, lavish, misuse, scatter, spend, waste. ANT.—accumulate, conserve, economize, preserve, save.

squeamish, SYN.—careful, fastidious, particular. ANT.—undiscriminating.

stability, SYN.—balance, composure, equilibrium, poise, steadiness; proportion, symmetry. ANT.—fall, imbalance, instability, unsteadiness.

stable, SYN.—constant, durable, enduring, established, firm, fixed, immovable, immutable. lasting, permanent, secure, staunch, steadfast, steady, unwavering. ANT.—changeable, erratic, irresolute, vacillating, variable.

staid, SYN.—earnest, grave, sedate, serious, sober, solemn. ANT.—boisterous, informal, joyful, ordinary.

stain, SYN.—befoul, blemish, blight, defile, discolor, disgrace, soil, spot, sully, tarnish; color, dye, tinge, tint. ANT.—bleach, cleanse, decorate, honor, purify.

stale, SYN.—dull, flat, insipid, tasteless, vapid. ANT.—savory, tasty.

stand, SYN.—abide, bear, continue, endure, suffer, sustain, tolerate; halt, pause, remain, rest, stay, stop. ANT.—advance, progress, run, submit, yield.

standard, SYN.—criterion, gauge, law, measure, principle, proof, rule, test, touchstone. ANT.—chance, fancy, guess, supposition.

start, SYN.—beginning, commencement, inception, opening, origin, outset, source. ANT.—close, completion, consummation, end, termination.

start, SYN.—arise, begin, commence, establish, found, inaugurate, initiate, institute, organize, originate. ANT.—complete, end, finish, termi-nate.

startle, SYN.—alarm, amaze, astonish, astound, disconcert, dumbfound, flabbergast, shock, stun, surprise, take aback. ANT.—admonish, caution, forewarn, prepare.

starved, SYN.—craving, famished, hungry, ravenous, voracious; avid, greedy, longing. ANT.—full, gorged, sated, satiated; satisfied.

state, SYN.—case, condition, circumstance, plight, predicament, situation.

state, SYN.—affirm, assert, avow, claim, declare, explain, express, propound, recite, recount, say, specify, tell, utter. ANT.—conceal, deny, imply, retract.

stately, SYN.—courtly, dignified, grand, imperial, kingly, lordly, majestic, monarchial, noble, princely, regal, royal, ruling, sovereign, supreme. ANT.—common, humble, low, plebian, proletarian, servile, vulgar.

statement, SYN.—allegation, announcement, declaration, mention, report; assertion, proposition, thesis.

status, SYN.—caste, condition, place, position, rank, standing, status.

statute, SYN.—act, decree, edict, law. ANT.—deliberation, inactivity, intention.

staunch, SYN.—constant, devoted, faithful, loyal, steadfast, true; reliable, trusty. ANT.—disloyal, false, fickle, treacherous, untrustworthy.

stay, SYN.—abide, arrest, check, delay, halt, hinder, linger, obstruct, remain, sojourn, stand, tarry, wait. ANT.—advance, expedite, hasten, leave, progress.

steadfast, SYN.—constant, fast, firm, inflexible, secure, solid, stable, steady, unswerving, unyielding. ANT.—insecure, loose, unstable, unsteady.

steadfastness, SYN.—constancy, industry, perseverance, persistence, persistency, pertinacity, tenacity. ANT.—cessation, idleness, laziness, rest, sloth.

steal, SYN.—burglarize, embezzle, loot, pilfer, pillage, plagiarize, plunder, purloin, rob, snitch, swipe. ANT.—buy, refund, repay, restore, return.

steep, SYN.—abrupt, hilly, precipitous, sharp, sheer, sudden. ANT.—flat, gradual, level.

steer, SYN.—conduct, direct, escort, guide, lead, control, manage, regulate, supervise.

stench, SYN.—aroma, fetidness, fume, odor, redolence, scent, smell, stink.

stern, SYN.—exacting, hard, harsh, intense, relentless, rigid, rigorous, severe, sharp, stringent, unmitigated, unyielding. ANT.—considerate, genial, indulgent, merciful, yielding.

stiff, SYN.—harsh, rigorous, severe, stern, strict, stringent, unyielding; inflexible, rigid, unbending. ANT.—compassionate, lax, lenient, mild, yielding; elastic, flexible, resilient, supple.

stigma, SYN.—brand, mark, scar, stain, trace, vestige.

still, SYN.—hushed, motionless, peaceful, placid, quiet, quiescent, tranquil, undisturbed; calm, gentle, meek, mild, modest, passive, patient, silent. ANT.—loud, strident; agitated, disturbed, perturbed.

stimulate, SYN.—arouse, awaken, disquiet, excite, incite, irritate, provoke, rouse, stir up. ANT.—allay, calm, pacify, quell, quiet.

stimulus, SYN.—arousal, encouragement, goad, incentive, motive, provocation, stimulant. ANT.—depressant, discouragement, discussion, response.

stingy, SYN.—acquisitive, avaricious, greedy, miserly, niggardly, parsimonious, penurious, tight. ANT.—altruistic, bountiful, extravagant, generous, munificent.

stipend, SYN.—allowance, compensation, earnings, fee, pay, payment, recompense, salary, wages.

ANT.—gift, gratuity, present.

stir, SYN.—agitate, impel, induce, instigate, move, persuade, propel, push, shift. ANT.—deter, halt, rest, stay, stop.

stock, SYN.—accumulation, fund, hoard, provision, reserve, store; breeJ, kind, sort, strain, subspecies. ANT.—homogeneity, likeness, monotony, sameness, uniformity.

stock, SYN.—fill, fill up, furnish, replenish, store, supply. ANT.—deplete, drain, empty, exhaust, void.

stoical, SYN.—assiduous, composed, forbearing, indulgent, long-suffering, passive, patient, resigned, uncomplaining. ANT.—chafing, clamorous, high-strung, hysterical, turbulent.

stolid, SYN.—blunt, dull, edgeless, obtuse, pointless, thick-witted, unsharpened. ANT.—polished, polite, suave, subtle, tactful.

stone, SYN.—boulder, gravel, jewel, pebble, rock.

stop, SYN.—abstain, arrest, bar, cease, check, close, cork, desist, discontinue, end, halt, hinder, impede, interrupt, obstruct, plug, seal, terminate. ANT.—begin, proceed, promote, speed, start.

store, SYN.—accrue, accumulate, amass, collect, gather, heap, hoard, increase. ANT.—diminish,

disperse, dissipate, scatter, waste.

stormy, SYN.—blustery, gusty, inclement, roaring, rough, tempestuous, turbulent, windy. ANT.—calm, clear, peaceful, quiet, tranquil.

story, SYN.—account, anecdote, chronicle, fable, fabrication, falsehood, fiction, history, narration, narrative, novel, report, tale, yarn.

stout, SYN.—chubby, corpulent, fat, obese, paunchy, plump, portly, pudgy, rotund, stocky, thickset. ANT.—gaunt, lean, slender, slim, thin.

straight, SYN.—direct, right, undeviating, unswerving, erect, unbent, upright, vertical, fair, honest, honorable, just, square. ANT.—circuitous, winding; bent, crooked; dishonest.

strain, SYN.—breed, kind, sort, stock, subspecies, variety.

strait, SYN.—condition, difficulty, dilemma, fix, plight, predicament, scrape, situation. ANT.—calmness, comfort, ease, satisfaction.

strange, SYN.—abnormal, bizarre, curious, eccentric, extraordinary, grotesque, irregular, odd, mysterious, peculiar, queer, singular, surprising, uncommon, unusual. ANT.—common, conventional, familiar, ordinary, regular.

stranger, SYN.—alien, foreigner, immigrant, new-comer, outsider. ANT.—acquaintance, associate, countryman, friend, neighbor.

stratagem, SYN.—cabal, conspiracy, design, intrigue, machination, plan, plot, scheme.

stray, SYN.—deviate, digress, err, ramble, range, roam, rove, saunter, stroll, traipse, wander. ANT.—halt, linger, settle, stay, stop.

stream, SYN.—flow, gush, run, spout, spurt; come, emanate, issue, originate, proceed, result; abound, be copious.

strength, SYN.—durability, force, fortitude, intensity, lustiness, might, potency, power, stamina, stoutness, sturdiness, toughness, vigor. ANT.—feebleness, frailty, infirmity, weakness.

strengthen, SYN.—confirm, corroborate, substantiate, verify; acknowledge, assure, establish, settle; approve, fix, ratify, sanction.

stress, SYN.—compulsion, exigency, press, pressure, urgency. ANT.—ease, lenience, recreation, relaxation.

stretch, SYN.—distend, distort, elongate, expand, extend, lengthen, protract, spread, strain. ANT.—contract, loosen, shrink, slacken, tighten.

strict, SYN.—harsh, rigorous, rough, rugged, severe, stringent. ANT.—gentle, mild.

strike, SYN.—beat, hit, hurt, knock, pound, pummel, smite.

striking, SYN.—affecting, arresting, august, commanding, exciting, forcible, grandiose, imposing, impressive, majestic, moving, over-powering, remarkable, splendid, stirring, thrilling, touching. ANT.—commonplace, ordinary, regular, unimpressive.

stringent, SYN.—grating, gruff, harsh, jarring, rigorous, rough, rugged, severe, strict. ANT.—gentle, mild.

stripped, SYN.—bare, exposed, naked, nude, unclad, uncovered; bald, barren, unfurnished; mere, plain, simple; defenseless, open, unprotected. ANT.—clothed, covered, dressed; concealed; protected.

strive, SYN.—attempt, endeavor, struggle, try, undertake; aim, aspire, design, intend, mean. ANT.—abandon, decline, ignore, neglect, omit.

strong, SYN.—athletic, cogent, concentrated, enduring, firm, forceful, forcible, fortified, hale, hardy, impregnanble, mighty, potent, powerful, robust, sinewy, sturdy, tough. ANT.—brittle, delicate, feeble, fragile, insipid.

struggle, SYN.—battle, combat, conflict, contest, fight, fray, skirmish, strife. ANT.— agreement, concord, peace, truce.

stubborn, SYN.—contumacious, determined, dogged, firm, head-strong, immovable, inflexible, intractable, obdurate, obstinate, pertinacious, uncompromising, unyielding. ANT.—amenable, compliant, docile, submissive, yielding.

student, SYN.—disciple, learner, observer, pupil, scholar.

study, SYN.—contemplate, examine, investigate, scrutinize, weigh; cogitate, meditate, muse, ponder, reflect; learn, master.

stuff, SYN.—material, matter, substance; subject, theme, thing, topic. ANT.— immateriality, phantom, spirit.

stuff, SYN.—fill, fill up, furnish, replenish; content, glut, gorge, sate, satiate, satisfy. ANT.—deplete, drain, empty, exhaust, void.

stumble, SYN.—collapse, drop, fall, sink, subside; topple, tumble. ANT.— arise, ascend, climb, mount, soar; steady.

stun, SYN.—alarm, amaze, astonish, astound, disconcert, dumbfound, flabbergast, shock, startle, surprise, take aback. ANT.—admonish, caution, forewarn, prepare.

stupid, SYN.—brainless, crass, dense, dull, dumb, foolish, obtuse, senseless, witless. ANT.—

alert, bright, clever, discerning, intelligent.

stupor, SYN.—daze, drowsiness, insensibility, languor, lethargy, numbness, stupefaction, torpor. ANT.—activity, alertness, liveliness, readiness, wakefulness.

sturdy, SYN.—enduring, firm, fortified, hale, hardy, mighty, potent, powerful, robust, strong, tough. ANT.—brittle, delicate, feeble, fragile, insipid.

subdue, SYN.—beat, conquer, crush, defeat, humble, master, overcome, quell, rout, subjugate, surmount, vanquish. ANT.—capitulate, cede, lose, retreat, surrender.

subject, SYN.—citizen, dependent, inferior, liegeman, subordinate, vassal; argument, matter, point, theme, thesis, topic; case, object, patient.

sublime, SYN.—elevated, exalted, glorious, grand, high, lofty, majestic, noble, raised, splendid, supreme. ANT.—base, ignoble, low, ordinary, ridiculous.

submerge, SYN.—dip, douse, dunk, immerse, plunge, sink; absorb, engage, engross. ANT.—elevate, recover, uplift.

submissive, SYN.—compliant, deferential, dutiful, obedient, tractable, yielding. ANT.—insubordinate, intractable, obstinate, rebellious.

submit SYN.—abdicate, accede, acquiesce, capitulate, cede, quit, relent, relinquish, resign, succumb, surrender, waive, yield. ANT.—deny, dissent, oppose, refuse; assert, resist, strive, struggle.

subordinate, SYN.—citizen, dependent, inferior, liegeman, subject, vasal.

subside, SYN.—collapse, decline, decrease, descend, diminish, drop, fall, sink; droop, extend downward, hang. ANT.—arise, ascend, climb, mount, soar; steady.

substance, SYN.—material, matter, stuff; consequence, importance, moment. ANT.—immateriality, phantom, spirit.

substantiate, SYN.—confirm, corroborate, verify; strengthen.

substitute, SYN.—agent, alternate, deputy, lieutenant, proxy; representative, understudy; equivalent, expedient, makeshift. ANT.—head, master, principal, sovereign.

substitution, SYN.—alteration, alternation, change, modification, mutation, variation, variety, vicissitude. ANT.—monotony, stability, uniformity.

subterfuge, SYN.—cloak, disguise, excuse, garb, mask, pretense, pretension, pretext, semblance, simulation. ANT.—actuality, fact, reality, sincerity, truth.

subtract, SYN.—curtail, deduct, decrease, diminish, lessen, reduce, remove, shorten. ANT.—amplify, enlarge, expand, grow, increase.

succeed, SYN.—achieve, flourish, gain, prevail, prosper, thrive, win; ensue, follow; inherit, supersede, supplant. ANT.—fail, miscarry, miss; anticipate, precede.

succession, SYN.—arrangement, chain, following, gradation, order, progression, sequence, series, string, succession, train.

succinct, SYN.—brief, compendious, concise, curt, laconic, pithy, short, terse. ANT.—extended, lengthy, long, prolonged, protracted.

succor, SYN.—comfort, consolation, contentment, ease, enjoyment, relief, solace. ANT.—affliction, discomfort, misery, suffering, torment, torture.

sudden, SYN.—abrupt, hasty, immediate, instantaneous, rapid, unexpected. ANT.—anticipated, gradual, slowly.

suffer, SYN.—bear, endure, feel, stand, sustain; allow, indulge, let, permit, tolerate; feel, undergo. ANT.—banish, discard, exclude, overcome.

suffering, SYN.—ache, agony, anguish, distress,

misery, pain, throe, torment, torture, woe. ANT.—comfort, ease, mitigation, relief.

sufficient, SYN.—adequate, ample, commensurate, enough, fitting, satisfactory. ANT.—deficient, lacking, scant.

suggest, SYN.—advise, allude, counsel, hint, imply, insinuate, intimate, offer, propose, recommend, refer. ANT.—declare, demand, dictate, insist.

suggestion, SYN.—admonition, advice, caution, counsel, exhortation, instruction, recommendation, warning; information, intelligence, notification.

suit, SYN.—accommodate, adapt, conform, fit. ANT.—disturb, misapply, misfit.

suitable, SYN.—acceptable, agreeable, gratifying welcome. ANT.—disagreeable, offensive.

sulley, SYN.—crabbed, dour, fretful, gloomy, glum, moody, morose, surly. ANT.—amiable, gay, joyous, merry, pleasant.

sullen, SYN.—crabbed, dour, fretful, gloomy, glum, moody, morose, sulky, surly. ANT.—amiable, gay, joyous, merry, pleasant.

sum, SYN.—aggregate, entirety, total, whole. ANT.—fraction, ingredient, part, sample.

sum, SYN.—add, adjoin, append, augment, increase, total. ANT.—deduct, detach, reduce, remove, subtract.

summarize, SYN.—abridge, abstract. ANT.—add, replace, restore, return, unite.

summit, SYN.—apex, crest, crown, head, pinnacle, top, zenith. ANT.—base, bottom, foot, foundation.

sundry, SYN.—different, divers, miscellaneous, various. ANT.—alike, congruous, identical, same, similar.

sunny, SYN.—clear, cloudless, fair. ANT.—cloudy, foul, overcast.

superannuated, SYN.—aged, ancient, antiquated, antique, archaic, elderly, obsolete, old, old-fashioned, senile, venerable. ANT.—modern, new, young, youthful.

supercilious, SYN.—arrogant, disdainful, haughty, overbearing, proud, stately, vain, vainglorious. ANT.—ashamed, humble, lowly, meek.

superficial, SYN.—cursory, exterior, flimsy, frivolous, imperfect, shallow, slight. ANT.—abstruse, complete, deep, profound, thorough.

superintend, SYN.—command, control, direct, dominate, govern, manage, regulate, rule. ANT.—abandon, follow, forsake, ignore, submit.

superintendence, SYN.—charge, control, inspection. management, oversight, supervision, surveillance.

superiority, SYN.—advantage, edge, mastery; benefit, good, profit, service, utility. ANT.—detriment, handicap, harm, impediment, obstruction.

superlative, SYN.—blameless, faultless, holy, immaculate, pure, sinless; complete, consummate, excellent, ideal, perfect, supreme; absolute, downright, unqualified, utter. ANT.—deficient, incomplete, lacking; blemished, defective, faulty, imperfect.

supernatural, SYN.—marvellous, metaphysical, miraculous, otherworldly, preternatural, spiritual, superhuman, unearthly. ANT.—common, human, natural, physical, plain.

supervise, SYN.—command, control, direct, dominate, govern, manage, regulate, rule, superintend. ANT.—abandon, follow, forsake, ignore, submit.

supervision, SYN.—charge, control, inspection, management, oversight, superintendence, surveillance.

supplant, SYN.—overcome, overthrow, overturn. ANT.—conserve, preserve, uphold.

supple, SYN.—elastic, flexible, lithe, pliable, pliant, resilient. ANT.—brittle, hard, rigid, stiff, unbending.

supplicate, SYN.—adjure, ask, beg, beseech, crave, entreat, implore, importune, petition, pray, request, solicit. ANT.—bestow, cede, favor, give, grant.

supplication, SYN.—appeal, entreaty, invocation, petition, plea, prayer, request, suit.

supply, SYN.—accumulation, fund, hoard, provision, reserve, stock, store.

supply, SYN.—endow, equip, fit, fit out, furnish, provide; give, produce, yield. ANT.—denude, despoil, divest, strip.

support, SYN.—base, basis, brace, buttress, foundation, groundwork, prop, stay; aid, assistance, backing, comfort, encouragement, favor, help, patronage, succor; livelihood, living, maintenance, subsistence; confirmation, evidence. ANT.—attack, enmity, opposition.

support, SYN.—advocate, assist, back, bear, brace, encourage, foster, further, help, keep, maintain, preserve, prop, sustain, uphold. ANT.—abandon, betray, destroy, discourage, oppose.

supporter, SYN.—adherent, attendant, devotee, disciple, follower, henchman, partisan, successor, votary. ANT.—chief, head, leader, master.

suppose, SYN.—apprehend, assume, believe, conjecture, deduce, guess, imagine, presume, speculate, surmise, think. ANT.—ascertain, conclude, demonstrate, know, prove.

supposition, SYN.—conjecture, hypothesis, theory. ANT.—certainty, fact, proof.

supress, SYN.—abate, decrease, diminish, lessen, lower, moderate, reduce. ANT.—amplify, enlarge, increase, intensify, revive.

supremacy, SYN.—ascendancy, domination, mastery, predominance, sovereignty, sway, transcendence. ANT.—inferiority.

supreme, SYN.—cardinal, chief, essential, first, foremost, highest, leading, main, paramount, predominant, principal. ANT.—auxiliary, minor, subordinate, subsidiary, supplemental.

sure, SYN.—assured, certain, definite, fixed, indubitable, inevitable, positive, secure, undeniable, unquestionable. ANT.—doubtful, probable, questionable, uncertain.

surly, ANT.—repellent; disagreeable, ill-natured, spiteful, ugly, vicious.

surname, SYN.—appellation, denomination, designation, epithet, name, style, title. ANT.—namelessness; anonymity.

surplus, SYN.—excess, extravagance, immoderation, intemperance, profusion, superabundance, superfluity. ANT.—dearth, deficiency, lack, paucity, want.

surprise, SYN.—curiosity, marvel, miracle, phenomenon, prodigy, rarity, spectacle; admiration, amazement, astonishment, awe, bewilderment, curiosity, wonder, wonderment. ANT.—familiarity, triviality; apathy, expectation, indifference.

surprise, SYN.—alarm, amaze, astonish, astound, disconcert, dumbfound, flabbergast, shock, startle, stun, take aback. ANT.—admonish, caution, forewarn, prepare.

surrender, SYN.—abandon, acquiesce, capitulate, cede, relinquish, renounce, resign, sacrifice, submit, yield. ANT.—conquer, overcome, resist, rout.

surround, SYN.—bound, circumscribe, confine, enclose, encompass, envelop, fence, limit. ANT.—distend, enlarge, expand, expose, open.

surveillance, SYN.—charge, control, inspection, management, oversight, superintendence, supervision.

suspect, SYN.—question, waver; distrust, doubt, mistrust. ANT.—believe, confide, decide, rely on, trust.

suspend, SYN.—adjourn, defer, delay, discontinue, interrupt, postpone, stay; balance, dangle, hang, poise, swing. ANT.—continue, maintain, persist, proceed, prolong.

suspicion, SYN.—distrust, doubt, incredulity, scruple, skepticism, suspense, unbelief, uncertainty. ANT.—belief, certainty, conviction, determination, faith.

sustain, SYN.—advocate, assist, back, bear, brace, encourage, foster, further, help, keep, maintain, preserve, prop, support, uphold. ANT.—abandon, betray, destroy, discourage, oppose.

sustenance, SYN.—diet, edibles, fare, feed, food, meal, nutriment, provisions, rations, repast, viands, victuals. ANT.—drink, hunger, starvation, want.

swallow up, SYN.—absorb, assimilate, consume, engulf, imbibe. ANT.—discharge, dispense, emit, expel, exude.

swarthy, SYN.—dark, dusky, sable. ANT.—light, bright.

sway, SYN.—actuate, affect, bias, control, impel, incite, influence, stir.

swear, SYN.—affirm, assert, aver, declare, maintain, protest, state. ANT.—contradict, demur, deny, dispute, oppose.

sweeping, SYN.—broad, expanded, extensive, large, vast, wide; liberal, tolerant. ANT.—confined, narrow, restricted.

sweet, SYN.—agreeable, delightful, engaging, gentle, honeyed, luscious, mellifluous, melodious, pleasing, saccharine, sugary, winning. ANT.—acrid, bitter, offensive, repulsive, sour.

swift, SYN.—expeditious, fast, fleet, quick, rapid, speedy. ANT.—slow, sluggish.

swindle, SYN.—artifice, cheat, chicanery, deceit, deception, duplicity, fraud, guile, imposition, imposture, trick. ANT.—fairness, honesty, integrity, sincerity.

swindle, SYN.—bilk, cheat, circumvent, deceive, defraud, dupe, fool, gull, hoax, hoodwink, outwit, trick, victimize.

symbol, SYN.—character, mark, sign.

symmetry, SYN.—balance, equilibrium; proportion. ANT.—imbalance, instability, unsteadiness.

sympathetic, SYN.—affable, benevolent, benign, compassionate, forbearing, gentle, good, humane, indulgent, kind, kindly, merciful, tender, thoughtful. ANT.—cruel, inhuman, merciless, severe, unkind.

sympathize, SYN.—cheer, comfort, console, encourage, gladden, solace, soothe. ANT.—antagonize, aggravate, depress, dishearten.

sympathy, SYN.—affinity, agreement, commiseration, compassion, concord, condolence, congeniality, empathy, harmony, pity, tenderness, warmth. ANT.—antipathy, harshness, indifference, malevolence, unconcern.

symptoms, SYN.—trace, vestige; characteristic, feature, indication, mark, property, trait.

synthetic, SYN.—artificial, bogus, counterfeit, ersatz, fake, feigned, fictitious, phony, sham, spurious, unreal. ANT.—genuine, natural, real, true.

system, SYN.—arrangement, method, mode, order, organization, plan, process, regularity, rule, scheme. ANT.—chance, chaos, confusion, disarrangement, disorder, irregularity.

T

tact, SYN.—address, adroitness, dexterity, diplomacy, finesse, knack, poise, savoir-faire, skill. ANT.—awkwardness, blunder, incompetence, rudeness, vulgarity.

tactful, SYN.—adroit, diplomatic, discreet, discriminating, judicious, politic. ANT.—boorish, churlish, coarse, gruff, rude.

tainted, SYN.—contaminated, corrupted, crooked, debased, depraved, dishonest, impure, profligate, putrid, spoiled, unsound, venal, vitiated.

take, SYN.—appropriate, capture, catch, confiscate, ensnare, gain, purloin, remove, steal; clasp, clutch, grasp, grip, seize; accept, get, obtain, receive; bear, endure, stand, tolerate; bring, carry, convey, escort; attract, captivate, charm, delight, interest; claim, demand, necessitate, require; adopt, assume, choose, espouse, select.

tale, SYN.—account, anecdote, chronicle, fable, fabrication, falsehood, fiction, history, narration, narrative, novel, report, story, yarn.

talent, SYN.—ability, aptitude, capability, cleverness, endowment, faculty, genius, gift, knack, skill. ANT.—incompetence, ineptitude, stupidity.

talented, SYN.—adroit, apt, clever, dexterous, quick, quick-witted, skillful, witty; bright, ingenious, sharp, smart. ANT.—awkward, bungling, clumsy, slow, unskilled; dull, foolish, stupid.

talk, SYN.—chatter, conference, conversation, dialogue, discourse, discussion, gossip, lecture, report, rumor, speech, ANT.— correspondence, meditation, silence, writing.

talk, SYN.—blab, chat, converse, gossip, jabber, mutter, prattle, speak, tattle; argue, comment, declaim, discourse, harangue, lecture, plead, preach, rant, spout; confer, consult, deliberate, discuss, reason.

talkative, SYN.—chattering, chatty, communicative, garrulous, glib, loquacious, verbose, voluble. ANT.—laconic, reticent, silent, taciturn, uncommunicative.

tall, SYN.—high, lofty, towering; elevated. ANT.—small, stunted, tiny.

tame, SYN.—docile, domestic, domesticated, gentle; meek, subdued, submissive; dull, flat, insipid, tedious. ANT.—fierce, savage, spirited, wild; animated, exciting, lively, spirited.

tamper, SYN.—interfere, interpose, interrupt, meddle, mix in, monkey.

tangible, SYN.—bodily, corporeal, material, palpable, physical, sensible. ANT.—mental, metaphysical, spiritual.

tardy, SYN.—delayed, late, overdue, slow. ANT.—early, timely.

tarnish, SYN.—befoul, blemish, blight, defile, discolor, disgrace, soil, spot, stain, sully. ANT.—bleach, cleanse, decorate, honor, purify.

tart, SYN.—acrid, biting, bitter, distasteful, pungent, sour. ANT.—delicious, mellow, pleasant, sweet.

task, SYN.—chore, job, labor, stint, toil, work, undertaking.

taste, SYN.—flavor, relish, savor, tang; discernment, disposition, inclination, judgment, liking, predilection, sensibility, zest. ANT.—antipathy, disinclination, indelicacy, insipidity.

taunt, SYN.—deride, fleer, flout, gibe, jeer, mock, scoff, sneer, tease. ANT.—compliment, flatter, laud, praise.

taunting, SYN.—acrimonious, biting, caustic, cutting, derisive, ironic, sarcastic, sardonic, satirical, sneering. ANT.—affable, agreeable, amiable, pleasant.

taut, SYN.—constricted, firm, snug, stretched, tight. ANT.—lax, loose, open, relaxed, slack.

tax, SYN.—assessment, custom, duty, exaction, excise, impost, levy, rate, toll, tribute; burden, strain. ANT.—gift, remuneration, reward, wages.

teach, SYN.—educate, inculcate, inform, instill, instruct, school, train, tutor. ANT.—misguide, misinform.

tear, SYN.—cleave, disunite, lacerate, rend, rip, rive, sever, shred, slit, split, sunder, wound. ANT.—join, mend, repair, sew, unite.

tease, SYN.—aggravate, annoy, badger, bother, disturb, harass, harry, irritate, molest, nag, pester, plague, provoke, tantalize, taunt, torment, vex, worry. ANT.—comfort, delight, gratify, please, soothe.

tedious, SYN.—boring, burdensome, dilatory, dreary, dull, humdrum, irksome, monotonous, slow, sluggish, tardy, tiresome, uninteresting, wearisome. ANT.—amusing, entertaining, exciting, interesting, quick.

teeming, SYN.—abundant, ample, bountiful, copious, overflowing, plenteous, plentiful, profuse, rich. ANT.—deficient, insufficient, scant, scarce.

tell, SYN.—describe, narrate, recount, rehearse, relate, report; communicate, express, mention, publish, speak, state, utter; announce, betray, confess, disclose, divulge, reveal; discern, discover, distinguish, recognize; acquaint, apprise, inform, instruct, notify; direct, order, request.

temerity, SYN.—audacity, boldness, foolhardiness, precipitancy, rashness, recklessness. ANT.—caution, hesitation, prudence, timidity, wariness.

temper, SYN.—anger, animosity, choler, exasperation, fury, indignation, ire, irritation, passion, petulance, rage, resentment, wrath. ANT.—conciliation, forbearance, patience, peace, selfcontrol.

temperament, SYN.—disposition, humor, mood, temper.

temperance, SYN.—abstention, abstinence, forbearance, moderation, self-denial, sobriety. ANT.—excess, gluttony, greed, intoxication, selfindulgence.

tempest, SYN.—blast, breeze, draft, gale, gust, hurricane, squall, storm, wind, zephyr.

temporal, SYN.—earthly, laic, lay, mundane, profane, worldly. ANT.—ecclesiastical, religious, spiritual, unworldly.

temporary, SYN.—brief, ephemeral, evanescent, fleeting, momentary, short-lived, transient. ANT.—abiding, immortal, lasting, permanent, timeless.

tenacity, SYN.—constancy, industry, perseverance, persistence, persistency, pertinacity, steadfastness. ANT.—cessation, idleness, laziness, rest, sloth.

tend, SYN.—accompany, attend, escort, follow, guard, lackey, protect, serve, watch.

tendency, SYN.—aim, bent, bias, drift, inclination, leaning, predisposition, proclivity, proneness, propensity, trend. ANT.—aversion, deviation, disinclination.

tender, SYN.—bland, gentle, kind, meek, mild, moderate, soft, soothing. ANT.—bitter, fierce, harsh, rough, severe.

tender, SYN.—advance, extend, offer, present, proffer, propose, volunteer. ANT.—accept, receive, reject, retain, spurn.

tenderness, SYN.—affection, attachment, endearment, fondness, kindness, love. ANT.—aversion, hatred, indifference, repugnance, repulsion.

tenet, SYN.—belief, creed, doctrine, dogma, precept, teaching. ANT.—conduct, deed, performance, practice.

term, SYN.—boundary, duration, limit, period, time; condition, expression, name, phrase, word.

terminal, SYN.—concluding, conclusive, decisive, ending, eventual, final, last, latest, ultimate. ANT.—first, inaugural, incipient, original, rudimentary.

terminate, SYN.—abolish, cease, close, complete, conclude, end, expire, finish, stop. ANT.—begin, commence, establish, initiate, start.

terrible, SYN.—appalling, awful, dire, dreadful, fearful, frightful, gruesome, hideous, horrible, horrid, severe, shocking. ANT.—happy, joyous, pleasing, safe, secure.

terrify, SYN.—affright, alarm, appall, astound, daunt, dismay, frighten, horrify, intimidate, scare, startle, terrorize. ANT.—allay, compose, embolden, reassure, soothe.

territory, SYN.—country, district, division, domain, dominion, land, place, province, quarter, region, section.

terror, SYN.—alarm, consternation, dismay, dread, fear, fright, horror, panic. ANT.—assurance, calm, peace, security.

terse, SYN.—brief, compact, concise, condensed, incisive, neat, pithy, succinct, summary. ANT.—lengthy, prolix, verbose, wordy.

testimony, SYN.—attestation, confirmation, declaration, evidence, proof, witness. ANT.—argument, contradiction, disproof, refutation.

testy, SYN.—fractious, fretful, ill-natured, ill-tempered, irritable, peevish, petulant, snappish, touchy, waspish. ANT.—affable, genial, good-natured, good-tempered, pleasant.

theatrical, SYN.—affected, artificial, ceremonious, dramatic, histrionic, melodramatic, showy, stagy. ANT.—modest, subdued, unaffected, unemotional.

theft, SYN.—burglary, depredation, larceny, pillage, plunder, robbery.

theme, SYN.—composition,

essay, motive, subject, text, thesis, topic.

theoretical, SYN.—academic, bookish, erudite, formal, learned, pedantic, scholarly, scholastic. ANT.— common-sense, ignorant, practical, simple.

theory, SYN.—conjecture, doctrine, hypothesis, opinion, postulate, presupposition, speculation. ANT.—fact, practice, proof, verity.

therefore, SYN.—accordingly, consequently, hence, so, then, thence.

thick, SYN.—close, compact, compressed, concentrated, crowded, dense. ANT.—dispersed, dissipated, sparse.

thin, SYN.—attenuated, diaphanous, diluted, emaciated, fine, flimsy, gaunt, gauzy, gossamer, lank, lean, meager, narrow, rare, scanty, scrawny, skinny, slender, slight, slim, spare, tenuous. ANT.—broad, bulky, fat, thick, wide.

think, SYN.—conceive, imagine, picture, recall, recollect, remember; cogitate, contemplate, deliberate, meditate, muse, ponder, reason, reflect, speculate; apprehend, believe, consider, deem, esteem, judge, opine, reckon, regard, suppose; devise, intend, mean, plan, purpose. ANT.—conjecture, forget, guess.

thorough, SYN.—complete, consummate, entire, finished, full, perfect, total, unbroken, undivided. ANT.—imperfect, lacking, unfinished.

thought, SYN.—cogitation, conception, consideration, contemplation, deliberation, fancy, idea, imagination, impression, judgment, meditation, memory, notion, opinion, recollection, reflection, regard, retrospection, sentiment, view.

thoughtful, SYN.—attentive, careful, cautious, concerned, considerate, heedful, provident, prudent, contemplative, dreamy, introspective, meditative, pensive, reflective. ANT.—heedless, inconsiderate, precipitous, rash, thoughtless.

thoughtless, SYN.—careless, heedless, imprudent, inattentive, inconsiderate, indiscreet, reckless, unconcerned; desultory, inaccurate, lax, neglectful, negligent, remiss. ANT.—accurate, careful, meticulous, nice.

threatening, SYN.—approaching, imminent, impending, menacing, nigh, overhanging, ANT.—afar, distant, improbable, remote, retreating.

thrifty, SYN.—economical, frugal, parsimonious, provident, saving, sparing, stingy, temperate. ANT.—extravagant, intemperate, self-indulgent, wasteful.

throb, SYN.—beat, palpitate, pulsate, pulse. ANT.—fail.

throe, SYN.—ache, pain, pang, paroxysm, twinge; agony, anguish, distress, grief, suffering. ANT.—comfort, ease, relief; happiness, pleasure, solace.

throng, SYN.—bevy, crowd, crush, horde, host, masses, mob, multitude, populace, press, rabble, swarm.

throw, SYN.—cast, fling, hurl, pitch, propel, thrust, toss. ANT.—draw, haul, hold, pull, retain.

thrust, SYN.—crowd, drive, force, impel, jostle, press, propel, push, shove; hasten, promote, urge. ANT.—drag, falter, halt, pull, retreat; ignore, oppose.

thwart, SYN.—baffle, balk, circumvent, defeat, disappoint, foil, frustrate, hinder, outwit, prevent. ANT.—accomplish, fulfill, further, promote.

tidings, SYN.—information, intelligence, message, news, report.

tidy, SYN.—clear, neat, nice, orderly, precise, spruce, trim. ANT.—dirty, disheveled, sloppy, slovenly, unkempt.

tie, SYN.—affinity, alliance, association, bond, conjunction, connection, link, relationship, union. ANT.—disunion, isolation, separation.

tie, SYN.—attach, bind, connect, engage, fasten, fetter, join, link, oblige,

restrain, restrict. ANT.—free, loose, unfasten, untie.

tight, SYN.—close, compact, constricted, contracted, firm, narrow, snug, stretched, taut, tense; close-fisted, niggardly, parsimonious, penny-pinching, stingy. ANT.—lax, loose, open, relaxed, slack.

time, SYN.—age, date, duration, epoch, era, interim, period, season, span, spell, tempo, term.

timely, SYN.—exact, precise, prompt, punctual, ready. ANT.—dilatory, late, slow, tardy.

timid, SYN.—abashed, bashful, coy, diffident, embarrassed, humble, modest, recoiling, shamefaced, sheepish, shy, timorous. ANT.—adventurous, daring, fearless, gregarious, outgoing.

tiny, SYN.—diminutive, insignificant, little, miniature, minute, petty, puny, slight, small, trivial, wee. ANT.—big, enormous, huge, immense.

tire, SYN.—bore, exhaust, fatigue, jade, tucker, wear out, weary. ANT.—amuse, invigorate, refresh, restore, revive.

tired, SYN.—exhausted, faint, fatigued, jaded, spent, weary, wearied, worn. ANT.—fresh, hearty, invigorated, rested.

title, SYN.—appellation, denomination, designa-

tion, epithet, name; claim, due, privilege, right.

toil, SYN.—achievement, business, drudgery, effort, employment, labor, occupation, opus, performance, production, task, travail, work. ANT.—ease, leisure, play, recreation, vacation.

tolerant, SYN.—broad, expanded, extensive, large, sweeping, vast, wide; liberal. ANT.—confined, narrow, restricted.

tolerate, SYN.—allow, permit; abide, bear, brook, endure, stand. ANT.—forbid, prohibit; protest.

toll, SYN.—assessment, custom, duty, exaction, excise, impost. levy, rate, tax, tribute; burden, strain. ANT.—gift, remuneration, reward, wages.

tongue, SYN.—cant, dialect, diction, idiom, jargon, language, lingo, phraseology, slang, speech, vernacular. ANT.—babble, drivel, gibberish, nonsense.

too, SYN.—also, besides, furthermore, in addition, likewise, moreover, similarly.

tool, SYN.—agent, apparatus, devise, instrument, means, medium, utensil, vehicle. ANT.—hindrance, impediment, obstruction, preventive.

top, SYN.—apex, chief, crest, crown, head, pinnacle, summit, zenith. ANT.—base, bottom, foot, foundation.

topic, SYN.—argument, matter, point, subject, theme, thesis.

torment, SYN.—ache, agony, anguish, distress, misery, pain, suffering, throe, torture, woe. ANT.—comfort, ease, mitigation, relief.

torment, SYN.—aggravate, annoy, badger, bother, disturb, harass, harry, irritate, molest, nag, pester, plague, provoke, tantalize, taunt, tease, vex, worry. ANT.—comfort, delight, gratify, please, soothe.

torpid, SYN.—idle, inactive, indolent, inert, lazy, slothful, sluggish, supine. ANT.—active, alert, assiduous, diligent.

torpor, SYN.—daze, drowsiness, insensibility, languor, lethargy, numbness, stupefaction, stupor. ANT.—activity, alertness, liveliness, readiness, wakefulness.

torrid, SYN.—burning, hot, scalding, scorching, warm; ardent, fervent, fiery, hotblooded, impetuous, intense, passionate. ANT.—cold, cool, freezing, frigid; apathetic, impassive, indifferent, passionless, phlegmatic.

torso, SYN.—body, form, frame. ANT.—intellect, mind, soul, spirit.

torture, SYN.—ache, agony, anguish, distress,

misery, pain, suffering, throe, torment, woe. ANT.—comfort, ease, mitigation, relief.

torture, SYN.—afflict, annoy, badger, harass, harry, hound, oppress, pester, plague, persecute, torment, vex, worry. ANT.—aid, assist, comfort, encourage, support.

toss, SYN.—cast, fling, hurl, pitch, propel, throw, thrust. ANT.—draw, haul, hold, pull, retain.

total, SYN.—complete, concluded, consummate, ended, entire, finished, full, perfect, thorough, unbroken, undivided. ANT.—imperfect, lacking, unfinished.

total, SYN.—aggregate, amount, collection, conglomeration, entirety, sum, whole. ANT.—element, ingredient, part, particular, unit.

total, SYN.—add, sum. ANT.—deduct, detach, reduce, remove, subtract.

touching, SYN.—affecting, heart-rending, impressive, moving, pitiable, poignant, sad, tender; adjacent, adjunct, bordering, tangent. ANT.—animated, enlivening, exhilarating, removed.

touchy, SYN.—choleric, excitable, fiery, hasty, hot, irascible, irritable, peevish, petulant, snappish, testy. ANT.—agreeable, calm, composed, tranquil.

tough, SYN.—cohesive, firm, hardy, stout, strong, sturdy, tenacious; difficult, formidable, hard, laborious, troublesome, trying; callous, incorrigible, obdurate, stubborn, vicious. ANT.—brittle, fragile, frail; easy, facile; compliant, forbearing, submissive.

toughness, SYN.—durability, force, fortitude, intensity, lustiness, might, potency, power, stamina, stoutness, strength, sturdiness, vigor. ANT.—feebleness, frailty, infirmity, weakness.

tour, SYN.—go, journey, ramble, roam, rove, travel. ANT.—stay, stop.

tow, SYN.—drag, draw, haul, pull, tug; extract, remove, take out, unsheathe. ANT.—drive, propel.

towering, SYN.—high, lofty, tall, towering; elevated, eminent, exalted, proud. ANT.—small, stunted, tiny; base, low, mean.

toy, SYN.—caper, frolic, gamble, gambol, play, revel, romp, sport, stake, wager.

trace, SYN.—mark, scar, stain, stigma, vestige; characteristic, feature, indication, property, symptoms, trait.

track, SYN.—chase, follow, hunt, persist, pursue, trail. ANT.—abandon, elude, escape, evade, flee.

tractable, SYN.—compliant, deferential, dutiful, obedient, submissive, yielding. ANT.—insubordinate, intractable, obstinate, rebellious.

traduce, SYN.—abuse, asperse, defame, disparage, ill-use, malign, revile, scandalize, vilify. ANT.—cherish, honor, praise, protect, respect.

trail, SYN.—chase, follow, hunt, persist, pursue, track. ANT.—abandon, elude, escape, evade, flee.

train, SYN.—aim, direct, level, point; bid, command, instruct, order. ANT.—deceive, distract, misdirect, misguide.

training, SYN.—cultivation, development, education, instruction, knowledge, learning, schooling, study, tutoring.

trait, SYN.—attribute, characteristic, feature, mark, peculiarity, property, quality.

traitorous, SYN.—apostate, disloyal, faithless, false, perfidious, recreant, treacherous, treasonable. ANT.—constant, devoted, loyal, true.

tramp, SYN.—beggar, bum, hobo, rover, vagabond, vagrant, wanderer. ANT.—gentleman, laborer, worker.

tranquil, SYN.—calm, composed, dispassionate, imperturbable, pacific, peaceful, placid, quiet, serene, still, undisturbed, unruffled. ANT.—excited, frantic, stormy, turbulent, wild.

tranquility, SYN.—calm, calmness, hush, peace, quiescence, quiet, quietude, repose, rest, serenity, silence, stillness. ANT.—agitation, disturbance, excitement, noise, tumult.

transact, SYN.—carry on, conduct, execute, manage, negotiate, perform, treat.

transaction, SYN.—affair, business, deal, deed, negotiation, occurrence, proceeding.

transfer SYN.—convey, dispatch, send, transmit, transport; remove, transplant; assign, consign, relegate.

transform, SYN.—alter, change, convert, modify, shift, transfigure, vary, veer. ANT.—continue, establish, preserve, settle, stabilize.

transgression, SYN.—affront, atrocity, indignity, insult, offense, outrage; aggression, crime, injustice, misdeed, sin, trespass, vice, wrong. ANT.—gentleness, innocence, morality, right.

transient, SYN.—brief, ephemeral, evanescent, fleeting, momentary, short-lived, temporary. ANT.—abiding, immortal, lasting, permanent, timeless.

translate, SYN.—construe, decipher, decode, elucidate, explain, explicate, intepret, render, solve, unravel. ANT.—confuse, distort, falsify, misconstrue, misinterpret.

transmit, SYN.—communicate, confer, convey, disclose, divulge, impart, inform, notify, relate, reveal, tell. ANT.—conceal, hide, withhold.

transparent, SYN.—clear, crystalline, limpid, lucid, thin, translucent; evident, explicit, manifest, obvious, open. ANT.—muddy, opaque, thick, turbid; ambiguous, questionable.

transpire, SYN.—bechance, befall, betide, chance, happen, occur, take place.

transport SYN.—bear, carry, convey, move, remove, shift, transfer; enrapture, entrance, lift, ravish, stimulate.

trap, SYN.—ambush, artifice, bait, intrigue, lure, net, pitfall, ruse, snare, strategem, trick, wile.

travel, SYN.—go, journey, ramble, roam, rove, tour. ANT.—stay, stop.

treachery, SYN.—cabal, collusion, combination, conspiracy, intrigue, machination, plot, treason.

treason, SYN.—cabal, collusion, combination, conspiracy, intrigue, machination, plot, treachery.

treasure, SYN.—appreciate, cherish, hold dear, prize, value; foster, nurture, sustain. ANT.—dislike, disregard, neglect; abandon, reject.

treat, SYN.—avail, employ, exploit, manipulate, operate, utilize; exercise, exert, practice; handle, manage, use. ANT.—ignore, neglect, overlook, waste.

treaty, SYN.—alliance, compact, covenant, marriage. ANT.—divorce, schism, separation.

tremble, SYN.—agitate, flutter, jar, jolt, quake, quaver, quiver, rock, shake, shiver, shudder, sway, totter, vibrate, waver.

trembling, SYN.—alarm, apprehension, dread, fear, fright, horror, panic, terror. ANT.—calmness, composure, serenity, tranquility.

trepidation, SYN.—alarm, apprehension, consternation, cowardice, dismay, dread, fear, fright, horror, panic, scare, terror, timidity. ANT.—assurance, boldness, bravery, courage, fearlessness.

trespass, SYN.—affront, atrocity, indignity, insult, offense, outrage; aggression, crime, injustice, misdeed, sin, vice, wrong. ANT.—gentleness, innocence, morality, right.

trespass, SYN.—attack, encroach, infringe, intrude, invade, penetrate, violate. ANT.—abandon, evacuate, relinquish, vacate.

trial, SYN.—examination,

experiment, ordeal, proof, test; attempt, effort, endeavor, essay; affliction, hardship, misery, misfortune, suffering, tribulation, trouble. ANT.—alleviation, consolation.

tribulation, SYN.—agony, anguish, distress, grief, misery, sorrow, suffering, torment, woe; calamity, disaster, evil, misfortune, trouble. ANT.—delight, elation, fun, joy, pleasure.

trick, SYN.—antic, artifice, cheat, deception, device, fraud, guile, hoax, imposture, ploy, ruse, stratagem, stunt, subterfuge, wile. ANT.—candor, exposure, honesty, openness, sincerity.

tricky, SYN.—artful, astute, clandestine, covert, crafty, cunning, foxy, furtive, guileful, insidious, shrewd, sly, stealthy, subtle, surreptitious, underhand, wily. ANT.—candid, frank, ingenuous, open, sincere.

trifling, SYN.—frivolous, insignificant, paltry, petty, small, trivial, unimportant. ANT.—important, momentous, serious, weighty.

trim, SYN.—clear, nice, orderly, precise, spruce, tidy, trim. ANT.—dirty, disheveled, sloppy, slovenly, unkempt.

trim, SYN.—adorn, beautify, bedeck, decorate, embellish, garnish, gild, ornament. ANT.—deface, deform, disfigure, mar, spoil.

trip, SYN.—cruise, expedition, jaunt, journey, passage, pilgrimage, tour, travel, voyage.

trite, SYN.—banal, common, hackneyed, ordinary, stale, stereotyped. ANT.—fresh, modern, momentous, novel, stimulating.

triumph, SYN.—achievement, conquest, jubilation, ovation, victory. ANT.—defeat, failure.

trivial, SYN.—frivolous, insignificant, paltry, petty, small, trifling, unimportant. ANT.—important, momentous, serious, weighty.

trouble, SYN.—affliction, anxiety, calamity, distress, grief, hardship, misery, pain, sorrow, woe; annoyance, bother, care, embarrassment, irritation, pains, torment, worry; disorder, disturbance, problem; care, effort, exertion, labor, toil.

trouble, SYN.—annoy, bother, chafe, disturb, inconvenience, irk, irritate, molest, pester, tease, vex. ANT.—accommodate, console, gratify, soothe.

troublesome, SYN.—annoying, bothersome, distressing, disturbing, irksome, trying, vexatious; arduous, burdensome, difficult, laborious, tedious. ANT.—accommodating, amusing, easy, gratifying, pleasant.

true, SYN.—accurate, actual, authentic, correct, exact, genuine, real, veracious, veritable; constant, faithful, honest, loyal, reliable, sincere, steadfast, trustworthy. ANT.—counterfeit, erroneous, false, fictitious, spurious; faithless, false, fickle, inconstant.

trust, SYN.—confidence, credence, dependence, faith, reliance, trust. ANT.—doubt, incredulity, mistrust, skepticism.

trust, SYN.—depend on, reckon on, rely on; believe, credit, hope; commit, confide, intrust. ANT.—doubt, impugn, question, suspect.

trustworthy, SYN.—certain, dependable, reliable, safe, secure, sure, tried, trust. ANT.—dubious, fallible, questionable, uncertain, unreliable.

truth, SYN.—accuracy, actuality, authenticity, correctness, exactness, fact, honesty, rightness, truthfulness, veracity, verisimilitude, verity. ANT.—falsehood, falsity, fiction, lie, untruth.

truthful, SYN.—candid, frank, honest, open, sincere, true, veracious; accurate, correct, exact, reliable. ANT.—deceitful, misleading, sly.

try, SYN.—attempt, endeavor, strive, struggle, undertake; afflict, prove, test, torment, trouble; aim, aspire, design, intend, mean. ANT.—abandon, decline, ignore, neglect, omit; comfort, console.

trying SYN.—annoying, bothersome, distressing, disturbing, irksome, troublesome, vexatious; arduous, burdensome, difficult, laborious, tedious. ANT.—accommodating, amusing, easy, gratifying, pleasant.

tumult, SYN.—agitation, chaos, commotion, confusion, disarrangement, disarray, disorder, ferment, jumble, stir, turmoil. ANT.—certainty, order, peace, tranquility.

tune, SYN.—air, concord, harmony, melody, strain.

turbulent, SYN.—blustery, gusty, inclement, roaring, rough, stormy, tempestuous, windy. ANT.—calm, clear, peaceful, quiet, tranquil.

turmoil, SYN.—agitation, chaos, commotion, confusion, disarrangement, disarray, disorder, ferment, jumble, stir, tumult. ANT.—certainty, order, peace, tranquility.

turn, SYN.—circle, circulate, invert, revolve, rotate, spin, twirl, twist, wheel, whirl; avert, deflect, deviate, divert, swerve; alter, change, transmute. ANT.—arrest, fix, stand, stop; continue, proceed; endure, perpetuate.

twist, SYN.—bend, bow, crook, curve, deflect, incline, lean, stoop, turn. ANT.—break, resist, stiffen, straighten.

type, SYN.—emblem, mark, sign, symbol; category, character, class, description, kind, nature, sort, stamp; examplar, model, pattern. ANT.—deviation, eccentricity, monstrosity, peculiarity.

typical, SYN.—accustomed, common, conventional, customary, familiar, habitual, normal, ordinary, plain, regular, usual, vulgar. ANT.—extraordinary, marvelous, remarkable, strange, uncommon.

tyrannous, SYN.—absolute, arbitrary, authoritative, despotic. ANT.—accountable, conditional, contingent, dependent, qualified.

tyrant, SYN.—autocrat, despot, dictator, oppressor, persecutor.

U

ugly, SYN.—deformed, hideous, homely, plain, repellant, repulsive, uncomely; disagreeable, ill-natured, spiteful, surly, vicious. ANT.—attractive, beautiful, fair, handsome, pretty.

ultimate, SYN.—concluding, extreme, final, hindmost, last, latest, terminal, utmost. ANT.—beginning, first, foremost, initial, opening.

unadulterated, SYN.—clean, clear, genuine, immaculate, pure, spotless,

untainted; absolute, bare, sheer. ANT.—foul, polluted, sullied, tainted, tarnished; corrupt, defiled.

unannounced, SYN.—abrupt, hasty, precipitate, sudden, unexpected. ANT.—anticipated, expected; courteous.

unassuming, SYN.—compliant, humble, lowly, meek, modest, plain, simple, submissive, unostentatious, unpretentious. ANT.—arrogant, boastful, haughty, proud, vain.

unbeliever, SYN.—apostate, dissenter, heretic, nonconformist, schismatic, sectarian, sectary.

unbiased, SYN.—equitable, fair, honest, impartial, just, reasonable. ANT. — dishonorable, frauduient, partial.

uncertain, SYN.—ambiguous, dim, hazy, indefinite, indistinct, obscure, unclear, undetermined, unsettled, vague. ANT.—clear, explicit, lucid, precise, specific.

uncertainty, SYN.—ambiguity, distrust, doubt, hesitation, incredulity, scruple, skepticism, suspense, suspicion, unbelief. ANT.—belief, certainty, conviction, determination, faith.

uncivilized, SYN.—barbarian, barbaric, barbarous, brutal, crude, cruel, inhuman, merciless, remorseless, rude, ruthless, savage, uncultured,

unrelenting. ANT.—civilized, humane, kind, polite, refined.

unclad, SYN.—bare, exposed, naked, nude, stripped, uncovered; defenseless, open, unprotected. ANT.—clothed, covered, dressed; concealed; protected.

uncompromising, SYN.—contumacious, determined, dogged, firm, headstrong, immovable, inflexible, intractable, obdurate, obstinate, pertinacious, stubborn, unyielding. ANT.—amenable, compliant, docile, submissive, yielding.

unconcern, SYN.—apathy, disinterestedness, impartiality, indifference, insensibility, neutrality. ANT.—affection, ardor, fervor, passion.

unconditional, SYN.—absolute, unqualified, unrestricted; arbitrary, authoritative, despotic, tyrannous. ANT.—accountable, conditional, contingent, dependent, qualified.

uncouth, SYN.—coarse, crude, green, harsh, illprepared, raw, rough, unfinished, unpolished, unrefined; crass, unrefined. ANT.—finished, well-prepared; cultivated, refined.

uncover, SYN.—betray, disclose, discover, divulge, expose, impart, reveal, show. ANT.—cloak, conceal, cover, hide, obscure.

under, SYN.—below, beneath, underneath. ANT.—above, over.

undergo, SYN.—bear, endure, feel, stand, suffer, sustain, tolerate; feel. ANT.—banish, discard, exclude, overcome.

understand, SYN.—appreciate, apprehend, comprehend, conceive, discern, grasp, know, learn, perceive, realize, see. ANT.—ignore, misapprehend, mistake, misunderstand.

understanding, SYN.—accordance, agreement, coincidence, concord, concurrence, harmony, unison; bargain, compact, contract, covenant, pact, stipulation. ANT.—difference, disagreement, discord, dissension, variance.

understudy, SYN.—agent, alternate, deputy, proxy, representative, substitute. ANT.—head, master, principal, sovereign.

undertaking, SYN.—attempt, effort, endeavor, essay, experiment, trial. ANT.—inaction, laziness, neglect.

undesigned, SYN.—accidental, casual, chance, contingent, fortuitous, incidental, unintended. ANT.—calculated, decreed, intended, planned, willed.

undivided, SYN.—all, complete, entire, intact, integral, perfect, total, unimpaired, whole. ANT.—incomplete, partial.

undying, SYN.—ceaseless, deathless, endless, eternal, everlasting, immortal, infinite, perpetual, timeless. ANT.—ephemeral, finite, mortal, temporal, transient.

unearthly, SYN.—marvellous, metaphysical, miraculous, other-worldly, preternatural, spiritual, superhuman, supernatural. ANT.—common, human, natural, physical, plain.

uneducated, SYN.—ignorant, illiterate, uncultured, uninformed, unlearned, unlettered, untaught. ANT.—cultured, educated, erudite, informed, literate.

unemployed, SYN.—idle, inactive, inert, unoccupied. ANT.—active, employed, industrious, occupied, working.

uneven, SYN.—odd, remaining, single, unmatched. ANT.—even, matched.

unexpected, SYN.—abrupt, hasty, immediate, instaneous, rapid, sudden. ANT.—anticipated, gradual, slowly.

unfasten, SYN.—exhibit, expand, open, spread, unbar, unfold, unlock, unseal. ANT.—close, conceal, hide, shut.

unfavorable, SYN.—adverse, antagonistic, contrary, hostile, opposed, opposite; counteractive, disastrous, unlucky. ANT.—benign, favorable, fortunate, lucky, propitious.

unfeeling, SYN.—cruel, hard, harsh, rigorous, severe, stern, strict. ANT.—gentle, lenient, tender.

unfold, SYN.—amplify, create, develop, elaborate, enlarge, evolve, expand, mature. ANT.—compress, contract, restrict, stunt, wither.

unfurnished, SYN.—bare, exposed, naked, stripped; mere, plain, simple; open. ANT.—covered, concealed; protected.

uniform, SYN.—customary, methodical, natural, normal, orderly, ordinary, periodical, regular, steady, systematic, unvaried. ANT.—abnormal, erratic, exceptional, rare, unusual.

uninformed, SYN.—ignorant, illiterate, uncultured, uneducated, unlearned, unlettered, untaught. ANT.—cultured, educated, erudite, informed, literate.

unintelligible, SYN.—abstruse, ambiguous, cloudy, cryptic, dark, dim, dusky, enigmatic, indistinct, mysterious, obscure, unintelligible, vague. ANT.—bright, clear, distinct, lucid.

uninteresting, SYN.—boring, burdensome, dilatory, dreary, dull, humdrum, irksome, monotonous, slow, sluggish, tardy, tedious, tiresome, wearisome. ANT.—

amusing, entertaining, exciting, interesting, quick.

union, SYN.—combination, concurrence, fusion, incorporation, joining, solidarity, unification; agreement, concord, harmony, unanimity; alliance, amalgamation, coalition, concert, confederacy, league, marriage. ANT.—division, schism, separation; disagreement, discord.

unique, SYN.—choice, distinctive, exceptional, matchless, peculiar, rare, singular, sole, solitary, uncommon, unequaled. ANT.—common, commonplace, frequent, ordinary, typical.

unite, SYN.—amalgamate, associate, attach, blend, combine, conjoin, connect, consolidate, embody, fuse, join, link, merge, unify. ANT.—disconnect, disrupt, divide, separate, sever.

universal, SYN.—common, familiar, frequent, general, ordinary, popular, prevalent, usual. ANT.—exceptional, extraordinary, odd, scarce.

unlawful, SYN.—criminal, illegal, illegitimate, illicit, outlawed, prohibited. ANT.—honest, law, legal, permitted.

unlike, SYN.—contrary, different, dissimilar, distinct, divergent, diverse, incongruous, opposite, variant; divers, miscellaneous, sundry, var-

ious. ANT.—alike, congruous, identical, same, similar.

unlimited, SYN.—boundless, endless, eternal, illimitable, immeasurable, immense, infinite, interminable, unbounded, vast. ANT.—bounded, circumscribed, confined, finite, limited.

unlocked, SYN.—ajar, open, unclosed; clear, passable, unobstructed; disengaged, free, unoccupied; accessible, exposed, unrestricted.

unmatched, SYN.—odd, remaining, single, uneven. ANT.—even, matched.

unmistakable, SYN.—apparent, clear, distinct, evident, manifest, obvious, palpable, patent, plain, self-evident. ANT.—abstruse, concealed, hidden, obscure.

unobstructed, SYN.—clear, free, loose, open, unfastened. ANT.—restricted; blocked, clogged, impeded.

unoccupied, SYN.—dormant, idle, inactive, indolent, inert, lazy, slothful, unemployed. ANT.—active, employed, industrious, occupied, working.

unpretentious, SYN.—candid, frank, open, plain, simple, sincere. ANT.—adorned, embellished, feigned, insincere.

unqualified, SYN.—absolute, unconditional, unrestricted; arbitrary, authoritative, despotic, tyr-

annous. ANT.—account-
able, conditional, contingent, dependent, quali-
fied.

unreasonable, SYN.—
absurd, foolish, inconsistent, irrational, nonsensical, preposterous, ridiculous, self-contradictory,
silly. ANT.—consistent,
rational, reasonable, sensible, sound.

unrestricted, SYN.—clear,
passable, unobstructed;
available, disengaged,
free, unoccupied; acces-
sible, exposed, open,
public.

unsafe, SYN.—critical, dangerous, hazardous, inse-
cure, menacing, perilous,
precarious, risky, threatening. ANT.—firm, pro-
tected, safe, secure.

unselfish, SYN.—beneficent, bountiful, gener-
ous, giving, liberal, magnanimous, munificent,
openhanded. ANT.—
covetous, greedy, miser-
ly, selfish, stingy.

unsophisticated, SYN.—artless, candid, frank, in-
genuous, innocent, na-
ive, natural, open, sim-
ple. ANT.—crafty, cun-
ning, sophisticated,
worldly.

unstable, SYN.—capricious,
changeable, fickle, fitful,
inconstant, restless, variable. ANT.—constant, re-
liable, stable, steady,
trustworthy.

unswerving, SYN.—con-
stant, fast, firm, inflexible, secure, solid, stable,
steadfast, steady, un-

yielding. ANT.—slow,
sluggish; insecure, loose,
unstable, unsteady.

untainted, SYN.—clean,
clear, genuine, immacu-
late, pure, spotless, un-
adulterated; chaste,
guiltless, innocent, mod-
est, sincere, undefiled,
virgin. ANT.—foul, pol-
luted, sullied, tainted,
tarnished; corrupt, de-
filed.

untamed, SYN.—barba-
rous, fierce, outlandish,
rude, savage, uncivi-
lized, undomesticated,
wild; desert, desolate,
rough, uncultivated,
waste; frantic, frenzied,
impetuous, mad, turbu-
lent, wanton, wayward;
boisterous, stormy, tem-
pestous; extravagant,
foolish, giddy, rash,
reckless. ANT.—civi-
lized, gentle; calm, placid, quiet.

untoward, SYN.—contrary,
disobedient, fractious,
peevish, petulant; for-
ward, intractable, obsti-
nate, perverse, stubborn,
ungovernable. ANT.—
agreeable, obliging; doc-
ile, tractable.

unusual, SYN.—aberrant,
abnormal, capricious,
devious, eccentric, irregular, unnatural, variable.
ANT.—fixed, methodical,
ordinary, regular, usual.

unyielding, SYN.—con-
stant, fast, firm, inflexible, secure, solid, stable,
steadfast, steady, un-
swerving, unyielding.
ANT.—slow, sluggish; in-

secure, loose, unstable, unsteady.

upbraid, SYN.—admonish, berate, blame, censure, lecture, rate, rebuke, reprehend, reprimand, scold, vituperate. ANT.—approve, commend, praise.

uphold, SYN.—assert, defend, espouse, justify, maintain, vindicate. ANT.—assault, attack, deny, oppose, submit.

upright, SYN.—direct, right, undeviating, unswerving; erect, straight, unbent, vertical; fair, honest, honorable, just, square. ANT.—circuitous, winding; bent, crooked; dishonest.

upset, SYN.—annoy, bother, disturb, harass, haunt, inconvenience, molest, perlex, pester, plague, tease, trouble, worry. ANT.—gratify, please, relieve, soothe.

urbane, SYN.—accomplished, civil, considerate, courteous, cultivated, genteel, polite, refined, well-bred, well-mannered. ANT.—boorish, impertinent, rude, uncivil, uncouth.

urge, SYN.—appetite, aspiration, craving, desire, hungering, longing, lust, wish, yearning. ANT.—abomination, aversion, distaste, hate, loathing.

urge, SYN.—coax, convince, exhort, incite, induce, influence, persuade, prevail upon, win over. ANT.—coerce, compel, deter, dissuade, restrain.

urgency, SYN.—crisis, emergency, exigency, juncture, pass, pinch, strait.

urgent, SYN.—cogent, compelling, critical, crucial, exigent, impelling, imperative, important, importunate, insistent, instant, necessary, pressing, serious. ANT.—insignificant, petty, trifling, trivial, unimportant.

use, SYN.—custom, habit, manner, practice, training, usage, wont. ANT.—disuse, idleness, inexperience, speculation, theory.

use, SYN.—apply, avail, employ, exploit, manipulate, operate, utilize; exercise, exert, practice, consume, exhaust, expend; handle, manage, treat; accustom, familiarize, inure, train. ANT.—ignore, neglect, overlook, waste.

useful, SYN.—advantageous, beneficial, good, helpful, profitable, salutary, serviceable, wholesome. ANT.—deleterious, destructive, detrimental, harmful, injurious.

usefulness, SYN.—excellence, merit, price, utility, value, virtue, worth, worthiness. ANT.—cheapness, uselessness, valuelessness.

useless, SYN.—abortive, bootless, empty, fruitless, futile, idle, ineffectual, pointless, unavailing, vain, valueless, vapid, worthless. ANT.—effective, potent, profitable; meek, modest.

usual, SYN.—accustomed, common, customary, every-day, familiar, general, habitual, normal, ordinary. ANT.—abnormal, exceptional, extraordinary, irregular, rare.

utensil, SYN.—apparatus, device, instrument, medium, tool, vehicle. ANT.—hindrance, impediment, obstruction, preventive.

utilize SYN.—avail, employ, occupy. ANT.—discard, discharge, reject.

utopian, SYN.—exemplary, fancied, faultless, ideal, imaginary, perfect, supreme, unreal, visionary. ANT.—actual, faulty, imperfect, material, real.

utter, SYN.—complete, entire, finished, full, perfect, whole; complete, consummate, excellent, ideal, superlative, supreme; absolute, downright, unqualified. ANT.—deficient, incomplete, lacking; faulty, imperfect.

V

vacant, SYN.—bare, barren, blank, empty, unoccupied, vacuous, void.

ANT.—busy, employed, engaged, full, replete.

vacate, SYN.—abandon, abdicate, abjure, relinquish, resign, surrender, waive; desert, forsake, leave, quit. ANT.—maintain, uphold; stay, support.

vacillate, SYN.—change, fluctuate, hesitate, oscillate, undulate, vary, waver. ANT.—adhere, decide, persist, resolve, stick.

vacillating, SYN.—contradictory, contrary, discrepant, illogical, inconsistent, incompatible, incongruous, irreconcilable, paradoxical, unsteady, wavering. ANT.—compatible, congruous, consistent, correspondent.

vagabond, SYN.—beggar, mendicant, pauper, ragamuffin, scrub, starveling, tatterdemalion, wretch.

vagrant, SYN.—beggar, bum, hobo, rover, tramp, vagabond, wanderer. ANT.—gentleman, laborer, worker.

vague, SYN.—ambiguous, dim, hazy, indefinite, indistinct, obscure, undertain, unclear, undetermined, unsettled. ANT.—clear, explicit, lucid, precise, specific.

vain, SYN.—abortive, bootless, empty, fruitless, futile, idle, ineffectual, pointless, unavailing, useless, valueless, vapid, worthless, conceited, proud, vainglorious.

ANT.—effective, potent, profitable, meek, modest.

vainglory, SYN.—arrogance, conceit, haughtiness, pride, self-esteem, superciliousness, vanity. ANT.—humility, lowliness, meekness, modesty, shame.

valiant, SYN.—adventurous, audacious, bold, brave, chivalrous, courageous, daring, dauntless, fearless, gallant, heroic, intrepid, magnanimous, valorous. ANT.—cowardly, cringing, fearful, timid, weak.

valid, SYN.—binding, cogent, conclusive, convincing, effective, efficacious, legal, logical, powerful, sound, strong, telling, weighty. ANT.—counterfeit, null, spurious, void, weak.

valuable, SYN.—costly, expensive, precious; dear, esteemed; profitable, useful. ANT.—cheap, mean, poor; trashy, worthless.

value, SYN.—excellence, merit, price, usefulness, utility, value, virtue, worth, worthiness. ANT.—cheapness, uselessness, valuelessness.

value, SYN.—appreciate, cherish, hold dear, prize, treasure; foster, nurture, sustain. ANT.—dislike, disregard; neglect; abandon, reject.

vanity, SYN.—complacency, conceit, egotism, pride, self-esteem; ca-price, conception, fancy, idea, imagination, notion, whim. ANT.—diffidence, humility, meekness, modesty.

vanquish, SYN.—beat, conquer, crush, defeat, humble, master, overcome, quell, rout, subdue, subjugate, surmount. ANT.—capitulate, cede, lose, retreat, surrender.

vapid, SYN.—banal, commonplace, hackneyed, inane, insipid, trite. ANT.—fresh, novel, original, stimulating, striking.

variable, SYN.—changeable, fickle, fitful, inconstant, shifting, unstable, vacillating, wavering. ANT.—constant, stable, steady, unchanging, uniform.

variant, SYN.—contrary, different, dissimilar, distinct, divergent, diverse, incongruous, opposite, unlike; divers, miscellaneous, sundry, various. ANT.—alike, congruous, identical, same, similar.

variation, SYN.—alteration, alternation, change, modification, mutation, substitution, variety, vicissitude. ANT.—monotony, stability, uniformity.

variety, SYN.—assortment, change, difference, dissimilarity, diversity, heterogeneity, medly, miscellany, mixture, multifariousness, variousness; breed, kind, sort, stock, strain, subspecies.

ANT.— homogeneity, likeness, monotony, sameness, uniformity.

various, SYN.—different, divers, miscellaneous, sundry. ANT.—alike, congruous, identical, same, similar.

vary, SYN.—change, exchange, substitute; alter, convert, modify, shift, transfigure, transform, veer. ANT.—continue, establish, preserve, settle, stabilize.

vassalage, SYN.—bondage, captivity, confinement, imprisonment, serfdom, servitude, slavery, thralldom. ANT.—freedom, liberation.

vast, SYN.—ample, big, capacious, colossal, extensive, great, huge, immense, large, wide. ANT.—little, mean, short, small, tiny.

vault, SYN.—bound, caper, hop, jerk, jump, leap, skip, spring, start.

vaunt, SYN.—boast, brag, crow, flaunt, glory. ANT.—apologize, deprecate, humble, minimize.

vaunting, SYN.—boasting, display, flourish, ostentation, pagentry, parade, pomp, show. ANT.—humility, modesty, reserve, unobtrusiveness.

vehement, SYN.—ardent, burning, excitable, fervent, fervid, fiery, glowing, hot, impetuous, irascible, passionate. ANT.—apathetic, calm, cool, deliberate, quiet.

veil, SYN.—cloak, clothe, conceal, cover, curtain, disguise, envelop, guard, hide, mask, protect, screen, shield, shroud. ANT.—bare, divulge, expose, reveal, unveil.

venal, SYN.—avaricious, corrupt, greedy, mercenary, sordid. ANT.—generous, honorable, liberal.

venerable, SYN.—aged, ancient, antiquated, antique, archaic, elderly, old, old-fashioned, superannuated. ANT.—modern, new, young, youthful.

venerate, SYN.—admire, appreciate, approve, esteem, respect. ANT.—abhor, despise, dislike.

vengeance, SYN.—reparation, reprisal, requital, retaliation, retribution, revenge, vindictiveness. ANT.—mercy, pardon, reconciliation, remission; forgiveness.

vent, SYN.—belch, breathe, discharge, eject, emanate, emit, expel, shoot, spurt.

venture, SYN.—risk, speculate. ANT.—insure, protect, secure.

verbal, SYN.—literal, oral, spoken, vocal. ANT.—documentary, recorded, written.

verbose, SYN.—chattering, chatty, communicative, garrulous, glib, loquacious, talkative, voluble. ANT.—laconic, reticent, silent, taciturn, uncommunicative.

verbosity, SYN.—long-windedness, redundancy, talkativeness, verboseness, wordiness. ANT.—conciseness, laconism, terseness.

verification, SYN.—confirmation, corroboration, demonstration, evidence, experiment, proof, test, testimony, trial. ANT.—failure, fallacy, invalidity.

verify, SYN.—corroborate, confirm, determine, substantiate; acknowledge, assure, establish, settle; approve, fix, ratify, sanction; strengthen.

veritable, SYN.—accurate, actual, authentic, correct, exact, genuine, real, true, veracious. ANT.—counterfeit, erroneous, false, fictitious, spurious.

versed, SYN.—acquainted, aware, cognizant, conversant, familiar, intimate, knowing. ANT.—unfamiliar.

vertical, SYN.—erect, perpendicular, plumb, straight, upright. ANT.—horizontal, inclined, level, oblique, prone.

vestige, SYN.—brand, mark, scar, stain, stigma, trace; characteristic, feature, indication, symptoms, trait.

vex, SYN.—aggravate, annoy, chafe, embitter, exasperate, inflame, irritate, nettle, provoke. ANT.—appease, mitigate, palliate, soften, soothe.

vexation, SYN.—annoyance, chagrin, exasperation, irritation, mortification, pique. ANT.—appeasement, comfort, gratification, pleasure.

vibrate, SYN.—agitate, flutter, jar, jolt, quake, quaver, quiver, rock, shake, shiver, shudder, sway, totter, tremble, waver.

vice, SYN.—crime, evil, guilt, iniquity, offense, sin, transgression, ungodliness, wickedness, wrong. ANT.—goodness, innocence, purity, righteousness, virtue.

vicinity, SYN.—district, environs, locality, neighborhood; adjacency, nearness. ANT.—distance, remoteness.

victory, SYN.—achievement, conquest, jubilation, ovation, triumph. ANT.—defeat, failure.

view, SYN.—observation, regard, review, sight, survey; outlook, panorama, perspective, prospect, range, scene, vista; belief, conception, impression, judgment, opinion, sentiment.

view, SYN.—behold, discern, eye, gaze, glance, look, scan, see, stare, survey, watch, witness; examine, inspect, observe, regard. ANT.—avert, hide, miss, overlook.

viewpoint, SYN.—attitude, disposition, standpoint; aspect, pose, position, posture, stand.

vigilant, SYN.—alert, anxious, attentive, careful, cautious, circumspect, observant, wakeful, wary, watchful. ANT.—careless, inattentive, lax, neglectful, oblivious.

vigor, SYN.—fortitude, liveliness, spirit, verve, vitality, zeal. ANT.—languor, listlessness.

vigorous, SYN.—active, animated, blithe, brisk, energetic, frolicsome, lively, spirited, sprightly, supple, vivacious. ANT.—dull, insipid, listless, stale, vapid.

vile, SYN.—base, debased, depraved, foul, loathsome, obscene, odious, revolting, sordid, vicious, vulgar, wicked; abject, despicable, ignoble, low, mean, worthless, wretched. ANT.—attractive, decent, laudable; honorable, upright.

vilify, SYN.—abuse, asperse, defame, disparage, ill-use, malign, revile, scandalize, traduce. ANT.—cherish, honor, praise, protect, respect.

villainous, SYN.—bad, base, deleterious, evil, immoral, iniquitous, noxious, pernicious, sinful, unsound, unwholesome, wicked. ANT.—excellent, good, honorable, moral, reputable.

vindicate, SYN.—absolve, acquit, assert, clear, defend, excuse, exonerate, justify, support, uphold. ANT.—abandon, accuse, blame, convict.

violate, SYN.—break, disobey, infringe, invade, transgress, defile, desecrate, dishonor, pollute, profane, debauch, deflower, ravish.

violence, SYN.—coercion, compulsion, constraint, force. ANT.—feebleness, frailty, impotence, weakness; persuasion.

violent, SYN.—boisterous, fierce, forceful, furious, impetuous, passionate, powerful, raging, raving, turbulent, vehement, wild; acute, extreme, intense, severe. ANT.—calm, feeble, gentle, quiet, soft.

virgin, SYN.—clean, clear, genuine, immaculate, spotless, unadulterated, untainted; chaste, guiltless, innocent, modest, pure, sincere, undefiled. ANT.—foul, polluted, sullied, tainted, tarnished; corrupt, defiled.

virile, SYN.—bold, hardy, lusty, male, manly, mannish, masculine, robust, strong, vigorous. ANT.—effeminate, emasculated, feminine, unmanly, weak, womanish.

virtue, SYN.—chastity, goodness, integrity, morality, probity, purity, rectitude, virginity; effectiveness, efficacy, force, power, strength; excellence, merit, worth. ANT.—corruption, lewdness, sin, vice; fault.

virtuous, SYN.—chaste, decent, ethical, good, honorable, just, moral, pure, right, righteous, scrupulous. ANT.—amoral, libertine, licentious, sinful, unethical.

virulent, SYN.—bitter, evil-minded, hostile, malevolent, malicious, malignant, rancorous, spiteful, wicked. ANT.—affectionate, benevolent, benign, kind.

visible, SYN.—cloudless, fair; limpid; apparent, clear, distinct, evident, intelligible, manifest, obvious, plain, unmistakable; open, unobstructed. ANT.—cloudy, foul, overcast; ambiguous, obscure, unclear, vague.

vision SYN.—apparation, daydream, dream, ghost, hallucination, mirage, phantasm, phantom, prophecy, revelation, specter. ANT.—reality, substance, verity.

visionary, SYN.—exemplary, fancied, faultless, ideal, imaginery, perfect, supreme, unreal, utopian. ANT.—actual, faulty, imperfect, material, real.

vital, SYN.—alive, animate, living; basic, cardinal, essential, indispensable, necessary, paramount, urgent. ANT.—inanimate, inert, lifeless; non-essential, unimportant.

vitality, SYN.—animation, being, buoyancy, existence, life, liveliness, spirit, vigor, vivacity. ANT.—death, demise, dullness, languor, lethargy.

vitiate, SYN.—abase, adulterate, alloy, corrupt, debase, defile, degrade, deprave, depress, humiliate, impair, lower, pervert, enhance, improve, raise, restore, vitalize.

vitiated, SYN.—contaminated, corrupt, corrupted, crooked, debased, depraved, dishonest, impure, profligate, putrid, spoiled, tainted, unsound, venal.

vivid, SYN.—bright, brilliant, intense, striking; animated, clear, expressive, fresh, graphic, lively, lucid. ANT.—dull, vague; dim, dreary, dusky.

vocation, SYN.—art, business, commerce, employment, engagement, enterprise, job, occupation, profession, trade, trading, work. ANT.—avocation, hobby, pastime.

void, SYN.—bare, barren, blank, empty, unoccupied, vacant, vacuous. ANT.—busy, employed, engaged, full, replete.

volatile, SYN.—buoyant, effervescent, light, resilient; animated, blithe, cheerful, elated, hopeful, jocund, lively, spirited, sprightly, vivacious. ANT.—dejected, depressed, despondent, hopeless, sullen.

volition, SYN.—choice, decision, desire, determination, intention, pleasure, preference, resolution, testament, will, wish. ANT.—coercion, compulsion, disinterest, indifference.

volume, SYN.—ability, capability, capacity, faculty, power, skill, talent; magnitude, size. ANT.—impotence, inability, incapacity, stupidity.

voluntary, SYN.—automatic, extemporaneous, impulsive, instinctive, offhand, spontaneous, willing. ANT.—compulsory, forced, planned, prepared, rehearsed.

volunteer, SYN.—advance, exhibit, extend, offer, present, proffer, propose, sacrifice, tender. ANT.—accept, receive, reject, retain, spurn.

voodoo, SYN.—black art, charm, conjuring, enchantment, legerdemain, magic, necromancy, sorcery, witchcraft, wizardry.

vulgar, SYN.—common, general, ordinary, plebian, popular; base, coarse, gross, low, obscene, ribald, rude, unrefined. ANT.—esoteric, select; aristocratic, polite, refined.

W

wager, SYN.—gamble, play, sport, stake.

wages, SYN.—allowance, compensation, earnings, fee, pay, payment, recompense, salary, stipend. ANT.—gift, gratuity, present.

wait, SYN.—abide, bide, delay, linger, remain, rest, stay, tarry; await, expect, watch; attend, minister, serve. ANT.—act, expedite, hasten, leave.

waive, SYN.—abandon, relinquish, renounce, surrender. ANT.—maintain, uphold.

wander, SYN.—deviate, digress, err, ramble, range, roam, rove, saunter, stray, stroll, traipse. ANT.—halt, linger, settle, stay, stop.

want, SYN.—destitution, indigence, necessity, need, penury, poverty, privation. ANT.—abundance, affluence, plenty, riches, wealth.

want, SYN.—covet, crave, desire, long for, wish; lack, need, require.

wariness, SYN.—care, caution, heed, prudence, vigilance, watchfulness. ANT.—abandon, carelessness, recklessness.

warlike, SYN.—antagonistic, hostile, inimical, opposed, unfriendly. ANT.—amicable, cordial, favorable.

warm, SYN.—ardent, cordial, earnest, gracious, hearty, sincere, sociable. ANT.—aloof, cool, reserved, taciturn.

warn, SYN.—admonish, advise, apprise, inform, notify.

warning, SYN.—admonition, advice, caution, indication, information, notice, portent, sign.

wary, SYN.—attentive, alert, alive, awake, aware, careful, heedful, mindful, observant, thoughtful, watchful. ANT.—apathetic, indifferent, oblivious, unaware.

wash, SYN.—bathe, clean, cleanse, launder, rinse, scrub, wet. ANT.—dirty, foul, soil, stain.

waspish, SYN.—fractious, fretful, ill-natured, ill-tempered, irritable, peevish, petulant, snappish, testy, touchy. ANT.—affable, genial, good-natured, good-tempered, pleasant.

waste, SYN.—abandoned, bare, bleak, deserted, desolate, forlorn, forsaken, lonely, solitary, uninhabited, wild. ANT.—attended, cultivated, fertile.

waste, SYN.—despoil, destroy, devastate, pillage, plunder, ravage, ruin, sack, strip; consume, corrode, dissipate, lavish, misuse, scatter, spend, squander, wear out; decay, diminish, dwindle, pine, wither. ANT.—accumulate, conserve, economize, preserve, save.

watch, SYN.—behold, contemplate, descry, discern, distinguish, espy, glimpse, inspect, look at, notice, observe, perceive, scan, scrutinize, see, view, witness.

waver, SYN.—doubt, hesitate, question; distrust, mistrust, suspect. ANT.—believe, confide, decide, rely on, trust.

wavering, SYN.—changeable, fickle, fitful, inconstant, shifting, unstable, vacillating, variable. ANT.—constant, stable, steady, unchanging, uniform.

wax, SYN.—accrue, amplify, augment, enhance, enlarge, expand, extend, grow, heighten, increase, intensify, magnify, multiply, raise. ANT.—atrophy, contract, decrease, diminish, reduce.

way, SYN.—avenue, channel, course, passage, path, road, route, street, thoroughfare, track, trail, walk; fashion, form, habit, manner, method, mode, plan, practice, procedure, process, style, system.

weak, SYN.—bending, fragile, frail, pliant, tender, yielding; debilitated, decrepit, delicate, feeble, impotent, infirm, illogical, inadequate, ineffective, lame, poor; vague; irresolute, pliable, vacillating, wavering; assailable, defenseless, exposed, vulnerable. ANT.—potent, powerful, robust, strong, sturdy.

weakness SYN.—disability, handicap, impotence, incapacity, incompetence. ANT.—ability, capability, power, strength.

wealth, SYN.—abundance, affluence, fortune, luxury, money, opulence, plenty, possessions, riches. ANT.—indigence, need, poverty, want.

wealthy, SYN.—affluent, costly, exorbitant, luxurious, opulent, prosperous, rich, sumptuous, well-to-do. ANT.—beggarly, destitute, indigent, needy, poor.

wearied, SYN.—faint, feeble, languid, irresolute, timid, weak. ANT.—vigorous, brave, forceful.

weary, SYN.—bored, exhausted, faint, fatigued, jaded, spent, tired, wearied, worn. ANT.—fresh, hearty, invigorated, rested.

wedlock, SYN.—espousal, marriage, matrimony, nuptials, union, wedding. ANT.—celibacy, divorce, virginity.

weigh, SYN.—consider, contemplate, deliberate, examine, heed, meditate, ponder, reflect, study. ANT.—ignore, neglect, overlook.

weight, SYN.—burden, gravity, heaviness, load, pressure; emphasis, import, importance, influence, significance, stress, value. ANT.—buoyancy, levity, lightness; insignificance, triviality.

welcome, SYN.—accept, gain, get, take; admit, shelter; entertain, receive. ANT.—bestow, give, impart, reject; discharge, turn away.

well, SYN.—hale, happy, healthy, hearty, sound; beneficial, convenient, expedient, good, profitable. ANT.—depressed, feeble, infirm, weak.

well-being, SYN.—contentment, delight, felicity, gladness, happiness, pleasure, satisfaction. ANT.—despair, grief, misery, sadness, sorrow.

well-bred, SYN.—courtly, cultivated, cultured, genteel, polished, polite, refined. ANT.—boorish, coarse, crude, rude, vulgar.

well-known, SYN.—celebrated, distinguished, eminent, famous, glorious, illustrious, noted, renowned. ANT.—hidden, ignominious, infamous, obscure, unknown.

whim, SYN.—caprice, fancy, humor, inclination, notion, quirk, vagary, whimsy.

whimsical, SYN.—curious, droll, eccentric, odd, peculiar, quaint, queer, singular, strange, unusual. ANT.—common, familiar, normal, ordinary, usual.

whole, SYN.—all, complete, entire, intact, integral, perfect, total, undivided, unimpaired; hale, healed, healthy, sound, well. ANT.—defective, deficient, imperfect, incomplete, partial.

wholesome, SYN.—hale, hearty, robust, sound, strong, well; healthy, hygienic, salubrious, salutary. ANT.—delicate, diseased, frail, infirm; injurious, noxious.

wicked, SYN.—bad, baleful, base, deleterious, evil, immoral, iniquitous, noxious, pernicious, sinful, unsound, unwholesome, villainous. ANT.—excellent, good, honorable, moral, reputable.

wide, SYN.—broad, expanded, extensive, large, sweeping, vast; liberal, tolerant. ANT.—confined, narrow, restricted.

wild, SYN.—barbarous, fierce, outlandish, rude, savage, uncivilized, undomesticated, untamed; desert, desolate, rough, uncultivated, waste; frantic, frenzied, impetuous, irregular, mad, turbulent, wanton, wayward; boisterous, stormy, tempestous; extravagant, foolish, giddy, rash, reckless. ANT.—civilized, gentle; calm, placid, quiet.

wilful, SYN.—contemplated, deliberate, designed, intended, intentional, premeditated, studied, voluntary. ANT.—accidental, fortuitous.

will, SYN.—choice, decision, desire, determination, intention, pleasure, preference, resolution, testament, volition, wish. ANT.—coercion, compulsion, disinterest, indifference.

win, SYN.—achieve, flourish, gain, prevail, prosper, succeed, thrive.

ANT.—fail, miscarry, miss.

wind, SYN.—blast, breeze, draft, gale, gust, hurricane, squall, storm, tempest, zephyr.

wisdom, SYN.—discretion, erudition, foresight, information, insight, intelligence, judgment, knowledge, learning, prudence, reason, sagacity, sageness, sense. ANT.—foolishness, ignorance, imprudence, nonsense, stupidity.

wise, SYN.—deep, discerning, enlightened, intelligent, penetrating, profound, sagacious, sound; erudite, informed, knowing, learned, scholarly; advisable, expedient, prudent. ANT.—foolish, shallow, simple.

wish, SYN.—appetite, aspiration, craving, desire, hungering, longing, lust, urge, yearning. ANT.—abomination, aversion, distaste, hate, loathing.

wish, SYN.—covet, crave, desire, hanker, hunger, long, thirst, want, yearn. ANT.—decline, despise, reject, repudiate, scorn.

wit, SYN.—comprehension, intellect, intelligence, mind, perspicacity, reason, sagacity, sense, understanding; banter, cleverness, fun, humor, irony, pleasantry, raillery, sarcasm, satire, witticism. ANT.—commonplace, platitude, sobriety, solemnity, stupidity.

witchcraft, SYN.—black

art, charm, conjuring, enchantment, legerdemain, magic, necromancy, sorcery, voodoo, wizardry.

withdraw, SYN.—abandon, depart, desert, forsake, give up, go, leave, quit, relinquish, renounce, retire. ANT.—abide, remain, stay, tarry.

wither, SYN.—droop, dry, sear, shrink, shrivel, waste, wilt, wizen; decline, fail, languish, sink, weaken. ANT.—refresh, rejuvenate, renew, revive.

withhold, SYN.—abstain, desist, forbear, refrain. ANT.—continue, indulge, persist.

withstand, SYN.—bar, combat, confront, contradict, counteract, defy, hinder, obstruct, resist, thwart. ANT.—agree, cooperate, submit, succumb, support.

witness, SYN.—attestation, confirmation, declaration, evidence, proof, testimony. ANT.—argument, contradiction, disproof, refutation.

witty, SYN.—adroit, apt, clever, funny, quick, quick-witted, talented; bright, ingenious, sharp, smart. ANT.—awkward, bungling, clumsy, slow, unskilled; dull, foolish.

wizardry, SYN.—black art, charm, conjuring, enchantment, legerdemain, magic, necromancy, sorcery, voodoo, witchcraft.

woe, SYN.—agony, anguish, distress, grief, misery, sorrow, suffering, torment, tribulation, calamity, disaster, evil, misfortune, trouble. ANT.—delight, elation, fun, joy, pleasure.

womanly, SYN.—female, feminine, girlish, ladylike, maidenly, womanish. ANT.—male, manly, mannish, masculine, virile.

wonder, SYN.—curiosity, marvel, miracle, phenomenon, prodigy, rarity, spectacle; admiration, amazement, astonishment, awe, bewilderment, curiosity, surprise, wonderment. ANT.—familiarity, triviality; apathy, expectation, indifference.

wont, SYN.—custom, habit, manner, practice, training, usage, use. ANT.—disuse, idleness, inexperience.

work, SYN.—achievement, business, drudgery, effort, employment, labor, occupation, opus, performance, production, task, toil, travail. ANT.—ease, leisure, play, recreation, vacation.

working, SYN.—active, operative; busy, industrious. ANT.—dormant, inactive, indolent, lazy, passive.

worldly, SYN.—animal, base, bodily, carnal, corporeal, fleshly, gross, lustful, sensual, voluptuous. ANT.—exalted, intellectual, refined, spiritual, temperate.

worn, SYN.—exhausted, faint, fatigued, jaded, spent, tired, wearied, weary. ANT.—fresh, hearty, invigorated, rested.

worry, SYN.—anxiety, apprehension, concern, disquiet, fear, trouble, uneasiness. ANT.—contentment, equanimity, peace, satisfaction.

worry, SYN.—annoy, bother, disturb, gall, harass, harry, haze, irritate, pain, persecute, tease, torment, trouble, vex; fret, fume, fuss. ANT.—comfort, console, solace.

worship, SYN.—adore, deify, honor, idolize, respect, revere, reverence, venerate. ANT.—blaspheme, curse, despise, loathe, scorn.

worth, SYN.—excellence, merit, price, usefulness, utility, value, virtue, worthiness. ANT.—cheapness, uselessness, valuelessness.

worthless, SYN.—abortive, bootless, empty, fruitless, futile, idle, ineffectual, pointless, unavailing, useless, vain, valueless, vapid. ANT.—effective, potent, profitable; meek, modest.

wound, SYN.—damage, disfigure, harm, hurt, impair, injure, mar. spoil; abuse, affront, dishonor, insult, wrong. ANT.—ameliorate, benefit, help, preserve; compliment, praise.

wrangle, SYN.—affray, altercation, argument, bickering, contention, disagreement, dispute, feud, quarrel, spat, squabble. ANT.—agreement, friendliness, harmony, peace, reconciliation.

wrap, SYN.—cloak, clothe, conceal, cover, curtain, disguise, envelop, guard, hide, mask, protect, screen, shield, shroud, veil. ANT.—bare, divulge, expose, reveal, unveil.

wrath, SYN.—anger, animosity, choler, exasperation, fury, indignation, ire, irritation, passion, petulance, rage, resentment, temper. ANT.—conciliation, forbearance, patience, peace, self-control.

wreck, SYN.—annihilate, demolish, destroy, devastate, eradicate, exterminate, extinguish, obliterate, ravage, raze, ruin. ANT.—construct, establish, make, preserve, save.

wretched, SYN.—comfortless, disconsolate, distressed, forlorn, heartbroken, miserable, pitiable; abject, contemptible, despicable, low, mean, paltry, worthless. ANT.—contented, fortunate, happy; noble, significant.

writer, SYN.—author, composer, creator, father, inventor, maker, originator.

wrong, SYN.—amiss, askew, awry, erroneous, fallacious, false, faulty, inaccurate, incorrect, mistaken, unprecise, untrue; improper, inappropriate, unsuitable; aberrant, bad, criminal, evil, immoral, iniquitous, reprehensible. ANT.—correct, right, true, suitable, proper.

Y

yearning, SYN.—appetite, aspiration, craving, desire, hungering, longing, lust, urge, wish. ANT.— abomination, aversion, distaste, hate, loathing.

yield, SYN.—crop, fruit, harvest, proceeds, produce, product, reaping, result, store.

yield, SYN.—afford, bear, bestow, breed, generate, impart, pay, produce, supply; accord, allow, concede, grant, permit; abdicate, accede, acquiesce, capitulate, cede, quit, relent, relinquish, resign, submit, succumb, surrender, waive. ANT.—deny, dissent, oppose, refuse; assert, resist, strive, struggle.

yielding, SYN.—compliant, deferential, dutiful, obedient, submissive, tractable. ANT.—insubordinate, intractable, obstinate, rebellious.

youthful, SYN.—boyish, callow, childish, childlike, girlish, immature, juvenile, puerile, young. ANT.—aged, elderly, mature, old, senile.

Z

zeal, SYN.—ardor, devotion, earnestness, enthusiasm, excitement, fanaticism, fervency, fervor, inspiration, intensity, vehemence, warmth. ANT.—apathy, detachment, ennui, indifference, unconcern.

zealous, SYN.—ardent, eager, enthusiastic, fervent, fervid, fiery, impassioned, intense, keen, passionate, vehement. ANT.—apathetic, cool, indifferent, nonchalant.

zenith, SYN.—acme, apex, climax, consummation, culmination, height, peak, summit. ANT.—anticlimax, base, depth, floor.

zone, SYN.—belt, climate, locality, region, sector, tract.

2. ABBREVIATIONS

a *ante* (L.), before.

a. about; accepted; acre; active; adjective; afternoon; aged, alto; ampere; *annus* (L.), year; answer; *ante* (L.) before; (Metric System) are; (Sports) assists; at.

A (Chem.) argon.

A. Academician; Academy; Alberta (Canada); America; American; Artillery.

a.a. author's alteration.

A.A. Antiaircraft Artillery; Associate in Accounting; Associate in, or of, Arts; Alcoholics Anonymous.

A.A.A. Agricultural Adjustment Administration; Amateur Athletic Association; American Automobile Association.

A.A.A.L. American Academy of Arts and Letters.

A.A.A.S. American Association for the Advancement of Science.

A.A.C. *anno ante Christum* (L.), in the year before Christ.

A.A.G. Assistant Adjutant General.

A.A.P.S.S. American Academy of Political and Social Science.

a.a.r. against all risks.

A.A.S. *Academiae Americanae Socius* (L.), Fellow of the American Academy (of Arts and Sciences); Associate in

Applied Science.

A.A.U. Amateur Athletic Union.

ab. about (times); (Baseball) at bat.

Ab (Chem.) alabamine.

A.B. able-bodied seaman; *Artium Baccalaureus* (L.), Bachelor of Arts.

A.B.A. American Bar Association; American Booksellers Association; Associate in Business Administration.

abbr. or **abbrev.** abbreviation; abbreviated.

ABC atomic, biologic and chemical (warfare); American Bowling Congress; American Broadcasting Co.; Australian Broadcasting Co.

A.B.C. Alcoholic Beverage Control; Argentina, Brazil, and Chile; (usually in reference to their mediation between the United States and Mexico in 1914.)

abd. abdicated.

A.B.F.M. American Board of Foreign Missions.

ab init *ab initio* (L.), from the beginning.

abl. ablative.

ABM Anti-ballistic missile.

Abp. Archbishop.

abr. abridged; abridgement.

abs. absent; absolute; abstract.

A.B.S. American Bible Society; American Bureau

of Shipping.

abs. re. *absente reo* (L.), the defendant being absent.

abt. about.

Abyss. Abyssinia; Abyssinian.

ac. account; acre.

a.c. account current; alternating current: *ante cibum* (L.), before meals (in prescriptions).

Ac (Chem.) actinium; acetate; acetyl.

A.C. *ante Christum* (L.), before Christ; Army Corps; Athletic Club; Automobile Club.

ACAA Agricultural Conservation and Adjustment Administration.

acad. academic; academy.

acc. accelerate; acceptance; accompanied; according; account; accusative.

accel. *accelerando* (It.), increasing in speed; (music) accelerate.

acct. account.

AC/DC alternating current or direct current.

ack. acknowledge.

A.C.L.U. American Civil Liberties Union.

A.C.P. American College of Physicians.

A.C.S. American Cancer Society; American Chemical Society.

act. active.

actg. acting.

ACW (Radio) alternating continuous waves.

ad. (pl. **ads.**) adapted; advertisement.

a.d. after date; *ante diem* (L.), before the day; av-

erage deviation.

AD (Mil.) Active Duty.

A.D. *anno Domini* (L.), in the year of our Lord.

A.D.A. American Dairy Association; American Dental Association; Americans for Democratic Action.

A.D.C. Aide-de-Camp; Aid to Dependent Children.

ad eund. *ad eundem gradum* (L.) to the same degree.

ad fin. *ad finem* (L.), to, or at, the end.

ad inf. *ad infinitum* (L.), to infinity.

ad init. *ad initium* (L.), to, or at, the beginning.

ad int. *ad interim* (L.), in the meantime.

adj. adjacent; adjective; adjourned; (Banking) adjustment.

Adj. or **Adjt.** Adjutant.

Adj. Gen. or **Adjt.Gen.** Adjutant General.

ad lib. *ad libitum* (L.), at pleasure, as one wishes, to the amount desired.

ad loc. *ad locum* (L.), to, or at, the place.

ad val. *ad valorem* (L.), according to value.

adm. administration; administrator; admission.

Adm. Admiral; Admiralty.

admr. administrator.

adv. *ad valorem* (L.), according to value; adverb; adverbial; *ad versus* (L.) against; advertisement; advertising; advise; advocate.

Adv. Advent.

advt. advertisement.

ae. *aetatis* (L.), of age;

aged.

A.E. Aeronautical Engineer; Agricultural Engineer; Associate in Education; Associate in Engineering.

A.E.A. Actor's Equity Association.

A. E. & P. Ambassador Extraordinary and Plenipotentiary.

A.E.F. American Expeditionary Forces.

aeron. aeronautics.

aet. or **aetat.** *aetatis* (L.), of age; aged.

a.f. audio frequency.

AF. or **A.F.** Anglo-French; Air-Force.

A.F.A.M. or **A.F. & A.M.** Ancient Free and Accepted Masons.

AFB air force base.

AFC automatic flight control; automatic frequency control.

aff. affectionate; affirmative; affirmatively.

afft. affidavit.

Afg. or **Afgh.** Afghanistan.

A.F.L. or **A.F. of L.** American Federation of Labor.

AFL-CIO American Federation of Labor-Congress of Industrial Organizations.

AFM American Federation of Musicians.

A.F.M. Air Force Medal (Brit.).

A.F. of L. See A.F.L.

Afr. Africa; African.

A. Fr. Anglo-French.

aft. afternoon.

A.F.T. American Federation of Teachers.

AFTRA American Federation of Television and Radio Artists.

Ag *argentum* (L.), (Chem.) silver.

Ag. August.

A.G. Adjutant General; Agent General; Attorney General.

AGCT Army General Classification Test.

agcy. agency.

agric. agricultural; agriculture.

agt. agent.

Ah or **a.h.** ampere

A.H. *anno Hejirae.* (L.), in the year of, or from, the Hejirae A.D. 622.

A.H.A. American Historical Association; American Hospital Association.

AHQ air headquarters; army headquarters.

A.I. artificial insemination.

A.I.A. American Institute of Architects.

AID Agency for International Development; American Institute of Decorators; artificial insemination by donor (Brit.).

A.I.E.E.E. American Institute of Electrical and Electronic Engineers.

A.I.M.E. American Institute of Mining Engineers.

AJ Associate Justice.

A.K.C. American Kennel Club.

Al (Chem.) aluminum.

Al. *alia* (L.) other things; *alii* (L.), other people.

A.L. (Baseball) American League; American Legion; Anglo-Latin.

Ala. Alabama.

A.L.A. American Library Association; Author's League of America; Association of Liberal Arts; Automobile Legal Association.

Alas. Alaska.

Alb. Albania; Albany; Albert.

Alba. Alberta (Canada).

ALBM air-launched ballistic missile.

alchem. alchemy.

ald. alderman.

alg. algebra.

Alg. Algeria; Algiers.

A.L.P. American Labor Party.

alt. alteration; alternate; altitude; alto.

Alta. Alberta (Canada).

a.m. *ante meridiem* (L.), before noon.

AM (Chem.) americium.

Am. America; American.

A.M. amplitude modulation; *anno mundi* (L.), in the year of the world; *ante meridiem* (L.), before noon; *Artium Magister* (L.), Master of Arts; *Ave Maria* (L.), Hail Mary.

A.M.A. American Management Association; American Medical Association.

Amb. Ambassador.

A.M.D.G. *ad majorem Dei gloriam* (L.), for the greater glory of God.

A.M.E. African Methodist Episcopal.

Amer. America; American.

AMORC Ancient Mystic Order Rosae Crucis.

amp. ampere.

AMPAS Academy of Motion Picture Arts and Sciences.

A.M.S. Army Medical Staff.

amt. amount.

amu atomic mass unit.

an. *anno* (L.), in the year; anonymous.

An (Chem.) actinon.

A.N. Anglo-Norman; Associate in Nursing.

anal. analogous; analogy; analysis; analytic; analytical; analyze.

anat. anatomical; anatomy.

anc. ancient.

ANC Army Nurse Corps.

Angl. Anglican; Anglicized.

ANG Air National Guard.

ann. *anni* (L.), years; annual; annuity.

annot. annotated; annotation; annotator.

anon. anonymous.

ANPA American Newspaper Publishers Association.

ans. answer.

ant. antiquary; antiquities; antonym.

anth. anthology.

anthro. or **anthrop.** or **anthropol.** anthropological; anthropology.

antiq. antiquary; antiquities; antiquity.

a/o account of.

AOL absent over leave.

aor. aorist; aoristic.

ap. *apud* (L.), in the writings of; as quoted by.

Ap. Apostle; apothecaries; April.

a/p account paid; account payable; authority to pay or purchase.

a.p. additional premium;

author's proof.

A.P. Associated Press.

A.P.A. American Pharmaceutical Association; American Philological Association; American Protective Association; American Protestant Association; American Psychological Association; American Psychiatric Association; Associate in Public Administration.

apo. apogee.

APO Army Post Office.

Apoc. Apocalypse; Apocrypha.

app. apparatus; apparent; apparently; appeal; appendix; applied; appointed; apprentice; approximate.

appar. apparent; apparently.

approx. approximately.

appx. appendix.

Apr. April.

A.P.S. American Peace Society; American Philatelic Society; American Philosophical Society; American Protestant Society.

A.P.S.A. American Political Science Association.

apt. (pl. **apts.**) apartment.

apx. appendix.

aq. *aqua* (L.), water.

aq. dest. *aqua destillata* (L.), distilled water.

ar. arrival; arrived; arrives.

Ar (Chem.) argon.

a.r. (Insurance) all risks; analytical reagent.

Ar. Arabic; Aramaic.

A.R. *anno regni* (L.), in the year of the reign; annual return; Army Registration.

A.R.A. American Railway Association; Associate of the Royal Academy.

Arab. Arabia; Arabian; Arabic.

Aram. Aramaic.

A.R.A.M. Associate of the Royal Academy of Music.

A.R.C. American Red Cross.

arch. archaic; archaism; archery; archipelago; architect; architectural; architecture; archives.

Arch. Archbishop.

archaeol. archaeological; archaeology.

Archd. Archdeacon; Archduke.

A.R.C.M. Associate of the Royal College of Music.

A.R.C.S. Associate of the Royal College of Science; Associate of the Royal College of Surgeons.

Arg. Argentina.

arith. arithmetic; arithmetical.

Ariz. Arizona.

Ark. Arkansas.

Arm. Armenian; Armoric.

arr. arranged; arrival; arrived; arrives.

A.R.R. *anno regni Regis* or *Reginae* (L.), in the year of the reign of the King or Queen.

ars. arsenal.

A.R.S.A. Associate of the Royal Scottish Academy.

a.s. at sight.

As (Chem.) arsenic.

As. or **A.S.** Anglo-Saxon.

A.S. *anno salutis* (L.), in the year of salvation.

A.S.A. American Standards Association; American Statistical Association.

ASCAP American Society of Composers, Authors and Publishers.

A.S.C.E. American Society of Civil Engineers.

A.S.M.E. American Society of Mechanical Engineers.

A.S.P.C.A. American Society for the Prevention of Cruelty to Animals.

ass. assistant; association; assorted.

assd. assessed; assigned; assured.

assn. association.

assoc. associate; associated; association.

ASSR Autonomous Soviet Socialist Republic.

asst. assistant.

astr. astronomer; astronomical; astronomy.

astrol. astrologer; astrological; astrology.

at. airtight; atmosphere; atomic, attorney.

At (Chem.) astatine.

ATC Air Traffic Control; Air Transport Command.

Atl. Atlantic.

at. no. atomic number.

att. attaché; attention; attorney.

attrib. attribute; attributive; attributively.

atty. attorney.

Atty. Gen. Attorney General.

at. wt. atomic weight.

Au *aurum* (L.), (Chem.) gold.

AU astronomical unit.

A.U.A. American Unitarian Association.

A.U.C. *ab urbe condita* or *anno urbis conditae* (L.), in the year since the founding of the city (Rome, 735 B.C.).

aud. auditor.

Aufl. *Auflage* (G.), edition.

aug. augmentative; augmented.

Aug. August; Augustus.

Aus. Austria; Austrian.

Ausg. *Ausgabe* (G.), edition.

Aust. Austria; Austrian.

Austral. Australasia; Australasian; Australia; Australian.

auth. author; authorized.

Auth. Ver. Authorized Version (of the Bible).

auto. automatic, automobile; automotive.

aux. or **auxil.** auxiliary.

av. avenue; average; avoirdupois.

a.v. *ad valorem* (L.), at the value; *annos vixit* (L.) he or she lived so many years; audio visual.

A.V. Authorized Version (of the Bible).

avdp. avoirdupois.

ave. avenue.

avg. average.

avn. aviation.

avoir. avoirdupois.

AW article of war.

A.W.L. absent with leave.

A.W.O.L. absent without leave.

ax. axiom.

A.Y.H. American Youth Hostels.

az. azimuth; azure.

B

b. base; (Sports) base or baseman; bass; book; born; brother.

B (Chem.) boron; (Chess) bishop.

B. Baron; Bay; Bible; British; brotherhood.

Ba (Chem.) barium.

B.A. Bachelor of Arts; British America.

B.A.A. Bachelor of Applied Arts.

bact. bacteriology.

B.A.E. Bachelor of Aeronautical Engineering; Bachelor of Agricultural Engineering; Bachelor of Architectural Engineering; Bachelor of Art Education; Bachelor of Arts in Education.

B. Ag. or **B. Agr.** Bachelor of Agriculture.

Bah. Bahamas.

bal. balance.

Bal. Baluchistan.

Balt. Baltic.

bap. baptized.

Bapt. Baptist.

bar. barometer; barometric; barrel; barrister.

Bar. Baruch (Apocrypha).

BAR Browning Automatic rifle.

Barb. Barbados.

barr. barrister.

Bart. Baronet.

B.A.S. Bachelor of Agricultural Sciences; Bachelor of Applied Science.

batt. battalion; battery.

Bav. Bavaria; Bavarian.

bb (Baseball) base on balls.

b.b. bill book.

B.B. bail bond; Blue Book; B'nai B'rith; Bureau of the Budget; ball bearing, best of breed.

B.B.C. British Broadcasting Corporation.

bbl. (pl. **bbls.**) barrel.

BBT basal body temperature.

B.C. Bachelor of Chemistry; before Christ; British Columbia.

BCD (Mil.) bad conduct discharge; (Computer Technology) binary-coded decimal.

B.C.E. Bachelor of Christian Education; Bachelor of Civil Engineering.

B. Ch. Bachelor of Chemistry; *Baccalaureus Chirurgiae* (L.), Bachelor of Surgery.

B.C.L. Bachelor of Civil Law.

B.C.M. Bachelor of Church Music.

B.C.P. Bachelor of City Planning.

B.C.S. Bachelor of Chemical Science.

bd. board; bond; bound.

B.D. Bachelor of Divinity; bills discounted.

B/D bank draft; (Accounting) brought down.

bd. or **bdl.** (pl. **bdls.**) bundle.

bdry. boundary.

Be (Chem.) beryllium.

b.e. bill of entry; bill of exchange.

B.E. Bachelor of Education; Bachelor of Engineering; Bank of England; Board of Education; Buddhist Era.

Bech. Bechuanaland.

B.E.E. Bachelor of Electrical Engineering.

bef. before.

B.E.F. British Expeditionary Forces.

Belg. Belgian; Belgium.

B.E.M. Bachelor of Engineering of Mines.

Beng. Bengal; Bengali.

B.E.P. Bachelor of Engineering Physics.

Berks. Berkshire.

B.E.S. Bachelor of Engineering Science.

bet. between.

bf. (Legal) brief.

bf. (Printing) bold face.

B/F (Accounting) brought forward.

B.F. Bachelor of Finance; Bachelor of Forestry.

B.F.A. Bachelor of Fine Arts.

B.F.S. Bachelor of Foreign Service.

B.F.T. Bachelor of Foreign Trade.

bg. (pl. **bgs.**) background; bag; being.

B.G. bonded goods.

B.G.E. Bachelor of Geological Engineering.

B. Gen. Ed. Bachelor of General Education.

bh. (Baseball) base hits.

B.H. base hospital; bill of health.

bhp brake horse power.

Bi (Chem.) bismuth.

B.I. British India.

Bib. Bible; Biblical.

bibliog. bibliographical; bibliography.

b.i.d. *bis in die* (L.), twice a day (in prescriptions).

B.I.D. Bachelor of Industrial Design.

B.I.E. Bachelor of Industrial Engineering.

biochem. biochemistry.

biog. biographer; biographical; biography.

biol. biological; biologist; biology.

B.I.S. Bank for International Settlements; British Information Service.

bk. (pl. **bks.**) bank; bark; black; block; book; brake.

BK (Chem.) berkelium.

bkcy. (Legal) bankruptcy.

bkg. banking.

Bklyn. Brooklyn.

bkpr. bookkeeper.

bkry. bakery.

bkt. (pl. **bkts.**) basket; bracket; bucket.

bl. (pl. **bls.**) bale; barrel; block; blue.

B/L bill of lading.

B.L. Bachelor of Laws; Bachelor of Letters.

B.L.A. Bachelor of Landscape Architecture; Bachelor of Liberal Arts.

bldg. (pl. **bldgs.**) building.

bldr. builder.

B. Lit. or **B. Litt.** *Baccalaureus Lit(t)erarum* (L.), Bachelor of Letters or Literature.

blk. black; block; bulk.

B.LL. *Baccalaureus Legum* (L.), Bachelor of Laws.

BLR breech-loading rifle.

bls. bales, barrels.

BLS Bureau of Labor Statistics.

B.L.S. Bachelor of Library Science.

blvd. boulevard.

BM basal metabolism; *Beatae Memoriae* (L.), of blessed memory; bench mark.

B.M. Bachelor of Medicine; Bachelor of Music; British Museum.

B.M.A. British Medical Association.

B. Mar. E. Bachelor of Marine Engineering.

B.M.E. Bachelor of Mechanical Engineering; Bachelor of Mining Engineering; Bachelor of Music Education.

B. Met. Bachelor of Metallurgy.

BMEWS (Mil.) ballistic missile early warning system.

B. Mgt. E. Bachelor of Management Engineering.

B. Min. E. Bachelor of Mining Engineering.

B.M.R. basal metabolic rate.

B.M.S. Bachelor of Marine Science.

B.M.T. Bachelor of Medical Technology.

B. Mus. Bachelor of Music.

B.M.V. *Beata Maria Virgo* (L.), Blessed Mary the Virgin.

B.N. Bachelor of Nursing.

B.N.S. Bachelor of Naval Science.

b.o. back order; branch office; broker's order; buyer's option.

B/O (accounting) brought over.

B.O. Board of Ordinance; (Informal) body odor; (Theatre) box office.

B.O.D. biochemical oxygen demand.

B. of E. Board of Education.

B. of H. Board of Health.

B. of T. Board of Trade.

Boh. or **Bohem.** Bohemia; Bohemian.

Bol. Bolivia.

bor. borough.

bot. botanical; botanist; botany; bought.

B.O.T. Board of Trade.

boul. boulevard.

bp. baptized; birthplace.

Bp. Bishop

b.p. (Com.) bills payable; (Phys., Chem.) boiling point; *Ebonum publicum* (L.), the public good.

B.P. Bachelor of Pharmacy; Bachelor of Philosophy; blood pressure.

B.P.A. Bachelor of Professional Arts.

B.P.E. Bachelor of Physical Education.

B. Pet. E. Bachelor of Petroleum Engineering.

B.P.H. Bachelor of Public Health.

B. Pharm. Bachelor of Pharmacy.

B. Phil. Bachelor of Philosophy.

b.p.d. barrels per day.

bpl. birthplace.

B.P.O.E. Benevolent and Protective Order of Elks.

Br (Chem.) bromine.

br. branch; brig; brother.

b.r. (Com.) bills receivable.

Br. Britain; British.

Braz. Brazil; Brazilian.

brev. brevet; brevetted.

brig. brigade; brigadier.

Brig. Gen. Brigadier General

Brit. Britain; British.

Brit. Mus. British Museum.

b.s. (Com.) balance-sheet; bill of sale.

B.S. Bachelor of Science; Bachelor of Surgery;

British Standard.

B.S.A. Bachelor of Science in Agriculture; Boy Scouts of America.

B.S.A.A. Bachelor of Science in Applied Arts.

B.S. Adv. Bachelor of Science in Advertising.

B.S.A.E. Bachelor of Science in Aeronautical Engineering; Bachelor of Science in Agricultural Engineering; Bachelor of Science in Architectural Engineering.

B.S. Arch. Bachelor of Science in Architecture.

B.S. Art Ed. Bachelor of Science in Art Education.

B.S.B.A. Bachelor of Science in Business Administration.

B.S. Bus. Bachelor of Science in Business.

B. Sc. Bachelor of Science.

B.S.C. Bachelor of Science in Commerce.

B.S.C.E. Bachelor of Science in Civil Engineering.

B.S. Ch. Bachelor of Science in Chemistry.

B.S. Ch. E. Bachelor of Science in Chemical Engineering.

B.S.D. Bachelor of Science in Design.

B.S.E. Bachelor of Science in Education; Bachelor of Science in Engineering.

B.S. Ec. Bachelor of Science in Economics.

B.S.E.M. Bachelor of Science in Engineering of Mines.

B.S.E.P. Bachelor of Science in Engineering Physics.

B.S.F. Bachelor of Science in Forestry

bsh. bushel

B.S.H.A. Bachelor of Science in Hospital Administration.

B.S.H.E. Bachelor of Science in Home Economics.

B.S.I.E. Bachelor of Science in Industrial Education; Bachelor of Science in Industrial Engineering.

B.S.J. Bachelor of Science in Journalism.

bskt. basket.

B.S.L. Bachelor of Science in Law.

B.S.L.S. Bachelor of Science in Library Science.

B.S.M. Bachelor of Science in Sacred Music; Bachelor of Science in Music.

B.S. Met. E. Bachelor of Science in Metallurgical Engineering.

B.S. Min. Bachelor of Science in Minerology.

bsmt. basement.

B.S.M.T. Bachelor of Science in Medical Technology.

B.S.N. Bachelor of Science in Nursing.

B.S.O.T. Bachelor of Science in Occupational Therapy.

B.S.P. Bachelor of Science in Pharmacy.

B.S.P.A. Bachelor of Science in Public Administration.

B.S.P.E. Bachelor of Science in Physical Education.

B.S.P.H. Bachelor of Science in Public Health.

B.S.P.H.N. Bachelor of Science in Public Health Nursing.

B.S.P.T. Bachelor of Science in Physical Therapy.

B.S.R.T. Bachelor of Science in Radiological Technology.

B.S.S.S. Bachelor of Science in Social Science.

bt. bought.

Bt. Baronet.

B. Th. Bachelor of Theology.

B.T.U. British thermal unit.

btwn. between.

bty. battery.

bu. bureau; bushel; bushels.

Bucks. Buckinghamshire.

bul. bulletin.

Bulg. Bulgaria; Bulgarian.

bull. bulletin.

bus. bushel; bushels; business; busmen.

b.v. book value.

B.V. *Beata Virgo* (L.), Blessed Virgin; *bene vale* (L.), farewell.

B.V.E. Bachelor of Vocational Education.

B.V.M. *Beata Virgo Maria* (L.), Blessed Virgin Mary.

bvt. brevet.

BW bacteriological warfare; biological warfare; bonded warehouse.

B.W.I. British West Indies.

bx. (pl. **bxs.**) box.

C

c *circa, circiter,* or *circum* (L.), about; cycle; cy-

cles.

c. carat; case; (Baseball) catcher; cathode; cent; (Football) center; centime; centimeter; century; chapter; child; *circa, circiter, circum* (L.), about; copyright; cost; coupon; cubic; current; cycle.

C calorie; carbon; Roman numeral for 100.

C. Cape; Catholic; Celsius; Centigrade; Chairman; Chancellor; Chancery; Church; Code; Commission; Congress; Conservative; Consult; Court.

ca. case; cathode; centiare; *circa* (L.), about.

Ca (Chem.) calcium.

CA chronological age.

C/A (Banking) capital account; cash account; credit account; current account.

C.A. Central America; Chartered Accountant; Chief Accountant; Commercial Agent; Consular Agent; Controller of Accounts; Court of Appeals.

CAA Civil Aeronautics Administration.

CAB Civil Aeronautics Board.

C.A.F. cost and freight; cost assurance and freight.

cal. calendar; calends; caliber; calorie.

Cal. California.

calc. calculate.

Calif. California.

c & sc (Printing) capitals and small capitals.

Camb. Cambridge.

can. canceled; cannon; canto.

Can. Canada; Canadian.

c. & f. cost and freight.

Cant. Canterbury; Canticles.

Cantab. *Cantabrigiensis* (L.), of Cambridge.

C.A.O. Civil Administrative Officer.

cap. (pl. **caps.**) capital; capital letter; capitalize; *capitulum* or *caput* (L.), chapter or section.

C.A.P. Civil Air Patrol.

caps. capital letters.

Capt. Captain.

car. carat.

Card. Cardinal.

Carib. Caribbean.

carp. carpenter; carpentry.

C.A.S. Certificate of Advanced Studies.

cash. cashier.

cat. catalogue; catechism.

Cat. Catalan.

cath. cathedral.

Cath. Catholic.

caus. causative.

cav. cavalry; caveat; cavity.

CAVU (Aeron.) ceiling and visibility unlimited.

c.b. cash book; (Mil.) confined to barracks; (Com.) currency bond.

Cb (Chem.) columbium.

C.B. *Chirurgiae Baccalaureus* (L.) Bachelor of Surgery; Common Bench; Companion of the Bath (Brit.).

C.B.C. contraband control; Canadian Broadcasting Corporation.

C.B.D. Central Business District.

C.B.E. Commander of the Order of the British Empire.

cc. cubic centimeter; chapters.

c.c. carbon copy; cash credit; cubic centimeter.

C.C. cashier's check; chief clerk; Chamber of Commerce; Circuit Court, City Councilor; Civil Code; Civil Court; Common Councilman; Country Club; County Clerk; County Commissioner; County Court.

C.C.A. Chief Clerk of the Admiralty; Circuit Court of Appeals; County Court of Appeals.

C.C.P. Code of Civil Procedure; Court of Common Pleas.

CCR Commission on Civil Rights.

cd. cord; could.

Cd (Chem.) cadmium.

C/D (Banking) certificate of deposit.

C.D. Civil Defense; Coast Defense; *corps diplomatique* (F), diplomatic corps.

C.D.S.O. Companion of the Distinguished Service Order (Brit.)

c.e. *caveat emptor* (L.), buyer's risk; compass error.

Ce (Chem.) cerium.

C.E. Chief Engineer; Church of England; Civil Engineer; Common Era; customs and excise.

CEA Council of Economic Advisors; County Education Authority.

CED Committee for Economic Development.

C.E.F. Canadian Expeditionary Forces.

Celt. Celtic.

cen. central; century.

cent. centigrade; central; century.

CENTO Central Treaty Organization.

cert. certificate; certify.

certif. certificate; certificated.

cet. par. *ceteris paribus* (L.), other things being equal.

Cf (Chem.) californium.

cf. (Baseball) center fielder; *confer* (L.), compare.

C/F. (Accounting) carried forward.

C.F. cost and freight.

c.f.i. cost, freight and insurance.

cg. centigram.

C.G. Captain of the Guard; Center of Gravity; Coast Guard; Consul-General.

cge. carriage.

C.G.H. Cape of Good Hope.

C.G.M. Conspicuous Gallantry Medal (Brit.).

c.g.s. (Scale of Units) centimeter-gram-second.

ch. chain; chapter; chief; child; church.

Ch. Champion; Chancery; Church; China.

C.B. Clearing House; Courthouse; Customs House; Companions of Honour (Brit.).

Chal. or **Chald.** Chaldaic; Chaldee.

Chanc. Chancellor; Chancery.

chap. chapel; chapter.

Chap. Chaplain.

Ch. H. *Chirurgiae Bacca-*

laureus (L.), Bachelor of Surgery.

Ch. E. Chemical Engineer.

chem. chemical; chemist; chemistry.

Ches. or **Chesh.** Cheshire.

Chev. Chevalier; Chevron.

chg. change.

chf. chief.

Chi. or **Chic.** Chicago.

Chin. China; Chinese.

Ch. J. Chief Justice.

Chmn. or **Chn.** Chairman.

CHQ Corps Headquarters.

Chr. Christian.

chron. chronological; chronology.

Chron. Chronicles.

CI cast iron; cephalic index; certificate of insurance; cost and insurance.

C.I. Channel Islands; Chief Inspector; Counter Intelligence; Imperial Order of the Crown of India (Brit.).

Cia. *Compañia* (Sp.), Company.

C.I.A. Central Intelligence Agency.

CIC Counter Intelligence Corps.

C.I.D. Criminal Investigation Department (Brit.)

Cie. *Compagñie* (Fr.), Company.

C.I.E. Companion of the Order of the Indian Empire (Brit.).

c.i.f. cost, insurance, and freight.

c.i.f. & c. cost, insurance, freight and commission.

c.i.f.c. & i. cost, insurance, freight, commission, and interest.

c.i.f.i. & e. cost, insurance, freight, interest, and exchange.

Cin. Cincinnati.

C. in C. Commander-in-Chief.

C.I.O. Congress of Industrial Organizations.

cir. *circa, circiter,* or *circum* (L.), about; circle.

circ. *circa, circiter,* or *circum* (L.), about; circuit, circulation, circumference.

cit. citation; cited; citizen; citrate.

C.J. Chief Justice.

ck. cask; check.

cl. carload; centiliter class; clause; clergyman; cloth.

Cl (Chem.) chlorine.

class. classic; classical; classification; classified.

cld. called; canceled; cleared; colored; cooled.

C.L.I. cost of living index.

clk. clerk, clock.

CLU Civil Liberties Union.

cm. centimeter.

Cm (Chem.) curium.

C.M. Certificated Master; Certificate of Merit; *Chirurgiae Magister* (L.), Master of Surgery; Church Missionary; Corresponding Member; court martial.

C.M.G. Companion of the Order of St. Michael and St.George (Brit.).

cml. commercial.

C.M.S. Church Missionary Society (Brit).

CNO Chief of Naval Operations.

CNS central nervous system.

c/o care of; carried over.

Co (Chem.) cobalt.

Co. Company, county.

C.O. Colonial Office; Commanding Officer; conscientious objector.

coch. *cochlear* or *cochleare* (L.), spoonful (in prescriptions).

C.O.D. cash, or collect, on delivery.

C. of C. Chamber of Commerce.

C. of M. certificate of merit.

C. of S. Chief of Staff.

cog. or cogn. cognate.

col. colonial; colony; color; column.

Col. Colonel; Colorado; Colossians; Colombia.

C.O.L. cost of living.

coll. collated; collateral; colleague; collected; collection; collective; collector; college; collegiate; colloquial.

collat. collateral.

colloq. colloquial; colloquialism; colloquially.

Colo. Colorado.

com. comedy; commentary; commerce; common; commonly; communication.

Com. commander; commission; commissioner; committee; commodore.

comb. combination; combined.

comdg. commanding.

Comdr. Commander.

Comdt. Commandant.

Com.-in-Chf. Commander-in-Chief.

comp. comparative; compiler; composer; composition; compositor; compound; comprising.

compar. comparative.

Comr. commissioner.

Com. Ver. Common Version (of the Bible).

con. concerto; consolidated; continued; *contra* (L.), against.

Con. conformist; consul.

cong. *congius* (L.), gallon; congregation.

Cong. Congregational; Congress; Congressional.

conj. conjugation; conjunction; conjunctive.

conn. connected; connotation.

Conn. Connecticut.

consgt. consignment.

consol. consolidated.

const. constable; constant; constituent; constitution; constitutional; construction.

constr. construction; construed.

cont. containing; contents; continent; continental; continued.

Cont. continental.

contd. continued.

contemp. contemporary.

contr. contracted; contraction; contractor; contralto; contrary; control.

conv. convalescent; convene; convenient; convention; convert; convertible; convocation.

coop. cooperation; cooperative.

cor. corner; corpus; corrected; correction; correlative; correspondent; corresponding.

Cor. Corinthians; coroner.

Corn. Cornish; Cornwall.

coroll. corollary.

corp. corporal; corporation.

corr. corrected; correspond; corrupt; corruption.

correl. correlative.

Cors. Corsica.

cor. sec. corresponding secretary.

cos cosine.

cosec cosecant.

cot cotangent.

covers. coversed sine.

cox. coxswain.

cp. compare; coupon.

c.p. candle power; carriage paid; cerebal palsy; charter party; chemically pure.

C.P. Chief Patriarch; Common Pleas; Common Prayer; Communist Party; Court of Probate.

C.P.A. Certified Public Accountant.

CPI Consumer Price Index.

Cpl. Corporal.

C.P.O. Chief Petty Officer.

cps cycles per second.

CQ (Radio) a signal sent at the beginning of radiograms, or sent by an amateur as an invitation for another amateur to reply.

cr. center; circular; created; credit; creditor; creek; crown; crowned.

Cr (Chem.) chromium.

CR conditioned reflex; critical ratio.

C.R. Costa Rica

craniol, craniology.

craniom. craniometry.

cres. or **cresc.** *crescendo* (It.), (Music) increasing in volume.

crit. critical; criticism.

CRT cathode ray tube.

cryst. or crystal. crystalline; crystallography.

cs. case; census; consciousness.

c.s. capital stock; current series.

Cs (Chem.) caesium.

C.S. Chief of Staff; Christian Science; Civil Service; Clerk of Session; Confederate States; court of sessions.

C.S.A. Confederate States of America; Confederate States Army.

csc cosecant.

CSC Civil Service Commission.

C.S.C. Conspicuous Service Cross (Brit.).

csk. cask.

C.S.O. Chief Signal Officer; Chief Staff Officer.

CST Central Standard Time.

ct. (pl. cts.) carat; cent; certificate; court; current.

c.t. cable transfer.

Ct. Connecticut; Count.

C.T. Central Time.

ctf. certificate.

ctge. cartage.

ctl. central.

cts. centimes; cents; certificates.

cu. cubic; cumulus.

Cu *cuprum* (L.), (Chem.) copper.

cur. currency; current (the current month).

C.V. Common Version (of the Bible).

C.V.O. Commander of the Royal Victorian Order (Brit.).

C.W. chemical warfare; child welfare; churchwarden; continuous wave.

C.W.A. Civil Works Administration.

c.w.o. cash with order.

C.W.O. Chief Warrant Officer.

cwt. hundredweight (for L. *centum*, and E. *weight*).

cy. capacity; currency; cycle.

cyc. cycle; cyclopedia; cyclorama.

C.Z. Canal Zone.

Czech. Czechoslovakia.

D

d. date; daughter; day; dead; degree; *denarius* or *denarii* (L.), penny or pence; deputy; died; dime; dividend; dollar; dose.

D Roman numeral for 500; (Chem.) deuterium.

D. Deacon; Democrat; *Deus* (L.); God; *Dominus* (L.), *Dom.* (Pg.); *Don* (Sp.), Lord; Dowager; Duchess; Duke; Dutch.

d.a. days after acceptance; deposit account.

D.A. District Attorney.

DAB Dictionary of American Biography.

Dan. Daniel; Danish.

D.A.R. Daughters of the American Revolution.

dat. dative.

DATA Defense Air Transportation Administration.

dau. daughter.

DAV Disabled American Veterans.

db decibel.

d.b. day book.

D.B. Bachelor of Divinity;

Doomsday Book.

D&B Dun and Bradstreet.

DBA doing business as.

D.B.E. Dame Commander of the Order of the British Empire.

D. Bib. Douay Bible.

dbk. drawback.

dbl. double.

d.c. direct current.

D.C. (Music) *da capo* (It.), repeat from the beginning; Dental Corps; Deputy Consul; District Court; District of Columbia.

D.C.L. Doctor of Civil Law.

D.C.M. Distinguished Conduct Medal (Brit.).

D. Cn. L. Doctor of Canon Law.

D.C.S. Deputy Clerk of Session; Doctor of Christian Science.

dd. delivered.

d.d. days after date; days after delivery; delayed delivery; demand draft.

DD dishonorable discharge.

D.D. Doctor of Divinity.

D.D.S. Doctor of Dental Surgery.

DE destroyer escort.

D.E. Doctor of Engineering.

Dea. Deacon.

deb. debenture; debutante.

dec. deceased; declension; (Music) *decrescendo* (It.), decrease.

Dec. December.

decd. deceased; declared; decreased.

decl. declension.

decres. or **decresc.** (Music) *decrescendo* (It.), de-

creasing in volume.

ded. dedicated; dedication.

def. defective; defendant; deferred; definite; definition.

deft. defendant.

deg. degree.

del. delegate; delete; *delineavite* (L.), he or she drew (it); deliver.

Del. Delaware.

Dem. Democrat; Democratic.

Den. Denmark.

D. Eng. Doctor of Engineering.

dent. dental; dentist; dentistry.

dep. departed; department; departs; deponent; depot; deputy.

dept. department.

der. derivation; derivative; derived.

deriv. derivation; derivative.

D. és L. *Docteur es Lettres* (Fr.), Doctor of Letters.

D. és S. *Docteur es Sciences* (Fr.), Doctor of Sciences.

det. detachment.

Deut. Deuteronomy.

Dev. Devonshire.

DEW Distant Early Warning.

DF (Telecom.) direction finding.

D.F. Dean of Faculty; *Defensor Fidei* (L.), Defender of the Faith; *Distrito Federal* (Sp.), Federal District, (Mexico); Doctor of Forestry.

D.F.A. Doctor of Fine Arts.

D.F.C. Distinguished Flying Cross (Brit.).

dft. defendant; draft.

dg decigram.

D.G. *Dei gratia* (L.), by the grace of God; *Deo gratias* (L.), thanks to God; Director-General.

d.h. *das heisst* (G.), that is to say.

D.H. Doctor of Humanities.

D.H.L. Doctor of Hebrew Letters.

d.i. *das ist* (G.), that is.

Di (Chem.) didymium.

dial. dialect; dialectical.

diam. diameter.

dict. dictator; dictation; dictionary.

diff. difference; different.

dig. digest.

dim. (Music) *diminuendo* (It.), decreasing in volume; diminutive.

dioc. diocesan; diocese.

dipl diploma; diplomatic.

dir. direction; director.

dis. discount; distance; distant, distribute.

disc. discount; discovered.

disp. dispatch; dispensary; dispensatory; dispenser.

diss. dissertation.

dist. distance; distinguish; district.

Dist. Atty. District Attorney.

Dist. Ct. district court.

div. divide; divided; dividend; divine; divinity; division, divisor; divorced.

D.J. (Colloq.) disc jockey; District Judge; *Doctor Juris* (L.), Doctor of Law.

dk. deck; dock.

dl. deciliter.

D. Lit. or **D. Litt** *Doctor*

Lit(t)erarum (L.), Doctor of Letters or Literature.

D.L.O. dead letter office.

D.L.S. Doctor of Library Science.

dly. daily; delivery.

dm decimeter.

D.M. *destra mano* (It.), right hand; Deutsche mark.

D.M.D. *Dentariae Medecinae Doctor* (L.), Doctor of Dental Medicine.

D.M.S. Doctor of Medical Science.

D. Mus. Doctor of Music.

DMZ demilitarized zone.

DNA deoxyribonucleic acid.

D.N.B. Dictionary of National Biography (Brit.).

d.o. delivery order.

D.O. district officer; Doctor of Optometry; Doctor of Osteopathy; duty officer.

D.O.A. dead on arrival.

doc. (pl. **docs.**) document.

dol. (pl. **dols.**) dollars; (Music) *dolce* (It.), soft, sweet.

dom. domestic; dominion.

D.O.M. *Deo Optimo Maximo* (L.), to God, the Best, the Greatest.

dom. econ. domestic economy.

Dor. Dorian; Doric.

D.O.R.A. Defense of the Realm Act (Brit.).

Dow. dowager.

doz. dozen; dozens.

D.P. displaced person.

D.P.A. Doctor of Public Administration.

D. Ph. Doctor of Philosophy.

D.P.H. Doctor of Public

Health.

dpt. department; deponent.

D.P.W. Department of Public Works.

dr. debtor; drachma; dram; draw; drawer.

d.r. dead reckoning; deposit receipt; differential rate.

Dr. Doctor; Drive (in street names).

D.R. Daughters of the (American) Revolution; District Registry; Dutch Reformed (Church).

dram. pers. *dramatis personae* (L.), the persons (characters) in the drama.

d.s. daylight saving; (Com.) days after sight.

D.S. (Music) *dal segno* (It.), repeat from the sign; Doctor of Science.

D. Sc. Doctor of Science.

D.S.C. Distinguished Service Cross (Brit.); Doctor of Surgical Chiropody.

D.S.M. Distinguished Service Medal (Brit.); Doctor of Sacred Music.

D.S.O. Distinguished Service Order (Brit.).

d.s.p. *decessit sine prole* (L.), died without issue.

D.S.T. Daylight Saving Time.

d.t. (usu. pl. **d.t.'s**) (Colloq.) delirium tremens.

D.T. or **D. Th.** Doctor of Theology.

Du. Duke; Dutch.

duo. duodecimo.

D.V. *Deo volente* (L.), God Willing; Douay Version (of the Bible).

D.V.M. Doctor of Veteri-

nary Medicine.

D.V.M.S. Doctor of Veterinary Medicine and Surgery.

d.v.p. *decessit vita patris* (L.), died in his, or her, father's lifetime.

dwt. pennyweight (from L. *denarius,* penny and E. *weight*).

d.w.t. deadweight tonnage.

DX (Radio) distance.

Dy (Chem.) dysprosium.

dyn. or **dynam.** dynamics.

dz. dozen; dozens.

E

e. eldest; entrance; (Baseball) errors.

E. Earl; earth; east; eastern; English; excellent.

ea. each.

e.a. educational age; enemy aircraft.

e. & o.e. errors and omissions excepted.

E.C. East Central (postal district of London); Engineering Corps; Established Church.

E.C.A. Economic Commission for Africa; Economic Cooperation Administration.

ECAFE Economic Commission for Africa and the Far East.

eccl. or **eccles.** ecclesiastical.

Eccl. or **Eccles.** Ecclesiastes.

Ecclus. Ecclesiasticus (Apocrypha).

ECG electrocardiogram.

econ. economic; economics; economy.

ECOSOC Economic and

Social Council (of UN).

ECT electroconvulsive therapy.

E.C.U. English Church Union.

Ecua. Ecuador.

ed. (pl. **eds.**) edited; edition; editor; educated.

E.D. election district; ex dividend.

Ed. B. Bachelor of Education.

Ed. D. Doctor of Education.

edit. edited; edition; editor.

Ed. M. Master of Education.

EDP electronic data processing.

eds. editors.

EDT. Eastern Daylight Time.

educ. educated; educational.

e.e. errors excepted.

E.E. early English; Electrical Engineer.

E.E. & M.P. Envoy Extraordinary and Minister Plenipotentiary.

EEC European Economic Community.

EEG electroencephalogram.

e.g. *exempli gratia* (L.), for example.

Eg. Egypt.

Egyptol, Egyptology.

E.I. East India; East Indies.

EKG (Med.) electrocardiogram.

elec. or **elect.** electric; electrical; electricity.

elem. element; elements; elementary.

Eliz. Elizabethan.

E. long. east longitude.

Em. (Physical Chem.) emanation.

EM electromagnetic; enlisted man.

E.M. Earl Marshall; Engineer of Mines.

embryol. embryology.

e.m.f. electromotive force.

e.m.h. educable mentally handicapped.

Emp. Emperor; Empire; Empress.

EMR electro magnetic response.

EMU electro magnetic unit.

ency. or **encyc.** encyclopedia.

E.N.E. east-northeast.

eng. engineer; engineering; engraver; engraving.

Eng. England; English.

enl. enlarged; enlisted.

Ens. Ensign.

E.O. errors and omissions; executive officer; ex officio.

e.o.m. end of the momth.

Ep. epistle.

Eph. Ephesians.

epil. epilogue.

Epiph. Epiphany.

Epis, or **Episc.** Episcopal; Episcopalian.

epit, epitaph; epitome.

EPNS electroplated nickel silver.

eq. equal; equation; equivalent.

EQ educational quotient.

equiv. equivalent.

Er (Chem.) erbium.

E.R. East Riding (Yorkshire); East River (New York); *Eduardus Rex* (L.), King Edward; *Elizabeth Regina* (L.), Queen Elizabeth.

ERA (Baseball) earned run average.

erron. erroneous; erroneously.

E.R.V. English Revised Version (of the Bible).

Es (Chem.) einsteinium.

Esd. Esdras (Apocrypha).

E.S.E. east-southeast.

esp. especially.

e.s.p. extrasensory perception.

est. established; estate; estimated; estuary.

E.S.T. Eastern Standard Time.

estab. established.

Esth. Esther; Esthonia.

Et (Chem.) ethyl.

E.T. Eastern Time; English Translation.

ETA estimated time of arrival.

et al. *et alibi* (L.), and elsewhere; *et alii* (L.), and others.

etc. *et cetera* (L.), and others; and so forth.

Eth. Ethiopia.

ethnog. ethnography.

ethnol. ethnological; ethnology.

et. seq. (pl. **et seqq.** or **et sqq.**) *et sequens* (L.), and the following.

etym. or **etymol.** etymological; etymology.

Eu (Chem.) europium.

E.U. (Thermodynamics) entropy unit.

Eur. Europe; European.

E.V. English Version (of the Bible).

Evang. Evangelical.

evg. evening.

ex. examination; examined; example; except; exception; exchange; ex-cursion; executed; executive; *exit* (L.), he or she goes out; *exeunt* (L.), they go out; export; extra; extract.

Ex. Exodus.

exam. examination; examined.

exc. excellent; except; exception; *excuit* (L.), he or she struck out, fashioned, or engraved (it), excursion.

Exc. Excellency.

exch. exchange; exchecquer.

excl. exclamation; exclamatory; excluding, exclusive.

ex d. or **ex div.** ex (without) dividend.

exec. executed; executive.

ex. gr. *exempli gratia* (L.), for example.

ex int. without interest.

ex lib. *ex libris* (L.), from the library (of).

Exod. Exodus.

ex off. *ex officio* (L.), by virtue of his office; officially.

exp. expense; expired; export; exporter; express.

exr. executor.

exrx. executrix.

ext. extended; extension; exterior; external; extinct; extra; extract; extreme.

Ez. Ezra.

Ezek. Ezekiel.

F

F. Fahrenheit; February; Fellow; folio; French; Friday.

FA Field Artillery.

FAA Federal Aviation Agency; Federal Alcohol Administration.

F.A.A.A.S. Fellow of the American Academy of Arts & Sciences; Fellow of the American Association for the Advancement of Science.

Fab. Soc. Fabian Society (Brit.).

fac. facsimile; factor; factory.

facet. facetious.

facsim. or facsm. facsimile.

Fahr. Fahrenheit.

F.A.I.A. Fellow of the American Institute of Architects.

fam. familiar; family.

F.A.M. or F.&A.M. Free and Accepted Masons.

FAO Food Agricultural Organization.

F.A.P.S. Fellow of the American Physical Society.

far. farad; farthing.

fath. fathom.

f.b. (Football) fullback.

F.B.A. Fellow of the British Academy.

F.B.I. Federal Bureau of Investigation.

F.B.S. Fellow of the Botanical Society (Brit.).

f.c. (Baseball) fielders choice; (Printing) follow copy.

F.C. Free Church (of Scotland).

F.C.A. Farm Credit Administration; Fellow of the Institute of Chartered Accountants (Brit.).

fcap. foolscap.

F.C.C. Federal Communications Commission; first-class certificate.

FCIC Federal Crop Insurance Corporation.

fco. *franco* (It.), franked, postage free.

fcp. foolscap.

F.C.P. Fellow of the College of Preceptors (Brit.).

F.C.S. Fellow of the Chemical Society (Brit.).

fd. fiord; fund.

F.D. *Fidei Defensor* (L.), Defender of the Faith; Fire Department; focal distance.

FDA Food and Drug Administration.

F.D.I.C. Federal Deposit Insurance Corporation.

Fe *ferrum* (L.), (Chem.) iron.

Feb. February.

fec. *fecit* (L.), he or she made (it).

Fed. Res. Bd. Federal Reserve Board.

Fed. Res. Bk. Federal Reserve Bank.

fem. female; feminine.

FEPC Fair Employment Practices Committee.

F.E.T. Federal Excise Tax.

feud. feudal, feudalism.

ff. folios; following (pages, chapters, verses, etc.); (Music) *fortissimo* (It.), very loud.

FFA Future Farmers of America.

fff. (Music) *fortississimo* (It.), very, very loud.

f.g. (Sports) field goal.

fgn. foreign.

F.G.S. Fellow of the Geological Society (Brit.).

F.G.S.A. Fellow of the Geological Society of America.

FHA Future Homemakers of America.

F.H.A. Federal Housing Administration.

F.I. Falkland Islands.

f.i.b. free into bunker.

F.I.C.A. Federal Insurance Contributions Act.

fict. fiction.

FIDO (Aeron.) Fog Investigation Dispersal Operation.

FIFO (Indust.) First-in, First-out.

fig. figurative; figuratively; figure.

fin. financial.

Fin. Finland, Finnish.

fir. firkin.

fl. florin; *floruit* (L.), flourished; fluid.

Fl. Flanders, Flemish.

Fla. Florida.

F.L.B. Federal Land Banks.

fld. field, fluid.

fl dr fluid dram, fluid drams.

Flem. Flemish.

F.L.N. Front de Libération Nationale (Algerian Nationalists).

flor. *floruit* (L.), flourished.

fl oz fluid ounces.

F.L.S. Fellow of the Linnean Society (Brit.).

fm. fathom; from.

Fm (Chem.) fermium.

F.M. Field Marshal; Foreign Mission; frequency modulation.

FMB Federal Maritime Board.

FMCS Federal Mediation and Conciliation Service.

fn. footnote.

fo. folio.

F.O. Field Officer; Foreign Office.

f.o.b. free on board.

F.O.E. Fraternal Order of Eagles.

fol. folio; following.

for. foreign; forester.

fort. fortification; fortified.

f.p. foot-pound; *forte-piano*, (It.), (Music) loud then soft; freezing point; fully paid.

F.P.C. Federal Power Commission.

FPHA Federal Public Housing Authority.

F.Ph.S. Fellow of the Philosophical Society (Brit.).

FPO field post office; fleet post office.

f.p.m. feet per minute.

f.p.s. feet per second.

Fr. *folio recto* (L.), on the front of the page.

fr. (pl. fr or frs.); fragment; franc; from.

Fr (Chem.) francium.

Fr. Father; France; Frau (G.); French; Friar; Friday.

F.R.A.M. Fellow of the Royal Academy of Music.

F.R.A.S. Fellow of the Royal Astronomical Society.

F.R.B. Federal Reserve Bank; Federal Reserve Board.

F.R.C.O. Fellow of the Royal College of Organists.

F.R.C.M. Fellow of the Royal College of Music.

F.R.C.P. Fellow of the Royal College of Physicians.

F.R.C.S. Fellow of the Royal College of Surgeons.

F.R.C.V.S. Fellow of the Royal College of Veterinary Surgeons.

freq. frequent; frequentative; frequently.

F.R.G.S. Fellow of the Royal Geographical Society.

F.R.H.S. Fellow of the Royal Horticultural Society.

Fri. Friday.

F.R.I.B.A. Fellow of the Royal Institute of British Architects.

F.R.I.C. Fellow of the Royal Institute of Chemistry.

Fris. Frisian.

Frl. Fraulein (G.).

F.R.Met.S. Fellow of the Royal Meteorological Society.

frs. francs.

FRS Federal Reserve System.

F.R.S.A. Fellow of the Royal Society of Arts.

F.R.S.L. Fellow of the Royal Society of Literature.

F.R.S.S. Fellow of the Royal Statistical Society.

frt. freight.

f.s. foot-second.

F.S.A. Fellow of the Society of Antiquaries (Brit.)

FSH follicle-stimulating hormone.

FSR Field Service Regulations.

F.S.S. Fellow of the Royal Statistical Society.

ft. feet; foot; fort.

FTC Federal Trade Commission.

fth. or **fthm.** fathom.

ft-lb. foot-pound.

fur. furlong; furlongs.

furl. furlough.

fut. future.

f.v. *folio verso* (L.), on the back of the page.

fwd. forward.

FWD four-wheel drive.

FYI (chiefly Mil.) for your information.

F.Z.S. Fellow of the Zoological Society (Brit.).

G

g. gauge; gender; genitive; (Sports) goalie; gram; guide; guinea.

G (Psychol.) general intelligence; (Slang) sum of one thousand dollars (Abbr. of Grand).

G. German; (specific) gravity; Gulf.

g.a. general average.

Ga (Chem.) gallium.

Ga. Gallic; Georgia.

G.A. General Assembly.

Gael. Gaelic.

gal. (pl. **gals.**) gallon.

Gal. Galatians.

galv. galvanism; galvanized.

G.A.R. Grand Army of the Republic.

GATT General Agreement on Tariffs and Trades.

Gaul. Gaulish.

G.A.W. guaranteed annual wage.

gaz. gazette; gazetteer.

G.B. Great Britain.

G.B.E. Knight, or Dame, Grand Cross of the Order of the British Empire.

GCA (Aeron.) ground controlled approach.

G.C.B. Knight Grand Cross of the Bath.

g.c.d. greatest common divisor.

g.c.f. greatest common factor.

G.C.I.E. Knight Grand Commander of the Indian Empire.

g.c.m. greatest common measure.

GCM (Mil.) General Court Martial.

G.C.M.G. Knight Grand Cross of St. Michael and St. George.

G.C.S.I. Knight Grand Commander of the Star of India.

G.C.T. (Navigation) Greenwich civil time.

G.C.V.O. Knight Grand Cross of the Royal Victorian Order.

Gd (Chem.) gadolinium.

g.d. granddaughter.

G.D. Grand Duchess; Grand Duchy; Grand Duke.

gdn. garden, guardian.

gds. goods.

Ge (Chem.) germanium.

geb. *geboren* (G.), born.

gen. gender; general; genitive; genus.

Gen. General; Genesis; Geneva.

geneal. geneaological; genealogy.

genit. genitive.

gent. gentleman.

geod. geodesy; geodetic.

geog. geographer; geographical; geography.

geol. geological; geologist; geology.

geom. geometrical; geometry.

ger. gerund.

Ger. German; Germany.

gest. *gestorben* (G.), died, deceased.

G.F.A. General Freight Agent.

G.F.T.U. General Federation of Trade Unions.

GG gamma globulin.

g.gr. great gross (144 dozen).

GHA (Navigation) Greenwich hour angle.

GHQ (Mil.) general headquarters.

gi. gill; gills.

G.I. galvanized iron; gastrointestinal; general issue; government issue; a member of the U.S. armed forces, especially an enlisted man.

Gib. Gibraltar.

gl. glass; gloss.

Gl (Chem.) glucinum.

G.L. grand lodge.

Glasg. Glasgow.

Glos. Gloucestershire.

gloss. glossary.

gm gram; grams.

G.M. general manager; grand marshal; grand master; guided missile.

G.M.&S. General Medical & Surgical.

GMT (Navigation) Greenwich mean time.

gn. (pl. **gns.**) guinea.

G.N. graduate nurse.

GNP gross national product.

G.O. general office; general order.

G.O.P. Grand Old Party (Republican Party).

Goth. Gothic.

gov. government.

Gov. Governor.

Gov.Gen. Governor General.

govt. government.

G.P. general practitioner; *Gloria Patri* (L.), Glory to the Father; Graduate in Pharmacy; Grand Prix.

gpd gallons per day.

gpm gallons per minute.

G.P.O. General Post Office; Government Printing Office.

G.Q. general quarters.

gr. grain; grand; great; gross.

Gr. Grecian; Greece; Greek.

G.R. *Georgius Rex* (L.), King George.

grad. (Math.) gradient; graduate; graduated.

gram. grammar; grammatical.

Gr. Br. or **Gr. Brit.** Great Britain.

gro. gross.

gr. wt. gross weight.

g.s. grandson.

G.S. general secretary; general staff.

G.S.A. General Services Administration; Girl Scouts of America.

G.S.R. galvanic skin response.

gt. gilt; great, *gutta* (L.), a drop (in prescriptions).

Gt. Br. or **Gt. Brit.** Great Britain.

g.t.c. good till canceled, or countermanded.

gtd. guaranteed.

gtt. (singular **gt.**) *guttae* (L.), drops (in prescriptions).

Guat. Guatamala.

Gui. Guiana.

Guin. Guinea.

gun. gunnery.

H

h. harbor; height; heller; heir; high; (Baseball) hits; hour; husband.

H (Phys.) enthalpy, intensity of magnetic field; (Chem.) hydrogen; (Slang) heroin.

H[1] (Chem.) protium.

H[2] (Chem.) deuterium.

H[3] (Chem.) tritium.

ha. hectare.

H.A. *hoc anno* (L.), this year; horse artillery.

Hab. Habakkuk.

hab. corp. *habeas corpus* (L.), you may have the body.

Hag. Haggai.

Hal (Chem.) halogen.

Hants. Hampshire.

hb. (Football) halfback.

Hb. (Biochem.) hemoglobin.

H.B.M. His, or Her, Britannic Majesty.

H.C. Holy Communion; House of Commons.

h.c.f. highest common factor.

h.c.l. (Colloq.) high cost of living.

H.C.M. His, or Her, Catholic Majesty.

hd. hand; head.

hdkf. handkerchief.

hdqrs. headquarters.

He (Chem.) helium.

H.E. high explosive; His Eminence; His Excellency.

Heb. Hebrew; Hebrews.

her. heraldic; heraldry.

herp. or **herpet.** herpetology.

H.E.W. Department of Health Education and Welfare.

hf. half.

Hf (Chem.) hafnium.

HF high frequency.

hg. hectogram.

Hg (Chem.) *hydrargyrum* (L.), mercury.

H.G. High German; His, or Her, Grace; Home Guards (Brit).

hgt. height.

H.H. His, or Her, Highness; High Holiness.

hhd. hogshead; hogsheads.

HHFA Housing and Home Finance Agency.

H.I. Hawaiian Islands.

H.I.H. His, or Her, Imperial Highness.

H.I.M. His, or Her, Imperial Majesty.

Hind. Hindustan; Hindustani.

hist. histology; historian; historical; history.

H.J. *hic jacet* (L.), here lies.

H.J.S. *hic jactet sepultus* (L.), here lies buried.

hl. hectoliter; hectoliters.

H.L. House of Lords.

hm. hectometer; hectometers.

H.M. His, or Her, Majesty.

H.M.G. His, or Her, Majesty's Government.

H.M.S. His, or Her, Majesty's Service; His, or Her, Majesty's Ship.

H.M.S.O. His, or Her, Majesty's Stationery Office.

ho. house.

Ho (Chem.) holmium.

H.O. head office; home of-

fice.

H.O.L.C. Home Owners' Loan Corporation.

Hon. Honorable; Honorary.

Hond. Honduras.

horol. horology.

hort. horticultural; horticulture.

Hos. Hosea.

hosp. hospital.

H.P. high pressure; hire purchase; horsepower; House of Parliament.

H.Q. headquarters.

hr. (pl. **hrs.**) hour.

Hr. Herr (G.).

H.R. Home Rule; House of Representatives.

H.R.E. Holy Roman Emperor; Holy Roman Empire.

H.R.H. His, or Her, Royal Highness.

H.R.I.P. *hic requiescit in pace* (L.), here rests in peace.

h.s. *hoc sensu* (L.), in this sense.

H.S. *hic sepultus* (L.), here is buried; *hic situs* (L.), here lies; High School, House Surgeon.

H.S.H. His, or Her, Serene Highness.

H.S.M. His, or Her, Serene Majesty.

ht. height.

HUAC House Un-American Activities Committee.

Hun. or **Hung.** Hungarian; Hungary.

hund. hundred.

Hunts. Huntingdonshire.

H.V. high voltage.

h.w.m. high water mark.

hyd. or **hydr.** hydraulics;

hydrostatics.

hyp. hypotenuse; hypothesis; hypothetical.

I

i incisor; interest; intransitive.

I (Chem.) iodine; Roman numeral for 1.

I. *Imperator* (L.), Emperor; *Imperatrix* (L.), Empress; independent; island; isle.

Ia. Iowa.

IAEA International Atomic Energy Agency.

I. & R. intelligence and reconnaissance.

I.A.S. Institute of Advanced Studies; Institute of the Aeronautical Sciences.

IAS indicated air speed.

IATA International Air Transport Association.

ib or **ibid.** *ibidem* (L.), in the same place.

i.b. invoice book.

IBT International Brotherhood of Teamsters.

I.C. *Iesus Christus* (L.), Jesus Christ.

I.C.A.A.A.A. Intercollegiate Association of Amateur Athletes of America.

ICBM intercontinental ballistic missile.

I.C.C. International Control Commission; Interstate Commerce Commission.

Ice. or **Icel.** Iceland; Icelandic.

ICFTU International Confederation of Free Trade Unions.

I.CH. TH.U.S. or **ICHTHUS** representing the initial letters of Gr. *Iesous Christos Theou Vios Soter,* Jesus Christ, Son of God, the Savior: the Gr. word *ichthus* meaning fish, and the fish having been used among the early Christians as a symbol for Christ.

ICJ International Court of Justice.

I.C.S. Indian Civil Service; International Correspondence School.

id. *idem* (L.), the same.

Id. Idaho.

I.D. identification; (Mil.) infantry division; Intelligence Department.

Ida. Idaho.

IDA International Development Association.

i.e. *id est* (L.), that is.

I.E. Indo-European; Industrial Engineer.

IFC International Finance Corporation; International Fisheries Commission (U.S. and Canada); International Freighting Corporation.

IFF (Mil.) identification, friend or foe.

I.F.S. Irish Free State.

I.G. Indo-Germanic; inspector general.

ign. ignition; *ignotus* (L.), unknown.

i.h.p. indicated horsepower.

I.H.S. *IESOUS* (Gr.), Jesus; also taken to represent *Iesus Hominum Salvator* (L.), Jesus, Savior of Men; *In Hoc*

Signo (vinces) (L.), in this sign the cross (shalt thou conquer); *In Hoc Salus* (L.), in this cross is salvation; and I (Christ) Have suffered.

Il (Chem.) Illinium.

ILA International Law Association; International Longshoremen's Association.

I.L.G.W.U. International Ladies' Garment Workers Union.

ill. illustrated; illustration.

Ill. Illinois.

illus. or **illust.** illustrated; illustration.

ILO International Labor Organization.

I.L.P. International Labour Party (Brit.).

ILS (Aeron.) instrument landing system.

I.M. Isle of Man.

IMF International Monetary Fund.

imit. imitative.

imp. imperative; imperfect; imperial; impersonal; import; important; imported; importer, *imprimatur* (L.), let it be printed, imprint; improve.

Imp. *Imperator* (L.), Emperor; *Imperatri* (L.), Empress.

imperf. imperfect.

impers. impersonal.

impv. imperative.

Impx. *Imperatrix* (L.), Empress.

in. (pl. **in.** or **ins.**) inch.

In (Chem.) indium.

inc. include; income; incorporated; increase; incumbent.

incl. inclosure; including; inclusive.

incog. incognito.

incor. incorporated.

ind. independent; index; indicative; indirect; industry.

Ind. India; Indian; Indiana; Indies.

I.N.D. *in nomine Dei* (L.), in the name of God.

indecl. indeclinable.

indef. indefinite.

indic. indicating; indicative.

indiv. individual.

inf. infantry; inferior, infinitive; information; *infra* (L.), below, after.

in f. *in fine* (L.), at the end of a title, law, or paragraph quoted.

infin. infinitive.

infl. influenced.

infra dig. *infra dignitatem* (L.), (Colloq.) beneath one's dignity.

in. Hg. (Chem.) inch of mercury.

in loc. cit. *in loco citato* (L.), in the place cited.

in mem. *in memoriam* (L.), in memory (of).

in pr. *in principio* (L.), in or at the beginning.

I.N.R.I. *Iesus Nazarenus Rex Iudaeorum* (L.), Jesus of Nazareth, King of the Jews.

ins. inches; inscribed; inspector; insulated; insurance.

I.N.S. International News Service.

insp. inspector.

Insp. Gen. Inspector General.

inst. instant (the present

month); instantaneous; institute; institution; instrument.

instr. instructor; instrumental.

int. interest; interior; interjection; internal; international; interpreter; intransitive.

intens. intensive.

inter. intermediate; interrogation; interrogative.

interj. interjection.

internat. international.

interrog. interrogation; interrogative; interrogatively.

intr. intransitive; introduce; introductory.

in trans. *in transitu* (L.), in transit, on the way.

Int. Rev. Internal Revenue.

intro. or **introd.** introduction; introductory.

inv. *invenit* (L.), he, or she, designed (it); inventor; inventory; invoice.

invt. inventory.

Io (Chem.) ionium.

Io. Iowa.

I.O.F. Independent Order of Foresters.

Ion. Ionic.

I.O.O.F. Independent Order of Odd Fellows.

I.O.R.M. Improved Order of Red Men.

I O U I owe you (an acknowledgement of indebtedness).

IPA International Phonetic Alphabet; International Phonetic Association; International Press Association.

IPBM interplanetary ballistic missile.

i.q. *indem quod* (L.), the same as.

I.Q. (Psychol.) intelligence quotient.

I.Q.E.D. *id quod erat demonstrandum* (L.), that which was to be demonstrated.

Ir (Chem.) iridium.

Ir. Ireland; Irish.

I.R. Inland Revenue; Intelligence Ratio; Internal Revenue.

I.R.A. Irish Republican Army.

IRBM intermediate range ballistic missile.

IRC International Red Cross.

Ire. Ireland.

I.R.O. Internal Revenue Office; Internal Revenue Officer; International Refugee Organization.

irreg. irregular; irregularly.

IRS Internal Revenue Service.

Is. Isaiah; Island.

I.S.C. interstate commerce.

ISG imperial standard gallon (Brit.).

isl. (pl. **isls.**) island; isle.

I.S.O. Imperial Service Order (Brit.).

iss. issue.

isth. isthmus.

It. Italian; Italy.

ITA Initial Teaching Alphabet.

ital. italic.

Ital. Italian.

ITO International Trade Organization.

ITU International Telecommunication Union.

i.v. increased value; initial velocity; intravenous; invoice value.

i.w. isotopic weight.
I.W. Isle of Wight.
I.W.W. Industrial Workers of the World.

J

j (Physics) joule.
J. (pl. **J.J.**) Journal; Judge; Justice.
j.a. joint account.
J.A. Joint Agent; Judge Advocate.
J.A.G. Judge Advocate General.
Jam. Jamaica.
J.A.M.A. Journal of the American Medical Association.
Jan. January.
Jap. Japan; Japanese.
Jas. James.
Jav. Javanese.
J.C. Jesus Christ; Julius Caesar; *juris consultus* (L.), jurisconsult.
J.C.C. Junior Chamber of Commerce.
J.C.B. *Juris Canonici Baccalaureus* (L). Bachelor of Canon Law; *Juris Civilis Baccalaureus* (L.), Bachelor of Civil Law.
J.C.D. *Juris Canonici Doctor* (L.), Doctor of Canon Law; *Juris Civilis Doctor* (L.), Doctor of Civil Law.
J.C.L. *Juris Canonici Licentiatus* (L.), Licentiate in Canon Law.
J.C.S. Joint Chief of Staff.
Jct. Junction.
J.D. *Juris Doctor* (L.), Doctor of Jurisprudence, Doctor of Law; *Jurum Doctor* (L.), Doctor of Laws; juvenile delin-

quency; juvenile delinquent.
Je. June.
Jer. Jeremiah; Jersey; Jerusalem.
j.g. junior grade.
JJ. judges; justices.
Jl. July.
Jno. John.
jnt. joint.
Josh. Joshua.
jour. or **journ.** journal; journalism.
J.P. Justice of the Peace.
Jr. junior.
jt. joint.
Jud. Judges; Judith (Apocrypha).
J.U.D. *Juris Utriusque Doctor* (L.), Doctor of Both Laws (canon and civil).
Judg. Judges.
Judge Adv. Judge Advocate.
Jun. June; Junior.
Junc. Junction.
JV Junior Varsity.
J.W.V. Jewish War Veterans.

K

k. (Elect.) capacity; karat; kilogram; knot.
K (Chem.) *kalium* (L.), potassium; (Chess) king.
K. Kaiser; Kelvin; King; Kings; Knight; krone; kronen.
kal. kalands, calends.
Kan. or **Kans.** Kansas.
K.B. King's Bench; Knight Bachelor (Brit.).
K.B.E. Knight Commander of the Order of the British Empire.
kc kilocycle.

K.C. King's Counsel; Knight Commander; Knight of Columbus.

K.C.B. Knight Commander of the Bath (Brit.).

K.C.I.E. Knight Commander of the Order of the Indian Empire (Brit.).

K.C.M.G. Knight Commander of St. Michael and St. George (Brit.).

K.C.S.I. Knight Commander of the Star of India (Brit.).

K.C.V.O. Knight Commander of the Royal Victorian Order (Brit.).

KD (Com.) knocked down.

Ken. Kentucky.

kg. keg; kilogram.

K.G. Knight of the Garter (Brit.).

Ki. Kings.

KIA (Mil.) killed in action.

KIAS (Aeron.) knot indicated airspeed.

kil. kilogram; kilometer.

kilom. kilometer; kilometers.

K.J.V. King James' Version (of the Bible).

K.K.K. Ku Klux Klan.

kl. kiloliter.

km. kilometer; kingdom.

Knt. Knight.

K.O. (Pugilism) knock-out.

K. of C. Knights of Columbus.

K. of P. Knights of Pythias.

K.P. kitchen police; Knight of the Order of St. Patrick (Brit.); Knight of Pythias.

kr. kreutzer; krona; kronor (Sweden and Faroe Isles); krona, kronur (Iceland); krona, kroner (Denmark and Norway).

Kr (Chem.) krypton.

kt. karat; carat; knot.

Kt (Chess) Knight.

Kt. Knight.

K.T. Knight of the Order of the Thistle (Brit.); Knights Templars.

K.V. *Kochel-Verzeichnis* (G.), (Music) the chronological listing of Mozart's works used with numbers to identify them.

kw. kilowatt.

Ky. Kentucky.

L

l. (pl. **ll.**) leaf; league; left; length; *liber* (L.), book; *libra* or *librae* (L.), pound, or pounds (British money); line; link; lira; liter; long; lost.

L elevated railroad, or railway; Roman numeral for 50; longitude.

L. lady; lake; Late; Latin; latitude; law; liberal; London; lord; (Theater) stage left.

La (Chem.) lanthanum.

La. Louisiana.

L.A. Latin America; law agent; library association; local agent; Los Angeles.

lab. laboratory.

Lab. Labrador.

lam. laminated.

Lam. Lamentations.

Lancs. Lancashire.

lang. language.

Lap. Lapland.

lat. latitude.

Lat. Latin; Latvia.

lb. (pl. **lbs.**) *libra* (L.),

(weight) pound.

L.B. *Litterarum Baccalaureus,* (L.), Bachelor of Letters or Literature; local board.

l.c. letter of credit; *loco citato* (L.), in the place cited; (Printing) lowercase.

L.C. Library of Congress; Lord Chamberlain; Lord Chancellor.

L.C.C. London County Council.

l.c.d. lowest common denominator.

LCI (Mil) landing craft infantry.

L.C.J. Lord Chief Justice.

l.c.m. least common multiple.

LCT (Mil.) landing craft tanks.

ld. land; limited.

Ld. Lord.

L.D. Low Dutch.

Ldp. Ladyship; Lordship.

L.D.S. Latter-Day Saints; Licentiate of Dental Surgery.

l.e. (Football) left end.

lea. league.

leath. leather.

lect. lecture; lecturer.

leg. legal; (Music) *legato* (It.), connected, smooth; legend; legislative; legislature.

legg. (Music) *leggiero* (It.) light and rapid.

Lev. Leviticus.

lex. lexical; lexicon.

lexicog. lexicographer; lexicographical; lexicography.

lf low frequency.

lf. (Baseball) left fielder.

l.g. (Football) left guard.

LG. or **L.G.** Low German.

L.G. life guard.

LGr. or **L.Gr.** Late Greek.

l.h. left hand.

L.H. lighthouse.

L.H.A. Lord High Admiral.

l.h.b. (Football) left halfback.

L.H.C. Lord High Chancellor.

L.H.D. *Litterarum Humaniorum Doctor* (L.), Doctor of Humane Letters; Doctor of the Humanities.

L.H.T. Lord High Treasurer.

Li (Chem.) lithium.

L.I. Light Infantry (Brit.); Long Island.

lib. *liber* (L.), book; librarian; library.

Lib. Liberal.

Lieut. Lieutenant.

LIFO (Ind.) Last-In, First-Out.

lin. lineal; linear; liniment.

Linc. or **Lincs.** Lincolnshire.

ling. linguistics.

l.i.p. life insurance policy.

liq. liquid; liquor.

lit. liter; literal; literally; literature.

Lit. B. *Lit(t)erarum Baccalaureus* (L.), Bachelor of Letters; Bachelor of Literature.

Lit. D. *Lit(t)erarum Doctor* (L.), Doctor of Letters; Doctor of Literature.

liter. literature; literary.

Lith. Lithuania, Lithuanian.

lithog. lithograph; lithography.

L.J. Lord Justice.

ll. lines.

l.l. *loco laudato* (L.) in the place cited; loose-leaf.

L.L. Late Latin; Lord Lieutenant; Low Latin.

LL.B. *Legum Baccalaureus* (L.), Bachelor of Laws.

LL.D. *Legum Doctor* (L.), Doctor of Laws.

LL.L. *Legum Licentiatus* (L.), Licentiate of Laws.

LL.M. *Legum Magister* (L.), Master of Laws.

L.M. Licentiate in Medicine; Licentiate in Midwifery; Lord Mayor.

L.M.T. local mean time.

loc. cit. *loco citato* (L.), in the place cited.

log. logarithm.

lon. longitude.

Lond. London.

long. longitude.

L.O.O.M. Loyal Order of Moose.

loq. *loquitur* (L.), he, or she, speaks.

L.P. Lord Provost; low pressure.

L.P.S. Lord Privy Seal.

L.R. Lloyd's Register.

LRBM long-range ballistic missile.

l.s. left side; lord speaker.

L.S. Linnean Society (Brit.); *locus sigilli* (L.), the place of the seal.

L.S.A. Licentiate of the Society of Apothecaries (Brit.).

l.s.c. *loco supra citato* (L.), in the place cited above or before.

l.s.d. *librae solidi denarii* (L.), pounds. shillings, pence.

LSD lysergic acid diethylamide; (U.S. Navy) landing ship deck.

L.S.E. London School of Economics.

L.S.T. Local Standard Time.

l.t. (Football) left tackle; long ton.

Lt. Lieutenant.

Lt. Col. Lieutenant Colonel.

ltd. limited.

Lt. Gen. Lieutenant General.

Lt. Gov. Lieutenant Governor.

L. Th. Licentiate in Theology.

Lt. Inf. Light Infantry.

Lu (Chem.) lutetium.

Luth. Lutheran.

lv. leaf; leaves; livre; livres.

Lw (Chem.) lawrencium.

l.w.m. low-water mark.

lwop leave without pay.

lwp leave with pay.

LXX Septuagint.

M

m. male; married; masculine; medium; meter; mile; minim; minute; molar; month; moon; morning; mouth.

M Roman numeral for 1000.

M. (pl. **MM.**) Majesty; Manitoba; mark (German money); Marquis; Marquess; Master; Medieval; Member; *meridies* (L.), noon; Middle; Monday; Monsieur (Fr.); mountain.

Ma (Chem.) masurium.

MA (Psychol.) mental age.

M.A. Master of Arts; Military Academy.

Mac. Maccabees (Apocrypha).

M. Ac. Master of Accounting.

Maced. Macedonia.

mach. machinery; machinist.

Mad. Madam; Madrid.

Madag. Madagascar.

M.A.E. Master of Aeronautical Engineering; Master of Art Education.

M.A. Ed. Master of Arts in Education.

mag. magazine; magnetism; magnitude.

M. Agr. Master of Agriculture.

Maj. Major.

Maj. Gen. Major General.

Mal. Malachi; Malayan.

M.A.L.D. Master of Arts in Law and Diplomacy.

man. manual.

Man. Manila; Manitoba.

Manit. Manitoba.

manuf. manufacturer; manufacturing.

mar. maritime; married.

Mar. March.

M.A.R. Master of Arts in Religion.

M. Arch. Master of Architecture.

March. Marchioness.

M. Arch. E. Master of Architectural Engineering.

marg. margin.

Marq. Marquis; Marquess.

mas. or **masc.** masculine.

Mass. Massachusetts.

mat. matins; matured.

M.A.T. Masters of Arts in Teaching.

math. mathematical; mathematician, mathematics.

MATS Military Air Transport Service.

Matt. Matthew.

max. maximum.

M.B. *Medicinae Baccalaureus* (L.), Bachelor of Medicine.

M.B.A. Master of Business Administration.

M.B.E. Member of the Order of the British Empire.

M.B.S. or **M.B. Sc.** Master of Business Science.

M.C. Marine Corps; Master Commandant; Master of Ceremonies; Medical Corps; Member of Congress; Military Cross (Brit.).

M.C.E. Master of Civil Engineering.

M. Ch. *Magister Chirurgiae* (L.), Master of Surgery.

M. Ch. E. Master of Chemical Engineering.

mcht. merchant.

M.C.J. Master of Comparative Jurisprudence.

M.C.L. Master of Civil Law.

M.C.P. Master of City Planning.

M.C.R. Master of Comparative Religion.

Md (Chem.) mendelevium

Md. Maryland.

m.d. *mano destra* (It.), (Music) right hand; memorandum of deposit; months after date.

M.D. *Medicinae Doctor* (L.), Doctor of Medicine; Middle Dutch.

Mdlle. Mademoiselle (Fr.).

Mdme. Madame (Fr.).

M.D.S. Master in Dental Surgery.

mdse. merchandise.

Me (Chem.) methyl.

Me. Maine.

M.E. Managing Editor; Master of Education; Master of Engineering; Mechanical Engineer; Methodist Episcopal; Middle English; Mining Engineer; Most Excellent.

M.E.A. Master of Engineering Administration.

meas. measure.

mech. mechanical; mechanics.

med. medical; medicine; medieval; medium.

Medit. Mediterranean.

Med. L. Medieval Latin.

Melan. Melanesia.

mem. member; memoir; memorandum; memorial.

memo. memorandum.

mensur. mensuration.

M.E.P. Master of Engineering Physics.

M.E.P.A. Master of Engineering and Public Administration.

mer. meridian; meridional.

merc. mercantile; mercurial; mercury.

Mesop. Mesopotamia.

Messrs. Messieurs (Fr.).

met. metaphor; metaphysics; Metropolitan.

metal. Metallurgical; metallurgy.

metaph. metaphysical; metaphysics.

Met. E. metallurgical engineer.

meteor. or **meteorol.** meteorological; meteorology.

Meth. Methodist.

Mex. Mexican; Mexico.

mf. *mezzo forte* (It.), (Music) moderately loud; microfarad.

M.F. Master of Forestry; Middle French.

M. Fr. Middle French.

M.F.A. Master of Fine Arts.

mfg. manufacturing.

M.F.H. Master of Fox Hounds.

mfr. (pl. **mfrs.**) manufacturer.

mg. milligram; milligrams.

Mg (Chem.) magnesium.

mgr. manager.

Mgr. *Monseigneur* (Fr.); (Eccles.) Monsignor.

MGr. or **M. Gr.** Middle Greek.

M.H. Medal of Honor.

M.H.E. Master of Home Economics.

M.H.A. Master in Hospital Administration.

MHG magnetohydrodynamics generation.

MHG or **M.H.G.** Middle High German.

M.H.L. Master of Hebrew Literature.

M.H.R. Member of the House of Representatives.

mi. mile; miles; mill; mills.

M.I. military intelligence; mounted infantry.

M.I.A. Master of International Affairs.

Mic. Micah.

M.I.C.E. Member of the Institution of Civil Engineers (Brit.).

Mich. Michaelmas; Michigan.

micros. microscopy.

mid. middle.

Mid. Midshipman.

M.I.D. Master of Industrial Design; Military Intelligence Division.

M.I.E. Master of Industrial Engineering; Master of Irrigation Engineering.

M.I.E.E. Member of the Institution of Electrical Engineers (Brit.).

mil. military.

M.I. Mar.E. Member of the Institution of Marine Engineers (Brit.).

M.I. Mech.E. Member of the Institution of Mechanical Engineers (Brit.).

min. mineralogical; mineralogy; minim; minimum; mining; minister; minor; minute.

M.I.N.A. Member of the Institution of Naval Architects (Brit.).

mineral. mineralogical; mineralogy.

Minn. Minnesota.

Min. Plen. Minister Plenipotentiary.

m.i.p. marine insurance policy.

M.I.S. Master of International Service.

misc. miscellaneous; miscellany.

Miss. Mississippi.

M.I.T. Massachusetts Institute of Technology.

M.J. Master of Journalism.

mks meter-kilogram-second (scale of units).

mkt. market.

ml. mail; milliliter.

M.L. *Magister Legum* (L.), Master of Laws; Middle Latin; muzzle-loading.

M.L.A. Master of Landscape Architecture; Modern Language Association.

MLB Maritime Labor Board.

MLF multilateral nuclear force.

M.L.G. Middle Low German.

Mlle. (pl. **Mlles.**) Mademoiselle (Fr.).

M.L.S. Master of Library Science.

MLW mean low water.

mm. millimeter; *millia* (L.), thousands.

m.m. *mutatis mutandis* (L.), the necessary change being made.

MM Messieurs (Fr.).

M.M. (Music) Maelzel's Metronome; Master Mason; Master Mechanic; Master of Music; Merchant Marine.

Mme. (pl. **Mmes.**) Madame (Fr.)

M.M.E. Master of Mechanical Engineering; Master of Mining Engineering; Master of Music Education.

MMRBM mobile midrange ballistic missile.

M. Mus. Master of Music.

Mn (chem.) manganese.

M.N.A. Master of Nursing Administration.

M.N.A.S. Member of the National Academy of Science.

M.N.E. Master of Nuclear Engineering.

mng. managing.

Mngr. Monsignor.

M.N.S. Master of Nutritional Science.

mo. (pl. **mos.**) month.

Mo (Chem.) molybdenum.

Mo. Missouri; Monday.

M.O. mail-order; manually operated; Medical Officer; *modus operandi* (L.), method of working; money order.

mod. moderate; *moderato* (It.), (Music) in moderate time; modern.

Mod. Fr. Modern French.

Mod. Gr. Modern Greek.

Mod. Heb. Modern Hebrew.

M.O.H. Medical Officer of Health.

Moham. Mohammedan.

mol. wt. molecular weight.

mon. monastery; monetary.

Mon. Monday; Monmouthshire; Monsignor.

Mons. Monsieur.

Mont. Montana.

Mor. Morocco.

morph. morphological; morphology.

mp. *mezzo piano* (It.) (Music), medium soft.

m.p. melting point.

M.P. Member of Parliament (Brit.); Minister Plenipotentiary; military police; mounted police.

M.P.A. Master of Professional Accounting; Master of Public Administration; Master of Public Affairs.

M.P.E. Master of Physical Education.

m.p.g. miles per gallon.

M.Ph. Master of Philosophy.

m.p.h. miles per hour.

M.P.H. Master of Public Health.

M.P.C. Member of Parliament, Canada.

M.P.P. Member of the Provincial Parliament.

Mr. (pl. **Messrs.**) Mister.

M.R. Master of the Rolls; motivation research.

M.R.A.S. Member of the Royal Academy of Science; Member of the Royal Asiatic Society.

MRBM medium-range ballastic missile.

M.R.C. Medical Reserve Corps.

M.R.C.P. Member of the Royal College of Physicians.

M.R.C.S. Member of the Royal College of Surgeons.

M.R.E. Master of Religious Education.

M.R.P. Master of Regional Planning.

Mrs. (pl. **Mmes.**) Mistress, Missis, a title prefixed to the name of a married woman.

ms. *mano sinistra* (It.), (Music).

Ms. or **ms.** (pl. **Mss.** or **mss.**) manuscript.

M.S. Master of Science; Master of Surgery; *memoriae sacrum* (L.), sacred to the memory (of); metric system; motor ship; multiple sclerosis.

M.S.A. Master of Science in Agriculture.

M.S.A.E. Master of Science in Aeronautical Engineering.

M.S.A.M. Master of Science in Applied Mathematics.

M.S. Arch. Master of Science in Architecture.

M.S.B.A. Master of Science in Business Administration.

M.S.B.C. Master of Science in Building Construction.

M.S. Bus. Master of Science in Business.

M.Sc. Master of Science.

M.Sc.D. Doctor of Medical Science.

M.S.C.E. Master of Science in Civil Engineering.

M.S.Ch.E. Master of Science in Chemical Engineering.

M.S.C.P. Master of Science in Community Planning.

MSD most significant digit.

M.S.D. Master of Science in Dentistry.

M.S.E. Master of Science in Education; Master of Science in Engineering.

M.S.Ed. Master of Science in Education.

M.S.E.E. Master of Science in Electrical Engineering.

M.S.E.M. Master of Science in Engineering Mechanics.

M.S. En. Master of Science in Entomology.

M.S.F. Master of Science in Forestry.

MSG monosodium glutamate.

M.S.G.M. Master of Science in Government Management.

Msgr. Monsignor.

MSH (Biochem.) melanocyte-stimulating hormone; Mohs scale of hardness.

M.S.H. Master of Stag-

hounds.

M.S.H.A. Master of Science in Hospital Administration.

M.S.H.E. Master of Science in Home Economics.

M.S. Hort. Master of Science in Horticulture.

M.S. Hyg. Master of Science in Hygiene.

M.S.I.E. Master of Science in Industrial Engineering.

M.S.J. Master of Science in Journalism.

m.s.l. mean sea level.

M.S.L. Master of Science in Linguistics.

M.S.M. Master of Sacred Music.

M.S.M.E. Master of Science in Mechanical Engineering.

M.S.N. Master of Science in Nursing.

M.S.P.E. Master of Science in Physical Education.

M.S.P.H. Master of Science in Public Health.

M.S. Phar. Master of Science in Pharmacy.

M.S.S. Master of Social Service.

M.S. Sc. Master of Social Science.

M.S.T. Master of Science in Teaching; Mountain Standard Time.

Ms-Th (Chem.) mesothorium.

MSTS (U.S. Navy) Military Sea Transport Service.

M.S.W. Master of Social Welfare; Master of Social Work.

mt. (pl. **mts.**) mount; mountain.

MT mechanical translation; megation; megatons.

M.T. metric ton.

mtg. meeting; mortgage.

mtgd. mortgaged.

mtge. mortgage.

M.Th. Master of Theology.

M T I moving target indicator.

Mt. Rev. Most Reverend.

mun. municipal.

M.U.P. Master of Urban Planning.

mus. museum; music; musical; musician.

Mus. B. *Musicae Baccalaureus,* (L.), Bachelor of Music.

Mus. D. *Musicae Doctor* (L.), Doctor of Music.

Mus. M. *Musicae Magister* (L.), Master of Music.

m.v. market value; mean variations; *mezza voce* (It.), (Music) with half the power of the voice, softly.

Mv (Elect.) megavolt; (Chem.) mendelevium.

MVA megavolt ampere.

MVD. *Ministerstvo Vnutrennikh Del* (R.), Ministry of Internal Affairs. Secret Police of U.S.S.R. since 1943, formerly NKVD.

M.V. Ed. Master of Vocational Education.

M.V.O. Member of the Royal Victorian Order.

Mw (Elect.) megawatt; megawatts.

M.W. Most Worshipful; Most Worthy.

M.W.A. Modern Wood-men of America.

Mx. Middlesex.

myl. myrialiter; myrialiters.

mym. myriameter; myriameters.

myth. or **mythol.** mythological; mythology.

N

n neutron.

n. *natus* (L.) born; nephew; net; neuter; new; night; nominative; note; noun; number.

N (Chem.) nitrogen; (Math) an indefinite constant whole number; (Chess) knight.

N. Nationalist; New; Noon; (Chem.) normal (strength solution); Norse; North; Northern; November.

Na *natrium* (L.), (Chem.) sodium.

N.A. National Academician; National Academy; National Army; Nautical Almanac; North America; North American; nursing auxiliary.

NAA National Aeronautic Association; National Automobile Association.

NAACP National Association for the Advancement of Colored People.

NAB National Association of Broadcasters; Naval Air Base.

N.A.D. National Academy of Design.

Nah. Nahum.

NAM National Association of Manufacturers.

N.Amer. North America;

North American.

N.A.S. National Academy of Sciences.

NASA National Aeronautics and Space Administration.

nat. national; native; natural; naturalist.

nat. phil. natural philosophy.

natl. national.

NATO North Atlantic Treaty Organization.

nat. sc. natural science.

naut. nautical.

nav. naval; navigation.

navig. navigation.

Nb (Chem.) niobium.

NB Naval Base; (Sports) no ball; *nota bene* (L.), note well, take notice.

N.B. New Brunswick.

NBA National Basketball Association; National Boxing Association.

N.B.S. National Bureau of Statistics.

NC (Mil.) Nurse Corps.

N.C. North Carolina.

N.C.A.A. National Collegiate Athletic Association.

N.C.C.J. National Conference of Christians and Jews.

N.C.C.M. National Council of Catholic Men.

N.C.C.W. National Council of Catholic Women.

N.C.O. noncommissioned officer.

n.c.v. no commercial value.

n.d. no date.

Nd (Chem.) Neodymium.

N.D. or **N. Dak.** North Dakota.

NDAC National Defense Advisory Commission.

Ne (Chem.) neon.

N.E. New England; northeast; northeastern.

N.E.A. National Editorial Association; National Education Association.

Neb. or **Nebr.** Nebraska.

N.E.B. New English Bible.

N.E.D. New English Dictionary (Oxford English Dictionary).

neg. negative; negatively.

Neh. Nehemiah.

nem. con. *nemine contradicente* (L.), no one contradicting, unanimously.

nem. diss. *nemine dissentiente* (L.), no one dissenting, unanimously.

N. Eng. New England; Northern England.

n.e.s. not elsewhere specified.

Neth. Netherlands.

neut. neuter.

Nev. Nevada.

Newf. Newfoundland.

n.f. no funds.

N.F. National Formulary; Newfoundland; Norman French.

Nfld. Newfoundland.

n.g. (Colloq.) no good.

NG (Chem.) nitroglycerin.

N.G. National Guard; New Guinea.

N. Gr. New Greek.

N.H. New Hampshire.

NHG. or **N.H.G.** New High German.

N.H.S. National Health Service (Brit.)

Ni (Chem.) nickel.

N.I. Northern Ireland.

Nicar. Nicaragua.

ni. pri. *nisi prius* (L.), unless before.

N.I.R.A. National Industrial Recovery Act.

N.J. New Jersey.

NKVD *Narodni Kommis-ariat Vnutrennikh Del*, People's Commissariat for Internal Affairs, the secret police of the Soviet Union (1935-1942).

n.l. (Printing) new line; *non licet* (L.), it is not permitted; *non liquet* (L.), it is not clear or evident.

N.L. (Baseball) National League; Neo-Latin; New Latin.

N. Lat. north latitude.

N.L.F. National Liberation Front.

N.L.R.B. National Labor Relations Board.

nm nautical mile.

N.M. or N. Mex. New Mexico.

N.M.U. National Maritime Union.

N.N.E. north-northeast.

NNP net national product.

N.N.W. north-northwest.

no. north; northern; *numero* (L.), number (pl. **nos.**).

No (Chem.) nobelium.

nol. pros. *nolle prosequi* (L.), to be unwilling to prosecute.

nom. nominative.

noncom. noncommissioned officer.

non obst. *non obstante* (L.), notwithstanding.

non pros. *non prosequitur* (L.), he does not prosecute.

non seq. *non sequitur* (L.), it does not follow.

n.o.p. not otherwise provided for.

nor. north; northern.

Nor. Norman; North; Norway; Norwegian.

Norf. Norfolk.

Norm. Norman.

Norw. Norway, Norwegian.

nos. numbers.

n.o.s. not otherwise specified.

Notts. Nottinghamshire.

Nov. November.

Np (Physics) neper; (Chem.) neptunium.

N.P. new paragraph; *nisi prius* (L.), no protest; Notary Public.

n.p. or d. no place or date (of publication).

n.p.t. normal pressure and temperature.

nr. near; number.

N.R. North Riding (Yorkshire); North River (New York).

N.R.A. National Recovery Act; National Recovery Administration.

N.R.C. National Research Council.

N.S. not specified; not sufficient funds.

N.S. new series; new style (in reckoning time); *Notre Seigneur* (F.), Our Lord; Nova Scotia.

NSA National Shipping Authority; National Standards Association; National Students Association.

NSC National Security Council.

n.s.f. not sufficient funds.

NSF National Science Foundation.

N.S.P.C.A. National Society for the Prevention of Cruelty to Animals.

N.S.P.C.C. National Society for the Prevention of Cruelty to Children.

N.S.W. New South Wales.

Nt (Chem.) niton.

N.T. National Trust (Brit.); New Testament; Northern Territory (Australia).

nt. wt. net weight.

n.u. name unknown.

Num. Numbers.

numis. numismatic; numismatics.

N.U.R. National Union of Railway Men.

N.U.T. National Union of Teachers.

N.W. North Wales; northwest; northwestern.

N.W.T. Northwest Territories (Canada).

N.Y. New York.

N.Y.C. New York City.

NYP not yet published.

N.Z. New Zealand.

O

o. *octarius* (L.), pint (in prescriptions); old; only; (Baseball) out, outs.

O (Elect.) ohm; (Chem.) oxygen.

O. ocean; octavo; October; Ohio; old; Ontario; order; Oregon.

o.a. on account.

OAS Organization of American States.

ob. *obiit.* (L.), he, or she, died.

Obad. Obadiah.

obdt. obedient.

O.B.E. Officer of the Order of the British Empire.

obj. object; objection; objective.

obl. oblique; oblong.

obs. observation; observatory; obsolete; obstetrics.

o.b.s.p. *obiit sine prole* (L.), he, or she, died without issue.

obstet. obstetrical; obstetrics.

oc. ocean.

occas. occasional; occasionally.

OCDM Office of Civil and Defense Mobilization.

OCS (Mil.) officer candidate school.

oct. or **8vo.** octavo.

Oct. October.

o.d. on demand; outside diameter; over-drive.

O.D. Officer of the Day; Old Dutch; olive drab (of military uniform); overdraft; Doctor of Optometry.

ODT Organization of Defense Transportation.

o.e. omissions expected.

OE. or **O.E.** Old English.

OECD Organization for Economic Cooperation and Development.

O.E.D. Oxford English Dictionary.

O.E.E.C. Organization for European Economic Community.

OEO Office of Economic Opportunity.

O.E.S. Order of the Eastern Star.

OF. or **O.F.** Old French.

off. office; officer; official.

O. Flem. Old Flemish.

O.F.M. *Ordo Fratrum Minorum* (L.), Order Friars Minor (Franciscan).

O.F.S. Orange Free State.

O.G. Officer of the Guard;

(Philat.) original gum.

O.G.O. orbiting geophysical observatory.

OHG. or O.H.G. Old High German.

O.H.M.S. On His, or Her, Majesty's Service.

O.K. (Colloq.) all right; correct.

Okla. Oklahoma.

OL. or O.L. Old Latin.

OLG. or O.L.G. Old Low German.

O.M. Order of Merit (Brit.).

ON. or O.N. Old Norse.

ONI Office of Naval Intelligence.

Ont. Ontario.

op. opera; operation; opposite; *opus* (L.), work

o.p. out of print.

O.P. *Ordo Praedicatorum* (L.), Order of Preachers (Dominican).

OPA Office of Price Administration, (1941-46).

op cit. *opere citato* (L.), in the work cited.

ophthalm. ophthalmology.

opp. opposed; opposite.

opt. optative; optical; optician; optics; optional.

o.r. owner's risk.

O.R.C. Officer's Reserve Corps.

ord. ordained; order; ordinal; ordinance; ordinary; ordnance.

ordn. ordnance.

Oreg. Oregon.

org. organic; organized.

orig. original; originally.

ornith. ornithological; ornithology.

o.s. out of stock.

Os (Chem.) osmium.

O.S. *oculus sinister*, (L.); the left eye (in prescriptions); Old Saxon; Old Series; Old Style (in reckoning time); ordinary seaman.

O.S.A. Order of St. Augustine (Augustinian).

O.S.B. Order of St. Benedict (Benedictine).

O.S.D. Order of St. Dominic (Dominican).

O.S.F. Order of St. Francis (Franciscan).

OSRD Office of Scientific Research and Development.

OSS Office of Strategic Services.

O.T. occupational therapy; Old Testament; overtime.

O.T.C. Officer Training Corps.

Oxf. Oxford; Oxfordshire.

Oxon. *Oxonia* (L.), Oxford, Oxfordshire; *Oxoniensis* (L.), of Oxford.

oz. (pl. **oz.** or **ozs.**) ounce.

P

p. (pl. **pp.**) page; part; participle; *partim* (L.), in part; past; *piano* (It.), (Music) soft; pint; pipe; (Baseball) pitcher; pole; population; *post* (L.), after; purl; peseta; peso.

P (Chess) pawn; (Chem.) phosphorus.

P. *Papa* (L.), Pope; *Pater* (L.), Father; President; pressure; Priest; Prince; progressive; Province.

p.a. participial adjective; *per annum* (L.), by the year.

Pa (Chem.) protactinium.

Pa. Pennsylvania.

PA public address system.

P.A. power of attorney; press agent; purchasing agent.

PABA (Chem.) para-aminobenzoic acid.

Pac. Pacific.

Pal. Palestine.

paleog. paleography.

paoleon. paleontology.

pam. or **pamph.** pamphlet.

Pan. Panama.

p. & l. profit and loss.

par. paragraph; parallel; parenthesis; parish.

Para. Paraguay.

paren. parenthesis.

Parl. Parliament; Parliamentary.

part. participle; particle; particular.

pass. passenger; *passim* (L.), here and there; passive.

pat. patent; patented.

PAT (Football) point, or points, after touchdown.

path. or **pathol.** pathological, pathology.

Pat. Off. patent office.

P.A.U. Pan American Union.

P.A.Y.E. Pay as you earn.

payt. payment.

p.b. (Baseball) passed ball.

Pb *plumbum* (L.), (Chem.) lead.

P.B. *Pharmacopoeia Britannica* (L.), British Pharmacopoeia; Prayer Book; Primitive Baptist.

PBA Public Buildings Administration.

PBX Private Branch Exchange (a telephone system for private use, as for routing interoffice calls, usually having outside lines.)

pc. (pl. **pcs.**) piece; price.

p.c. per cent; petty cash; *post cibum* (L.), after meals; post card; price current.

P.C. Penal Code; Perpetual Curate; Police Constable; Privy Council; Privy Councilor.

pd. paid.

Pd (Chem.) palladium.

P.D. *per diem* (L.), by the day; Police Department.

Pd. B. Bachelor of Pedagogy.

Pd. D. Doctor of Pedagogy.

Pd. M. Master of Pedagogy.

p.d.q. (Slang) pretty damned quick.

P.E. Physical Education; Presiding Elder; printer's error; probable error (statistics); Protestant Episcopal.

ped. (Music) pedal; pedestal.

P.E.I. Prince Edward Island.

pen. peninsula.

P.E.N. International Association of Poets; Playwrights, Editors, Essayists, and Novelists.

Penn. or **Penna.** Pennsylvania.

Pent. Pentecost.

per an. *per annum* (L.), by the year.

perf. perfect; perforated.

perh. perhaps.

perp. Perpendicular.

per pro. or **per proc.** *per procurationem* (L.), by procuration, by the agency of another.

pers. person; personal.
Pers. Persia; Persian.
persp. perspective.
pert. pertaining.
Pet. Peter.
petrog. petrography.
petrol. petrology.
pf. perfect; pfennig; preferred (of stock).
p.f. *piu forte* (It.), (Music) louder.
Pfc. (Mil.) private first class.
pfd. preferred (of stock).
pfg. pfennig, or *phennig* (G.), penny.
pg. page.
Pg. Portugal; Portuguese.
P.G. paying guest; postgraduate.
PGA Professional Golfer's Association.
P.G.M. Past Grand Master.
Ph (Chem.) phenyl.
P.H. Public Health.
PHA Public Housing Administration.
phar. or **pharm.** pharmaceutical; pharmacology; pharmacopoeia; pharmacy.
Phar. D or **Pharm. D.** Doctor of Pharmacy.
Phar. or **Pharm.** of Pharmacy.
Ph. B. *Philosophiae Baccalaureus* (L.), Bachelor of Philosophy.
Ph. D. *Philosophiae Doctor* (L.), Doctor of Philosophy.
phil. philosophical; philosophy.
Phil. Philadelphia; Philemon; Philip; Philippians; Philippine.
Phila. Philadelphia.
Philem. Philemon.

philol. philological; philology.
philos. philosopher; philosophical; philosophy.
phon. phonetics.
phonol. phonology.
phot. or **photog.** photographic; photography.
photom. photometry.
phr. phrase.
phren. or **phrenol.** phrenological; phrenology.
PHS Public Health Service.
phys. physical; physician; physics; physiological; physiology.
physiol. physiological; physiologist; physiology.
P.I. Philippine Islands.
pinx. *pinxit* (L.), he or she, painted (it).
PIO (Mil.) public information office or offices.
pizz. *pizzicato* (It.), pinched; (Music) played by plucking with the finger.
pk. (pl. **pks.**) pack; park; peak; peck.
PK psychokinesis.
pkg. (pl. **pkgs.**) package.
pkt. (pl. **pkts.**) packet.
pl. place; plate; plural.
P.L. Poet Laureate.
plat. plateau; platoon.
plf. or **plff.** plaintiff.
plupf. pluperfect.
plur. plural; plurality.
pm. premium.
Pm (Chem.) promethium.
P.M. Past Master; Paymaster; Postmaster; *post meridiem* (L.), afternoon; post mortem; Prime Minister; Provost Marshal.
P.M.G. Paymaster Gener-

al; Postmaster General.

PMLA Publication of the Modern Language Association.

p.n. please note; promissory note.

PNA (Biochem.) pentose nucleic acid.

pneum. pneumatic; pneumatics.

pnxt. *pinxit* (L.), he, or she, painted (it).

po. (Baseball) put-outs.

Po (Chem.) polonium.

P.O. Petty Officer; postal order; post office; Province of Ontario.

P.O.B. post office box.

poet. poetic; poetry.

POGO polar orbiting geophysical observatory.

pol. political; politics.

Pol. Poland; Polish.

pol. econ. political economy.

polit. political; politics.

poly. polytechnic.

pop. popular; population.

P.O.P. print-out paper.

Port. Portugal; Portuguese.

pos. position; positive; possession; possessive.

poss. possessive; possible.

pot. potential.

POW prisoner of war.

p.p. past participle; *per procurationem* (L.), by procuration, by the agency of another; post-paid or prepaid.

P.P. parcel post; Parish Priest.

P.P.C. *pour prendre conge* (F.), to take leave.

pph. pamphlet.

ppr. or **p. pr.** present participle.

P.P.S. *post postscriptum*

(L.), a second postscript.

P.Q. previous question; Province of Quebec.

pr. (pl. **prs.**) pair; preference; preferred; present; price; priest; printing; pronoun.

Pr (Chem) praseodymium.

Pr. Prince; Provencal.

P.R. Parliamentary Reports; *populus Romanus* (L.), Roman people; Press Release; proportional representation; Public Relations; Puerto Rico.

PRA Public Roads Administration.

P.R.B. Pre-Raphaelite Brotherhood.

prec. preceding.

pred. predicate.

pref. preface; prefatory; preference; preferred; prefix.

prelim. preliminary.

prem. premium.

Prem. Premier.

prep. preparation; preparatory; preposition.

pres. present; pressure; presumptive.

Pres. President.

Presb. Presbyterian.

pret. preterit.

prin. principal; principally; principle.

print. printing.

priv. private; privative.

p.r.n. *pro re nata* (L.), as the occasion may require (in prescriptions).

PRO Public Relations Officer.

prob. probable; probably; problem.

proc. procedure; proceedings; process; proclamation; proctor.

prod. produced; production.

Prof. Professor.

Prog. Progressive.

prom. promontory; promoted.

pron. pronominal; pronoun; pronounced; pronunciation.

prop. proper; properly; property; proposition; proprietor.

propr. proprietor.

pros. proscenium; prosody.

Pros. Atty. Prosecuting Attorney.

Prot. Protestant.

pro. tem. *pro tempore* (L.), for the time, temporarily.

prov. provident; province; provincial; provisional.

Prov. Provençal; Proverbs; Province; Provost.

prox. *proximo (mense)* (L.), of the next or coming month.

prs. pairs.

P.R.S. President of the Royal Society.

Prus. Prussia; Prussian.

ps. pieces, pseudonym.

Ps. Psalms.

P.S. Permanent Secretary; *postscriptum* (L.), postscript; Privy Seal; (Theat.) prompt side; Public School; Public Service.

PSAT Preliminary Scholastic Aptitude Test.

PSC Public Service Commission.

pseud. pseudonym.

P.S.T. Pacific Standard Time.

psych. or **psychol.** psycho-

logical; psychologist; psychology.

psychoanal. psychoanalysis.

p.t. past tense; *pro tempore* (L.), for the time, temporarily.

Pt (Chem.) platinum.

P.T. patrol torpedo boat; physical therapist; Physical Training; pupil teacher.

P.T.A. Parent-Teacher Association.

p.t.o. please turn over.

Pu (Chem.) plutonium.

pub. public; publication; published; publisher; publishing.

punct. punctuation.

PVC polyvinyl chloride.

Pvt. private.

P.W.A. Public Works Administration.

P.W.D. Public Works Department.

pwt. pennyweight.

PX post exchange.

pxt. *pinxit* (L.), he, or she, painted (it).

Q

q. *quadrans* (L.), farthing; quart, quasi; query; question; quintal; quire.

Q. quarto; Quebec; Queen; Queensland; query; question.

q.b. (Football) quarterback.

Q.B. Queen's Bench.

Q.C. Queen's Counsel.

q.d. *quasi dicat* (L.), as if one should say; *quasi dictum* (L.), as if said; *quaque die* (L.), daily (in prescriptions).

q.e. *quod est* (L.), which is.

Q.E.D. *quod erat demonstrandum* (L.), which was to be demonstrated.

Q.E.F. *quod erat faciendum* (L.), which was to be done.

ql. quintal.

q.l. or **q. lib.** *quantum libet* (L.), as much as you please (in prescriptions).

Q.M. Quartermaster.

Q.M.C. Quartermaster Corps.

Q.M.G. Quartermaster General.

q.p. or **q.pl.** *quantum placet* (L.), as much as you please (in prescriptions).

qq.v. *quae vide* (L.), which (words, etc.) see.

qr. (pl. **qrs.**) *quadrans* (L.), farthing; quarter; quire.

q.s. quarter section.

qt. (pl. **qts.**) quart; quality.

q.t. (Slang) quiet.

qu. query; question.

qu. quadrangle.

quar. or **quart.** quarter; quarterly.

Que. Quebec.

ques. question.

quot. quotation.

q.v. *quantum vis* (L.), as much as you wish (in prescriptions); *quod vide* (L.), which see.

qy. query.

R

r. (pl. **rs.**) radius; railroad; railway; rare; received; *recto* (L.), right-hand page; residence; resides; retired; right; rises; rod; rood; ruble; (Baseball)

runs; rupee.

R (Chem.) radical; (Math.) ratio; (Elect.) resistance; (Theat.) stage right; (Physics) roentgen; (Chess) rook.

R. *Réaumur* (L.), thermometer; *recipe* (L.), take (in prescriptions); *Regina* (L.), Queen; Republican; response; *Rex* (L.), king; River; ruble.

Ra (Chem.) radium.

R.A. Rear Admiral; (Astron.) right ascension; Royal Academician; Royal Academy; Royal Artillery.

R.A.A.F. Royal Australian Air Force.

rad. (Math.) radical; radix.

Rad. Radical.

R.A.F. Royal Air Force.

rail. railroad; railways.

rall. (Music) *rallentando* (It.), slackening; becoming slower.

R & D research and development.

R. & I. *Regina et Imperatrix* (L.), Queen and Empress; *Rex et Imperator* (L.), King and Emperor.

Rb (Chem.) rubidium.

R.B.I. (Baseball) run, or runs, batted in.

R.C. Reserve Corps; Red Cross; Roman Catholic.

R.C.A.F. Royal Canadian Air Force.

R.C.M.P. Royal Canadian Mounted Police.

R.C.P. Royal College of Physicians.

R.C.S. Royal College of Surgeons.

Rct. (Mil.) recruit.

rd. rendered; road; rod; round.

r.d. (Banking) refer to drawer.

Rd (Chem.) radium.

R.D. Royal Naval Reserve Decoration (Brit.); Rural Dean; rural delivery.

Rd Ac (Chem.) radio actinium.

RDF radio direction finder.

Re (Chem.) rhenium.

r.e. (Football) right end.

Re rupee.

R.E. Reformed Episcopal; Royal Engineers.

R.E.A. Railway Express Agency; Rural Electrification Administration.

Réaum. Réaumur (thermometer).

rec. receipt; recipe; record; recorded; recorder.

recd. received.

Recit. (Music) recitative.

rec. sec. recording secretary.

rect. receipt; rectangle; rector; rectory.

redupl. reduplicated; reduplication.

ref. referee; reference; referred; refined; reformation; reformed; refund.

Ref. Ch. Reformed Church.

refl. reflex; reflexive.

refrig. refrigeration.

reg. region; register; registered; regular.

Reg. Regent; Regiment; *Regina* (L.), Queen.

regd. registered.

Reg. Prof. Regius Professor.

regr. registrar.

regt. regiment.

rel. relative; relatively; re-

ligion; religious.

relig. religion.

rep. repair; repeat; report; reporter; representative; republic.

Rep. Republican.

repr. represented; representing; reprint; reprinted.

repts. reports.

Repub. Republican.

res. reserve; residence; resides; resigned.

ret. or **retd.** retained; returned.

rev. revenue; reverse; review; revised; revision; revolution; revolving.

Rev. Revelation; Reverend.

Rev. Stat. or **Rev. Stats.** Revised Statutes.

Rev. Ver. Revised Version (of the Bible).

rf. (Baseball) right fielder.

r.f. radio frequency; range finder; rapidfire; (Baseball) right field.

R.F. *Republique Francaise* (F.); Reserve Force.

R.F.A. Royal Field Artillery.

R.F.C. Reconstruction Finance Corporation; Royal Flying Corps.

R.F.D. rural free delivery.

r.g. (Football) right guard.

R.G.S. Royal Geographical Society.

Rh (Chem.) rhodium.

R.H. Royal Highlanders; Royal Highness.

r.h. relative humidity; right hand.

r.h.b. (Football) right halfback.

rhet. rhetoric; rhetorical.

R.H.S. Royal Historical

Society; Royal Horticultural Society; Royal Humane Society.

R.I. Religious Instructions; Rhode Island; Royal Institute of Painters in Water Colours; Royal Institution of Great Britain.

R.I.B.A. Royal Institutes of British Architectures.

R.I.I.A. Royal Institute of International Affairs.

R.I.P. *requiescat* (or *requiescant*) *in pace* (L.), may he or she (or they) rest in peace.

rit. or **retard.** *ritardando* (It.), (Music) retarding.

riv. river.

rm. (pl. **rms.**) ream; room.

R.M. Resident Magistrate; Royal Mail; Royal Marines.

R.M.A. Royal Marine Artillery; Royal Military Academy; Royal Military Asylum.

R.M.C. Royal Military College (Sandhurst).

R.M.S. Railway Mail Service; Royal Mail Steamer.

Rn (Chem.) radon.

R.N. Registered Nurse; Royal Navy.

RNA (Biochem.) ribonucleic acid.

R.N.A.S. Royal Naval Air Service.

R.N.R. Royal Naval Reserve.

ro. *recto* (L.), the right-hand page; rood.

R.O. Royal Observatory.

Rom. Roman; Romance; Romans.

Rom. antiq. Roman antiquities.

Rom. Cath. Roman Catholic.

R.O.T.C. Reserve Officers Training Corps.

R.P. Reformed Presbyterian; Regius Professor.

R.P.D. *Rerum Politicarum Doctor* (L.), Doctor of Political Science.

r.p.m. revolutions per minute.

R.P.O. Railway Post Office.

RPQ (Commercial) request for price quotation.

rpt. report.

R.R. railroad; Right Reverend.

r.s. right side.

R.S. Recording Secretary; reformed spelling; revised statutes.

R.S.A. Royal Scottish Academician; Royal Scottish Academy; Royal Society of Arts.

R.S.F.S.R. Russian Soviet Federated Socialist Republic.

R.S.P.C.A. Royal Society for the Prevention of Cruelty to Animals.

R.S.V.P. *repondez s'il vous plait* (F.), reply, if you please.

rt. right.

r.t. (Football) right tackle.

Rt. Hon. Right Honorable.

Rt. Rev. Right Reverend.

Ru (Chem.) ruthenium.

Rum. Rumania; Rumanian.

Russ. Russia; Russian.

R.V. Revised Version (of the Bible).

R.W. Right Worshipful; Right Worthy.

R.W.S. Royal Watercolour Society.

Rwy. Railway.

R.Y.S. Royal Yacht Squadron.

S

s. (pl. **ss.**) second; section; series; *siécle* (Fr.), century; see, singular; *solidus,* or *solidi* (L.), shilling or shillings; son; soprano; substantive; succeeded; sun.

S (Chem.) sulfur.

S. (pl. **SS.**) Sabbath; Saint; Saskatchewan; Saturday; Saxon; school; sea; senate; September; *signa* (L.), mark; (Phar.) label; Signor (It.); Socialist; Society; *Socius* (L.), Fellow; south; southern; Sunday; surplus.

s.a. *sine anno* (L.), without year or date; subject to approval.

Sa (Chem. Obs.) samarium.

S.A. Salvation Army; sex appeal; *Son Altesse* (Fr.), His, or Her, Highness; *Societe anonym* (Fr.); South Africa; South African; South America; South American; South Australian.

Sab. Sabbath.

S.A.E. Society of Automotive Engineers.

S. Afr. South Africa; South African.

Salv. Salvador.

Sam. or **Saml.** Samuel.

SAM Surface-to-air-missile.

S. Amer. South American.

Sans. Sanskrit.

Sar. Sardinia.

S.A.R. Sons of the American Revolution.

Sask. Saskatchewan.

Sat. Saturday; Saturn.

SAT Scholastic Aptitude Test.

Sax. Saxon; Saxony.

sb. substantive.

Sb *stibium* (L.), (Chem.) antimony.

S.B. *Scientiae Baccalaureus* (L.), Bachelor of Science; South Britain (England and Wales).

SBA Small Business Administration.

sc. scale; scene; science; scientific; *scilicet* (L.), to wit, namely, that is to say; screw; scruple; *sculpsit* (L.), he, or she, carved (it).

s.c. small capitals.

Sc (Chem.) scandium.

Sc. Scotch; Scotland; Scots; Scottish.

S.C. Security Council (of U.N.); Signal Corps; South Carolina; Staff Corps; Supreme Court.

Scand. Scandinavia; Scandinavian.

s. caps. small capitals.

Sc. B. *Scientiae Baccalaureus* (L.), Bachelor of Science.

Sc. D. *Scientiae Doctor* (L), Doctor of Science.

sch. school; schooner.

sci. science; scientific.

scil. *scilicet* (L.), to wit, namely.

Sc. M. *Scientiae Magister* (L), Master of Science.

Scot. Scotch, Scotland; Scottish.

scr. scruple.

Script. Scriptural; Scripture.

SCS Soil Conservation Service.

sculp. sculptor; sculpture.

sd. sound.

s.d. sight draft; *sine die* (L.), without day, without day fixed for meeting again.

S.D. *Scientiae Doctor* (L.), Doctor of Science; South Dakota; (Statistics) Standard Deviation.

S.D.A. Seventh Day Adventists.

S. Dak. South Dakota.

S.D.S. Students for a Democratic Society.

Se (Chem.) selenium.

SE southeast; southeastern.

SEATO South East Asia Treaty Organization.

sec secant.

sec. second; secondary; secretary; section; sector; *secundum* (L.), according to.

S.E.C. Securities and Exchange Commission.

sec. art. *secundum artem* (L), according to rule.

sect. section.

secy. secretary.

Sem. Seminary; Semitic.

Sen. Senate; Senator; Senior.

sep. sepal; separate.

Sept. September; Septuagint.

seq. (pl. **seqq.**) sequel; *sequens* (L.), the following.

ser. series; sermon.

Serb. Serbian.

Serg. or **Sergt.** Sergeant.

s.f. sinking fund.

SF science fiction.

S.F. San Francisco.

Sfc (Mil.) sergeant first class.

sfz. *sforzando* (It.), (Music) with force or emphasis.

s.g. specific gravity.

S.G. Solicitor General.

sgd. signed.

Sgt. Sergeant.

sh. share; shilling; shillings.

SHA (Navig.) sidereal hour angle.

Shp shaft house power.

shpt. shipment.

Si (Chem.) silicon.

S.I. Sandwich Island; Staten Island.

Sib. Siberia; Siberian.

Sic. Sicilian; Sicily.

sig. *signa* (L.), mark, label (in prescriptions); signature.

Sig. *Signore* (It.) Signor.

sin sine.

sing. singular.

S.J. Society of Jesus (Jesuit).

S.J.D. *Scientiae Juridicae Doctor* (L.), Doctor of Juridicial Science.

Skr. or **Skt.** Sanskrit.

s.l. *sine loco* (L.), without place (of publication).

S. lat. south latitude.

Slav. Slavic; Slavonic.

SLBM satelite-launched ballistic missile.

sld. sailed; sealed; sold.

Sm (Chem.) samarium.

S.M. *Santa Maria* (It.), Saint (or Holy) Mary; *Scientiae Magister* (L.), Master of Science; Sergeant Major; State Militia.

sm. c. or **sm. caps.** small

capitals.

s.n. *sine nomine* (L), without name.

Sn *stannum* (L.), (Chem.) tin.

so. south; southern.

s.o. seller's option; shipping order.

soc. socialist; society.

sociol. sociological; sociology.

S. of Sol. Song of Solomon.

sol. solicitor; solution.

Sol. Solomon.

sop. soprano.

SOP Standard Operating Procedure.

SOS the letter represented by the radio telegraphic signal (...—...) used especially by ships in distress as an internationally recognized call for help.

sou. south; southern.

sp. special; species; specific; specimen; spelling; spirit.

s.p. *sine prole* (L.), without issue.

Sp. Spain; Spaniard.

S.P. Shore Patrol; Socialist party; submarine patrol.

S.P.A.S. *Societatis Philosophicae Americanae Socius* (L.), Member of the American Philosophical Society.

S.P.C.A. Society for the Prevention of Cruelty to Animals.

S.P.C.C. Society for the Prevention of Cruelty to Children.

S.P.C.K. Society for Promoting Christian Knowledge (Brit.).

spec. special; specially; specific; specifically.

S.P.G. Society for the Propagation of the Gospel.

sp. gr. specific gravity.

Spgs. Springs.

S.P.Q.R. *Senatus Populusque Romanus* (L.), the Senate and the People of Rome.

S.P.R. Society for Physical Research (Brit.).

spt. seaport.

sq. (pl. **sqq.**) *sequens* (L.), the following; squadron; square.

Sq. Squadron; Square.

Sr (Chem.) strontium.

Sr. Senior; *Señor* (Sp.).

Sra. *Señora* (Sp.).

SRBM short-range ballistic missile.

S.R.N. State Registered Nurse. (Brit.).

S.R.O. standing room only.

Srta. *Señorita* (Sp.).

SS. *scilicet* (L.), to wit; namely; sections; (Baseball) shortstop.

SS. Saints.

S.S. Secret Service; steamship; Sunday School.

S.S.C. Solicitor Before the Supreme Courts (Scotland).

S.S.D. *Sanctissimus Dominus* (L.), Most Holy Lord (a title of the Pope).

S.S.D. *Sacrae Scripturae Doctor* (L.), Doctor of the Sacred Scripture.

S.S.E. south-southeast.

S.S.L. *Sacrae Scripturae Licentiatus* (L.), Licentiate of Sacred Scripture.

SSM surface-to-surface missile.

SSS Selective Service System.

SST supersonic transport.

S.S.W. south-southwest.

st. stanza; statute; (Printing) *stet* (L.), let it stand or remain; (pl. **st.,** weight) stone; (pl. **sts.**) strait; (pl. **sts.**) street.

s.t. short ton.

St. Saint; Strait; Street.

sta. station.

Sta. *Santa* (It.), Saint (female); Station.

stacc. *staccato* (It.), (Music) detached, disconnected.

stat. statute.

S.T.B. *Sacrae Theologiae Baccalaureus* (L.), Bachelor of Sacred Theology; *Scientiae Theologicae Baccalaureus* (L.), Bachelor of Theology.

std. standard.

S.T.D. *Sacrae Theologiae Doctor* (L.), Doctor of the Sacred Theology.

Ste. *Sainte* (F.), Saint (female).

ster. sterling.

St. Ex. Stock Exchange.

stg. sterling.

str. steamer.

sub. subaltern; subscription; substitute; suburb; suburban; subway.

subj. subject; subjunctive.

subst. substantive; substantively; substitute.

suff. suffix.

Sun. or **Sund.** Sunday.

sup. superior; superlative; supine; supplement; *supra* (L.), above, before.

Sup. Ct. Superior Court; Supreme Court.

superl. superlative.

supp. supplement.

supt. superintendent.

Sur. Surrey.

surg. surgeon; surgery; surgical.

surv. surveying; surveyor; surviving.

sus. per. coll. *suspendatur* (or *suspensio,* or *suspensus*) *per collum* (L.), let him be hanged (or hanging, or hanged) by the neck.

s.v. *sub verbo* or *sub voce* (L.), under the word or heading.

S.V. *Sancta Virgo* (L.), Holy Virgin.

S.V.P. *s'il vous plait* (F.), if you please.

Sw. Sweden; Swedish; Swiss.

S.W. South Wales; southwest; southwestern.

Swed. Sweden, Swedish.

S.W.G. standard wire gauge.

Switz. Switzerland.

syll. syllable; syllabus.

sym. symbol.

syn. synonym; synonymous.

synop. synopsis.

Syr. Syria; Syriac.

syst. system.

T

t. teaspoon; temperature; *tempore* (L.), in the time of; tenor; tense; *tome* (F.), volume; ton; town; transitive; tun.

T. Tablespoon; Territory; Testament; Tuesday; Turkish.

Ta (Chem.) tantalum.

tab. *tabella* (L.), tablet (in prescriptions); table.

TAC (Mil.) Tactical Air Command.

tan tangent.

Tasm. Tasmania.

TAT Thematic Apperception Test.

t.b. torpedo boat; trial balance.

Tb (Chem.) terbium.

T.B. turbercle bacillus, tuberculosis.

tbs. or **tbsp.** tablespoon, tablespoons.

Tc (Chem.) technetium.

TCBM transcontinental ballistic missile.

TD touchdown; touchdowns.

T.D. Territorial Decoration (Brit.); Traffic Director; Treasury Department.

Te (Chem.) tellurium.

tech. technical; technology.

technol. technology.

tel. telegram; telegraph; telephone.

teleg. telegram; telegraph; telegraphy.

temp. temperature; temporary; *tempore* (L.), in the time of.

ten. tenor; *tenuto* (It.), (Music) held, sustained.

Tenn. Tennessee.

ter. terrace; territory.

term. terminal; termination.

Test. Testament.

Teut. Teutonic.

Tex. Texas.

t.g. (Biol.) type genus.

Th (Chem.) thorium.

Th. Thursday.

T.H. Territory of Hawaii.

Th.D. *Theologiae Doctor* (L.), Doctor of Theology.

theat. theatrical.

theol. theologian; theological; theology.

theor. theorem.

theos. theosophical; theosophy.

therap. therapeutic; therapeutics.

Thes. or **Thess.** Thessalonians.

T.H.I. temperature-humidity index.

Thos. Thomas.

Thurs. Thursday.

Ti (Chem.) titanium.

Tim. Timothy.

tinct. tincture.

tit. title.

Tit. Titus.

TKO (Boxing) technical knockout.

Tl (chem.) thallium.

t.l.o. (Insurance) total loss only.

Tm (Chem.) thulium.

tn. ton.

Tn (Chem.) thoron.

TNT or **T.N.T.** trinitrotoluene; trinitrotoluol.

t.o. telegraph office; turn over.

Tob. Tobit (Apocrypha).

tonn. tonnage.

topog. topographical; topography.

tox. toxicology.

tp. township; troop.

t.p. title page.

tr. tincture; trace; train; transaction; transitive; translated; transpose; treasurer; *trillo* (It.), (Music) trill; trustee.

Tr (Chem.) terbium.

T.R. *tempore regis* (L.), in the time of the King; tons registered; trust receipts.

trans. transactions; transfer; transformer; transitive; translation; transparent; transportation; transpose; transverse.

transf. transferred.

trav. traveler; traveling.

treas. treasurer; treasury.

trig. or **trigon.** trigonometric; trigonometry.

trop. tropic; tropical.

T. Sgt. (Mil.) Technical Sergeant.

tsp. teaspoon; teaspoons.

T.T. telegraphic transfer; tuberculin tested.

Tu. Tuesday.

T.U. trade union; training unit.

Tues. Tuesday.

Turk. Turkey; Turkish.

TV television.

T.V.A. Tennessee Valley Authority.

twp. township.

ty. territory.

typ. or **typog.** typographer; typographical; typography.

U

u. uncle; *und* (G.), and; uniform; unit; upper.

U (Chem.) uranium.

U, Union; Unionist; University.

UAM underwater to air missile.

u. & l.c. (Print.) upper and lower case.

U.A.R. United Arab Republic.

UAW United Automobile Workers.

U.B. United Brethren.

u.c. *una corda* (It.), (Music) one string, soft pedal; (Print.) upper case.

U.C. Upper Canada; under construction.

UCMJ (Mil.) Uniform Code of Military Justice.

U.C.V. United Confederate Veterans.

U.D.C. United Daughters of the Confederacy; Urban District Council (Brit.).

U.E.L. United Empire Loyalists.

U.F.C. United Free Church (of Scotland).

UFO unidentified flying object.

UHF ultra high frequency.

U.J.D. *Utriusque Juris Doctor* (L.), Doctor of Civil and Canon Law.

U.K. United Kingdom.

Ukr. Ukraine.

ult. ultimate; ultimately; *ultimo mense* (L.), of the last month.

UMW United Mine Workers.

UN *or* **U.N.** United Nations.

UNESCO United Nations Educational, Scientific and Cultural Organization.

UNICEF United Nations International Children's Emergency Fund.

Unit. Unitarian.

univ. universal; universally; university.

Univ. Universalist.

UNRRA United Nations Relief and Rehabilitation Agency.

U. of S. Afr. Union of South Africa.

up. upper.

U.P. United Press.

U.P.I. United Press International.

Uru. Uruguay.

u.s. *ubi supra* (L.), in the place above (mentioned); *ut supra* (L.), as above.

U.S. United States.

U.S.A. United States Army; United States of America.

U.S.A.E.C. United States Atomic Energy Commission.

U.S.A.F. United States Air Force.

U.S.A.R. United States Army Reserve.

U.S.C.G. United States Coast Guard.

U.S.D.A. United States Department of Agriculture.

U.S.I.A. United States Information Agency.

U.S.I.S. United States Information Service.

U.S.M. United States Mail; United States Marine(s); United States Mint.

U.S.M.A. United States Military Academy.

U.S.M.C. United States Marine Corps; United States Maritime Commission.

U.S.N. United States Navy.

U.S.N.A. United States National Army; United States Naval Academy.

U.S.N.G. United States National Guard.

U.S.O. United Service Organization.

U.S.P. or **U.S. Pharm.** United States Pharmaco-

poeia.

U.S.P.O. United States Post Office.

U.S.P.H.S. United States Public Health Service.

U.S.S. United States Senate; United States Service; United States Ship.

U.S.S.B. United States Shipping Board.

U.S.S.R. Union of Soviet Socialist Republics.

U.S.S.S. United States Steamship.

usu. usual; usually.

U.S.V. United States Volunteers.

Ut. Utah.

ut dict. *ut dictum* (L.), as directed (in prescriptions).

UV ultraviolet.

ux. *uxor* (L.), wife.

V

v. (pl. **vv.**) vector; verb; verse; version; verso; *versus* (L.), against; *vert* (L.), turn over; vice; *vide* (L.), see; village; violin; vocative; volt; volume; *von* (G.), of (in personal names).

V (Chem.) vanadium; Roman numeral for 5.

V. Valve; Venerable; Vicar; Village; Viscount; Volunteers.

v.a. verb active; verbal adjective.

Va. Virginia.

V.A. Royal Order of Victoria and Albert (Brit.); Veterans Administration; Vicar Apostolic; Vice-Admiral.

val. valuation.

var. variant; variation; variety; various.

Vat. Vatican.

v. aux. verb auxiliary.

vb. verb.

vb.n. verbal noun.

V.C. Veterinary Corps; Vice-Chairman; Vice-Chancellor; Vice-Consul; Victoria Cross (Brit.); Viet Cong.

v.d. various dates.

V.D. venereal disease; Volunteer Officers' Decoration (Brit.).

Ven. Venerable; Venice.

Venez. Venezuela.

verb. sap., or **verb. sat.**, or **verbum sap.** *verbum sapienti sat est* (L.), a word to the wise is sufficient.

vers (Math.) versed sine.

vet. veteran; veterinarian; veterinary.

V.F. Vicar Forane; video frequency; voice frequency.

V.F.W. Veterans of Foreign Wars.

v.g. *verbi gratia* (L.), for example.

V.G. Vicar General.

VHF very high frequency.

v.i. verb intransitive; *vide infra* (L.), see below.

Vi (Chem.) virginium.

V.I. Vancouver Island; Virgin Islands.

Vic. Vicar; Vicarage; Victoria.

vil. village.

Visc. Viscount; Viscountess.

VISTA Volunteer in Service to America.

viz. *videlicet* (L.), to wit; namely; that is to say.

v.l. (pl. **vv.ll.**) *varia lectio* (L.), variant reading.

V.L. Vulgar Latin.

V.M.D. *Veterinariae Medecinae Doctor*, (L.), Doctor of Veterinary Medicine.

v.n. verb neuter.

vo. *versa* (L.), left-hand page.

VOA Voice of America; Volunteers of America.

voc. vocative.

vocab. vocabulary.

vocat. vocative.

vol. (pl. **vols.**) volcanic; volcano; volume; volunteer.

v.p. verb passive.

V.P. or **V. Pres.** Vice-President.

v.r. verb reflexive.

V.R. *Victoria Regina* (L.), Queen Victoria.

V.Rev. Very Reverend.

vs. verse; *versus* (L.), against.

v.s. *vide supra* (L.), see above.

V.S. Veterinary Surgeon.

v.t. verb transitive.

Vt. Vermont.

Vte. *Vicomte* (Fr.), Viscount.

Vtesse. *Vicomtesse* (Fr.), Viscountess.

VTO (Aeron.) vertical take-off.

VTOL (Aeron.) vertical take-off and landing.

Vul. or **Vulg.** Vulgate.

vulg. vulgar; vulgarly.

vv. verses, violins.

v.v. *vice versa* (L.), the order being changed.

vv. ll. *variae lectiones* (L.), variant readings.

v.y. various years.

W

w. wanting; warehouse; watt; week; wide; width; wife; with; won; (Physics) work.

W *wolframium* (L.), (Chem.) tungsten.

W. Wales; Warden; Washington; Wednesday; Welsh; west; western.

W.A. West Africa; Western Australia.

W.A.A.C. Women's Army Auxiliary Corps (Brit.).

War. or **Warw.** Warwickshire.

Wash. Washington.

w.b. warehouse book; water ballast; waybill.

w.c. water-closet; without charge.

W.C. West Central (postal district, London).

WCC World Council of Churches.

W.C.T.U. Woman's Christian Temperance Union.

wd. ward, word.

W.D. War Department.

Wed. Wednesday.

Westm. Westminster.

wf (Printing) wrong font.

WFTU World Federation of Trade Unions.

W. Ger. West Germany.

W. Gmc. West Germanic.

whf. wharf.

WHO World Health Organization.

w.i. (Finance) when issued.

W.I. West Indian; West Indies.

Wilts. Wiltshire.

Wis. or **Wisc.** Wisconsin.

Wisd. Wisdom of Solomon (Apocrypha).

wk. (pl. **wks.**) week; work.

wkly. weekly.

w.l. water line; wave length.

W.L. or **W. long.** west longitude.

Wm. William.

WMO World Meteorological Organization.

W.N.W. west-northwest.

W.O. warrant officer; War Office (Brit.).

Worc. or **Worcs.** Worcestershire.

wp. (Baseball) wild pitch; wild pitches.

W.R. West Riding (Yorkshire).

WRAC Women's Royal Army Corps.

WRAF Women's Royal Air Force.

WRNS Women's Royal Naval Service (Brit.).

W.S. Writer to the Signet; West Saxon.

W. Sax. West Saxon.

W.S.W. west-southwest.

wt. weight.

W. Va. West Virginia.

W.V.S. Women's Voluntary Service (Brit.).

w.w. warehouse warrant.

WW world war.

Wy. or **Wyo.** Wyoming.

X

X (Chem.) xenon; Christ; Christian; Roman numeral for 10.

xc. or **xcp.** (Stock Exchange) ex (without) coupon.

xd. or **xdiv.** (Stock Exchange) ex (without) dividend.

Xe (Chem.) xenon.

xi. or **xint.** (Stock Exchange) ex (without) interest.

XL extra large.

Xmas Christmas.

Xn. Christian.

Xnty. Christianity.

XP *Christos* (Gr.), Christ.

x pr (Stock Exchange) without privileges.

xr (Stock Exchange) without rights.

Xt. Christ.

Xtian. Christian.

Xty. Christianity.

Y

y. yard; yards; year; years.

Y (Chem.) yttrium.

Y. Young Men's Christian Association; Young Men's Hebrew Association; Young Women's Christian Association; Young Women's Hebrew Association.

Yb (Chem.) ytterbium.

Y.B. yearbook.

yd. (pl. **yds.**) yard.

yeo. yeoman; yeomanry.

YHA Youth Hostels Association.

Y.M.C.A. Young Men's Christian Association.

Y.M.C.U. Young Men's Christian Union.

Y.M.H.A. Young Men's Hebrew Association.

Yorks. Yorkshire.

Y.P.S.C.E. Young People's Society of Christian Endeavor.

yr. (pl. **yrs.**) year; younger; your.

yrs. years; yours.

Yt (Chem.) yttrium.

Y.T. Yukon Territory.

Yugo. Yugoslavia.

Y.W.C.A. Young Women's Christian Association.

Y.W.H.A. Young Women's Hebrew Association.

Z

z. zero; zinc.

Zach. Zacharias (Douay Version).

z.B. *zum Beispiel* (G.), for example.

Zech. Zechariah.

Zeph. Zephaniah.

Zn (Chem.) zinc.

zod. zodiac.

zoochem. zoochemical; zoochemistry.

zoogeog. zoogeographical; zoogeography.

zool. zoological; zoologist; zoology.

Zr (Chem.) zirconium.

Z.S. Zoological Society (London).

3. COUNTRIES OF THE WORLD

This chapter contains the names of all the countries in the world together with their chief cities and rivers, the language or languages spoken in each, and the currency used. The capital of each country is listed together with the cities but is followed by (c.).

Afghanistan
  Cit.: Kabul (c.), Herat, Kandahar, Jalalabad; *Riv.:* Helamand; *Lang.:* Persian, Pushtu; *Curr.:* Afghani

Albania
  Cit.: Tirane (c.); *Riv.:* Drin; *Lang.:* Gheg, Tosk; *Curr.:* Lek

Algeria
  Cit.: Algiers (c.), Oran, Annaba, Constantine; *Lang.:* French, Arabic, Berber; *Curr.:* Algerian dinar

Andorra
  Cit.: Andorra la Vella (c.); *Lang.:* Catalan; *Curr.:* French franc, Spanish peseta

Angola
  Cit.: Luanda (c.), Buengela, Moçamedes, Lobito; *Lang.:* Tribal languages, (Portuguese); *Curr.:* Escudo (Portuguese)

Argentina
  Cit.: Buenos Aires (c.), Rosario, La Plata, Cordoba; *Riv.:* Paraná, Uruguay, Rio de la Plata, Rio Negro; *Lang.:* Spanish; *Curr.:* Peso

Australia
  Cit.: Canberra (c.), Sydney, Newcastle, Greater Wallongong, Geelong, Melbourne, Brisbane, Adelaide, Perth, Hobart, Port Darwin; *Riv.:* Murray, Darling, Murrumbidgee, Lachlan; *Lang.:* English; *Curr.:* Australian dollar

Austria
  Cit.: Vienna (c.), Graz, Linz, Salsburg, Innsbruck, Klagenfurt; *Riv.:* Danube, Inn, Enns, Drau, Ill, Mur; *Lang.:* German; *Curr.:* Schilling

Bahamas
  Cit.: Nassau (c.), Freeport; *Lang.:* English; *Curr.:* Bahaman dollar

Bangladesh
  Cit.: Dacca (c.), Chittagong, Chalna; *Riv.:* Brahmaputra, Ganges; *Lang.:* Bengali, English; *Curr.:* Bangladesh rupee

Barbados
  Cit.: Bridgetown (c.); *Lang.:* English; *Curr.:* East Caribbean dollar

Belgium
  Cit.: Brussels (c.), Antwerp, Mons, Charleroi, Namur, Liège, Ghent, Bruges, Verviers; *Riv.:* Meuse, Scheldt; *Lang.:* Dutch, French, Walloon;

Curr.: Belgian franc

Bhutan
Cit.: Thimbu (c.), Punakha, Tashi Cho Dzong; *Lang.:* Dialect of Tibetan; *Curr.:* Indian rupee

Bolivia
Cit.: La Paz (c.), Sucre, Santa Cruz; *Lang.:* Spanish, Aymará, Quechua; *Curr.:* Peso Boliviano

Botswana
Cit.: Gabrone (c.), Kayne, Serowe; *Lang.:* English, Tswana, tribal languages; *Curr.:* South African rand

Brazil
Cit.: Brasília (c.), Rio de Janeiro, São Paulo, Belo Horizonte, Recife, Salvador, Belem, Pôrto Alegre, Fortaleza; *Riv.:* Amazon, Paraíba do Sul, São Francisco, Paraguay, Paraná, Uruguay; *Lang.:* Portuguese; *Curr.:* Cruzeiro

Bulgaria
Cit.: Sofia (c.), Dimitrovo, Dimitrovgrad, Pleven, Plovdiv, Stara Zagora, Sliven, Kolarovgrad, Burgas, Ruse, Tolbuhin, Varna; *Riv.:* Danube, Iskar, Maritsa; *Lang.:* Bulgarian, Turkish; *Curr.:* Lev

Burma
Cit.: Rangoon (c.); *Riv.:* Irrawaddy, Sittang; *Lang.:* Burmese, English; *Curr.:* Kyat

Burundi
Cit.: Bujumbura (c.); *Lang.:* French, tribal languages; *Curr.:* Burundi franc

Cameroon
Cit.: Yaoundé (c.), Douala; *Lang.:* French, English, tribal languages; *Curr.:* CFA franc

Canada
Cit.: Ottawa (c.), Montreal, Toronto, Vancouver, Winnipeg, Hamilton, Edmonton, Calgary, Quebec, Windsor, London, Halifax, Verdun, Saskatoon, Kitchener, Sherbrooke, St. John's, Victoria, Oshawa, Hull, St. Catherines; *Riv.:* St. John, St. Lawrence, Nelson, Albany, Churchill, Saskatchewan, Athasbasca, Peace, Mackenzie, Fraser, Thompson, Columbia; *Lang.:* English, French; *Curr.:* dollar

Cape Verde Islands
Cit.: Praia (c.); *Lang.:* Portuguese, local dialects; *Curr.:* Escudo (Portuguese)

Central African Republic
Cit.: Bangui (c.); *Riv.:* Ubangi, Shari; *Lang.:* French, tribal languages; *Curr.:* CFA franc

Chad
Cit.: Fort-Lamy (c.); *Riv.:* Shari, Logone, Bahr el Ghazal; *Lang.:* French, Arabic, tribal languages; *Curr.:* CFA franc

Chile
Cit.: Santiago (c.), Valparaiso, Concepción, Viña del Mar, Temuco; *Riv.:* Aconcagua, Bió-Bió, Copiacó; *Lang.:*

Spanish; *Curr.:* Escudo

China
Cit.: Peking (c.), Shanghai, Nanking, Canton, Tientsin, Mukden, Chungking, Harbin; *Riv.:* Yangtze, Yellow, West, Pai; *Lang.:* Chinese; *Curr.:* Yuan

Colombia
Cit.: Bogotá (c.), Mendellin, Cali, Barranquilla; *Riv.:* Magdalena, Cauca; *Lang.:* Spanish; *Curr.:* Peso

Comoro Islands
Cit.: Moroni (c.); *Lang.:* Arabic; *Curr.:* CFA franc

Congo
Cit.: Brazzaville (c.), Pointe-Noire, Dolisie; *Riv.:* Congo, Niari, Ubangi, Ogowel; *Lang.:* French, tribal languages, Lingala, Kongo; *Curr.:* CFA franc

Costa Rica
Cit.: San José (c.), Limón, Puntarenas; *Lang.:* Spanish; *Curr.:* Colon

Cuba
Cit.: Havana (c.), Santiago, Guantánamo; *Riv.:* Cauto; *Lang.:* Spanish; *Curr.:* Peso

Cyprus
Cit.: Nicosia (c.), Limassol, Larnaca, Famagusta; *Lang.:* Turkish, English; *Curr.:* Cyprus pound

Czechoslovakia
Cit.: Prague (c.), Brno, Bratislava, Ostrava; *Riv.:* Elbe, Vltava, Oder, Vistula, Morava, Danube; *Lang.:* Czech, Slovak, German, Hungarian, Ukrainian, Polish; *Curr.:* Koruna

Dahomey
Cit.: Porto Novo (c.), Cotonou; *Lang.:* Sudani, French; *Curr.:* CFA franc

Denmark
Cit.: Copenhagen (c.), Aarhus, Odense, Aalborg; *Lang.:* Danish; *Curr.:* Krone

Dominican Republic
Cit.: Santo Domingo (c.), Santiago, San Cristobal, La Vega, San Pedro de Marcorís, La Romana, Puerto Plata; *Riv.:* Yaque del Norte, Yaque del Sur, Yuna, Ozama; *Lang.:* Spanish; *Curr.:* Peso

Ecuador
Cit.: Quito (c.), Guayaquil, Cuena, Ambato; *Riv.:* Guayas, Esmeraldas; *Lang.:* Spanish; *Curr.:* Sucre

Egypt
Cit.: Cairo (c.), Alexandria; *Riv.:* Nile; *Lang.:* Arabic; *Curr.:* Egyptian pound

El Salvador
Cit.: San Salvador (c.), Santa Ana, San Miguel, Neuva San Salvador; *Lang.:* Spanish; *Curr.:* Colon

Equatorial Guinea
Cit.: Santa Isabel (c.), Bata; *Lang.:* Spanish, Fang; *Curr.:* Spanish peseta

Ethiopia
Cit.: Addis Ababa (c.),

Diredawa, Harar, Dabra-Mark'os, Gondar, Gambela, Asmara; *Riv.*: Blue Nile, Webi Shebeli; *Lang.*: Amharic, English; *Curr.*: Ethiopian dollar

Finland
Cit.: Helsinki (c.), Turku, Tampere; *Riv.*: Kemi, Oulu, Kymi, Kokemäki, Vuoksi; *Lang.*: Finnish, Swedish, Lapp; *Curr.*: Markka

France
Cit.: Paris (c.), Marseilles, Lyons, Toulouse, Nice, Bordeaux, Nantes; *Riv.*: Seine, Loire, Rhone, Saône, Garonne; *Lang.*: French; *Curr.*: Franc

Gabon
Cit.: Libreville (c.); *Lang.*: French, tribal languages; *Curr.*: CFA franc

Gambia
Cit.: Banjul (c.); *Riv.*: Gambia; *Lang.*: English, tribal languages; *Curr.*: Gambian pound

Germany, East
Cit.: East Berlin (c.), Leipzig, Dresden, Karl-Marx-Stadt, Magdeburg, Halle; *Riv.*: Elbe, Oder, Saale, Spree; *Lang.*: German; *Curr.*: East German mark

Germany, West
Cit.: Bonn (c.), Hamburg, Bremen, West Berlin, Munich, Cologne, Dusseldorf, Essen, Frankfurt am Main, Dortmund, Stuttgart; *Riv.*: Danube, Rhine, Ems, Weser, Elbe; *Lang.*: German; *Curr.*: West German mark

Ghana
Cit.: Accra (c.), Takoradi; *Riv.*: Volta; *Lang.*: English, tribal languages; *Curr.*: Cedi

Greece
Cit.: Athens (c.), Volos, Salonika, Piraenus, Patras, Candia, Larissa; *Riv.*: Vardar, Peneus, Achelous, Alpheus; *Lang.*: Greek; *Curr.*: Drachma

Guatemala
Cit.: Guatemala City (c.), Quelzaltenago, Cobán, Zacapa, Puerto Barrios; *Riv.*: Montagua, Usumacinta, Dulce; *Lang.*: Spanish, Indian dialects; *Curr.*: Queztal

Guinea
Cit.: Conakry (c.); *Riv.*: Gambia, Niger, Senegal; *Lang.*: French, tribal languages; *Curr.*: Guinea franc

Guinea-Bissau
Cit.: Bissau (c.); *Riv.*: Geba; *Lang.*: Tribal languages, Portuguese, Cape Verde-Guinea Creole

Guyana
Cit.: Georgetown (c.); *Riv.*: Essequibo, Demerara, Berbice; *Lang.*: English; *Curr.*: Guyana dollar

Haiti
Cit.: Pourt-au-Prince (c.), Cap-Haïtien, Les Cayes; *Riv.*: Artibonite; *Lang.*: French, Creole; *Curr.*: Gourde

Honduras
Cit.: Tegucigalpa (c.);
Riv.: Ulóa; Lang.: Spanish, Indian dialects;
Curr.: Lempira

Hungary
Cit.: Budapest (c.), Cebrecen, Szeged, Miskolc, Diosgyör, Györ, Ozd, Salgotarjan, Pecs, Hodmezövasarhely, Bekescsaba, Szolnok, Kecskemet; Riv.: Danube, Tisza, Leitha, Raab, Sio-Sarviz, Ipel, Sajo, Zagyva, Somes; Lang.: Hungarian; Curr.: Florint

Iceland
Cit.: Reykjavik (c.); Riv.: Jokulsa a Fjollum, Thjorsa, Hvita, Fnjoska; Lang.: Icelandic; Curr.: Króna

India
Cit.: New Delhi (c.), Calcutta, Bombay, Delhi, Madras, Hyderabad, Ahmedabad; Riv.: Ganges, Mahanadi, Godavari, Krishna, Cauvery, Narbada, Tapti, Brahmaputra; Lang.: Hindi, English, Tamil, Sanskrit, Malayalam, Kanarese, Telugu, Bengali, Assamese, Oriya, Marathi, Gujarati, Punjabi, Sindhi, Kashmiri, Urdu; Curr.: Rupee

Indonesia
Cit.: Djarkarta (c.), Surabaya, Bandung; Riv.: Solo, Brantas, Musi, Kapuas; Lang.: Bahasa Indonesia; Curr.: Rupiah

Iran
Cit.: Teheran (c.), Meshed, Tabriz, Isfahan,

Abadan, Shiraz, Hamadan, Bushire, Astara;
Riv.: Karun, Atrek, Safid, Karkhek; Lang.: Persian, Kurdish, Azerbaijani; Curr.: Real

Iraq
Cit.: Baghdad (c.), Mosul, Kirkuk, Basra; Riv.: Tigris, Euphrates, Shatt al Arab; Lang.: Arabic, Kurdish; Curr.: Dinar

Ireland
Cit.: Dublin (c.), Cork, Limerick, Dún Laoghaire, Waterford; Riv.: Shannon, Barrow, Suir, Blackwater; Lang.: English, Gaelic; Curr.: Irish pound

Israel
Cit.: Jerusalem (c.), Haifa, Tel Aviv, Ramat Gan, Beersheba; Riv.: Jordan, Yarkon, Kishon; Lang.: Hebrew, Arabic, English; Curr.: Israeli pound

Italy
Cit.: Rome (c.), Milan, Naples, Turin, Genoa, Palermo, Bologna, Florence, Catania, Venice, Bari, Trieste, Messina, Verona, Padua; Riv.: Po, Adige, Piave, Tagliamento, Tiber, Arno; Lang.: Italian; Curr.: Lira

Ivory Coast
Cit.: Abidjan (c.), Bouaké; Riv.: Bandama, Sassandra, Comoé; Lang.: French, tribal languages; Curr.: CFA franc

Jamaica
Cit.: Kingston (c.); Lang.: English; Curr.: Jamaican pound

Japan
Cit.: Tokyo (c.), Osaka, Nagoya, Yokohama, Kyoto, Kobe; *Riv.:* Ishikari, Shinano, Tone; *Lang.:* Japanese; *Curr.:* Yen

Jordan
Cit.: Amman (c.), Aquaba; *Riv.:* Jordan; *Lang.:* Arabic; *Curr.:* Jordan dinar

Kenya
Cit.: Nairobi (c.), Mombasa, Kilidini; *Riv.:* Tana; *Lang.:* English, Swahili, other tribal languages; *Curr.:* East African shilling

Khmer Republic
Cit.: Phnom Penh (c.), Battambang, Kompong Som; *Riv.:* Mekong; *Lang.:* Khmer, French; *Curr.:* Riel

Korea, North
Cit.: P'yongyang (c.), Wonsan, Ch'ongjin; *Riv.:* Taedong, Yalu; *Lang.:* Korean; *Curr.:* Won

Korea, South
Cit.: Seoul (c.), Taegu, Pusan, Inchon; *Riv.* Han, Naktong; *Lang.:* Korean; *Curr.:* Won

Kuwait
Cit.: Kuwait (c.), Hawalli; *Lang.:* Arabic; *Curr.:* Kuwait dinar

Laos
Cit.: Vientiane (admin. c.), Luang Prabang (royal c.); *Riv.:* Mekong; *Lang.:* Laotian, French; *Curr.:* Kip

Lebanon
Cit.: Beirut (c.), Tripoli, Zahle, Saida, Tyre; *Riv.:* Orontes, Litani; *Lang.:* Arabic, French, English; *Curr.:* Lebanese pound

Lesotho
Cit.: Maseru (c.); *Lang.:* English, Sesotho; *Curr.:* South African rand

Liberia
Cit.: Monrovia (c.); *Riv.:* Cavalla, St. Paul; *Lang.:* English, tribal languages; *Curr.:* Liberian dollar, U.S. dollar

Libya
Cit.: Tripoli (c.), Benghazi, Sebba; *Lang.:* Arabic, Italian; *Curr.:* Libyan pound

Lichtenstein
Cit.: Vaduz (c.); *Riv.:* Rhine; *Lang.:* German; *Curr.:* Swiss franc

Luxembourg
Cit.: Luxembourg (c.); *Riv.:* Moselle; *Lang.:* French, Letzeburgesch, German; *Curr.:* Luxembourg franc

Malawi
Cit.: Zomba (c.), Blantyre-Limbe; *Lang.:* Bantu, English; *Curr.:* Malawi pound

Malaysia
Cit.: Kuala Lumpur (c.), Penang (George Town); *Riv.:* Pahang, Perak; *Lang.:* Malay, English, Chinese, Tamil; *Curr.:* Malaysian dollar

Maldive Islands
Cit.: Male (c.); *Lang.:* Maldivian (Sinhalese), Arabic; *Curr.:* Rupee

Mali
Cit.: Bamako (c.), Kayes, Segou; *Riv.:* Ni-

ger; *Lang.*: French, tribal languages; *Curr.*: Mali franc

Malta
Cit.: Valetta (c.); *Lang.*: Maltese, English; *Curr.*: Maltese pound

Mauritania
Cit.: Nouakchott (c.), Port-Etienne; *Riv.*: Sénégal; *Lang.*: Arabic, tribal languages, French; *Curr.*: CFA franc

Mexico
Cit.: Mexico City (c.), Guadalajara, Monterrey, Puebla, Mérida, Torreón, San Luis Potosí, León, Cuidad Juárez, Veracruz, Tampico, Mexicali; *Riv.*: Rio Grande, Pánuco, Santiago-Lerma, Nazas, Rio de la Balsas, Fuerte, Casas Grandes; *Lang.*: Spanish, Indian dialects; *Curr.*: Peso

Monaco
Cit.: Monaco-Ville (c.); *Lang.*: French; *Curr.*: Monégasque franc

Mongolia
Cit.: Ulan Bator (c.), Darkhan, Choibalsan, Kobdo, Sukhe Bator; *Riv.*: Ongin, Baidarik, Kerulen, Selenge, Orhon, Dzhabhan; *Lang.*: Mongolian, Russian; *Curr.*: Tugrik

Morocco
Cit.: Rabat (c.), Casablanca, Tangier, Fez, Marrakesh, Meknès, Oujda, Tetuan; *Lang.*: Arabic, Berber, French; *Cur.*: Dirham

Mozambique
Cit.: Lourenço, Marques, Beira; *Riv.*: Limpopo, Rovuma, Zambezi, Savi; *Lang.*: Native languages, Portuguese; *Curr.*: Escudo (Portuguese)

Nepal
Cit.: Katmandu (c.); *Riv.*: Kali, Karnali, Gandak, Kosi; *Lang.*: Nepali, Newari, Photia; *Curr.*: Nepalese rupee

Netherlands
Cit.: Amsterdam (legal c.), The Hague (actual c.), Rotterdam, Utrecht, Haarlem, Eindhoven, Groningen, Tilburg; *Riv.*: Rhine, Scheldt, Maas; *Lang.*: Dutch; *Curr.*: Guilder

New Zealand
Cit.: Wellington (c.), Auckland, Christchurch, Dunedin, Hutt; *Riv.*: Waikato, Wanganui, Rangitikei, Manawatu, Clutha, Waitaki; *Lang.*: English; *Curr.*: New Zealand dollar

Nicaragua
Cit.: Managua (c.), León, Granada; *Riv.*: Rio Grande, Escondido, San Juan; *Lang.*: Spanish; *Curr.*: Córdoba

Niger
Cit.: Niamey (c.), Zinder; *Riv.*: Niger; *Lang.*: French, tribal languages; *Curr.*: CFA franc

Nigeria
Cit.: Lagos (c.), Kano, Ibadan, Ogbomosho; *Riv.*: Niger, Benue; *Lang.*: English, tribal languages, Arabic; *Curr.*: Nigerian pound

Norway
Cit.: Oslo (c.), Bergen, Trondheim, Stavanger, Drammen, Kristiansand, Skien, Tromso; Riv.: Glomma; Lang.: Norwegian; Curr.: Krone

Oman
Cit.: Muscat (c.), Matrah; Lang.: Arabic, Indian dialects; Curr.: Persian Gulf rupee

Pakistan
Cit.: Islamabad (c.), Karachi, Lyallpur, Lahore, Hyderabad, Multan, Rawalpindi, Gujranwala, Peshawar; Riv.: Indus, Jhelum, Chenab, Sutlej; Lang.: Urdu, English, Punjabi, Pushtu, Sindhi, Baluchi; Curr.: Pakistani rupee

Panama
Cit.: Panama City (c.), Colón; Riv.: Chagres, Chepo, Tuira; Lang.: Spanish; Curr.: Balboa

Paraguay
Cit.: Asunción (c.), Concepción, Encarnación, Villarrica; Riv.: Paraguay, Alto Paraná, Pilcomayo; Lang.: Spanish, Guaraní; Curr.: Guaraní

Peru
Cit.: Lima (c.), Callao, Arequipa, Cuzco, Iquitos, Chiclayo, Trujillo, Ica, Chimbote, Huancayo; Riv.: Marañón, Huallaga, Ucayali, Apurimac, Urubamba; Lang.: Spanish, Indian dialects; Curr.: Sol

Philippines
Cit.: Quezon City (c.), Cebu, Manila, Iliolo, Davao, Basilan City; Riv.: Agusan, Cagayan; Lang.: Tagalog, English, Spanish, Malayo-Polynesian dialects; Curr.: Peso

Poland
Cit.: Warsaw (c.), Lodz, Cracow, Poznan, Wroclaw, Gdansk, Szczecin, Katowice; Riv.: Vistula, Western Bug, Oder, Narew, San, Warta, Pilica, Drweca; Lang.: Polish; Curr.: Zloty

Portugal
Cit.: Lisbon (c.), Oporto, Setubal, Coimbra; Riv.: Tagus, Douro, Guadiana; Lang.: Portuguese; Curr.: Escudo

Qatar
Cit.: Doha (c.), Dukhan, Umm Sa'id; Lang.: Arabic; Curr.: Riyal

Rhodesia
Cit.: Salisbury (c.), Bulaway; Riv.: Zambesi, Limpopo, Sabi; Lang.: English, Shona, Ndebele, other Bantu dialects; Curr.: Rhodesian dollar

Rumania
Cit.: Bucharest (c.), Cluj, Timisoara, Ploesti, Braila, Constanta; Riv.: Danube, Olt, Jiu, Siret, Prut; Lang.: Rumanian, Hungarian, Turkish, German; Curr.: Leu

Rwanda
Cit.: Kigali (c.); Lang.: French, tribal languages; Curr.: Franc

San Marino
Cit.: San Marino (c.); Lang.: Italian; Curr.: Italian lira

São Tomé and Principe
  Cit.: São Tomé and Santo Antonio; *Lang.*: Portuguese, native languages; *Curr.*: Escudo (Portuguese)

Saudi Arabia
  Cit.: Riyadh (c.), Mecca (c), Jidda, Medina; *Lang.*: Arabic; *Curr.*: Riyal

Senegal
  Cit.: Dakar (c.), Saint-Louis, Kaolack, Thies, Diourbel; *Riv.*: Senegal, Gambia, Saloum, Casamance; *Lang.*: Tribal languages, French; *Curr.*: CFA franc

Sierra Leone
  Cit.: Freetown (c.); *Lang.*: Tribal languages, English; *Curr.*: Leone

Singapore
  Cit.: Singapore (c.); *Lang.*: English, Chinese, Malay, Tamil; *Curr.*: Singapore dollar

Somalia
  Cit.: Mogadishu (c.), Berbera, Hargeisa, Merca, Kismayu; *Riv.*: Juba, Webi Shebeli; *Lang.*: Somali, Italian, Arabic, English; *Curr.*: Somali shilling

South Africa
  Cit.: Pretoria (admin. c.), Cape Town (legis. c.), Bloemfontein (judic. c.), Johannesburg, Durban, Port Elizabeth, Germiston, Benoni, Springs, East London; *Riv.*: Orange, Vaal, Caledon; *Lang.*: English, Afrikaans; *Curr.*: Rand

Spain
  Cit.: Madrid (c.), Barcelona, Valencia, Seville; *Riv.*: Ebro, Douro, Tagus, Guadiana, Guadalquivir; *Lang.*: Spanish, Catalan, Galician, Basque; *Curr.*: Peseta

Sri Lanka
  Cit.: Colombo (c.), Jaffna, Kandy, Galle; *Lang.*: Sinhalese, Tamil, English; *Curr.*: Sri Lanka rupee

Sudan
  Cit.: Khartoum (c.), Port Sudan, Omdurman; *Riv.*: White Nile, Blue Nile, Nile; *Lang.*: Arabic, tribal languages, English; *Curr.*: Sudanese pound

Swaziland
  Cit.: Mbabane (c.), Manzini; *Riv.*: Usutu, Komati; *Lang.*: English, Swazi; *Curr.*: South African rand

Sweden
  Cit.: Stockholm (c.), Goteborg, Malmo, Norrkoping, Halsingborg, Orebro, Uppsala, Vasteras, Boras, Linkoping; *Riv.*: Ljusna, Indal, Angerman, Lule, Torne; *Lang.*: Swedish, Lapp; *Curr.*: Krona

Switzerland
  Cit.: Bern (c.), Zurich, Basel, Geneva, Lausanne, St. Gall, Winterthur, Lucerne; *Riv.*: Rhine, Aar, Rhone, Inn; *Lang.*: German, French, Italian, Romansh; *Curr.*: Swiss franc

Syria
  Cit.: Damascus (c.),

Aleppo, Latakia, Homs, Hama; *Riv.:* Euphrates, Orontes; *Lang.:* Arabic, Kurdish, Armenian, Turkish, Circassian; *Curr.:* Syrian pound

Taiwan (Republic of China)
Cit.: Taipei (c.), Kaohsiung, Tainan, Taichung; *Lang.:* Chinese; *Curr.:* New Taiwan dollar

Tanzania
Cit.: Dar es Salaam (c.), Tanga, Moshi, Kigoma, Lindi; *Riv.:* Pangani, Rufiji, Lukuledi, Ruvuma; *Lang.:* Swahili, English, Bantu, Arabic; *Curr.:* Tanzanian shilling

Thailand
Cit.: Bangkok (c.), Nakhon Ratchasima, Ayutthaya, Chiangmai; *Riv.:* Chao Phraya; *Lang.:* Thai, Chinese; *Curr.:* Baht

Togo
Cit.: Lomé (c.); *Riv.:* Mono; *Lang.:* French, tribal languages; *Curr.:* CFA franc

Tonga (Friendly Islands)
Cit.: Nuku'alofa (c.); *Lang.:* Tonganese; *Curr.:* Tongan pound

Trinidad and Tobago
Cit.: Port of Spain (c.), San Fernando, Scarborough; *Riv.:* Caroni, Ortoire; *Lang.:* English, Indian and Chinese dialects; *Curr.:* Trinidad and Tobago dollar

Tunisia
Cit.: Tunis (c.), Bizerte, Sousse, Sfax, Gabes, Kairouan; *Riv.:* Medjer-

da; *Lang.:* Arabic, French, Italian; *Curr.:* Dinar

Turkey
Cit.: Ankara (c.), Istanbul, Izmir, Adana, Bursa; *Riv.:* Tigris, Euphrates, Kizil Irmak; *Lang.:* Turkish, Kurdish, Arabic; *Curr.:* Turkish lira

Uganda
Cit.: Kampala (c.), Entebbe, Jinja, Mbale; *Riv.:* White Nile; *Lang.:* English, tribal languages; *Curr.:* Uganda shilling

Union of Soviet Socialist Republics
Cit.: Moscow (c.), Leningrad, Kiev, Baku, Tashkent, Gorky, Kharkov, Novosibirsk, Kuibyshev, Sverdlovsk, Donetsk, Tbilisi, Chelyabinsk, Odessa, Dnepropetrovsk; *Riv.:* Volga, Kama, Don, Ural, Dnieper, Dniester, Yenisey, Ob, Lena, Amur, Onega; *Lang.:* Russian, Ukrainian, Belorussian, Uzbek Tatar; *Curr.:* Ruble

United Arab Emirates
Cit.: Abu Dhabi (c.), Dubai, Ajman, Ras al-Khaimah, Sharjah, Umm al-Qaiwan, Fujairah; *Lang.:* Arabic; *Curr.:* UAE dirham

United Kingdom of Great Britain and Northern Ireland
Cit.: London (c.), Birmingham, Leeds, Sheffield, Manchester, Liverpool, Clydebank, Glasgow, Edinburgh, Dun-

dee, Bristol, Belfast, Londonderry, Bangor, Lurgan, Ballymena, Lisburn, Portadown; *Riv.:* Spey, Avon, Dee, Tay, Forth, Tweed, Tyne, Ouse, Trent, Thames, Severn, Clyde; *Lang.:* English, Welsh, Gaelic; *Curr.:* pound

United States of America (see also Chapter 5)
Cit.: Washington D.C. (c.), New York, Chicago, Los Angeles, Detroit, Boston, Pittsburgh, Toledo, Cleveland, Minneapolis, St. Louis, Richmond, Birmingham, New Orleans, Portland, Philadelphia, Baltimore, Houston, San Francisco, Seattle, Milwaukee, Dallas, Atlanta; *Riv.:* St. Lawrence, Mississippi, Missouri, Ohio, Arkansas, Rio Grande, Colorado, Columbia, Snake; *Lang.:* English; *Curr.:* U.S. dollar

Upper Volta
Cit.: Ouagadougou (c.); *Lang.:* French, tribal languages; *Curr.:* CFA franc

Uruguay
Cit.: Montevideo (c.), Salto, Rivera, Mercedes, Paysandú; *Riv.:* Rio de la Plata, Uruguay, Rio Negro; *Lang.:* Spanish; *Curr.:* Peso

Venezuela
Cit.: Caracas (c.), Maracaibo, Barquisimeto, Valencia, Maracay; *Riv.:* Orinoco; *Lang.:* Spanish; *Curr.:* Bolivar

Vietnam
Cit.: Hanoi (c.), Haiphong, Nam Dinh, Thai Nguyen, Saigon, Da Nang, Hue; *Riv.:* Black, Red, Mekong; *Lang.:* Vietnamese, Chinese, French; *Curr.:* Dong

Western Samoa
Cit.: Apia (c.); *Lang.:* Samoan (Polynesian), English; *Curr.:* Tala

Yemen
Cit.: Sanaa (c.), Taiz, Hodeida, Moucha; *Lang.:* Arabic; *Curr.:* Riyal

Yemen, People's Democratic Republic of
Cit.: Madinat al-shaab (c.), Aden; *Lang.:* Arabic; *Curr.:* South Arabian dinar

Yugoslavia
Cit.: Belgrade (c.), Zagreb, Ljubljana, Skopje, Rijeka, Sarajevo, Sibernik, Split, Kardeljevo, Dubrovnik; *Riv.:* Danube, Bojana, Neretva, Morava; *Lang.:* Slovene, Macedonian, Serbo Croatian; *Curr.:* Dinar

Zaire
Cit.: Kinshasa (c.), Mbandaka, Bandundu, Kisangani, Lubumbashi; *Riv.:* Congo, Ubangi; *Lang.:* French, tribal languages and dialects; *Curr.:* Zaire

Zambia
Cit.: Lusaka (c.), Ndola, Kitwe, Luanshya; *Riv.:* Zambesi, Kafue, Luangwa, Luapula; *Lang.:* Bantu, English; *Curr.:* Kwacha

4. THE UNITED STATES

This chapter contains the names of all of the states together with principal cities, rivers, lakes, mountains and islands. State capitals are followed by (c.).

Alabama
Cit.: Montgomery (c.), Birmingham, Mobile; Riv.: Mississippi, Tennessee, Mobile

Alaska
Cit.: Juneau (c.), Anchorage, Fairbanks; Riv.: Yukon

Arizona
Cit.: Phoenix (c.), Tucson; Riv.: Gila, Colorado

Arkansas
Cit.: Little Rock (c.), North Little Rock, Fort Smith; Riv.: Mississippi, Arkansas, Ouachita, Saline, Red

California
Cit.: Sacramento (c.), Los Angeles, San Francisco, San Diego, Oakland, San Jose, Long Beach; Mtns.: Sierra Nevada Range, Coast Range

Colorado
Cit.: Denver (c.), Pueblo, Colorado Springs; Riv.: Colorado, Arkansas, South Platte, Rio Grande; Mtn.: Rocky Mountains, Colorado Plateau

Connecticut
Cit.: Hartford (c.), Bridgeport, New Haven, Waterbury; Riv.: Connecticut, Thames, Naugatuck, Housatonic

Delaware
Cit.: Dover (c.), Wilmington, Newark

District of Columbia
Riv.: Potomac

Florida
Cit.: Tallahassee (c.), Miami, Tampa, Jacksonville, St. Petersburg; Lake: Lake Okeechobee

Georgia
Cit.: Atlanta (c.), Savannah, Columbus, Macon; Riv.: Okefenokee Swamp; Mtn.: Piedmont Plateau

Hawaii
Cit.: Honolulu (c.), Kailua, Hilo; Mtn.: Mauna Kea; Isl.: Niihau, Kauai, Oahu, Molokai, Lanai, Maui, Hawaii

Idaho
Cit.: Boise (c.), Idaho City, Pocatello; Riv.: Columbia, Snake; Mtn.: Rocky Mountains

Illinois
Cit.: Springfield (c.), Chicago, Rockford, Peoria; Riv.: Mississippi, Ohio, Wabash; Lake: Lake Michigan

Indiana
Cit.: Indianapolis (c.), Gary, Fort Wayne, Evansville, South Bend, Hammond; Riv.: Wabash, White, Tippecanoe; Lake: Lake Michi-

gan

Iowa
Cit.: Des Moines (c.), Cedar Rapids, Sioux City, Davenport; *Riv.*: Mississippi, Des Moines, Skunk, Iowa, Cedar, Wapsipinicon, Turkey

Kansas
Cit.: Topeka (c.), Kansas City, Wichita; *Riv.*: Kansas, Smoky Hill, Arkansas

Kentucky
Cit.: Frankfort (c.), Louisville, Lexington, Covington; *Riv.*: Mississippi, Ohio, Big Sandy, Licking, Kentucky, Green

Louisiana
Cit.: Baton Rouge (c.), New Orleans, Shreveport; *Riv.*: Mississippi

Maine
Cit.: Augusta (c.), Portland, Lewiston, Bangor

Maryland
Cit.: Annapolis (c.), Baltimore; *Riv.*: Potomac

Massachusetts
Cit.: Boston (c.), Worcester, Springfield; *Mtn:* Hoosac, Taconic, Berkshire Hills

Michigan
Cit.: Lansing (c.), Detroit, Flint, Grand Rapids; *Lake:* Ontario, Huron, Michigan, Superior

Minnesota
Cit.: St. Paul (c.), Minneapolis, Duluth; *Riv.*: Mississippi; *Lake:* Superior, Itasca

Mississippi
Cit.: Jackson (c.), Meridian, Biloxi; *Riv.*: Mississippi, Yazoo, Big Black,

Pearl

Missouri
Cit.: Jefferson City (c.), St. Louis, Kansas City, Springfield; *Riv.*: Mississippi, Missouri

Montana
Cit.: Helena (c.), Great Falls, Billings, Butte; *Mtn.*: Bitterroot Range, Lewis Range, Cabinet Mountains, Big Belt Mountains

Nebraska
Cit.: Lincoln (c.), Omaha; *Riv.*: Missouri, Platte, Niobrara, Nemaha, Republican

Nevada
Cit.: Carson City (c.), Las Vegas, Reno

New Hampshire
Cit.: Concord (c.), Manchester, Nashua; *Mtn.*: White Mountains, Mt. Washington

New Jersey
Cit.: Trenton (c.), Newark, Jersey City, Paterson, Camden, Elizabeth; *Riv.*: Delaware, Hudson, Raritan, Passaic, Hackensack; *Mtn.*: Kittatinny, New Jersey, Palisades

New Mexico
Cit.: Santa Fe (c.), Albuquerque, Roswell; *Mtn.*: Rocky Mountains

New York
Cit.: Albany (c.), New York, Buffalo, Rochester, Syracuse, Yonkers; *Mtn.*: Catskill Mountains, Appalachian Mountains

North Dakota
Cit.: Bismarck (c.), Far-

go, Grand Forks; *Riv.:*
Missouri

Ohio
Cit.: Columbus (c.),
Cleveland, Cincinnati,
Toledo, Akron, Dayton,
Youngstown, Canton;
Riv.: Ohio, Great Miami,
Scioto, Muskingum;
Lake: Erie

Oklahoma
Cit.: Oklahoma City (c.),
Tulsa; *Riv.:* Arkansas,
Cimarron, North Cana-
dian, Canadian, Red;
Mtn.: Ozark Plateau

Oregon
Cit.: Salem (c.), Port-
land, Eugene; *Riv.:* Co-
lumbia, Snake; *Mtn.:*
Coast Range, Cascade
Range, Mt. Hood

Pennsylvania
Cit.: Harrisburg (c.),
Philadelphia, Pittsburgh,
Erie, Scranton, Allen-
town; *Riv.:* Ohio, Alle-
gheny, Monongahela,
Delaware, Susquehanna;
Mtn.: Appalachians

Rhode Island
Cit.: Providence (c.),
Warwick, Pawtucket

South Carolina
Cit.: Columbia (c.),
Greenville, Charleston;
Mtn.: Blue Ridge

South Dakota
Cit.: Pierre (c.), Sioux
Falls, Rapid City, Aber-
deen; *Riv.:* Missouri,
James, Vermillion, Big
Sioux; *Mtn.:* Black Hills

Tennessee
Cit.: Nashville (c.),
Memphis, Chattanooga,
Knoxville; *Riv.:* Tennes-
see, Mississippi; *Mtn.:*
Appalachian, Cumber-
land Plateau, Highland
Rim

Texas
Cit.: Austin (c.), Hous-
ton, Dallas, San Antonio,
Fort Worth, El Paso,
Corpus Christi; *Riv.:* Ca-
nadian

Utah
Cit.: Salt Lake City (c.),
Ogden; *Mtn.:* Wasatch
Range, Colorado Pla-
teau, Uinta Mountains,
Kings Peak; *Lake:* Great
Salt Lake

Vermont
Cit.: Richmond (c.), Nor-
folk, Virginia Beach,
Portsmouth, Newport
News; *Mtn.:* Appalachi-
ans

Washington
Cit.: Olympia (c.), Seat-
tle, Spokane, Tacoma;
Mtn.: Cascade Range,
Mt. Rainier, Olympic
Mountains

West Virginia
Cit.: Charleston (c.),
Huntington, Wheeling;
Mtn.: Allegheny Plateau

Wisconsin
Cit.: Madison (c.), Mil-
waukee, Racine; *Riv.:*
Wisconsin, Chippewa,
Black, Rock, Fox, Wolf

Wyoming
Cit.: Cheyenne (c.), Cas-
per, Laramie; *Mtn.:*
Rocky Mountains, Gan-
nett Peak

5. FAMOUS PERSONALITIES

ONE-LETTER NAMES

Q (Quiller-Couch, Sir Arthur Thomas)

TWO-LETTER NAMES

Ky, Nguyen Cao

THREE-LETTER NAMES

Arp, Jean (also Hans)
Bok, Edward W.
Boz (Charles Dickens)
Cid, El (in Spanish: El Cid Campeador, "the Lord Champion"; real name Rodrigo Díaz de Vivar)
Dam, Carl Peter Henrik
Day, Clarence Shepard
Dee, John
Eck, Johann Maier von
Fox, George
Fry, Christopher
Gay, John
Jay, John
Key, Francis Scott
Law, Andrew Bonar
Lee, Harper Nelle
Lee, Henry
Lee, Robert Edward
Lee, Tsung-Dao
Leo I-XIII (popes); I-IV, IX, Saint
Leo I-VI (Byzantine [East Roman] Emperors); I (called "Leo the Great"); III (called "Leo the Isaurian"); IV (called "Leo the Khazar"); V (called "Leo the Wise," called "The Philosopher")
Low, Juliette Gordon
Nye, Russell Blaine

Ohm, Georg Simon
Orr, Sir John Boyd
Poe, Edgar Allen
Pym, John
Ray, Man
Sax, Antoine Joseph (called "Adolphe")
Zog I (original name: Ahmed Zogu; king)

FOUR-LETTER NAMES

Abbe, Cleveland
Abel, John Jacob
Adam, Robert
Agar, Herbert S.
Agee, James
Agis IV (king of Sparta)
Amis, Kingsley
Anne
Arne, Thomas Augustine
Asch, Sholem
Bach, Johann Sebastian
Ball, Hugo
Baum, Lyman Frank
Bean, Alan L.
Bede
Bell, Alexander Graham
Benz, Karl
Berg, Alban
Bock, Jerry
Bohr, Niels Henrik David
Boll, Heinrich Theodor
Born, Max
Broz, Joseph
Buck, Paul Herman
Buck, Pearl
Byng, Julian H. G. (Viscount)
Byrd, Richard E.
Cage, John Milton, Jr.
Cato, Marcus Porcius
Clay, Henry
Cody, William Frederick

Cook, James
Cori, Carl Ferdinand
Cori, Gerty Theresa
Cuyp, Albert
Dale, Sir Henry Hallett
Dali, Salvador
Dana, Charles Anderson
Dana, Richard Henry
Davy, Sir Humphrey
Debs, Eugene Victor
Dias, Bartholomeu (also Diaz)
Diem, Ngo-Dinh
Doré, Paul Gustave
Dufy, Raoul
Eddy, Mary Morse (née Baker)
Edel, Joseph Leon
Eden, Sir (Robert) Anthony
Edwy (also Eadwig)
Eric I-VII (kings of Denmark); I (also Erik, also Erick; called "Evergood"); IV (also Eric VI, also Erik, also Erick; called "Ploughpenny"); V (also Erik VII, also Erick; called "Klipping"); VII of Pomerania (also Erik, also Erick)
Feis, Herbert
Fife, Duncan
Fish, Hamilton
Foch, Ferdinand
Ford, Ford Madox
Ford, Gerald Rudolph
Ford, Henry
Gage, Thomas
Gale, Zona
Galt, Sir Alexander Tilloch
Geta, Publius Septimius
Gide, André
Grau, Shirley Ann
Gray, Elisha
Gray, Thomas
Grey, Earl (Albert H. George)

Grey, Zane
Gris, Juan (José Victoriano González)
Hahn, Otto
Hale, Nathan
Hall, Charles Francis
Hall, Granville Stanley
Hals, Frans
Hart, Moss
Hess, Victor Francis
Hess, Walter Rudolf
Hill, Archibald Vivian
Howe, Julia Ward
Howe, Mark Antony DeWolfe
Hugo, Victor Marie
Hull, Cordell
Hume, David
Hunt, William Holman
Husa, Karel
Inge, William M.
Ivan I-IV (grand dukes of Moscow) I (also Ivan Kalita; called "Moneybags"); II (also Ivan Krasny; called "Ivan the Red"); III Vasilievich (also czar of Russia; called "Ivan the Great"); IV Vasilievich (also czar of Russia; called "Ivan the Terrible")
Ives, Charles Edward
Ives, James Merritt
John (John Lackland; king of England)
John II (king of France; also called "John the Good")
John II (John Casimir, also Casimir V; king of Poland)
John III (John Sobieski; king of Poland)
John I-XXIII (popes); I (Saint), II (John Murcurius)
José, Miguel

Jung, Carl Gustav
Kant, Immanuel
Katz, Sir Bernard
Khan, Anver Bey
Kidd, William
King, B. B. (Riley King)
King, Martin Luther, Jr.
King, Riley (B. B. King)
King, William Lyon Mackenzie
Klee, Paul
Knox, John
Koch, Robert
Kuhn, Richard
Lamb, Charles
Lamb, William
Lamb, Willis Eugene, Jr.
Lear, Edward
Levi, Carlo
Levy, Leonard William
Lind, Jenny
Livy (also Titus Livius)
Mann, Horace
Mann, Thomas
Marc, Franz
Mark, Saint (also Marcus; pope)
Marx, Groucho (real name: Julian)
Marx, Karl
Mary I (called "Bloody Mary")
Mary II (queen)
Mary (also Mary Anjou; queen)
Mayo, William James
Mayo, Charles Horace
Mays, David John
Mead, George Herbert
Mead, Margaret
Meir, Golda
Mill, James
Mill, John Stuart
Miró, Joan
More, Sir Anthony
More, Sir Thomas
Moro, Antonio
Mott, Frank Luther

Mott, John Raleigh
Muir, John
Nash, Ogden
Nast, Thomas
Néel, Louis Eugéne Félix
Nero (Nero Claudius Caesar Drusus Germanicus)
Olaf I-II (kings of Denmark); I (called "Hunger")
Olaf I-V (kings of Norway); I (called "Olaf Tryggvesson',); II (called "Saint Olaf," called "Olaf Haraldsson," called "Olaf the Fat")
Orff, Carl
Otho, Marcus Salvius
Otis, James
Otto I-IV (Holy Roman Emperors); I (called "Otto the Great"); III (called "Wonder of the World")
Ovid (full name: Publius Ovidius Naso)
Páez, José Antonio
Paré, Ambroise
Park, Chung Hee
Parr, Catherine
Paul I-VI (popes); I, Saint
Paul I (czar of Russia)
Paul, John
Peel, Sir Robert
Penn, William
Pepo, Cenni di
Peri, Jacopo
Pike, Zebulon Montgomery
Pire, Georges Henri
Pitt, William (called "the Elder Pitt")
Pitt, William (called "the Younger Pitt")
Pius I-XII (popes); I, Saint; V, Saint; X, Saint
Polk, James Knox

Polo, Marco
Pope, Alexander
Post, Emily
Pu Yi, Henry (Chinese emperor reign title: Hsüan T'ung)
Rabi, Isidor
Reed, Walter
Reid, Benjamin Lawrence
Reni, Guido
Rice, Elmer L. (real name: Reizenstein)
Root, Elihu
Ross, Betsy
Ross, Sir James Clark
Ross, Sir John
Ross, Sir Ronald
Rous, Francis Peyton
Ruth, George Herman
Ryle, Martin
Salk, Jonas Edward
Sand, George
Sato, Eisaku
Shaw, George Bernard
Shaw, Robert
Sims, William Sowden
Snow, Sir Charles Percy
Taft, Lorado
Taft, Robert Alphonso
Taft, William Howard
Tamm, Igor Yevgenyvich
Tate, Allen
Tito (real name: Joseph Broz)
Toch, Ernst
Todd, Sir Alexander Robertus
Tojo, Eiki (also Hideki Tojo)
Urey, Harold Clayton
Wald, George
Ward, Robert
Watt, James
Watt, Sir Robert Alexander Watson
Webb, Sidney James
West, Benjamin
West, Mae

West, Nathanael
West, Dame Rebecca
Wolf, Hugo
Wood, Grant
Wood, John
Wood, Leonard
Wouk, Herman
Wren, Sir Christopher
Yang, Chen Ning
Zola, Émile
Zorn, Anders Leonhard

FIVE-LETTER NAMES

Aalto, Alvar Henrick
Abbas (full name: al-'Abbas ibn-'Abd-al-Muttalib)
Abbas I
Abbas II (full name: Abbas Hilme Pasha)
Abbas I (called "Abbas the Great")
Abbey, Edwin Austin
Abbot, Henry Larcom
Adams, Abigail
Adams, Henry Brooks
Adams, James Truslow
Adams, John
Adams, John Quincy
Adams, Samuel
Adler, Alfred
Adler, Felix
Adolf of Nassau (also Adolphus)
Aesop
Agnew, Spiro Theodore
Agnon, Samuel J.
Aiken, Conrad P.
Akins, Zoe
Albee, Edward
Alder, Kurt
Alger, Horatio
Allen, Ethan
Allen, Frederick L.
Arrow, Kenneth Joseph
Asser, Tobias M. C.
Aston, Francis W.

Astor, John Jacob
Auden, Wystan Hugh
Bacon, Francis
Bacon, Roger
Baeda (Bede)
Bajer, Fredrik
Baker, Ray S.
Balch, Emily G.
Balfe, Michael William
Barry, Phillip
Barth, John
Barth, Karl
Basil I-II (Byzantine Emperors); I (called "Basil the Macedonian"), II (called "Bulgaroctonus")
Basov, Nikolai G.
Beard, Charles A.
Behan, Brendan
Bemis, Samuel F.
Benes, Eduard
Benét, Stephen Vincent
Benét, William Rose
Beria, Lavrenti Pavlovich
Bethe, Hans Albrecht
Bevin, Ernest
Beyle, Marie Henri
Bizet, Georges (Alexandre Cesar Léopold Bizet)
Black, Hugo La Fayette
Blair, Eric (George Orwell)
Blake, William
Bloch, Felix
Bloch, Konrad E.
Boone, Daniel
Booth, John Wilkes
Booth, William
Boris III (king of Bulgaria)
Bosch, Hieronymus (also Bos; real name: Hieronymus van Aeken; also van Aken)
Bosch, Karl
Bothe, Walter
Bouts, Dierick (also Dirk, also Thierry)
Bovet, Daniel
Bowen, Elizabeth Dorothea Cole
Boyer, Jean Pierre
Boyle, Robert
Brady, Mathew B.
Bragg, Sir William Henry
Bragg, Sir William Lawrence
Brahe, Tycho
Braun, Karl Ferdinand
Bruer, Marcel Lajos
Brown, Ford Madox
Brown, John
Bruce, David (David II)
Bruce, William Cabell
Bryan, William Jennings
Buley, R. Carlyle
Bunin, Ivan Alekseyevich
Burke, Edmund
Burns, Robert
Byron, George Gordon Noel (called "Lord Byron")
Cabell, James Branch
Cabot, John (Giovanni Caboto)
Caius, Saint (also Gaius)
Camus, Albert
Capek, Karel
Capet, Hugh
Carus, Marcus Aurelius
Cecil, Edgar Algernon Robert
Cecil, Robert
Chain, Sir Ernst Boris
Chanel, Gabrielle (called "Coco")
Chase, Mary Coyle
Chase, Salmon Portland
Clapp, Margaret
Clark, George Rogers
Clive, Robert
Cohan, George Michael
Cohen, Georg Morris (Georg Morris Brandes)
Coles, Robert M.
Colum, Padraic
Conon (pope)
Corot, Jean Baptiste

Camille
Crane, H. Hart
Crane, Stephen
Crick, Francis Harry Compton
Crome, John
Crumb, George
Curie, Marie Sklodowska
Curie, Pierre
Curti, Merle Eugene
Dalén, Nils Gustaf
Daley, Richard J.
Dalin, Olof von
Dance, George
Dante (full name: Dante Alighieri)
David I-II (kings of Scotland); II (also David Bruce)
David, Jacques Louis
Davis, Bette
Davis, David Brion
Davis, Harold Lenoir
Davis, Jefferson
Davis, Owen
Dawes, Charles Gates
Dayan, Moshe
Debye, Peter Joseph Wilhelm
Deere, John
Defoe, Daniel
Degas, Hilaire Germain Edgar
Dewey, George
Dewey, John
Diels, Otto
Doisy, Edward Adelbert
Donne, John
Donus (also Domnus, pope)
Doyle, Sir Arthur Conan
Drake, Sir Francis
Drury, Allen
Dubos, René Jules
Dugan, Alan
Dumas, Alexandre
Dürer, Albrecht
Dylan, Bob (original name:

Robert Zimmerman)
Ebert, Friedrich
Edgar (king)
Edred (king)
Eigen, Manfred
Eliot, George (real name: Mary Ann (also Marian) Evans)
Eliot, T. S. (Thomas Stearns)
Elman, Mischa
Ernst, Max
Essex, Second Earl of (Robert Devereux)
Eudes (also Odo)
Euler, Ulf Svante von
Evans, Mary Ann (George Eliot)
Fëdor I Ivanovich (czar of Russia)
Fëdor III Alekseevich (czar of Russia)
Felix I-III (popes); I (also St. Felix I); II (also III, also St. Felix II, also III); III (also IV, also St. Felix III; also IV)
Fermi, Enrico
Field, Eugene
Fitch, W. Clyde
Frank, Ilya Mikhailovich
Freud, Sigmund
Frick, Henry Clay
Fried, Alfred Hermann
Friml, Charles Rudolf
Frost, Robert Lee
Gable, Clark
Galba, Servius Sulpicius
Galen
Garbo, Greta
Geber (also Jabir; original name: Jabir ibn-Hayyan)
Gerry, Elbridge
Getty, J. Paul
Ghazi I (king of Iraq)
Gibbs, James
Glenn, John Herschel Jr.
Gluck, Alma (real name:

Reba Fiersohn)

Gluck, Christoph Willibald

Gobat, Charles Albert

Gogol, Nikolai Vasilievich

Golgi, Camillo

Gorki, Maxim (real name: Aleksei Maksimovich Peshkov)

Grant, Cary

Grant, Ulysses Simpson

Grass, Gunter Wilhelm

Green, Constance McLaughlin

Green, Paul Eliot

Green, William

Grieg, Edvard Hagerup

Grimm, Jacob Ludwig Karl

Grimm, Wilhelm

Grisi, Charlotta

Grosz, George

Guidi, Tommaso (Masaccio)

Haber, Fritz

Handy, W. C.

Hardy, Thomas

Harte (Francis) Bret

Haydn, Franz Joseph

Hayes, Rutherford B.

Hearn, Lafcadio (in Japanese: Yakumo Koizumi)

Heath, Edward Richard George

Hecht, Anthony

Hegel, Georg Wilhelm Friedrich

Heine, Heinrich

Hench, Philip Showalter

Henry I-VIII (kings of England); I (also Henry Beauclerc); II (also Henry of Anjou); IV (also Henry of Bolingbroke)

Henry I-IV (kings of France); IV (called "Henry of Navarre"; called "Henry the Great")

Henry I-VII (kings of Germany); I (called "Henry the Fowler"); II-VII (and Holy Roman Emperors); III (called "Henry the Black"); VII (called "Henry of Luxemburg")

Henry, O. (real name: William Sydney Porter)

Henry, Patrick

Herod I (called "Herod the Great")

Hertz, Gustav

Hesse, Hermann

Heyse, Paul Johann Ludwig

Hicks, Sir John Richard

Hiner, Cincinnatus (Joaquin Miller)

Hofer, Karl

Hoffa, James

Homer

Homer, Winslow

Hooch, Pieter de (also Hoogh)

Ibsen, Henrik

Jacob, François

James I-II (kings of England): I (also VI of Scotland)

James I-VI (kings of Scotland)

James, Henry

James, Frank

James, Jesse Woodson

James, Marquis

James, William

Jesus (also Jesus Christ, also Jesus of Nazareth)

Johns, Jasper

Jones, Howard Mumford

Jones, James

Jones, John Paul (original name: John Paul)

Joule, James Prescott

Joyce, James

Kafka, Franz
Keats, John
Kelly, Emmett Leo
Kelly, George
Kenny, Elizabeth
Kramm, Joseph
Krebs, Hans Adolf
Krogh, August
Krupp, Alfred
Kubik, Gail
Kumin, Maxine Winokur
Kusch, Polykarp
Lange, Christian Louis
Laval, Pierre
Lazar I (prince)
Leahy, William Daniel
Leech, Margaret Kernochan
Léger, Alexis (Saint-John Perse)
Léger, Fernand
Léger, Jules
Lenin, Vladimir Ilyich (real name: Vladimir Ilyich Ulyanov)
Leone, Giovanni
Lewis, Cecil Day
Lewis, C. S. (full name: Clive Staples Lewis)
Lewis, John Llewellyn
Lewis, Sinclair
Lewis, Wyndham (full name: Percy Wyndham Lewis)
Libby, Willard Frank
Linus, Saint (pope)
Lippi, Filippino
Lippi, Fra Filippo
Liszt, Franz
Locke, John
Loewi, Otto
Logan, Joshua
Lorne, Marquis of (real name: John D. S. Campbell)
Louis I-XVIII (kings of France); I (called "Louis the Pious," and "Louis the Debonnaire"); II (called "the Stammerer"); IV (called "d'Outremer"); V (called "the Sluggard"); VI (called "the Fair"); VII (called "the Young"); VIII (called "the Lion"); IX (also Saint Louis); X (called "the Quarreler"); XII (called "Père du Peuple"); XIV (called "the Great," called "le Roi Soleil"); XV (called "the Well-Beloved"); XVII (called "Louis Charles de France"); XVIII (full name: Louis Xavier Stanislas).
Louis I-IV (kings of Germany); I (called "Louis the Pious," called "Louis the Debonnaire"); II (called "Louis the German"); III (called "Louis the Child"); IV (called "Louis the Bavarian").
Louis I-II (kings of Hungary); I (called "Louis the Great")
Luncan, Marcus Anneus
Luria, Salvador
Lwoff, André Michel
Lyell, Sir Charles
Lynen, Feodor
Mabee, Fred Carleton
Manet, Edouard
Manzu, Giacomo
Marat, Jean Paul
Mayer, Maria Goeppert
Mayer, René
Meade, George Gordon
Milan (full name: Milan Obrenovich)
Milne, A. A. (full name: Alan Alexander Milne)
Milos (full name: Milos

Obrenovich)
Minot, George Richards
Minto, Earl of (real name: Gilbert J. Elliot)
Monck, Charles Stanley
Monet, Claude
Moniz, Antonio Coetano de Abreu Freire Egas
Monod, Jacques L.
Moody, Dwight Lyman
Moody, Douglas Stuart
Moore, Henry
Moore, Marianne Craig
Moore, Stanford
Morse, Samuel Finley Breese
Mosel, Tad
Moses, Anna Mary Robertson (called "Grandma Moses")
Mozee, Phoebe Anne Oakley (Annie Oakley)
Munch, Edvard
Murry, Kathleen Beauchamp (Katherine Mansfield)
Nader, Ralph
Natta, Giulio
Nehru, Jawaharlal
Nepos, Cornelius
Nepos, Julius
Nerva, Marcus Cocceius
Nervi, Pier Luigi
Nixon, Richard Milhous
Nobel, Alfred Bernhard
Nolde, Emil
North, Frederick
Noyes, Alfred
Oates, Joyce Carol
Ochoa, Severo
Odets, Clifford
O'Hara, John Henry
Ojeda, Alonso de
Olson, Charles
Oppen, George
Oscar I-II (kings of Sweden and Norway)
Paine, Thomas

Palma, Jacopo (also Ciacomo)
Parks, Gordon R.
Passy, Frédéric
Paton, Alan Stewart
Patti, Adelina
Pauli, Wolfgang
Peary, Robert Edwin
Philo (also Philo Judaeus, also Philo of Alexandria)
Plato
Poole, Ernest
Pound, Ezra Loomis
Pratt, Edwin John
Pregl, Fritz
Price, Leontyne
Pupin, Michael Idvorsky
Pusey, Edward Bouverie
Pusey, Merlo John
Raman, Sir Chandrasekhara Venkata
Rauch, Christian Daniel
Ravel, Maurice
Riley, James Whitcomb
Rilke, Rainer Maria
Rodin, François Auguste René
Roget, Peter Mark
Romer, Olaus (Olaus Roemer)
Rurik
Sabin, Albert Bruce
Sachs, Hans
Sachs, Nelly
Sadat, Anwar Al-
Scott, David R.
Scott, Robert Falcon
Scott, Sir Walter
Scott, Winfield
Segal, George
Segrè, Emilio Gino
Serra, Junipero (original name: Miguel José Serra)
Smith, Adam
Smith, Alfred Emanuel
Smith, Ian Douglas
Smith, Joseph

Smith, Justin Harvey
Smith, Samuel Francis
Smith, Sydney
Soane, Sir John
Soddy, Frederick
Sousa, John Philip (called "the March King")
Speke, John Hanning
Stark, Johannes
Steen, Jan
Stein, Gertrude
Stein, William Howard
Steno, Nicolaus (in Danish: Niels Stensen)
Stern, Isaac
Stern, Otto
Stoss, Veit
Stowe, Harriet Elizabeth Beecher
Sturt, Charles
Sully, Thomas
Sweyn I-II (kings of Denmark); I (also Svend; called "Sweyn Forkbeard"); II (called "Sweyn Estrithson")
Swift, Jonathan
Synge, John Millington
Synge, Richard Laurence Millington
Tasso, Torquato
Tatti, Jacopo (Jacopo Sansovino)
Tatum, Edward Lawrie
Teale, Edwin Way
Thant, U
Thieu, Nguyen Van
Titov, Gherman Stepanovich
Tutus (Titus Flavius Sabinus Vespasianus)
Tobey, Mark
Tracy, Spencer
Truth, Sojurner
Tunis, Earl of (real name: Harold R. L. G. Alexander)
Twain, Mark (real name:

Samuel Langhorne Clemens)
Tweed, William Marcy (called "Boss Tweed")
Tyler, John
Unger, Irwin
Urban I-VIII (popes); I, Saint
Valla, Lorenzo
Varro, Marcus Terentius
Verdi, Giuseppe
Verne, Jules
Verus, Lucius Aurelius (original name: Lucius Ceionius Commodus)
Vigny, Comte Alfred Victor de
Villa, Francisco (real name: Doroteo Arango; called "Pancho Villa")
Vivar, Rodrigo Diaz de (El Cid)
Volta, Count Alessandro
Watts, Alan Wilson
Watts, George Frederic
Watts, Issac
Waugh, Evelyn Arthur St. John
Wayne, Anthony (called "Mad Anthony")
Weber, Karl Maria Friedrich Ernst von
Weber, Max
Weiss, Ehrich (Harry Houdini)
Wells, H. G. (full name: Herbert George Wells)
Welty, Eudora
White, Edward H., II
White, Hugh Lawson
White, Leonard
White, Stanford
White, Theodore Harold
White, Walter Francis
White, William Allen
White, William Smith
Wilde, Oscar
Wolfe, James

Wolfe, Linnie Marsh
Wolfe, Thomas Clayton
Woolf, Virginia
Wyeth, Andrew Newell
Wylie, Elinor
Wylie, Philip Gordon
Yeats, William Butler
Young, Brigham
Young, John (Baron Lisgar)
Young, Jown W.
Young, Whitney M.
Ysaë, Eugène
Zelle, Gertrud Margarete (Mata Hari)
Zweig, Arnold

SIX-LETTER NAMES

Abbott, George
Abbott, Sir John Joseph Caldwell
Addams, Jane
Adrian I-VI (popes); I (also Hadrian I); III (Saint); IV (real name: Nicholas Breakspear)
Adrian, Edgar
Agatho, Saint (pope)
Aitken, William Maxwell (First Baron Beaverbrook)
Albert, Josef
Albert I-II (kings of Germany); II (also Albert V of Austria)
Albert I (margrave of Brandenburg; called "Albert the Bear")
Albert I (king of Belgium; full name: Albert Leopold Clement Marie Meinrad)
Albert, Arthur William Patrick (Duke of Connaught)
Albert, Prince
Alcott, Louisa May

Aldrin, Edwin E., Jr.
Alexis I Mikhailovich (czar)
Alfred (called "Alfred the Great")
Alfven, Hannes Olof Gosta
Amadeo I (king)
Amedeo, Luigi, Prince of Savoy-Aosta (Duke of the Abruzzi)
Ampère, André Marie
Anders, William A.
André, John
Angell, Sir Norman
Arango, Doroteo (Francisco Villa)
Arcaro, George Edward (Eddie)
Arendt, Hannah
Armour, Phillip Danforth
Arnold, Benedict
Arnold, Matthew
Arnulf
Arouet, Francois Marie (Voltaire)
Artaud, Antonin
Arthur, Chester Allen
Ashley, Lord (Anthony Ashley Cooper)
Ashton, Sir Frederick
Atilla (called "the Hun," called "the Scourge of God")
Attlee, Clement Richard
Austen, Jane
Avitus, Marcus Maecilius
Bacall, Lauren
Baeyer, Adolf von
Baffin, William
Bailey, Frederick Augustus Washington (Frederick Douglass)
Balboa, Vasco Núñez de
Baline, Israel (Irving Berlin)
Baloil, Edward de
Baloil, John de

Balzac, Honore de

Barany, Robert

Barber, Samuel

Barkla, Charles G.

Barnes, Margaret A.

Barnum, P. T. (full name: Phineas Taylor)

Baroja, Pio

Barrie, Sir James Matthew

Barrow, Sir John

Bartók, Bèla

Barton, Clara

Barton, Derek H. R.

Baruch, Bernard Mannes

Baskin, Leonard

Baxter, James Phinney, III

Beadle, George W.

Becket, Thomas à

Békésy, Georg von

Belloc, Hilaire (full name: Joseph Hilary Pierre Belloc)

Bellow, Saul

Benton, Thomas Hart

Bering, Vitus

Berlin, Irving (real name: Israel Baline)

Bhutto, Zulfikar Ali

Bierce, Ambrose Gwinnett

Bishop, Elizabeth

Bodoni, Giambattista

Boleyn, Anne

Bonsal, Stephen

Borden, Sir Robert Laird

Bordet, Jules Jean Baptiste Vincent

Borges, Jorges Juis

Borgia, Cesare

Borgia, Lucrezia

Borman, Frank

Bowell, Sir Mackenzie

Brahms, Johannes

Braine, John

Brandt, Willy

Braque, Georges

Brecht, Bertolt

Bremer, Fredrika

Breton, André

Briand, Aristide

Brontë, Charlotte (pseudonym: Currer Bell)

Brontë, Emily Jane (pseudonym: Ellis Bell)

Brooke, Edward W.

Brooks, Gwendolyn

Brooks, Van Wyck

Bryant, William Cullen

Buchan, John (Baron Tweedsmuir)

Buffon, Comte Georges Louis Leclerc de

Bunche, Ralph Johnson

Bunyan, John

Burger, Warren Earl

Burnet, Sir F. Macfarlane

Burton, Richard

Burton, Sir Richard Francis

Butler, Nicholas Murray

Butler, Reg (full name: Reginald Cotterall Butler)

Cadman, Charles Wakefield

Caesar, Gaius (Caligula)

Caesar, Gaius Julius

Calder, Alexander

Callot, Jacques

Calvin, John (original name: Jean Chauvin, also Caulvin)

Calvin, Melvin

Canute

Capone, Alphonse (called "Scarface Al")

Capote, Truman

Carman, William Bliss

Carpio, Lope Felix de Vega (Lope de Vega)

Carrel, Alexis

Carter, Elliott Cook, Jr.

Caruso, Enrico (original name: Errico)

Carver, George Washington

Casals, Pablo

Cassin, René
Castro, Fidel
Cather, Willa Sibert
Catlin, George
Catton, Bruce
Cavell, Edith Louisa
Cavour, Conte Camillo Benso di
Céline, Louis-Ferdinand (real name: Louis Fuch Destouches)
Cernan, Eugene A.
Chávez, Carlos
Chávez, Cezar
Chopin, Frederic François
Cletus, Saint (Saint Anacletus)
Conrad I-IV (kings of Germany)
Conrad, Charles Jr.
Conrad, Joseph (original name: Teodor Jozef Konrad Korzeniowski)
Cooper, Anthony Ashley
Cooper, Gary
Cooper, James Fenimore
Cooper, Leon N.
Cooper, Leroy Gordon, Jr.
Copley, John Singleton
Cortés, Hernando
Coward, Noel
Cremer, Sir William Randal
Cronyn, Hume
Crouse, Russel
Cunard, Sir Samuel
Curtis, Charles
Custer, George Armstrong
Dallas, George Mifflin
Dalton, John
Darius (kings of Persia); I (called "Darius the Great"); II (called "Darius the Bastard"); III (called "Darius Codomannus")
Darrow, Clarence Seward
Darwin, Charles Robert

Decius (Gaius Messius Quintus Trajanus Decius)
Dekker, Thomas
Delany, Martin R.
Derain, André
De Sade, Comte Donatien Alphonse François (called "Marquis de Sade")
De Soto, Hernando
de Vega, Lope (full name: Lope Felix de Vega Carpio; called "El Fenix de Espana")
De Voto, Bernard Augustine
Dickey, James
Diesel, Rudolf
Dillon, George
Disney, Walter E.
Donald, David
Dubcek, Alexander
Du Bois, William Edward Burghardt
Du Gard, Roger Martin
Dulles, John Foster
Dunant, Jean Henri
Duncan I (king of Scotland)
Duncan, Isadora
Du Pont, Eleuthère Irénée
Durant, Ariel
Durant, William James
Dvorak, Anton
Eadwig (also Edwy)
Eakins, Thomas
Eccles, Sir John Carey
Edison, Thomas Alva
Edmund, (also Eadmund I; called the "Deed-doer" or the "Magnificent")
Edmund II (called "Edmund Ironside")
Edward (also Eadward; called "Edward the Martyr")
Edward (also Eadward;

called "Edward the Confessor")

Edward I-VIII (kings of England)

Egbert, (also Ecgberht, king)

Eiffel, Alexandre Gustave

Eisele, Donn Fulton

Elliot, Gilbert J. (Earl of Minto)

Elliot, Maud

Enders, John Franklin

Engels, Friedrich

Erhard, Ludwig

Eucken, Rudolf Christoph

Euclid

Eugene (also Eugenius, popes); I, Saint

Fabian (also St. Fabian, pope)

Faisal I (also Feisal, also Feisul; king)

Faisal II

Faisil, Ibn al Saud

Farouk I (king)

Fawkes, Guy

Ferber, Edna

Fichte, Johann Gottlieb

Fields, W. C. (full name: William Claude Fields)

Finsen, Niels R.

Fisher, Vardis Alvero

Flavin, Martin

Flores, Juan José

Florey, Sir Howard W.

Fokine, Michel

Fokker, Anton Herman Gerard

Forbes, Esther

Foster, Stephen Collins

France, Anatole (real name: Jacques Anatole Thibault)

Franck, César Auguste

Franck, James

Franco, Francisco (full name: Francisco Paulino Hermengildo Teódulo Franco-Bahamonde)

Frings, Ketti

Frisch, Ragnar

Fuller, Richard Buckminster

Fulton, Robert

Furphy, Joseph (Tom Collins)

Gallus, Caius Vibius Trebonianus

Da Gama, Vasco

Gandhi, Shrimati Indira

Gandhi, Mohandas Karamchand (called "Mahatma Gandhi")

Garner, John Nance

Garvey, Marcus

Gasser, Herbert S.

Gehrig, Henry Louis (called "Lou Gehrig," called "The Iron Horse")

Geijer, Erik Gustaf

George I-VI (kings of England)

George, Albert H. (Earl Grey)

George, Henry

Gibbon, Edward

Gibson, Charles Dana

Gilroy, Frank Daniel

Gipson, Lawrence Henry

Glaser, Donald A.

Goethe, Johann Wolfgang von

Gordon, Charles George

Gordon, George Hamilton

Gordon, John C. (Earl of Aberdeen)

Gordon, Richard F.

Gorton, John G.

Goujon, Jean

Gounod, Charles François

Graham, Billy (full name: William Franklin Graham)

Graham, Ernest Robert

Graham, Martha

Granit, Ragnar A.

Graves, Robert Ranke
Greene, Graham
Greene, Nathanael
Haakon I (called "Haakon the Good"); IV (full name: Haakon Haakonsson; called "Haakon the Old"); VII (kings of Norway)
Halévy, Jacques François Fromental Elie
Halley, Edmund
Halsey, William Frederick
Hamlin, Talbot Faulkner
Hamsun, Knut
Handel, George Frederick
Hansen, Marcus Lee
Hanson, Howard Harold
Harden, Sir Arthur
Harlan, John Marshall
Harold I-II kings of England; I (called "Harold Harefoot")
Harold I (called "Harold the Fairhaired," called "Harald Haarfagre"); III (called "Harold the Stern," called "Harald Haardraade"); (kings of Norway)
Harris, Joel Chandler
Harvey, William
Hassel, Odd
Hearst, William Randolph
Heller, Joseph
Hersey, John R.
Herzog, Emile Salomon Wilhelm (André Maurois)
Hesiod
Hevesy, Georg von
Hewish, Antony
Hickok, James Butler (called "Wild Bill")
Hideki (Eiki Tojo)
Hilary, Saint (also Hilarius)
Hitler, Adolph

Hobbes, Thomas
Hobson, John Atkinson
Holley, Robert W.
Holmes, Oliver Wendell
Hoover, John Edgar (also J. Edgar Hoover)
Horace
Horgan, Paul
Howard, Catherine
Howard, Sidney Coe
Hudson, Henry
Hughes, Charles Evans
Hughes, Hatcher
Hughes, (James) Langston
Huxley, Aldous Leonard
Huxley, Andrew Fielding
Huxley, Julian
Huxley, Thomas Henry
Ieyasu (also Iyeyasu; full name: Ieyasu Tokugawa)
Ingres, Jean Auguste Dominique
Inness, George
Irving, Washington
Jansen, Cornelis
Jenner, Edward
Jensen, Hans Daniel
Jensen, Johannes Vilhelm
Joffre, Joseph Jacques Césaire
Jonson, Ben (full name: Benjamin Jonson)
Joseph I-II (Holy Roman Emperors)
Joseph, Ferdinand Maximilian (Maximilian)
Jovian (Flavius Claudius Jovianus)
Juárez, Benito
Julian (Flavius Claudius Julianus) (called "Julian the Apostate")
Julius I-III (popes); I, Saint
Jung, Carl Gustav
Kaiser, Henry John
Kantor, MacKinlay
Kaplan, Justin
Karrer, Paul

Keller, Gottfried
Keller, Helen Adams
Kelvin, First Baron William Thomson
Kennan, George Frost
Kepler, Johannes
Keynes, John Maynard
Kilmer, Alfred Joyce
Kinsky, Countess (Bertha von Suttner)
Kocher, Emile Theodor
Kodály, Zoltán
Kossel, Albrecht
Kramár, Karel
Kremer, Gerhard (Gerardus Mercator)
Krylov, Ivan Andreyevich
Kunitz, Stanley Jasspon
Landau, Lev Davidovich
Landor, Walter Savage
Landus (also Lando, pope)
Lanier, Sidney
Lao-tze (also Lao-tse, also Lao-tzu)
Larkin, Oliver Waterman
LeLoir, Luis Federico
Lenard, Philipp Eduard Anton
Lennon, John Winston
Leonov, Alexei Arkhipovich
Lister, Joseph
Little, Malcolm (Malcolm X)
London, Jack
Lovell, James A., Jr.
Lowell, Amy
Lowell, James Russell
Lowell, Robert
Lucian
Lucius I-III (popes) I, Saint
Ludwig, Emil
Luther, Martin
Maddox, Lester G.
Mahler, Gustav
Mailer, Norman
Malory, Sir Thomas

Marcos, Ferdinand Edralin
Marion, Francis (called "the Swamp Fox")
Martin I-V (popes) I (Saint)
Martin, Archer John Porter
Massey, Vincent
Massys, Quentin (also Matsys, also Messys, also Metsys)
Mather, Cotton
Medici, Cosimo de'
Medici, Giovanni de'
Medici, Lorenzo de'
Medill, Joseph
Mellon, Andrew William
Mendel, Gregor Johann
Merton, Robert K.
Millay, Edna St. Vincent
Miller, Arthur
Miller, Caroline
Miller, Heine (Joaquin Miller)
Miller, Henry
Miller, Joaquin (pseudonym: Cincinnatus Hiner, also Heine Miller)
Miller, Perry
Millet, Jean François
Milton, John
Moberg, Carl Artur Vilhelm
Mobutu, Sese Seko
Molnár, Ferenc
Moneta, Ernesto Teodoro
Monroe, James
Monroe, Marilyn (real name: Norma Jean Mortensen)
Morgan, John Pierpoint
Morgan, Thomas Hunt
Moroni, Giambattista
Morris, Robert
Morris, William
Mozart, Wolfgang Amadeus
Muller, Hermann Joseph
Müller, Paul Herman (also Mueller)

Murphy, William Parry
Murrow, Edward Roscoe
Musset, Alfred de (full name: Louis Charles Alfred de Musset)
Myrdal, Gunnar
Nansen, Fridtjof
Napier, John (also Neper)
Nasser, Gamal Abdel
Nation, Carry Amelia
Necker, Jacques
Nelson, Horatio
Nernst, Walther
Neruda, Pablo
Nevins, Allan
Newman, Charles
Newman, John Henry
Newton, Sir Isaac
Nonnus
Norris, Frank (full name: Benjamin Franklin Norris)
Oakley, Annie (real name: Phoebe Anne Oakley Mozee)
O'Casey, Sean
Ockham, William of (also Occam; called "Doctor Invincibilis," called "Venerabilis Inceptor")
Olbers, Heinrich Wilhelm Matthäus
O'Neill, Eugene
Orosco, José Clemente
Orsini, Felice
Orwell, George (real name: Eric Blair)
Ostade, Adraen van
Palade, George E.
Palmer, Daniel David
Pascal, Blaise
Patton, George Smith
Pavlov, Ivan Petrovich
Paxon, Frederic Logan
Pelayo, Francisco de Asís Fernando Pío Juan María Gregorio (Alfonso XII, king of Spain)

Perrin, Jean Baptiste
Perutz, Max Ferdinand
Pétain, Henri Philippe
Pétion, Alexandre Sabès
Philip (called "Philip the Arabian": full name: Marcus Julius Phillipus; Roman emperor)
Philip II (king of Macedon)
Philip I-VI (kings of France); II (also Philip Augustus; III (called "Philip the Bold"); IV (called "Philip the Fair"); V (called "Philip the Tall")
Philip I-V (kings of Spain)
Pierce, Franklin
Pindar
Pinter, Harold
Pisano, Andrea
Pisano, Antonio (Pisanello)
Pisano, Giovanni
Pisano, Nicola
Piston, Walter
Planck, Max Karl Ernst Ludwig
Porter, George
Porter, Katherine Anne
Porter, Quincy
Porter, Rodney Robert
Porter, William Sydney (O. Henry)
Potter, Beatrix
Potter, Edward Clark
Powell, Anthony
Powell, Cecil Frank
Powell, John Wesley
Powell, Lewis Franklin, Jr.
Powell, Sumner Chilton
Powers, Hiram
Probus, Marcus Aurelius
Proust, Marcel
Pyrrho
Quidde, Ludwig
Racine, Jean Baptiste
Rahman, Mujibur
Rameau, Jean Philippe

Ramsay, Sir William
Ramses I-III (kings of Egypt)
Ransom, John Crowe
Renoir, Pierre Auguste
Revere, Paul
Rhodes, Cecil John
Ribera, Jusepe (also José Giuseppe)
Richet, Charles Robert
Rivera, Diego
Rivera, José Fructuoso
Robert I-II (kings of France); II (called "Robert the Pious")
Robert I-III (kings of Scotland); I (also Robert the Bruce); III (original name: John Stuart, earl of Carrick)
Roemer, Olaus (also Ole)
Rogers, Randolph
Rogers, Robert
Rogers, Will (full name: William Penn Adair Rogers)
Rommel, Erwin (called "the Desert Fox")
Romney, George
Rothko, Mark
Rubens, Peter Paul
Rudolf (also Raoul)
Rudolf I-II (kings)
Rudolf, Karl August (Charles Proteus Steinmenz)
Rupert
Ruskin, John
St. John, Henry (Viscount Bolingbroke)
Sanger, Frederick
Sanger, Margaret
Sappho
Sartre, Jean-Paul
Schurz, Carl
Scopas
Scopes, John Thomas
Scribe, Augustin Eugéne

Seeger, Pete
Seneca, Lucius Annaeus
Seurat, Georges
Seward, William Henry
Sexton, Anne Harvey
Sforza, Count Carlo
Sforza, Giacomuzzo (also Muzio Attendolo)
Sforza, Lodovico (also Ludovico; called "Il Moro")
Shalom (Solomon Rabinowitz)
Saara, Michael
Shonin, Georgi S.
Sidney, Sir Philip
Sisley, Alfred
Sixtus I-V (popes) I, Saint; II, Saint; III, Saint.
Snyder, Gary
Sperry, Elmer Ambrose
Speyer, Leonora
Stalin, Joseph Vissarionovich (real name: Dzugashvili)
Steele, Sir Richard
Steele, Wilbur Daniel
Sterne, Laurence
Strutt, John William
Stuart, Charles Edward Louis Philip Casimir (called "Bonnie Prince Charlie")
Stuart, Gilbert Charles
Stuart, James Ewell Brown (called "Jeb")
Stuart, James Francis Edward (called "the Old Pretender")
Stuart, John
Styron, William
Sumner, Charles
Sumner, James Batcheller
Sutter, John Augustus
Tagore, Sir Rabindranath
Tanaka, Kakuei
Tandem, Carl Felix (Carl Freidrich Spitteler)

Taylor, Robert Lewis
Taylor, Zachary
Tegner, Esaias
Téllez, Gabriel (Tirso de Molina)'
Temple, Henry John (Third Viscount of Palmerston)
Thales
Thiers, Louis Adolphe
Thomas, Ambroise
Thomas, Dylan Marlais
Thomas, Norman Mattoon
Titian (real name: Tiziano Vecellio)
Toledo, Francisco de
Townes, Charles Hard
Trajan, (Marcus Ulpius Trajanus)
Truman, Harry S.
Tubman, Harriet
Tubman, William Vacanarat Shadrach
Tupper, Sir Charles
Turner, Frederick Jackson
Turner, Joseph Mallord William
Turner, Nat
Tz'u Hsi
Undset, Sigrid
Updike, John Hoyer
Valens
Vanier, Georges P.
Vasari, Giorgio
Vasili I-III grand dukes of Moscow; I (also Basil I Dmitrievich) II (also Basil; called "Temny the Blind"); III, Ivanovich (also Basil)
Vasili, Shuiski (also Basil)
Veblen, Thorstein Bunde
Vergil (also Virgil)
Victor I-III (popes); I (Saint)
Villon, François
Villon, Jacques (real name: Gaston Duchamp)

Volkov, Vladislav N.
Wagner, Richard (full name: Wilhelm Richard Wagner)
Walter, Bruno (real name: Bruno Walter Schlesinger)
Walton, Ernest Thomas Sinton
Walton, Izaak
Walton, Sir William Turner
Warhol, Andy
Warren, Charles
Warren, Earl
Warren, Robert Penn
Waters, Ethel
Watson, James Dewey
Weaver, Robert C.
Weller, Thomas Huckle
Welles, Orson
Welles, Sumner
Werfel, Franz
Werner, Alfred
Wesley, John
Weyden, Rogier van der
Wiener, Norbert
Wigner, Eugene Paul
Wilder, Thornton Niven
Wilson, Allen Benjamin
Wilson, Angus
Wilson, Charles Thomas Rees
Wilson, Colin Henry
Wilson, Edmund
Wilson, Forrest
Wilson, Henry (original name: Jeremiah James Colbath)
Wilson, Harold (full name: James Harold Wilson)
Wilson, Margaret
Wilson, Richard
Wilson, Thomas Woodrow
Wister, Owen
Wolsey, Thomas
Wright, Frank Lloyd
Wright, James
Wright, Orville

Wright, Richard
Wright, Wilbur
Xavier, Saint Francis
Xerxes Iyukawa, Hideki
Zeeman, Pieter
Zhukov, Georgi Konstantinovich

SEVEN-LETTER NAMES

Abbadie, Antoine Thomson d'
Abbadie, Arnaud Michel d'
á Becket, Saint Thomas
Abruzzi, Duke of the (Prince Luigi Amedeo of Savoy-Aosta)
Acheson, Dean Gooderham
Addison, Joseph
Agassiz, Louis (full name: Jean Louis Rodolphe Aggasiz)
Agrippa, Marcus Vipsanius
á Kempis, Thomas
Alarcón, Hernando de
Alarcón, Pedro Antonio de
Alberti, Leon Battista
Aldrich, Nelson W.
Aldrich, Thomas B.
Alfieri, Vittorio
Alfonso XII (full name: Francisco de Asís Fernando Pío Juan María Gregorio Pelayo)
Alfonso XIII (full name: León Fernando María Isidro Pascual Antonio)
Alinsky, Saul
Amagro, Diego De
Altgeld, John Peter
Alvarez, Luis W.
Amherst, Jeffrey
Adreev, Leonid Nikolaevich (also Adreyev)
Andrews, Charles McLean
Andrews, Roy Chapman

Anterus, Saint (also Anteros)
Anthony, Susan Brownell
Antonio, Leónj Fernando María Isidro Pascual (Alfonso XIII)
Aquinas, Saint Thomas
Ariosto, Lodovico
Artigas, José Gervasio
Asquith, Herbert Henry
Attucks, Crispus
Aubigne, Théodore Agrippa d'
Audubon, John James
Axelrod, Julius
Bakunin, Mikhail Aleksandrovich
Baldwin, James
Baldwin, Robert
Baldwin, Stanley
Balfour, Arthur James
Banting, Sir Frederick G.
Bardeen, John
Barkley, Alben William
Barlach, Ernst
Basedow, Johann Bernhard
Bassett, Leslie R.
Batista, Zaldivar (called "Fulgencio")
Beckett, Samuel B.
Beecham, Sir Thomas
Beecher, Henry Ward
Behring, Emil A. von
Behrman, Samuel N.
Bellini, Gentile
Bellini, Giovanni
Bellini, Jacopo
Bellini, Vincenzo
Bellows, George Wesley
Bennett, Arnold (full name: Enoch Arnold Bennett)
Bennett, James Gordon
Bennett, First Viscount (real name: Richard Bedford Bennett)
Bentham, Jeremy

Bergman, Ingrid
Bergson, Henri L.
Berlioz, Louis Hector
Bernard, Rosine (Sara Bernhardt)
Bernini, Giovanni Lorenzo
Bidault, Georges
Bigordi, Domenico di Tommaso (Ghirlandajo)
Bolivar, Simon (called "the Liberator")
Bonheur, Rosa (full name: Marie Rosalie)
Bonnard, Pierre
Borlaug, Norman Ernest
Borodin, Aleksandr Profirevich
Boswell, James (called "Bozzy")
Boyd-Orr, John
Brandes, George Morris (original surname: Cohen)
Bridges, Robert Seymour
Britten, Edward Benjamin
Broglie, Prince Louis-Victor de
Buchner, Eduard
Buffalo Bill (real name: William Frederick Cody)
Buisson, Ferdinand Edward
Burrows, Abe
Calhoun, John Caldwell
Calvert, George
Candela, O. Félix
Canning, George
Carinus, Marcus Aurelius
Carlyle, Thomas (called "Sage of Chelsea")
Carroll, Lewis (real name: Charles Lutwidge Dodgson)
Cartier, Jacques
Casimir III (king of Poland; called "Casimir the Great")
Cellini, Benevenuto

Cernuda, Luis
Cézanne, Paul
Chaffee, Roger B.
Chagall, Marc
Chapman, George
Chapman, John
Chardin, Jean Baptiste Siméon
Charles I-II (kings of England)
Charles (prince of Wales)
Charles I-X (kings of France); III (called "Charles the Simple"); IV (called "Charles the Fair"); V (called "Charles the Wise"); VI (called "Charles the Well-Beloved"); VII (called "Charles the Victorious")
Charles I-VIII (Holy Roman Emperors); I (Charlemagne); II (called "Charles the Bald"); III (called "Charles the Fair"); IV (called "Charles of Luxemburg").
Charles I-IV (kings of Hungary)
Charles I-IV (kings of Spain)
Charles I-XV (kings of Sweden); X (also Charles Gustavus); XII (called "Alexander of the North"); XIV John (original name: Jean Baptiste Jules Bernadotte).
Charles Albert
Charlot, Jean
Chaucer, Geoffrey
Chauvin, Jean (John Calvin)
Chekhov, Anton Pavlovich (also Chekov; also

Tchekhov)
Chirico, Giorgio de
Cimbue, Giovanni (original name: Cenni di Pepo)
Claudel, Paul Louis Charles
Cleaver, Eldridge
Clemens, Samuel Langhorne (Mark Twain)
Clement I-XIV (popes); I, Saint
Clinton, DeWitt
Clinton, George
Cocteau, Jean
Colette (real name: Sidonie Gabrielle Claudine Colette)
Collins, Michael
Compton, Arthur Holly
Copland, Aaron
Courbet, Gustave
Cozzens, James Gould
Cranach, Lucas (also Kranach, also Kronach)
Cranmer, Thomas
Creeley, Robert White
Currier, Nathaniel
Cushing, Harvey
Damasus I-II (popes); I, Saint
Daumier, Honoré
da Vinci, Leonardo
Debussy, Claude Achille
Decatur, Stephen
de Kruif, Paul
de Siloe, Diego
Delibes, Leo
De Mille, Agnes
Dennett, Tyler
de Rojas, Ferdinand
Dickens, Charles
Diderot, Denis
di Paoli, Pasquale
Dodgson, Charles Lutwidge (Lewis Carroll)
Doenitz, Karl
Douglas, Sir John Sholto

Douglas, Stephen Arnold
Dreiser, Theodore
Dreyfus, Alfred
Du Barry, Comptesse Marie Jeanne Bécu
Duchamp, Gaston (Jacques Villon)
Duchamp, Marcel
Durrell, Lawrence
Earhart, Amelia
Eastman, George
Edelman, Gerald Maurice
Ehrlich, Paul
Eijkman, Christiaan
El Greco (real name: Domingo Teotocopuli)
Emerson, Ralph Waldo
Epstein, Sir Jacob
Erasmus, Desiderius
Ericson, Leif (also Ericsson)
Faraday, Michael
Farnese, Alessandro
Farnese, Pierluigi
Farrell, James T.
Fechner, Gustav Theodor
Feynman, Richard P.
Fibiger, Johannes A. G.
Fischer, Emil H.
Fischer, Hans
Fitsroy, Augustus Henry
Flaxman, John
Fleming, Sir Alexander
Florian (Marcus Annius Florianus)
Fonteyn, Dame Margot (original name: Margoret Hookham)
Forster, Edward Morgan
Francis I-II (kings of France)
Francis I-II (Holy Roman Emperors)
Francis Joseph (also Franz Joseph)
Freeman, Douglas Southall
Fremont, John Charles
Freneau, Philip Morin

Froding, Gustaf
Gadsden, James
Galileo (full name: Galileo Galilei)
Galvani, Luigi (also Aloisio)
Gardner, Erle Stanley
Garland, Hamlin
Garrick, David
Gatling, Richard Jordan
Gauguin, (Eugene Henri) Paul
Gellius, Aulus
Giaque, William F.
Gielgud, Sir John
Gilbert, Sir William Schwenck
Glasgow, Ellen Anderson Gholson
Gleizes, Albert Léon
Godunov, Boris
Goering, Hermann Wilhelm (also Göring)
Golding, William Gerald
Gompers, Samuel
Gordian I-III (Roman emperors); I, Marcus Antonius; III, Marcus Antonius; (called "Gordianus Pius")
Greeley, Horace
Gregory I-XVI (popes); I, Saint (called "Gregory the Great"); II, Saint; III Saint
Grissom, Virgil I.
Gromyko, Andrei Andreyevich
Gropius, Walter
Grotius, Hugo
Guevara, Ernesto "Che"
Gunther, John
Guthrie, Alfred Bertram, Jr.
Hackett, Albert
Hadrian, (Publius Aelius Hadrianus)
Halleck, Henry Wagner

Hammett, Dashiell
Hammond, Bray
Hancock, John
Handlin, Oscar
Harding, Warren Gamaliel
Harnick, Sheldon Mayer
Hawkins, Sir John (also Hawkyns)
Haywood, William Dudley
Hazlitt, William
Heifetz, Jascha
Hellman, Lillian
Herbart, Johann Friedrich
Herbert, Victor
Herrick, Robert
Hershey, Alfred D.
Heymans, Corneille J. F.
Heyward, DuBose
Hillyer, Robert Silliman
Himmler, Heinrich
Hobbema, Meindert
Hodgkin, Alan Lloyd
Hodgkin, Dorothy Crowfoot
Hogarth, William
Hokusai, Katsushika
Holbein, Hans
Hopkins, Sir Frederick Gowland
Houdini, Harry (real name: Ehrich Weiss)
Housman, Alfred Edward
Houston, Sam
Howells, William Dean
Hueffer, Ford Madox (Ford Madox Ford)
Huggins, Charles B.
Humbert I-II, kings of Italy (in Italian: Umberto); I (called "Humbert the Good"); II (also Count di Sarre)
Hussein I (king of Jordan)
Hyginus, Saint
Ionesco, Eugène
Jackson, Andrew
Jackson, Thomas Jonathan
Jacobsz, Lucas (Lucas van

Leyden)
Jarrell, Randall
Jeffers, Robinson
Jiménez, Juan Ramón
Joffrey, Robert (Anver Bey Khan)
Johnson, Andrew
Johnson, Eyvind
Johnson, Josephine Winslow
Johnson, Lyndon Baines
Johnson, Samuel (called "Dr. Johnson" or the "Great Cham of Literature")
Jolliet, Louis (also Joliet)
Jouhaux, Léon
Juvenal (Decimus Junius Juvenalis)
Kastler, Alfred
Kaufman, George Simon
Kaunitz, Count Wenzel Anton von (from 1764, Prince von Kaunitz-Rietberg)
Kellogg, Frank Billings
Kendall, Edward Calvin
Kendrew, John Cowdery
Kennedy, John Fitzgerald
Kennedy, Robert Francis
Kenneth I (king of Scotland; called "MacAlpine")
Kerouac, Jack (full name: Jean-Louis Kerouac)
Khorana, Hargobind
Krumov, Yevgeny V.
Kipling, Joseph Rudyard
Komarov, Vladimir M.
Kossuth, Louis (in Hungarian: Lajos Kossuth)
Kosygin, Alexi Nikolayevich
Kubasov, Valery
Kubelik, Jan
Kuznets, Simon Smith
La Farge, Oliver Hazard Perry

Laffite, Jean (also Lafitte)
Lamarck, Jean Baptiste Pierre Antoine de Monet, Chevalier de
Laplace, Pierre Simon, Marquis de
Lardner, Ring (full name: Ringgold Wilmer Lardner)
LaSalle, Robert Cavelier, Sieur de
Laurier, Sir Wilfred
Laveran, Charles Louis Alphonse
Laxness, Halldor Kiljan
Leacock, Stephen Butler
Leopold I-III (kings of Belgium)
Leopold I-II (Holy Roman Emperors)
Lesseps, Ferdinand Marie, Vicomte de
Lincoln, Abraham
Lindsay, Howard
Lindsay, Vachel
Lipmann, Fritz Albert
Lippman, Gabriel
Lorentz, Hendrik Antoon
Lorrain, Claude
Lothair I-III (kings of Germany)
Lumumba, Patrice E.
Luthuli, Albert John
Macbeth
MacKaye, Percy
Macleod, John James Richard
McMahon, William
Madison, James
Malamud, Bernard
Malcolm III of Scotland (also Malcolm Canmore)
Malcolm IV of Scotland (called "Malcolm the Maiden")
Malcolm X (original name: Malcolm Little)
Malraux, André (full

name: Georges André Malraux)

Mansart, François (also Mansard; full name: Nicholas François Mansart)

Manzoni, Alessandro Francesco Tommaso Antonio

Marconi, Marchese Guglielmo

Marinus I-III (popes) I (also Martin II); II (also Martin III)

Marison (full name: Marison Escubar)

Markham, Edwin (full name: Charles Edwin Markham)

Marlowe, Christopher

Martial, Marcus Valerius

Martini, Simone

Marvell, Andrew

Masaryk, Jan Garrigue

Masaryk, Tomás Garrigue

Massine, Léonide

Masters, Edgar Lee

Matisse, Henri

Maugham, William Somerset

Mauldin, William

Mauriac, François

Maurois, André (real name: Émile Salomon Wilhelm Herzog)

Maximus (Magnus Clemens Maximus)

Maxwell, James Clerk

Medawar, Sir Peter Brian

Meighen, Arthur

Meinrad, Albert Leopold Clement Marie (Albert I)

Memling, Hans (also Memlinc)

Mencken, Henry Louis

Menotti, Gian-Carlo

Mieszko I (also Mieczyslaw)

Mieszko II (also Mieczyslaw)

Milhaud, Darius

Millais, Sir John Everett

Mistral, Frédéric

Mistral, Gabriela (real name: Lucila Godoy de Alcayage)

Moissan, Henri

Molière (real name: Jean Baptiste Poquelin)

Momaday, N. Scott

Mommsen, Theodor

Montagu, Ashley (full name: Montague Francis Ashley Montagu)

Montagu, John

Montagu, Lady Mary Wortley

Morales, Luis de

Moravia, Alberto (real name: Alberto Pincherle)

Morison, Samuel Eliot

Morisot, Berthe

Morrice, James Wilson

Mumford, Lewis

Murdoch, Jean Iris

Murillo, Bartolomé Estéban

Nabokov, Vladimir

Neville, Richard

Nicollé, Charles Jules Henri

Nkrumah, Kwame

Noguchi, Isamu

Norrish, Ronald George Wreyford

Noverre, Jean Georges

Nyerere, Julius K.

O'Connor, Edwin

O'Connor, Frank

O'Connor, Thomas Power (called "Tay Pay")

O'Keeffe, Georgia

Orléans, Louis Philippe Joseph duc d' (called "Philippe-Egalité")

Ostwald, Wilhelm

Ottocar I-II (kings of Bohemia); II (called "Ottocar the Great")
Parnell, Charles Stewart
Paschal I-II (popes); I, Saint
Pasteur, Louis
Patrick, John
Pauling, Linus Carl
Pavlova, Anna
Pearson, Lester Bowles
Pekeris, Chaim Leib
Persius
Peshkov, Aleksei Maxsimovich (Maxim Gorki)
Peterkin, Julia Mood
Petrovic, George (Karageorge)
Phidias (also Pheidias)
Picabia, Francis
Picasso, Pablo Ruiz y
Piccard, Auguste
Piccard, Jean Felix
Pickett, George Edward
Pinchot, Gifford
Plautus, Titus Maccius
Pollock, Jackson
Pontian (Saint)
Poulenc, Francis
Poussin, Nicolas
Prandtl, Ludwig
Pringle, Henry Fowles
Prud'hon, Pierre Paul
Ptolemy I (full name: Ptolemy Soter)
Ptolemy (Claudius Ptolamaeus)
Puccini, Giacomo
Pulaski, Casimir
Purcell, Edward Mills
Purcell, Henry
Pushkin, Aleksandr Sergeyevich
Pynchon, William
Quintana, Manual José
Raeburn, Sir Henry
Raleigh, Sir Walter (also Ralegh)

Raphael (full name: Raphael Santi; also Sanzio)
Rayburn, Sam
Redmond, John Edward
Renault, Louis
Reuther, Walter Philip
Reymont, Wladyslaw Stanislaw
Reynaud, Paul
Rhodius, Appolonius (Appolonius of Rhodes)
Ribalta, Francisco de
Ricardo, David
Richard I-III (kings of England); I (called "Lion-Hearted")
Richter, Conrad Michael
Rimbaud, Arthur
Robbins, Frederick Chapman
Robbins, Jerome
Roberts, Kenneth Lewis
Robeson, Paul
Rodgers, Richard Charles
Roethke, Theodore
Rolland, Romain
Rolvaag, Ole Edvart
Romains, Jules (pseudonym: Louis Farigoule)
Romanus
Rossini, Gioacchino Antonio
Rostand, Edmond
Rouault, Georges
Rudolph, Paul Marvin
Russell, Bertrand Arthur William
Russell, Charles Edward
Russell, Charles Taze (called "Pastor Russell")
Russel, John
Ruzicka, Leopold
Rydberg, Abraham Viktor
Sackler, Howard
Salazar, Antonio de Oliveira
Sallust (Gaius Sallustinus Crispus)

Samuels, Ernest
Sargent, John Singer
Saroyan, William
Sassoon, Siegfried
Schadow, Johann Gott-
fried
Schirra, Walter Marty, Jr.
Schmitt, Bernadotte Ever-
ly
Schuman, William
Schwann, Theodor
Seaborg, Glenn Theodore
Seferis, George (Giorgios
Stylianou Seferiades)
Segovia, Andrés
Semenov, Nikolai Niko-
laevich
Sergius I-VI (popes); I
(Saint)
Service, Robert William
Severus, Flavius Valerius
Severus, Livius (also Vibi-
us)
Severus, Lucius Septimius
Seymour, Hane
Shapiro, Karl Jay
Shelley, Mary Wollstone-
craft
Shelley, Percy Bysshe
Shepard, Alan Bartlett, Jr.
Shepard, Odell
Sherman, James School-
craft
Sherman, William Tecum-
seh
Siddons, Sarah Kemble
Simpson, Louis
Sitwell, Dame Edith
Smetana, Friedrich (also
Bedrich Smetana)
Sorokin, Pitirim Alesan-
drovich
Soterus, Saint (also Soter)
Southey, Robert
Sowerby, Leo
Spemann, Hans
Spencer, Herbert
Spender, Stephen Harold

Spenser, Edmund
Spinoza, Baruch (also
Benedict)
Stanley, Charles (Viscount
Monck)
Stanley, Edward George
Geoffrey Smith
Stanley, Sir Henry Morton
(original name: John
Rowlands)
Stanley, Wendell Meredith
Stanton, Edwin McMas-
ters
Statius, Publius Papinius
Stegner, Wallace Earle
Steiger, Rod
Stengel, Charles Dillon
(called "Casey")
Stephen (king of England)
Stephen I (called "Saint
Stephen," king of Hun-
gary)
Stephen I-IX (popes); I,
Saint
Stevens, Wallace
Stimson, Henry Lewis
Strauss, Johann
Strauss, Richard George
Suharto
Sukarno, Dr. Achmed (also
Soekarno)
Suttner, Bertha von
Tacitus, Marcus Claudius
Tacitus, Cornelius
Temujin (Genghis Kahn)
Teniers, David
Terence (Publius Terentius
Afer)
Terrell, Mary Church
Theiler, Max
Thomson, Sir George
Paget
Thomson, James
Tyndale, William (also
Tindal, also Tindale)
Uccello, Paolo (real name:
Paolo di Dono)
Ulyanov, Vladimir Ilyich

(Vladimir Ilyich Lenin)
Unamuno, Miguel de
Ustinov, Peter Alexander
Utamaro, Kitagawa
Utrillo, Maurice
Vandyke, Sir Anthony (also Van Dyck)
van Eyck, Hubert
van Eyck, Jan
van Gogh, Vincent
van Rijn, Rembrandt
Van Tyne, Claude Halstead
Vermeer, Jan (also Johannes)
Viereck, Peter Robert Edwin
Vignola, Giacomo da
Virchow, Rudolf
Vischer, Peter
Vivaldi, Antonio
Vorster, Balthazar Johannes
Waksman, Selman Abraham
Wallace, Alfred Russel
Wallace, George C.
Wallace, Henry Agard
Wallach, Otto
Walpole, Horace
Walpole, Sir Hugh Seymour
Walpole, Sir Robert
Warburg, Otto Heinrich
Warwick, Richard Neville, earl of
Watteau, Jean Antoine
Webster, Daniel
Webster, Noah
Weidman, Jerome
Wharton, Edith Jones
Wheeler, Joseph
Wheeler, William Alman
Whipple, George Hoyt
Whitlam, Gough
Whitman, Marcus
Whitman, Walt
Whitney, Eli

Wieland, Heinrich
Wilkins, Sir George Hubert
Wilkins, Maurice Hugh Frederick
Willard, Francis Elizabeth
William I-IV (kings of England); I (called "William the Conqueror"); II (also William Rufus).
William I-II (kings of Prussia)
William I-III (kings of Netherlands)
Willkie, Wendell Lewis
Windaus, Adolf
Winslow, Ola Elizabeth
Yegorov, Boris B.
Zachary, Saint (also Sacharias)
Zeeland, Paul van
Zernike, Frits
Ziegler, Karl
Zozimus, Saint (also Zosimus)
Zwingli, Huldreich (also Ulrich)

EIGHT-LETTER NAMES

Aberdeen, Earl of (real name: John C. Gordon)
Adenauer, Konrad
Adolphus (Adolf of Nassau)
Agapetus I-II (popes); I, Saint
Alcayaga, Lucila Godoy de (Gabriela Mistral)
Aleichem, Sholom (Solomon Rabinowitz)
Ammianus, Marcellinus
Amundsen, Roald
Anacreon
Andersen, Hans Christian
Anderson, Carl David
Anderson, Dame Judith

Anderson, Marian
Anderson, Maxwell
Anderson, Sherwood
Anfinsen, Christian Bohmer
Angelico, Fra (real name: Giovanni da Fiesole)
Angström, Anders Jonas
Anicetus
Appleton, Sir Edward V.
Apuleius
Arcadius
Armitage, Kenneth
Asturias, Miguel Angel
Augustus (original name: Gaius Octavius)
Augustus II (called "Augustus the Strong")
Augustus, Titus Flavius Domitianus (Domitian)
Aurelian (Lucius Domitius Aurelianus)
Aurelius, Marcus (Alexander Severus)
Avogadro, Count Amadeo
Balbinus, Decimus Caelius
Bankhead, Tallulah
Barbusse, Henri
Baudouin (king of Belgium)
Beauvoir, Simone de
Beckmann, Max
Beerbohm, Sir Max
Bellmann, Karl Mikael
Belyayev, Pavel I.
Benchley, Robert Charles
Benedict I-XV (popes)
Bentinck, William Henry Cavendish
Berkeley, George
Berryman, John
Bessemer, Sir Henry
Betjeman, Sir John
Bismarck, Prince Otto Eduard Leopold von (full name: Bismarck-Schönhausen; called "the Iron Chancellor")

Björnson, Björnstjerne
Blackett, Patrick
Boethius, Anicius Manilus Severinus
Boniface I-IX (popes); I, Saint
Boniface, Saint (original name: Winfrid; called "Apostle of Germany")
Bonnefoy, Yves Jean
Bontemps, Arna
Borromeo, Saint Carlo
Bradford, William
Bramante, Donato d'Agnolo
Brancusi, Constantin
Brandeis, Louis Dembitz
Branting, Karl Hjalmar
Brattain, Walter H.
Brezhnev, Leonid Ilyich
Bridgman, Percy Williams
Brisbane, Sir Thomas Makdougall
Browning, Elizabeth Moulton Barrett
Browning, Robert
Bruckner, Anton
Brummell, George Bryan (called "Beau Brummell")
Buchanan, James
Burgoyne, John
Burnside, Ambrose Everett
Bykovsky, Valery F.
Caldwell, Erskine Preston
Caligula (real name: Gaius Caesar)
Calixtus (also Callistus), I-III (popes) I, Saint.
Campbell, John D. S. (Marquis of Lorme)
Carducci, Giosuè
Carloman
Carnegie, Andrew
Cassatt, Mary
Castagno, Andrea del
Catullus, Gaius Valerius

Chadwick, Sir James
Chadwick, Lynn Russell
Chambers, Sir William
Champlain, Samuel de
Channing, Edward
Claudian (Claudius Claudianus)
Claudius I (Tiberius Claudius Drusus Nero Germanicus)
Claudius II (Marcus Aurelius Claudius)
Columbus, Christopher (in Italian: Cristofore Colombo; in Spanish Cristóbal Colón)
Commodus, Lucius Aelius Aurelius
Congreve, William
Connelly, Marc
Conradin
Constans (Flavius Julius Constans); II (Flavius Heraclius Constans)
Contucci, Andrea (Andrea Sansovino)
Converse, Frederick Shepherd
Coolidge, Calvin (full name John Calvin Coolidge)
Coronado, Francisco Vasquez de
Couperin, François
Cournand, Andre Ferderic
Crockett, David (called "Davy")
Cromwell, Oliver
Cromwell, Richard
Cromwell, Thomas
cummings e e (full name: Edward Estlin Cummings)
Daguerre, Louis Jacques Mandé
Daladier, Edouard
Damrosch, Walter Johannes

Danilova, Alexandra
Davisson, Clinton Joseph
Day Lewis, Cecil
de Gaulle, Charles André Joseph Marie
Delbrück, Max
De Medici, Catherine
de Molina, Tirso (real name: Gabriel Téllez)
de Rivera, José
De Valera, Eamon
Devereux, Robert
di Cosimo, Piero (original name: Piero de Lorenzo)
Disraeli, Benjamin
Dollfuss, Engelbert
Domitian (Titus Flavius Domitianus Augustus)
Donleavy, J. P.
Douglass, Frederick (real name: Frederick Augustus Washington Bailey)
DuBuffet, Jean
Ducommun, Elie
Dudevant, Amandine Aurore Lucie Baronne (George Sand)
Dufferin, Earl of (real name: Frederick T. Hamilton-Temple-Blackwood)
Durkheim, Émile
Duvalier, François
Eberhart, Richard
Eichmann, Adolf
Einstein, Albert
Epicurus
Ericsson, John
Erlanger, Joseph
Ethelred
Ethelred II (called "Ethelred the Unready")
Eugenius
Eusebius, Saint
Farquhar, George
Farragut, David Glasgow
Faulkner, William
Fielding, Henry

Fillmore, Millard
Flagstad, Kirsten
Flanagan, Edward Joseph
Flaubert, Gustave
Fletcher, John Gould
Forester, Cecil Scott
Formosus
Fournier, Alain Henry (Henri Alain-Fournier)
Franklin, Benjamin
Franklin, John Hope
Fukuzawa, Yukichi
Gagliari, Paolo (Paolo Veronese)
Galerius (Gaius Galerius Valerius Maximianus)
Gallatin, Abraham Alfonse Albert
Gallieni, Joseph Simon
Gambetta, Leon
Garamond, Claude
Garfield, James A.
Garrison, William Lloyd
Gelasius I-II (popes); I, Saint
Gell-Mann, Murray
Geronimo (Indian name: Goyathlay, in English: "One who Yawns")
Gershwin, George
Gershwin, Ira
Ghiberti, Lorenzo
Ginsberg, Allen
Glaspell, Susan
Godowsky, Leopold
Goebbels, Joseph Paul
Goethals, George Washington
Goncourt, Edmond Louis Antoine Huot de
Gonzáles, Julio
Goodrich, Frances
Goodyear, Charles
Gorbatko, Victor V.
Grignard, Francois August Victor
Gustavus I-V (kings of Sweden); I (full name:

Gustavus Vasa, also Gustavus .Erikson); II (full name: Gustavus Adolphus; called "Lion of the North," called "Snow King")
Gustavus, Charles (Charles X)
Hamilton, Alexander
Hannibal
Harrison, Benjamin
Harrison, George
Harrison, William Henry
Hartline, Haldan Keffer
Harunobu, Suzuki
Hastings, Warren
Hendrick, Burton Jesse
Hepworth, Barbara
Herschel, Sir William
Hirohito (reign name: Showa)
Holloway, Emory
Honecker, Erich
Honorius I-IV (popes)
Honorius, Flavius
Horowitz, Vladimir
Humphrey, Hubert Horatio
Innocent I-XIII (popes); I, Saint
Isabella I-II (queens of Spain); I (called "Isabella the Catholic")
Karlfeldt, Erik Axel
Kawabata, Yasunari Kenyatta
Kenyatta, Jomo
Kerenski, Aleksandr Feodorovich
Kingsley, Henry
Kingsley, Sidney
Kirchner, Leon
Koestler, Arthur
Kollwitz, Käthe
Kornberg, Arthur
Kreisler, Fritz
Lagerlöf, Selma
Landseer, Sir Edwin

Henry
Langland, William
Langmuir, Irving
Larousse, Pierre Athanase
Lawrence, D. H. (full name: David Herbert Lawrence)
Lawrence, Ernest Orlando
Lawrence, Sir Thomas
Lawrence, Thomas Edward (called "Lawrence of Arabia"; changed surname to Shaw in 1924)
Leibnitz, Baron Gottfried Wilhelm von (also Leibniz)
Levertov, Denise
Licinius (Gaius Flavius Valerius Licinianus Licinius)
Linnaeus, Carolus (in Swedish: Karl von Linné)
Lipchitz, Jacques
Longinus, Dionysius Cassius
Lovelace, Richard
Lucilius, Gaius
Lysippus
Macaulay, Thomas Babington
Macbride, Sean
McCarthy, Eugene J.
McCarthy, Joseph R.
McCarthy, Mary
McDivitt, James Alton
McGinley, Phillis
McGuffey, William Holmes
McIlwain, Charles Howard
McKinley, William
MacLeish, Archibald
McMillan, Edwin Mattison
Macrinus (Marcus Opelius Macrinus)
Magellan, Ferdinand (in Portuguese: Fernão de Magalhães)

Magritte, René
Majorian (Julius Valerius Majorianus)
Makarios III (original name: Michael Christedoulos Mouskos)
Malenkov, Georgi M.
Mallarmé, Stéphane
Malpighi, Marcello
Mantegna, Andrea
Margaret, Princess (also Countess of Snowdon)
Maritain, Jacques
Marquand, John Phillips
Marshall, George Catlett
Marshall, John
Marshall, Thomas Riley
Marshall, Thurgood
Masaccio (real name: Tommaso Guidi; called "Father of Modern Art")
Mascagni, Pietro
Mata Hari (real name: Gertrud Margarete Zelle)
Matthias
Maximian (Marcus Aurelius Valerius Maximianus)
Mazzuoli, Girolamo Francesco Maria (Parmigiano)
Meleager
Melville, Herman
Menander
Mercator, Gerardus (original name: Gerhard Kremer)
Meyerhof, Otto
Michener, James Albert
Michener, Roland
Millikan, Robert Andrews
Mirabeau, Comte de Honoré Gabriel Victor Riqueti
Mitchell, Margaret
Mohammed (also Muhammad)
Mondrian, Piet (full name: Pieter Cornelis Mondri-

an)
Montcalm, Louis Joseph de
Mortimer, Roger de
Moultrie, William
Mulliken, Robert Sanderson
Nanteuil, Robert
Napoleon I-III (emperors of France); I (full name: Napoleon Bonaparte; called "The Little Corporal"); II (full name: Francois Charles Joseph Bonaparte; called "L'Aiglon"); III (full name: Charles Louis Napoleon Bonaparte: called "Louis Napoleon")
Nicholas I-IV (popes); I, Saint (called "Nicholas the Great")
Nicholas I-II (czars of Russia)
Nicholas, Roy Franklin
Niemeyer, Oscar
Nijinsky, Waslaw
Nobunaga (also Nobunago Oda)
Northrop, John Howard
O'Connell, Daniel (called "The Liberator")
Octavius, Gaius (Augustus)
O'Donovan, Michael (Frank O'Connor)
O'Higgins, Bernardo (called "Liberator of Chile")
Olybrius, Anicius
Overbeck, Johan Friedrich
Pagnini, Niccolò
Paladio, Andrea
von Papen, Franz
Pelagius I-II (popes)
Perceval, Spencer
Pericles
Perrault, Claude

Pertinax, Publius Helvius
Philips, Wendell
Picherle, Alberto (Alberto Moravia)
Piranesi, Giovanni Batsita
Pissarro, Camille
Plotinus
Plutarch
Poincaré, Raymond
Polybius
Pompidou, Georges J. R.
Ponselle, Rosa Melba (real name: Ponzillo)
Ponsonby, Vere B. (Earl of Bessborough)
Pontian, Saint
Popovich, Pavel Romanovich
Poquelin, Jean Baptiste (Molière)
Powhatan (Indian name Wahunsen-a-cawh)
Primrose, Archibald Philip
Proudhon, Pierre Joseph
Pulitzer, Joseph
Quisling, Vidkun
Rabelais, François
Raimondi, Marcantonio
Randolph, A. Philip
Randolph, Edmund
Randolph, John
Rasputin, Grigori Yefimovich
Rattigan, Terence Mervyn
Rawlings, Marjorie Kinnan
Rayleigh, Third Baron (John William Strutt)
Redgrave, Sir Michael
Remarque, Erich Maria
Respighi, Ottorino
Reynolds, Sir Joshua
Richards, Dickinson Woodruff, Jr.
Richards, Laura Elizabeth
Richards, Theodore William
Robinson, Edwin Arlington

Robinson, Frederick John

Robinson, Jack Roosevelt (called "Jackie")

Robinson, Sir Robert

Roebling, John Augustus

Roentgen, Wilhelm Conrad

Rossetti, Christina Georgina

Rossetti, Dante Gabriel

Rossetti, Gabriele

Rousseau, Henri

Rousseau, Jean Jacques

Rosseau, Théodore

Rowlands, John (Sir Henry Morton Stanley)

Runeberg, Johan Ludvig

Saarinen, Gottlieb Eliel

Sabatier, Paul

Salinger, Jerome David

Sandburg, Carl

Sandwich, Fourth Earl of (John Montagu)

Scharoun, Hans

Schiller, Johann Christoph Friedrich von

Schubert, Franz Peter

Schumann, Clara (full name: Clara Josephine Wieck Schumann)

Schumann, Robert Alexander

Secondat, Charles Louis de (Baron de La Brede et de Montesquieu)

Secundus, Gaius Plinius Caecilius (Pliny the Younger)

Selassie, Haile

Shatalov, Vladimir A.

Sheraton, Thomas

Sheridan, Philip Henry

Sheridan, Richard Brinsley

Sherwood, Robert Emmet

Shockley, William Bradford

Sholokov, Mikhail Aleksandrovich

Sibelius, Jean Julius Christian

Siegbahn, Karl Manne Georg

Sinclair, Upton Beall

Siricius, Saint

Snoilsky, Count Johan Carl Gustav

Socrates

Spengler, Oswald

Sprengel, Herman Johann Philipp

Stafford, Thomas Patten

Standish, Miles (also Myles Standish)

Stanhope, Charles

Stanhope, Philip Dormer (Fourth Earl of Chesterfield)

Steichen, Edward

Stendhal (pseudonym of Marie Henri Beyle)

Strachey, Lytton (full name: Giles Lytton Strachey)

Suckling, Sir John

Suleiman I (sultan of Turkey; called "Suleiman the Magnificent")

Sullivan, Sir Arthur Seymour

Sullivan, Louis Henry

Svedberg, Theodor

Taglioni, Maria

Tecumseh (also Tecumtha, also Tecumthe, also Tikamthi)

Tenerani, Pietro

Tennyson, Alfred

Theodore I-II (popes)

Theorell, Axel Hugo Teodor

Thompson, David

Thompson, Dorothy

Thompson, Francis

Thompson, Sir John Sparrow David

Tiberius (Tiberius Julius Caesar Augustus; original name: Tiberius Claudius Nero)

Tibullus

Timoleon

Tiselius, Arne Wilhelm Karin

Tolbert, William Richard, Jr.

Tomonaga, Sin-Itiro

Tompkins, Daniel D.

Trollope, Anthony

Trumbull, John

Turgenev, Ivan Sergeyevich

Ulbricht, Walter

Valdemar (Waldemar)

Valdivia, Pedro de

Valerian (Publius Licinius Valerianus)

van Aeken, Hieronymus (Hieronymus Bosch)

Van Allen, James Alfred

Vanbrugh, Sir John

Van Buren, Martin

Van Doren, Carl

Van Doren, Mark

Van Rijn, Rembrandt

van't Hoff, Jacobus Hendricus

Verlaine, Paul

Veronese, Paolo (real name: Paolo Caliari)

Vesalius, Andreas

Vespucci, Amerigo

Victoria (full name: Alexandrina Victoria)

Vigeland, Adolf Gustav

Vigilius

Villiers, George William Frederick

Vertanen, Artturi Ilmari (also Wirtanen)

Vitalian, Saint

Vizcáino, Sebastián

Vlaminck, Maurice de

Voltaire (real name: François Marie Arouet)

Volyanov, Boris V.

von Hayek, Friederich August

von Laue, Max

Vuillard, Jean Edouard

Waldemar I-IV (also Valdemar; kings of Denmark); I (called "Waldemar the Great"); (also Valdemar II; called "Waldemar the Victorious"); (also Valdemar IV; called "Waldemar Atterdag")

Waldheim, Kurt

Walworth, Arthur

Wedgwood, Josiah

Weismann, August

Whistler, James Abbott McNeill

Whittier, John Greenleaf

Williams, Daniel Hale

Williams, Jesse Lynch

Williams, Roger (original name: Thomas Lanier Williams)

Williams, Tennessee

Williams, William Carlos

Woodhull, Victoria Claflin

Woodward, Robert Burns

Wycliffe, John (also Wyclif)

Xenophon

Yamasaki, Minoru

Yoritomo (Yoritomo Minamoto)

Zeppelin, Count Ferdinand Graf von

Zurbarán, Francisco de

NINE-LETTER NAMES

Abdul-Aziz

Adeodatus II (pope; also Saint)

Aeschines

Aeschylus

Agrippina, Julia

Aguinaldo, Emilio
Aldington, Richard
Alekseyev, Constantin Sergeyevich (Constantin Stanisslavsky)
Alexander I-VIII (popes); I, Saint
Alexander I-III (czars of Russia)
Alexander I-III, kings of Scotland; II (called "Alexander the Peaceful")
Alexander I Obrenovich (king of Serbia)
Alexander I (king of Yugoslavia)
Alexander, Harol R. L. G. (Earl of Tunis)
Altdorfer, Albrecht
Anacletus, Saint (also Saint Cletus)
Anthemius
Antoninus, Marcus Aurelius (Caracalla)
Appleseed, Johnny (John Chapman)
Arbuthnot, John
Aristotle
Armstrong, Louis
Armstrong, Neil A.
Arnoldson, Klas P.
Arrhenius, Svante A.
Athelstan
Athanaeus
Baltimore, George Calvert (George Calvert)
Bannister, Roger Gilbert
Barrymore, Ethel
Barrymore, John
Barrymore, Lionel
Bathelme, Donald
Bartholdi, Frederic Auguste
Beardsley, Aubrey Vincent
Becquerel, Antoine H.
Beernaert, August M. F.
Beethoven, Ludwig van

Benavente, y Martínez Jacinto
Ben-Gurion, David
Beregovoi, Georgi T.
Bernhardt, Sarah (real name: Rosine Bernard)
Bernoulli, Daniel
Bernoulli, Jakob (also Jacques)
Bernoulli, Johann (also Jean)
Bernstein, Leonard
Beveridge, Albert Jeremiah
Boleslaus I-III (also Boleslav; kings of Poland); I (called "Boleslaus the Brave"); II (called "Boleslaus the Bold")
Bonaparte, Joseph
Borromini, Francesco
Bourgeois, Leon
Brautigan, Richard
Bromfield, Louis
Bronstein, Lev Davidovich (Leon Trotski)
Burroughs, Edgar Rice
Butenandt, Adolf F. J.
Cambridge, Alexander A. F. W. A. G. (Earl of Athlone)
Canaletto, Antonio
Caracalla (real name: Marcus Aurelius Antoninus)
Carpenter, Malcolm Scott
Catherine I-II (czarinas of Russia); II (called "Catherine the Great")
Cavendish, George
Cavendish, Henry
Cavendish, Victor C. W. (Duke of Devonshire)
Cavendish, William
Ceausescu, Nicolae
Celestine I-V (popes); I, Saint
Cervantes, Saavedra, Miguel de

Chaliapin, Feodor Ivanovich

Chennault, Claire Lee

Cherenkov, Pavel Alekseyevich

Chou En-lai

Christian I-X, kings of Denmark; II (called "Christian the Cruel")

Christina

Chung-cheng, Chiang (Chiang Kai-shek)

Churchill, Sir Winston Leonard Spencer

Cleopatra VII, queen of Egypt

Cleveland, Grover

Cockcroft, Sir John Douglas

Coleridge, Samuel Taylor

Confucius (in Chinese: K'ung Fu-tzu, also Kung Fu-tse, also K'ung Ch'iu)

Connaught, Duke of (real name: Arthur William Patrick Albert)

Constable, John

Corneille, Pierre

Cornelius, Saint

Cornelius, Peter von

Correggio, Antonio Allegri da

Da Fiesole, Giovanni (Fra Angelico)

D'Annunzio, Gabriele

de Broglie, Louis-Victor

de Herrara, Juan

De Kooning, Willem

de la Roche, Mazo

Dello Joio, Norman

de Mendoza, Antonio

De Quincey, Thomas

Descartes, René

Diaghilev, Sergei Pavlovich

Dickinson, Emily

Dionysius, Saint

Donatello, Donato

Donizetti, Gaetano

Doolittle, Hilda (pseudonym: H. D.)

Doolittle, James Harold

Dos Passos, John Roderigo

Echegaray, Jose

Ehrenburg, Ilya Grigoryevich

Einthoven, Willem

Einstein, Sergei Mikhailovich

Elizabeth I-II (queens of England)

Ellington, Duke (real name: Edward Kennedy Ellington)

Epictetus

Ethelbald

Ethelbert

Ethelwulf

Euripides

Evaristus, Saint

Fairbanks, Charles Warren

Fairbanks, Douglas

Fairfield, Cicily Isabel (Dame Rebecca West)

Farigoule, Louis (Jules Romains)

Feininger, Lyonel

Ferdinand

Ferdinand I-III (Holy Roman Emperors)

Ferdinand I-VII (kings of Spain)

Firestone, Harvey Samuel

Forssmann, Werner

Frederick I (margrave of Brandenburg)

Frederick II-IX (kings of Denmark)

Frederick I-III (Holy Roman Emperors); I (called "Frederick Barbarossa")

Frederick I-III (kings of Prussia; II (called "Frederick the Great"); III (also Frederick William)

Luxemburg, Rosa
MacArthur, Douglas
McCartney, Paul (full name: James Paul McCartney)
McClellan, George Brinton
McCormack, John
McCormick, Cyrus Hall
McCullers, Carson Smith
MacDonald, James Ramsay
Macdonald, Sir John Alexander
Mackenzie, Sir Alexander
Mackenzie, Alexander
Macmillan, Harold (full name: Maurice Harold Macmillan)
Mansfield, Katherine (real name: Kathleen Murry)
Marcellus I, Saint
Marcellus II
Marcianus (also Marcian)
Margrethe II, queen of Denmark
Marquette, Jacques (called "Père Marquette")
Martinson, Harry Edmund
Masefield, John
Massenet, Jules Emile Frédéric
Maxentius, Marcus Aurelius Valerius
Mendeleev, Dmitri Ivanovich (also Mendelejeff)
Mestrovic, Ivan
Michelson, Albert Abraham
von Moltke, Count Helmuth Karl Bernhard
Montaigne, Michel Eyquem de
Mortensen, Norma Jean (Marilyn Monroe)
Mössbauer, Rudolf (also Moessbauer)
Musorgsky, Modest Petrovich (Mussorgsky)

Mussolini, Benito (called "Il Duce")
Mutsuhito (reign name: Meiji)
Navarrete, Martín Fernández de
Nicholson, Ben
Nietzsche, Friedrich Wilhelm
Nikolayev, Adrian Grigoryevich
Nirenberg, Marshall Warren
Noel-Baker, Philip John
Offenbach, Jacques Levy
Oldenburg, Claes Thure
Ossietzky, Carl von
Ostrovski, Aleksandr Nikolaevich
Pasternak, Boris Leonidovich
Pechstein, Max
Pergolesi, Giovanni Batista (also Pergolese)
Pilsudski, Jozef
Pisanello (real name: Antonio Pisano)
Pompadour, Jeanne Antoinette Poisson Le Normant d'Etioles, Marquise de
Pretorius, Andries Wilhelmus Jacobus
Priestley, Joseph
Procopius
Prokhorov, Aleksander Mikhailovich
Prokofiev, Sergei Sergeyevich
Quantrill, William Clarke
Quasimodo, Salvatore
Rasmussen, Knud Johan Victor
Rehnquist, William Hubbs
Remington, Frederic
Richelieu, Armand Jean du Plessis, duc de
Roosevelt, Anna Eleanor

Roosevelt, Franklin Delano

Roosevelt, Theodore

Sacagawea (also Sacajawea, also Sakajawea; called "Bird Woman")

St. Laurent, Louis Stephen

Salisbury, First Earl of (Robert Cecil)

Salisbury, Third Marquis of (Robert Arthur Talbot Gascoyne-Cecil)

Samuelson, Paul Anthony

San Martin, Jose de

Sansovino, Andrea (real name: Andrea Contucci)

Sansovino, Jacupo (real name: Jacopo Tatti)

Santa Anna, Antonio Lopez de

Santa Cruz, Andres

Santayana, George

Scarlatti, Alessandro

Scarlatti, (Giuseppe) Domenico

Schelling, Friedrich Wilhelm Joseph von

Schleiden, Matthias Jakob

Schonberg, Arnold (also Schoenberg)

Schwinger, Julian Seymour

Severinus

Sigismund III (king of Poland)

Sillanpää, Frans Eemil

Silverius, Saint

Siqueiros, David Alfaro

Sisinnius

Snodgrass, William DeWitt

Soderblom, Nathan

Sophocles

Southwell, Robert

Spitteler, Carl Friedrich Georg (pseudonym: Carl Felix Tandem)

Stanislas, Louis Xavier (Louis XVIII)

Steinbeck, John Ernst

Steinmetz, Charles Proteus (original name: Karl August Rudolf)

Stevenson, Adlai Ewing

Stevenson, Robert Louis Balfour

Stieglitz, Alfred

Stockton, Frank R. (full name: Francis Richard Stockton)

Stokowski, Leopold Antoni Stanislaw

Stribling, Thomas Sigismund

Suetonius (Gaius Suetonius Tranquillus)

Sun Yat-sen (also Sun Wen)

Swinburne, Algernon Charles

Sylvester I-III (popes); I, Saint

Summachus, Saint (also Symmacus)

Thackeray, William Makepeace

Tinbergen, Jan

Toscanini, Arturo

Townshend, Charles (called "the Weathercock")

Valentine (pope)

Valentine, Saint

Vancouver, George

van Leyden, Lucas (original name: Lucas Jacobsz)

Vannucchi, Andrea Domenico d'Agnolo di Francesco (Andrea del Sarto)

van Ostade, Adraen

van Scorel, Jan

Velasquez, Diego Rodriguez de Silva y

Venizelos, Eleutherios

Verhaeren, Emile

Verrazano, Giovanni da
Vespasian (Titus Flavius Sabinus Vespasianus)
Vishinsky, Andrei Yanuarievich
Vitellius, Aulus
Vittorini, Elio
von Moltke, Count Helmuth Johannes Ludwig
Wellesley, Arthur
Whitehead, Alfred North
Wodehouse, Pelham Grenville (P.G.)
Woollcott, Alexander
Wurdemann, Audrey May
Yeliseyev, Aleksei S.
Zimmerman, Robert (Bob Dylan)
Zoroaster
Zsigmondy, Richard Adolf

TEN-LETTER NAMES

Abd-al-Kader
Abdul-Hamid II (called the "Great Assassin," or the "Red Sultan")
Aemilianus
Alcibiades
Aleixandre, Vincente
Anastasius I-IV (popes); I, Saint
Anaxagoras
Archimedes
Argelander, Friedrich Wilhelm August
Balanchine, George
Barbarelli, Giorgione (Giorgione)
Baudelaire, Charles
Beauregard, Pierre Gustave Toutant de
Bellarmine, Saint Robert (full name: Roberto Francesco Romolo Bellarmino)
Bernadotte, Count Folke (full name: Count Folke

Bernadotte of Wisborg)
Bernadotte, Jean Baptiste Jules (Charles XIV John)
Blackstone, Sir William
Botticelli, Sandro
Breakspear, Nicholas (Pope Adrian IV)
Buonarroti, Michelangelo
Burne-Jones, Sir Edward Coley
Caravaggio, Michalangelo Amerigi da
Chesterton, Gilbert Keith
Christophe, Henri
Chrysostom, Saint John
Chung-cheng, Chiang (Chiang Kai-shek)
Clemenceau, Georges Eugene Benjamin (called "le Tigre," the tiger)
Copernicus, Nicolas (in Polish: Nikolaj Kopernik)
Cornwallis, Charles
Cunningham, Ronnie Walter
Democritus
Destouches, Louis Fuch (Louis-Ferdinand Celine)
Devonshire, Duke of (real name: Victor C. W. Cavendish)
Diocletian (Gaius Aurelius Valerius Diocletianus)
Dostoevski, Fyodor Mikhailovich
Drinkwater, John
Duns Scotus, John
Dürrenmatt, Friedrich
du Vigneaud, Vincent
Elagabalus (Heliogabalus)
Empedocles
Eric the Red
Fahrenheit, Gabriel Daniel
Feoktistiv, Konstantin P.
FitzGerald, Edward
Fitzgerald, F. Scott (full

name: Francis Scott Key Fitzgerald)
Galli-Curci, Amelita
Galsworthy, John
Germanicus, Nero Claudius Caesar Drusus (Nero)
Giacometti, Alberto
Guggenheim, Solomon Robert
Gullstrand, Allvar
Heisenberg, Werner
Heraclitus
Hofstadter, Richard
Hofstadter, Robert
Karageorge (also Karadjordje, also Czerny Djordje; original name: George Petrovic)
Khrushchev, Nikita Sergeyevich
Kublai Khan (also Khubilai Khan, also Kubla Khan)
La Follette, Robert Marion
La Fontaine, Henri
La Fontaine, Jean de
Lagerkvist, Pär Fabian
La Montaine, John
Liebermann, Max
Longfellow, Henry Wadsworth
McLaughlin, Andrew Cunningham
Magnentius, Flavius Popilius
Malinowski, Bronislaw
Mao Tse-tung (also Mao Tze-tung)
Maximilian (full name: Ferdinand Maximilian Joseph)
Maximilian I-II (Holy Roman Emperors)
Melchaides, Saint (also Miltiades)
Metternich, Prince Klemens Wenzel Nepomuk Lothar von (family

name: Metternich-Winneburg)
Mickiewicz, Adam
Mindszenty, Jozsef
Modigliani, Amedeo
Moholy-Nagy, László
Montessori, Maria
Monteverdi, Claudio (also Monteverde)
Motherwell, Robert
Mussorgsky, Modest Petrovich (also Musorgsky, also Moussorgsky)
Obrenovich, Milan (Milan)
Obrenovich, Milos (Milos)
Oglethorpe, James Edward
Paderewski, Ignace Jan
Palestrina, Giovanni Pierluigi da (called "Prince of Music")
Palmerston, Third Viscount of (real name: Henry John Temple)
Parrington, Vernon Louis
Pauncefote, Julian
Pirandello, Luigi
Pocahontas
Polygnotus
Praxiteles
Propertius, Sextus
Protagoras
Queensbury, Eighth Marquis of (John Sholto Douglas)
Quintilian, Marcus Fabius
Rabinowitz, Solomon (pseudonym: Shalon, also Sholom Aleichem)
Reichstein, Tadeus
Ribbentrop, Joachim von
Richardson, Sir Owen Willans
Richardson, Samuel
Rochambeau, Comte de Jean Baptiste Donatien de Vimeur
Rosenquist, James Albert
Rothschild, Baron Lionel

Nathan de
Rothschild, Mayer Anselm
(also Meyer Anschel)
Rothschild, Nathan Mayer
(also Meyer)
Rubinstein, Anton Gregor
Rubinstein, Artur
Rutherford, Ernest
Sabinianus
Saint-Saëns, Charles Camille
Saint-Simon, Comte
Claude Henri de Rouvroy de
Santa Maria, Domingo
Savonarola, Girolamo
Schreiffer, John Robert
Schweitzer, Albert
Seferiades, Giorgos Stylianou (pseudonym:
George Seferis)
Signorelli, Luca d'Egidio
di Ventura de
Simplicius, Saint
Stanislaus, kings of Poland; I (original name:
Stanislaus Leszczynski);
II (original name: Stanislaus Augustus Poniatowski)
Staudinger, Hermann
Stefansson, Vilhjalmur
Stradivari, Antonio
Stravinsky, Igor Fëdorovich
Stresemann, Gustav
Strindberg, Johan August
Stuyvesant, Peter
Sutherland, Earl W., Jr.
Sutherland, Graham
Tarkington, Booth (full
name: Newton Booth
Tarkington)
Tertullian (full name:
Quintus Septimius Florens Tertullianus)
Tetrazzini, Luisa
Theocritus

Theodosius I, Flavius
(called "Theodosius the
Great")
Theodosius II
Torquemada, Tomas de
Torricelli, Evangelista
Tranquilli, Secundo (Ignazio Silone)
Tvardovsky, Alexandr Trifonovich
Tweedsmuir, Baron (real
name: John Buchan)
Uladislaus II (also Ladislas
II)
Vanderbilt, Cornelius
(called "Commodore
Vanderbilt")
van der Goes, Hugo
Villa-Lobos, Heitor
von Steuben, Baron Friedrich Willhelm Ludolf
Gerhard Augustin
Voroshilov, Kliment Yefremovich
Washington, Booker Taliaferro
Washington, George
Wassermann, August von
Wassermann, Jakob
Wenceslaus
Whitefield, George
Willingdon, Marquis (real
name: Freeman
Freeman-Thomas)
Wordsworth, William
Xenophanes
Zaturenska, Marya
Zeno of Elea
Zephyrinus, Saint

**ELEVEN-LETTER
NAMES**

Abderhalden, Emil
Abd-er-Rahman
Abdul-Medjid I (also
Abdul-Mejid)
Albuquerque, Alfonso de

Anaximander

Apollinaire, Guillaume (full name: Guillaume Apollinaire de Kostrowitsky)

Baden-Powell, Robert Stephenson Smyth

Baskerville, John

Beaverbrook, First Baron (real name: William Maxwell Aitken)

Bessborough, Earl of (real name: Vere B. Ponsonby)

Bolingbroke, Viscount (full name: Henry St. John, Viscount Bolingbroke)

Boumedienne, Houari

Callimachus

Cartier-Bresson, Henri

Castiglione, Giovanni Benedetto (called "Il Grechetto")

Chamberlain, Arthur Neville

Chamberlain, Owen

Chamberlain, Sir Joseph Austen

Charlemagne (also Charles I; called "Charles the Great")

Chippendale, Thomas

Constantine (pope)

Constantine I-II (Roman Emperors); I (called "Constantine the Great"; full name: Flavius Valerius Aurelius Constantinus); II (Flavius Julius Constantinus)

Constantius I-III (Roman Emperors); I (Flavius Valerius Constantius, surnamed Chlorus); II (Flavius Julius Constantius)

Covarrubias, Miguel

Czartoryski, Prince Adam Jerzy

Dangerfield, George

della Robbia, Andrea

della Robbia, Luca

Demosthenes

Diefenbaker, John George

Douglas-Home, Rt. Hon. Sir Alexander Frederick

Eleutherius, Saint (also Eleutheros)

Filipchenko, Anatoli V

Frankfurter, Felix

Friedenberg, Edgar Z.

Garcia Lorca, Federico

Genghis Khan (also Jenghiz, also Jinghis; original name: Temujin, also Temuchin)

Ghirlandajo (also Ghirlandaio, also Grillandajo; original name: Domenico di Tommaso Bigordi)

Hammerstein, Oscar, II

Hardicanute (also Harthacanute)

Hinshelwood, Sir Cyril Norman

Hippocrates

Humperdinck, Englebert

Jesus Christ

Joliot-Curie, Irène

Kazantzakis, Nikos

Kierkegaard, Sören Aabye

Kochanowski, Jan

Landsteiner, Karl

Le Corbusier (real name: Charles Edouard Jeanneret)

Leeuwenhoek, Anton van

Leoncavallo, Ruggiero

Leszczynski, Stanislaus (Stanislaus I)

Liddell Hart, Sir Basil Henry

Li Hung-chang (called "the Bismarck of Asia")

Livingstone, David

Lloyd George, David
Machiavelli, Niccolo
Maeterlinck, Count Maurice
Marcellinus, Saint
Marlborough, First Duke of (real name: John Churchill)
Mendelssohn, Felix (full name: Jakob Ludwig Felix Mendelssohn-Bartholdy)
Metchinkoff, Elie
Montesquieu, Baron de la Brède et de (real name: Charles Louis de Secondat)
Moussorgsky, Modest Petrovich (Mussorgsky)
Nightingale, Florence (called "the Lady with the Lamp")
Numerianus, Marcus Aurelius
Omar Khayyám
Oppenheimer, J. Robert
Ponce de Leon, Juan
Poniatowski, Stanislaus Augustus (Stanislaus II)
Pontoppidan, Henrik
Prajadhipok
Rachmaninov, Sergei Vasilyevich
Ramon y Cajal, Santiago
Reizenstein, Elmer L. (Elmer L. Rice)
Robespierre, Maximilien Marie Isidore
Rockefeller, John Davidson
Rockefeller, Nelson Aldrich
Schlesinger, Arthur Meir, Jr.
Schlesinger, Bruno Walter (Bruno Walter)
Schrodinger, Erwin
Schweickart, Russell

Shaftesbury, Earl of (Anthony Ashley Cooper)
Shakespeare, William
Sherrington, Sir Charles Scott
Sienkiewicz, Henryk
Sitting Bull
Stiernhielm, Georg (original name: Georgius Olai)
Tchaikovsky, Peter Ilyich
Teotocopulo, Domenico (El Greco)
Thorvaldsen, Albert Bertel (also Thorwaldsen)
Thucydides
Tutankhamen
Valentinian I-III Roman Emperors, I (Flavius Valentinianus); III (Flavius Placidus Valentinianus)
van Ruisdale, Jacob (also Ruysdael)
van der Waals, Johannes D.
Wallenstein, Albrecht Eusebois Wenzel von
Wheelwright, William
Wilberforce, William
Willstätter, Richard
Wolf-Ferrari, Ermanno
Yevtushenko, Yevgeny Aleksandrovich
Zarathustra (Zoroaster)

TWELVE-LETTER NAMES

Alcala Zamora, Niceto (Niceto Alcala Zamora y Torres)
Anna Ivanovna (also Ioannovana)
Anne of Cleves
Aristophanes
Bandaranaike, Sirimavo
Blasco-Ibanez, Vicente
Breckinridge, John Cabell

Brunelleschi, Filippo
Charles Felix
Chesterfield, Fourth Earl of (real name: Philip Dormer Stanhope)
de Maupassant, Guy (full name: Henri René Albert Guy de Maupassant)
Eratosthenes
Ferlinghetti, Lawrence
Hammarskjöld, Dag
Heliogabalus (also Elagabalus; full name: Varius Avitus Bassianus)
Korzeniowski, Teodor Józef Konrad (Joseph Conrad)
Koussevitzky, Sergei Alexandrovich
Lichtenstein, Roy F.
Liliuokalani (Lydia Kamehameha)
Machado y Ruiz, Antonio
Maria Theresa
Martin du Gard, Roger
Martinez Ruiz, José (called "Azorin")
Michelangelo (full name: Michelangelo Buonarroti)
Nordenskjold, Baron Nils Adolf Erik
Parmigianino II (also Parmigiano; real name: Girolamo Francesco Maria Mazzuoli or Massola)
Pelham-Holles, Thomas
Pérez de Ayala, Ramón
Quiller-Couch, Sir Arthur Thomas (pseudonym: Q)
Rickenbacker, Edward Vernon
Sacher-Masoch, Leopold von
Saint-Gaudens, Augustus
Schopenhauer, Arthur
Shostakovich, Dimitri
Solzhenitsyn, Aleksandr I.

Stanislavsky, Constantin (real name: Constantin Sergeyevich Alekseyev)
Szent-Györgyi, Albert von
Themistocles
Theophrastus
Viollt-le-Duc, Eugène Emmanuel
Westinghouse, George
Zeno of Citium

THIRTEEN-LETTER NAMES

Alain-Fournier (pseudonym of Henri Alain Fournier)
Antoninus, Pius (Titus Aurelius Fulvus Boionoius Arrius Antoninus)
Charles Albert (Charles VII)
Châteaubriand, Vicomte François René de
Chiang Kai-shek (real name: Chiang Chungcheng)
Chiang Kai-shek, Madam
de Tocqueville, Alexis Charles Henri Maurice Clerel
Francis Joseph (also Franz Joseph)
Freeman-Thomas, Freeman (Marquís Willingdon)
Gascoyne-Cecil, Robert Arthur Talbot
Louis Philippe
Moreto y Cavaña, Agustin
Ortega y Gasset, José
Pepin the Short
Pliny the Elder
Radhakrishnan, Sir Sarvepalli
Rain-in-the-Face
Saavedra Lamas, Carlos

Stephen Dushan (also Dusan)
Timon of Philius
Van Renssaelaer, Stephen
Victor Amadeus I-III (dukes of Savoy)
Vincent de Paul, Saint
von Heidenstam, Verner
von Hindenburg, Paul
von Keyserling, Count Hermann Alexander
von Richthofen, Baron Alfred
von Richthofen, Baron Ferdinand
von Schlieffen, Count Alfred
Wagner-Jauregg, Julius
Wa-hun-sen-a-cawh (Powhatan)
Zamora y Torres, Niceto Alcala

FOURTEEN-LETTER NAMES

Albertus Magnus
della Francesca, Piero
Didius Julianus (Marcus Didius Salvius Julianus)
Ercilla y Zúñiga, Alonso de
Goya y Lucientes, Francisco José de
Marcus Aurelius (Marcus Aurelius Antoninus)
Oehlenschläger, Adam Gottlob
Philip of Swabia
Prévost d'Exiles, Antoine François
Rimsky-Korsakov, Nikolai Andreevich
Silius Italicus, Tiberius Catius
Stephen Nemanya
Sully-Prudhomme, Rene François Armand

Ulrika Eleonora
Velez de Guevara, Luis
Victor Emmanuel I-II (kings of Sardinia); III (king of Italy)
von Krafft-Ebing, Baron Richard
von Schuschnigg, Kurt
William the Lion

FIFTEEN-LETTER NAMES

Abd-er-Rahman Khan (also Abdurrahaman Khan)
Alarcón y Mendoza, Juan Ruiz de
Charles Emmanuel I-IV (dukes of Savoy)
Cueva de la Garoza, Juan de la
Diodorus Siculus
Euler-Chelpin, Hans Karl August Simon von
Giotto de Bondone
Jesus of Nazareth
Kamerlingh-Onnes, Heike
La Rochefoucauld, François, Duc de
La Tour d'Auvergne, Henri de (Vicomte de Turenne)
Marie Antoinette (full name: Josèphe Jeanne Marie Antoinette)
Pliny the Younger
Pupienus Maximus (Marcus Clodius)
Saxo Grammaticus
Simonides of Ceos
Toulouse-Lautrec, Henri Marie Raymond de
Vaughan Williams, Ralph
Vitruvius Pollio
Watson-Wentworth, Charles

SIXTEEN-LETTER NAMES

Alexander Severus (Marcus Aurelius; original name: Alexianus Bassianus)
Cyrano de Bergerac, Savinien
Frederick William (called the "Great Elector")
Frederick William I-IV (kings of Prussia)
Mary Queen of Scots (real name: Mary Stuart)
Matthias Corvinus
Petronius Maximus
Petty-Fitzmaurice, Henry C. K. (Marquis of Lansdowne)
Stanley of Preston, Baron (real name: Frederick A. Stanley)
Synesius of Cyrene
von Schwarzenberg, Prince Karl Philipp

SEVENTEEN-LETTER NAMES

Calderón de la Barca, Pedro
Campbell-Bannerman, Sir Henry
Catherine of Aragon
Chillida Juantegui, Eduardo
Dunoyer de Segonzac, André
Elizabeth Petrovna
Emmanuel Philibert
Gentile da Fabriano
Michael Fëdorovich
Romulus Augustulus
Theodoric the Great

EIGHTEEN-LETTER NAMES

Appolonius of Rhodes (also Apollonius Rhodius)
Aristarchus of Samos
Casanova de Seingalt, Giovanni Jacopo (also Giacomo)
Eleanor of Aquitaine

NINETEEN-LETTER NAMES

Toussaint L'Ouverture, Pierre Dominique

TWENTY-LETTER NAMES

Margaret Maid of Norway

TWENTY-ONE-LETTER NAMES

Jean Baptiste de la Salle, Saint

TWENTY-TWO LETTER NAMES

Estournelles de Constant, Paul Henri Benjamin, Baron d'

TWNETY-THREE LETTER NAMES

Hamilton-Temple-Blackwood, Frederick T. (Earl of Dufferin)

TWENTY-FOUR LETTER NAMES

Dionysius of Halicarnassus

6. MYTHOLOGICAL NAMES

TWO-LETTER NAMES

Ge
Io
Ra
Re
Ve

THREE-LETTER NAMES

Atë
Ban
Eos
Nox
Nyx
Pan
Set
Sol

FOUR-LETTER NAMES

Acis
Aias
Ares
Argo
Arne
Clio
Dido
Dike
Echo
Eris
Eros
Gaea
Geri
Hebe
Hera
Hero
Iris
Isis
Juno
Kore
Leda

Leto
Loki
Mars
Mors
Odin
Ossa
Rhea
Siva
Styx
Thor
Troy
Vili
Zeus

FIVE-LETTER NAMES

Aegis
Aeson
Aikos (or
    Aeacus)
Amata
Ammon
Argus
Arion
Atlas
Attis (Atys)
Cacus
Ceres
Chaos
Circe
Creon
Cupid
Danaë
Diana
Dione
Dirce
Erato
Eurus
Fates
Flora
Freki
Frigg
Galli

Hades
Helen
Helle
Hodur
Horae
Horus
Hours
Hydra
Hylas
Hymen (or
    Hymenaeus)
Ixion
Janus
Jason
Laius
Lares
Medea
Midas
Minos
Muses
Nanna
Niobe
Nisus
Notus
Orion
Paris
Pluto
Priam
Remus
Shiva
Sibyl
Uther
Venus
Vesta
Wotan

SIX-LETTER NAMES

Acamas
Admete (or
    Admeta)
Adonis
Aeacus (or

Aikos)
Aeëtes
Aegeus
Aegina
Aeneas
Aeolus
Aerope
Agenor
Aglaia
Alecto
Althea
Amycus
Anubis (Inpu Hermanubis)
Apollo
Arthur (King Arthur)
Asgard
Athena (Pallas Athene)
Atreus
Augeas
Aurora
Auster
Baldur (Balder)
Baucis
Boreas
Brahma
Cadmus
Castor
Charon
Chiron
Clotho
Clytie
Cronus
Cybele
Danaus
Daphne
Deimos
Delphi
Dryads
Eirene
Elaine
Erebus
Europa
Evadne
Faunus
Furies

Gawain
Genius
Graces
Haemon
Hecate
Hector
Hecuba
Helios
Hermes
Hestia
Hygeia
Icarus
Isolde (and Tristram)
Klotho
Kyrene
Latona
Medusa
Mentor
Merlin
Modred (or Mordred)
Moirai
Naiads
Nereus
Nessus
Nestor
Nymphs
Oenone
Oreads
Osiris
Pallas (or Pallas Athene)
Parcae
Peleus
Pelias
Pelion
Pelops
Peneus
Pollux
Psyche
Pyrrha
Python
Saturn
Satyrs
Scylla
Semele
Sibyls

Sirens
Somnus
Sphinx
Tereus
Tethys
Thalia
Themis
Thetis
Thisbe
Titans
Tityos
Triton
Turnus
Uranie
Uranus
Vishnu
Vivien
Vulcan
Zethus

SEVEN-LETTER NAMES

Abderos
Acarnan
Acestes
Achates
Acheron
Actaeon
Admetus
Alcmene (or Alcmena)
Alcmeon
Alfadur
Alpheus
Amazons
Amphion
Amymone
Ancaeus
Antaeus
Antiope
Arachne
Ariadne
Artemis
Astarte
Asteria
Astraea
Atlanta

Atlamas
Atropos
Avernus
Bacchus
Bellona
Briseis
Busiris
Calaeno
Calchas
Çalydon
Calypso
Camelot
Camenae
Camilla
Cecrops
Chloris
Clymene
Curetes
Daidale
Danaids
Daphnis
Demeter
Diomede
Electra
Elysion
Epigoni
Euterpe
Evander
Galahad (Sir)
Galatea
Glaucus
Gorgons
Harpies
Helenus
Helicon
Incubus
Jocasta
Jupiter
Kuretes
Laertes
Laocoön
Leander
Maenads
Megaera
Mercury
Midgard
Minerva
Mordred (or

Modred)
Nemesis
Nephele
Neptune
Nereids
Oceanus
Oedipus
Olympus
Omphale
Orestes
Orpheus
Ouranos
Pandora
Perseus
Phaedra
Phaeton
Phoebus
Phrixus
Priapus
Proteus
Pylades
Pyramus
Pyrrhus
Romulus
Silenus
Theseus
Ulysses

EIGHT-LETTER NAMES

Achelous
Achilles
Aconteus
Acrisius
Adrastus
Aegyptus
Alcestis
Alcionüs
Alcithoë
Ambrosia
Anaxibia
Anchises
Antigone
Arethusa
Astyanax
Atlantis
Atreidae

Briareos
Brunhild
Caduceus
Calliope
Callisto
Capaneus
Castalia
Centaurs
Cerberus
Charites
Chimaera
Cyclopes
Daedalus
Dardanus
Deianira
Dionysus
Dioscuri
Endymion
Eteocles
Eurydice
Ganymede
Heracles
Hercules
Hormonia
Hyperion
Kerberos
Lachesis
Laodamia
Laomedon
Lapithae
Meleager
Menelaus
Minotaur
Morpheus
Nausicaä
Oceanids
Odysseus
Oenomaus
Oenopion
Paladium
Pasiphae
Pasithea (or
   Aglaia)
Penelope
Pentheus
Philemon
Pleiades
Poseidon

Ragnarok
Sangreal
Sarpedon
Sisyphus
Tantalus
Tartarus
Thanatos
Thyestes
Tiresias
Tithonus
Tristram (and
    Isolde)
Valhalla
Valkyrie
Zephyrus

NINE-LETTER NAMES

Aegisthus
Agamemnon
Alcathous
Amaltheia
Androcles
Andromeda
Aphrodite
Argonauts
Aristaeus
Asklepios
Autolycus
Cassandra
Charybdis
Chryseies
Deucalion
Eumenides
Eurytheus
Excalibur
Guinevere
Hippolyte
Holy Grail

Hymenaeus (or
Hymen)
Kassandra
Labyrinth
Launcelot (Sir)
Melpomene
Mnemosyne
Narcissus
Parnassus
Palamedes
Parmassus
Patroclus
Polynices
Pygmalion
Siegfried
Telegonus
Tisiphone
Trojan War
Tyndareus

TEN-LETTER NAMES

Acheliodes
Amphiaraus
Amphitrite
Amphitryon
Amphoteros
Andromache
Antilochus
Ascalaphos
Bacchantes
Bucephalus
Cassiopeia
Cornucopia
Euphrosyne
Hamadryads
Hephaistos
Hesperides
Hippocrine

Iphigeneia
King Arthur
Niebelungs
Persephone
Polydeuces
Polyhymnia
Polyphemus
Prometheus
Proserpina
Telemachus

ELEVEN-LETTER NAMES

Aescalapius
Bacchanalia
Bellerophon
Hyancinthos
Neoptolemus (or
    Pyrrhus)
Penthesilea
Round Table
Terpsichore

TWELVE-LETTER NAMES

Clytemnestra
Golden Fleece
Hypermnestra
Pallas Athene
Rhadamanthus

FOURTEEN-LETTER NAMES

Inpu Hermanu-
    bis (or Anubis)
Launcelot du
    Lac

7. ALPHABETS

ARABIC	**GREEK**	**HEBREW**
1. alif	1. alpha	1. aleph
2. ba	2. beta	2. beth
3. ta	3. gamma	3. gimmel
4. sa	4. delta	4. daleth
5. jim	5. epsilon	5. he
6. ha	6. zeta	6. vav
7. kha	7. eta	7. zayin
8. dal	8. theta	8. kheth
9. zal	9. iota	9. teth
10. ra	10. kappa	10. yod
11. za	11. lambda	11. kaph
12. sin	12. mu	12. lamed
13. shin	13. nu	13. mem
14. sad	14. xi	14. nun
15. dad	15. omicron	15. samekh
16. ta	16. pi	16. ayin
17. ain	17. rho	17. pe
18. ghain	18. sigma	18. tsadi
19. fa	19. tau	19. koph
20. qaf	20. upsilon	20. resh
21. kaf	21. phi	21. sin
22. lam	22. chi	22. dhin
23. min	23. psi	23. tav
24. nun	24. omega	
25. ha		
26. waw		
27. ya		

8. GEOLOGIC TIME

Cambrian: earliest period of the Paleozoic era.

Carboniferous: period preceding the Permian period of the Paleozoic era.

Cenozoic: most recent era.

Cretaceous: most recent period of the Mesozoic era.

Devonian: period preceding the Permian period of the Paleozoic era.

Eocene: epoch of the Tertiary period of the Cenozoic era.

Jurassic: intermediate period of the Mesozoic era.

Mesozoic: era preceding the Cenozoic.

Miocene: epoch of the Tertiary period of the Cenozoic era.

Mississippian: more distant of the Carboniferous periods of the Paleozoic era.

Oligocene: epoch of the Tertiary period of the Cenozoic era.

Ordovician: period preceding the Carboniferous period of the Paleozoic era.

Paleocene: epoch of the Tertiary period of the Cenozoic era.

Paleozoic: era preceding the Mesozoic era.

Pennsylvanian: more recent of the Carboniferous periods of the Paleozoic era.

Permian: most recent period of the Paleozoic era.

Pleistocene: epoch of the Quaternary period of the Cenozoic era.

Precambrian: earliest era of geologic time, preceding the Paleozoic era.

Quaternary: more recent period of the Cenozoic era.

Recent: epoch of the Quaternary period and the Cenozoic era.

Tertiary: older period of the Cenozoic era.

Triassic: most distant period of the Mesozoic era.

9. CHEMICAL ELEMENTS AND THEIR ABBREVIATIONS

Actinium, Ac
Aluminum, Al
Americium, Am
Antimony, Sb
Argon, Ar
Arsenic, As
Astatine, At
Barium, Ba
Berkelium, Bk
Beryllium, Be
Bismuth, Bi
Boron, B
Bromine, Br
Cadmium, Cd
Calcium, Ca
Californium, Cf
Carbon, C
Cerium, Ce
Cesium, Cs
Chlorine, Cl
Chromium, Cr
Cobalt, Co
Copper, Cu
Curium, Cm
Dysprosium, Dy
Einsteinium, Es
Erbium, Er
Europium, Eu
Fermium, Fm
Flourine, F
Francium, Fr
Gadolinium, Gd
Gallium, Gal
Germanium, Ge
Gold, Au

Hafnium, Hf
Helium, He
Holmium, Ho
Hydrogen, H
Indium, In
Iodine, I
Iridium, Ir
Iron, Fe
Krypton, Kr
Lanthanum, La
Lawrencium, Lw
Lead, Pb
Lithium, Li
Lutenium, Lu
Magnesium, Mg
Manganese, Mn
Medelevium, Md
Mercury, Hg
Molybdenum, Mo
Neodymium, Nd
Neon, Ne
Neptunium, Np
Nickel, Ni
Niobium, Nb
Nitrogen, N
Nobelium, No
Osmium, Os
Oxygen, O
Palladium, Pd
Phosphorus, P
Platinum, Pt
Plutonium, Pu
Polenium, Po
Potassium, K

Praseodymium, Pr
Promethium, Pm
Protactinium, Pa
Radium, Ra
Radon, Rn
Rhenium, Rh
Rhodium, Rh
Rubidium, Rb
Ruthenium, Ru
Samarium, Sm
Scandium, Sc
Selenium, Se
Silicon, Si
Silver, Ag
Sodium, Na
Strontium, Sr
Sulfur, S
Tantalum, Ta
Technetium, Tc
Tellurium, Te
Terbium, Tb
Thallium, Tl
Thorium, Th
Thulium, Tm
Tin, Sn
Titanium, Ti
Tungsten, W
Uranium, U
Vanadium, V
Xenon, Xe
Ytterbium, Yb
Yttrium, Y
Zinc, Zn
Zirconium, Zr